The Kingdom of Science

PAUL A. OLSON

The Kingdom of Science

*Literary Utopianism
and British Education,*
1612–1870

University of Nebraska Press
Lincoln and London

Library of Congress Cataloging-in-Publication Data
Olson, Paul A.
The kingdom of science : literary utopianism and
British education, 1612–1870 / Paul A. Olson.
p. cm. Includes bibliographical references and index.
ISBN 0-8032-3568-2 (cloth : alkaline paper)
1. Education – Great Britain – History. 2. Utopias
in literature. 3. Educational change – Great
Britain – History. 4. Education – Social aspects –
Great Britain. 1. Title.
LA631.O48 2002   370'.941—dc21   2002003091

Dedicated to the memory of B E T T Y   O L S O N , 1929–1999

Wife
Mother
Teacher
Peace and Justice Activist

Winter is past, the rains are over and gone. . . .
come then, my beloved, my lovely one.
. . . to become temperate, just, loving, and modest,
innocent mankinde.

Contents

Preface

THIS BOOK had its genesis in a plan developed in the early 1980s to publish a series of essays written during the 1960s–80s. The essays concerned literature and education, culture and education, the education of teachers, and the treatment of poor people in America by higher and secondary education. While I taught medieval and Renaissance literature at the University of Nebraska, I had also led a series of federal projects and commissions: the Nebraska Project English, the Tri-University Project, a Teaching the Teachers of Teachers project, the United States Office of Education Study Commission on Education and the Education of Teachers, and the Center for Great Plains Studies. In the process of leading these efforts, I was called upon to deliver papers and speeches addressing the educational issues of the period of the Civil Rights movement and its aftermath. Since these were nonce presentations, I thought I should do the research to fill in the background of what I had said to make them more serious pieces.

I wrote one version of this book, but as I contemplated it, I began to realize that it would quickly become dated and that I needed to understand the relationship between literary texts and the construction of education at a deeper level. Hence, I began the writing that led to *The Journey to Wisdom* on medieval self-education and the editing that led to *The Struggle for the Land* on small group societies and the environment. Working with those two books made me aware that I might contribute more to our understanding of the topics at issue if I traced the modern decline of faith in our capacity to learn and the imaginative forces ensuring that education in England and the United States took a different course in the post-Reformation/Renaissance period from that pursued on the Protestant or Catholic continents. As I view the matter, this course was utopia centered, and its utopianism had a good deal to do with why we have ravaged the natural environment, often in ways that would have been impossible or unthinkable to earlier small group societies. Anglo-American utopia-based education after Bacon emphasized capitalistic-style competition, the basics, and science and technology to the elimination of almost all other serious study. (I have not traced the American part of the story as it is close to the English side save that compulsory education came late to the whole nation in the United States because of the presence of slavery; genuine compulsory education did not exist in parts of the South even in the early 1960s lest African American children become educated.) When I worked recently with the Annenberg Rural Challenge and the School at the Center project, both relating the community factor in education with the environmental factor, I began to see that my theme should be how we have created an education to take us away from our surroundings and from each other.

I began serious work on this version of the book in 1987 when I was a fellow at the Institute for Advanced Studies in the Humanities in Edinburgh and continued it in Lincoln in 1987–2000 and in Edinburgh at the Institute again in 1997. My wife, now deceased and the person to whom this book is dedicated, talked through most of the chapters with me and suggested wholesale changes in my argument, which I often adopted, though she was too ill when I was finishing the book to read the latter parts of it. I have had assistance with the Shakespeare chapter from Clifford Ronan of Southwest Texas University and from Steve Buhler of the University of Nebraska at Lincoln; with the Bacon and Comenius chapters from Esther Cope, the seventeenth-century historian, and from Les Whipp in seventeenth-century literature; with the Scribleran chapter from Robert Stock, my colleague, and from my long-time friend and student Lawrence Freeman, formerly dean of education at Governor's State University; with Adam Smith and the Utilitarians from my son Lars Olson, who is a resource economist at the University of Maryland; with the Utilitarians, the second generation Utilitarians, and Dickens from Linda Lewis, a nineteenth-century scholar, and from Gerri Brooks, a Victo-

rian scholar. Les Whipp and Linda Lewis have read the whole manuscript and given me many valuable suggestions, especially on chapter
7 and the conclusion. Finally, my use of Karl Mannheim and my differences with him come out of discussions concerning the sociology
of knowledge that I have had with the Disciplines Committee of the
Study Commission on Undergraduate Education and the Education
of Teachers, headed by Edward Rose, and out of other conversations
with Les Whipp, Philipp Fehl, and my colleagues in theory at the Department of English of the University of Nebraska. Jean and Peter
Jones of the Institute for Advanced Studies made a number of very
helpful scholarly suggestions. The mistakes of the work are my own.

I am deeply indebted for editorial and scholarly help to two of
my students and friends, Jennifer Moore and William Paul Ward,
both of whom helped me refine the scholarly side of the argument
and polish its rhetoric. At an earlier stage, Karma Larsen helped
me with editing and with Combe manuscript material. The George
Combe collection at the Scottish National Library includes that
reformer's books, pamphlets, journals, and letters to hundreds of
prominent educators and political leaders. Its material was indispen-
sible to this study. For help in accessing the manuscripts used in this
book, I am indebted to the Scottish National Library; University College, London; Sheffield University; and the University of Edinburgh;
I shall also be forever grateful to the librarians of those collections.

As to financial aid, I have had assistance from the University of Nebraska Research Council, the UNL sabbatical program, and the Institute for Advanced Studies both in 1987 and 1997. Much of the work
on the seventeenth century was done when I was a Fulbright scholar
many years ago.

Much of the book was written during the period when my wife
was dying of ovarian cancer, and I am aware of a certain irony in my
dependence on advanced science and technology to prolong her life
and what may appear to be the anti-technological stance of this book.
I can only say that part of what creates the illness of our time derives
from our mistakes in employing education, science, and technology
to dominative ends. I have no quarrel with the domain of scientific

inquiry; I do have a quarrel with the dominative science, pseudo-science, and exploitative scientific and technological education that make up too much of what the state compels children to undertake now in Great Britain, the United States, and the rest of the world that emulates them.

The Kingdom of Science

Karl Mannheim and the Utopian Educational Project

THE ARROGANCE OF A CHILD

WHILE IT IS our wont to dream of better worlds in all ages, we dream different worlds from age to age. The utopias that we who are children of normal science, capitalism, and radical environmental manipulation have dreamed—and to some degree realized in the nineteenth and twentieth centuries—began with the seventeenth- and eighteenth-century visions of Bacon, the Commonwealth utopians, Adam Smith, and the early Utilitarians. Their sorts of fantasies were what authors such as Swift and Dickens (who did not believe in the myths of full human empire over the natural world) endeavored to reduce to nightmare. Those skeptical of the dream of science, technology, education, and capitalism—linked together to complete the conquest of the natural world—performed a service. When action is the aim, the worlds created in the shadow of utopian images often come into being with relatively little critical reflection and exist for most of their real-world subjects without those subjects having any knowledge of the images' origins, their basis for existence, or their possible destructive side. In consequence, the critiquing of utopia comes not from within utopia itself but from the dystopian response, which reminds us that in creating its own future, the human race has had a choice. At least, the elites have. In the case of this book, the alternative futures proposed by the Scriblerans and Dickens include the possibility that we could have chosen something other than capitalism, other than competitive scientific/industrial education, and other than compulsion as the motive power for change. We might have chosen something other than environmental degradation, understanding that the alternative choices would also have had their price. This book is about how we might have changed the world differently.

When I was a child in northern Wisconsin in the early 1930s, my elementary school class was as competitive a jungle as our unsupervised playground. I recall the little reading half-circle in which we sat according to the teacher's estimation of our strengths as readers. From time to time, some people would move up and others down. One boy always remained in the lowest status place in the half-circle, sounding out each word as the teacher gave him sounds and then pronouncing it haltingly as the teacher gave it to him or as he guessed. Most of us thought he wet his pants and he deserved to remain in the lowest place. At the top, a small group of "good readers" remained perpetually in their places. In between, a group of middling readers would change places from day to day. The same logic of competition and separation applied to spelling bees. Our arithmetic papers were posted so that everyone could see who received the best grades and who the worst, and for coloring and other "artistic" pursuits we received silver or gold stars for "exceptional" work.

When we finished our assigned lessons, we were allowed to read in our comic books of Superman and Batman and their conquests of space, time, and material impediments through special chemical compounds and a scientific knowledge of physics as well as through superior birth. Since this was during World War II, we all played with paper airplanes that emulated in imaginative power the force of Spitfires or B-29s. We made motor noises as we soared and dived, and I shot many a Nazi schoolmate out of the sky. I knew I could make anything and destroy evil with what I made. Winning the competition was the essence of school. I did not know what the competition was for and did not necessarily connect winning it with being able to do anything in the material world, but I did know that both the competition and the making of B-29s counted.

As I have grown older, I have wondered whence arose this schoolboy vision positing competition as the essential form of learning in compulsory school. Where did I learn to love the sense that I could master the material universe without imagining that this mastery might have negative consequences? Explaining my uncritical vision is the central concern of this book, and it essentially treats only the English-speaking world because that is where the crucial elements of the vision arose. Part of the answer also includes examining where intelligence and aptitude testing, compensatory education, and secular compulsory schooling came from in the English-speaking world— what motives and visions led to their rise. How did we come to a somewhat linear model of education, often based on rote, mechanical learning that is easily tested?

Clearly things were not always as I have described. Earlier, little meritocracy existed, and the assumption that the material world could be conquered was absent. The larger medieval English town educated its elite young through school training in a grammar school where rote learning and noncompetitive individual recitation prevailed. The smaller villages sometimes provided exceptional prospects with tutoring by the priest or other clerics.[1] Those youths who did not go to school in the towns or cities were apprenticed to a tradesman and learned by imitation of an adult (or at least an older master or journeyman); a similar system, albeit a more informal one, must have trained young people to do the work of the villages on the manor farms.

Young women had roughly parallel, though skimpier, education through doing. The learning of worldly skills must have come partly from losing oneself in places like Breughel's village squares. As for formal work of an advanced character, Augustine and most medieval and Renaissance students of education describe advanced learning as consisting of two kinds of activity: rote learning conducted by the school masters; and searching carried out alone, based on an impulse to learn that supposedly came from within.[2]

Apprenticeship and schooling forms of education had a long life in medieval and Renaissance culture, but neither was very like the schooling I knew. In the preindustrial world, face-to-face competition for academic place among groups of several students seems to have been minimal, save for the occasional competition between two students in a disputation or for a prize to enable a poor scholar to go on to university. Of course, there must have been some sort of competition among the various roles in society and for pride of place within the roles, but this was not explicit head-to-head competition for a grade or a number.[3] And some teaching nearly precluded competition because it took place in one-to-one tutorials by the family priest or appointed tutor. Some accounts tell us that the medieval and Renaissance school students were assigned a lesson, and those who did not learn it by the time of the next lesson were beaten.

As to the scientific and technological assumptions I made in my paper airplane world: in Renaissance England, the medieval elementary or "little" school or the monastic song school for children offered no science, only Latin reading, some writing, and perhaps a little training in comparable subjects in English (the song school added some training in liturgical singing).[4] The secondary, or grammar, school offered more advanced training in Latin reading and composition, perhaps including some initial training in Latin rhetoric. Elementary and secondary schools offered no training in disciplines analogous to the modern scientific ones, even in their medieval and early modern versions. Few people other than magicians assumed that the physical universe could be mastered, and theirs was a marginal domain even after the rediscovery of white magic in the Florentine Renaissance. A few academics and court figures influenced by the new Platonism seem to have assumed that culture itself could also provide a sort of general education through architecture, art, music, poetry, and drama. In consequence of the assumption of a nonmanipulable natural world, a great portion of education went into teaching people endurance and the perception of the providence in apparently untoward events. Teaching about accepting what comes as providential came through readings in such scriptures as standard fables by Avianus, sermons on Job, and the "consider the lilies" passage. It came for advanced students from the study of such philosophic works as Boethius's *Consolation of Philosophy*. The lessons had to be learned because one could not do a great deal about unpredictable disease, famine, or cold.

Introduction

My education was different from that known by the medieval and early Renaissance child not only because it assumed a constantly changing ranking of students to be the center of the educational process and the end of learning to be mastery over the material universe. It was also different in that it was compulsory and inescapable. Since the burden of this book is to trace the rise of the form of compulsory education designed to teach humankind to master the physical universe, it may appear to require concern with continental education. However, I do not treat the first appearances of compulsory education in the early modern continental Protestant towns that followed Luther and the Swiss Protestants, since that education largely centers on language and does so in the Protestant continental countries until well into the eighteenth century.[5] The education described in the present work—the sort that anticipates my childhood experience—is hard-facts education of the kind that Dickens presents in *Hard Times* in his portrait of Gradgrind's school. Such education is, in my opinion, crucial in the development not only of modern education but of essential structures in modern industrial society.

The discussion begins with static-state utopias, More's *Utopia* and Shakespeare's *Tempest*, as benchmarks that demonstrate how similar in surface and yet how different in implication are the new dynamic perfect places that follow after these models and essentially emerge from Bacon's *New Atlantis*. Since static-state utopias ratify the status quo or at least a possible status quo envisaged from within the primary assumptions of their period, they promote no vision of long-term change and do not energize movements. It took several centuries and a spate of socialistic "strong misreadings" before More's utopia became part of serious mobilizing to create a world in its reinterpreted image. *The Tempest*, as an educational utopia, stands at the head of no utopian movement. In contrast, the authors of the dynamic utopian schemes discussed in this book—Bacon, the Commonwealth educators, Adam Smith, the first and second generation Utilitarians—write to change the world through the communities that they propose for winning knowledge and through the uses that they envisage for human understanding.

There are reactions to this tradition, however—powerful ones suggesting that we were not without choice in creating the environmental and education cul-de-sacs that we now face. As every critic of Dickens knows, *Hard Times* presents two forms of education not envisaged in the medieval and early Renaissance periods. One of these occurs in Sleary's circus as a metonymic figure for romantic faith in the imagination as an educational and redemptive force. In Sleary's circus, the free play of imagination transforms the participant's and the spectator's understanding of life through the development of empathy and a holistic imagination of other people's situations and of the natural world. It is, in Buber's terms, "thou" education. The other, "it" oriented education, occurs under Gradgrind, the utilitarian educator allied with Bounderby, the archetypical capitalist and creator of Coketown. Gradgrind's concern is only with "the facts": information numbered, aggregated, and productive of human "utility."[6]

The two worlds of *Hard Times* did not come into existence through Dickens's fiction-making powers alone but had a historical reality some time before Dickens invented Sleary's circus. The equivalents of the circus existed in early nineteenth-century romantic poems, fairy tales, Gothic novels, and the like, all of which looked to the romantic imagination as the guiding principle for development of a sense of ethics and human compassion. The other world, Gradgrind's school, was embodied in a myriad of schools that offered a utilitarian education in Baconian science, its industrial applications, and its competitive ethos.

The forebears of Gradgrind's school can be found in the genealogy of English "knowledge" utopias and dystopias constructed in the period 1600–1870 and in the real-life schools constructed in the later part of that period to imitate utopian conditions. These schools were to create a better next generation, to enable humankind to control nature and make it a willing servant. The early educational utopias, Shakespeare's *Tempest* and Bacon's *New Atlantis*, though common-

6

place reading, differ vastly in their assumptions. While Shakespeare presents no prospect of permanent change and offers what is essentially a stable-state society, Bacon tells us that the world can be radically transformed. And after Bacon, the assumptions change in the more obscure Baconian educational utopias constructed by the members of the Hartlib circle (especially Comenius), before and during England's Commonwealth period, and in the utopian designs of the moderate Royalists that underlay the creation of the Royal Society.

But there was an attempt at braking the march toward the earthly paradise. To counter the appeal of Commonwealth utopianism and Chiliasm and their successors, the Tory wits created the utopias and dystopias that ask for caution in leaving behind the old stable-state societies lacking a transformative science and technology. Pope's translation of Homer, the *Dunciad*, and *Gulliver's Travels*, the Scriblerus papers, and the documents in the ancient vs. modern controversy warn the English-speaking world against the new project. To little effect!

Baconian utopian dreams revive in Adam Smith, especially those parts of his works dealing with education, the scientific enterprise, the ameliorative effects of competition, and the necessity for compulsory schooling. The utopian visions of Smith's followers, the Baconian Utilitarians (e.g., the schooling proposals contained in Bentham's *Chrestomathia*, Lancaster's proposals for monitorial schools, J. S. Mill's writings on education, and William Ellis's and George Combe's writings and schools) bring the Baconian vision to full realization. In the process of being realized, the vision changes to include mass compulsory education.

This Smithian/Utilitarian group of dreams is answered in Dickens as the first group is answered by Swift and his colleagues, but Dickens too goes largely ignored. Bacon's republic of scientists where the scientific elites know and do everything important materializes in the nineteenth- and twentieth-century competitive industrial order, where the elites have critical knowledge and the masses have technical information. In late nineteenth century and the twentieth, under the tutelage of those who inherited Bacon's utopianism and added to it the utopianism of Comenius and Bentham, mass compulsory education and social and natural transformation became the order of the day. When the English-speaking world founded its efforts on their assumptions, it knew that it could change the earth's ecosystems, alter the air, water, and soil, and change the temperature, and it assumed that the alterations would be for the better. At least until recently, most of us have assumed that massive environmental transformations and the educational transformation of human nature were a price that we had to pay on the road to a better life.

MANNHEIM, HOPE, AND SOCIAL CONSTRUCTION

This is a book about literature and history—specifically about literary utopias rehearsing the rise to power of new groups and the historical arrangements for the production of knowledge and myth demanded by those groups. It is about how power creates knowledge and knowledge creates power. The study of utopias as the rehearsal of possible future states begins with Karl Mannheim's *Ideology and Utopia*, which contrasts the roles of ideologies and utopias in the development of knowledge-creating societies such as the ones found in educational institutions. Ideologies are systems of belief promulgated by a dominant society to legitimize its activities, and these, in Mannheim's view, exist in tension with the utopias created to mobilize forces moving toward a new social order. For example, the conservative *ideology* of the feudal classes proclaimed all human beings to be "brothers" and, at the same time, in practice insisted on serfdom, apparently without noticing an incompatibility.[7]

In contrast to ideological thinking, Mannheim's *utopian thinking* develops among rising social groups that look to the future, seeking to transform present social reality on the basis of some imaginative but apparently "rational" vision. While ideologues suppress or reinterpret information that does not support the hegemony of the dominant group, utopianists look to some proposed new city that answers to widely felt anguish about the present situation. Though Mannheim does not explicitly address what utopian thinking does to knowledge, it must also suppress facts or opinions that lie in its way

8

or are perceived to lie in its way. Mannheim's utopian idea, though often the product of an individual imagination, is not a fantastic vision of the future that has no moorings in material reality. It criticizes the present order, arousing a conscious or unconscious yearning for a better situation in significant groups of people. It mobilizes human will and intelligence until the idea of a better life becomes a "dominant wish" that determines the sequence, order, and evaluation of single experiences and even "molds the way that we experience time."[8] In short, it selects what is to be observed, researched, and recorded.[9] In the landscape of this book, Baconian utopianism both creates communities for the production of scientific knowledge and constructs the myths that deny the possible destructive consequences of its technological application.

Mannheim grounds his thought in the work of Thomas More, indicating that he wishes to broaden the concept of the utopian from what More articulates to include "much of which is unrelated to this historical point of departure."[10] Thus, he includes fictions and ideas that go beyond the literary phenomena of "ideal commonwealths" to mass shared vision; his category of the utopian encompasses both literary ideal commonwealths *and* a broader group of visions of historically constructed ideal futures that have impelled historical action.[11] Mannheim argues that he is not beginning with an arbitrary definition but with a conception of utopia "already present in the utopias as they have appeared in history" and in the literary and nonliterary dreams that have led to social change.[12] He is thus interested both in utopia as *genre* and in utopia as *impulse to mass social movement*, in what Diane Knight calls the utopian gesture.[13] It is somewhat idle, however, to separate the utopian genre from the utopian gesture, except in the cases of works having a very limited circulation and no appeal to a general social group, perhaps such a work as Ursula Le Guin's *The Dispossessed*. Utopian works, by definition, create social movements, though the movement may exist primarily, as Roland Barthes puts it, as "a pure imaginary, of a theatre of discourse."[14]

Utopian discourse offering educational and technological change that will make material conditions much easier represents a reaching for hope, and Ernest Bloch has created a useful taxonomy of kinds of desire leading to hope and, in some cases, to action to create the incarnation of hope. He begins with the least and proceeds to the most authentic forms of dreams: (1) manipulated *daydreams* such as the anti-Jewish daydreams of middle-class Germans in the period prior to the rise of Hitler; (2) *dreams that relate to basic human needs* such as the need for self-preservation (e.g., the need to eat); (3) *enacted dreams making our "wishes" become "horses"* (e.g., in the world of the circus, the dance, travel, gardening, movies, the search for wild scenery and wild weather); (4) *enactable dreams of a better world* (e.g., the basic utopian dreams calculated from the perspective of the needs of the times in which they are created (the feminist utopia or the ecological utopia in our time); and, (5) *dreams rehearsing and enacting the possibility of human liberation* (e.g., those found in great religious visions or great music).[15] The dreams I am examining fall largely into Bloch's classes (3) and (4), have their foundation in the need for food, health, shelter, and a stable life. They empower social movements because they create ends for desire. Renaissance utopias derive from the various fabulous loci in the *Odyssey* and *Aeneid* and are icons that, when contemplated, inspire *social* effort in the quotidian world to imitate their pattern. They do so in something of the fashion that an emblem in Caesario Ripa's *Iconologia* was supposed to woo its *individual* "reader" to become what it represents.

In the early utopias, the ideal place appears in consequence of odysseys like those the fifteenth-century explorers made into strange parts of the ocean. The place is an island set off from "civilization" and represents a possible social moral state similar in kind to the allegorized lands of the Lotus-Eaters or the Phaeacians in Renaissance *Odyssey* comment. Later, when the dynamic utopianism that forms the subject of most of my discussion appears, the utopian place turns into a technological or educational ideal. Though Knight speaks of utopia as an "ideal society located in a future place, a geographically other place, or a different place within," in the Renaissance and seventeenth and early eighteenth century, the literal fiction of the utopia generally presents a "geographically other place" that is a metaphor for a state of society that Europe can reach by the long-term exercise of human will.[16] Renaissance letters dedicatory and comments on utopian works treat them as representing the possible. A Renaissance-Enlightenment utopia is not simply a satiric artifact but rehearses *a possible moral or material state* accessible to society if it has the will to get there. Beginning with Bacon's *New Atlantis*, the emphasis goes to a possible material state, accessible through scientific or educational progress.[17] By the mid-eighteenth century, with the decline of the classical languages and literatures as live objects, the intertexts from Plato's works and from the epic tradition drop out of the educational utopias and dystopias altogether. The knowledge utopia becomes a disembodied fiction unrelated to the classical tradition; utopia becomes a school building set in a journey that takes one no more distant from the everyday world than the distance across a playground. Such utopianism continues into our own time, in the rhetoric of most political administrations and of almost every educational reformer. Though both Mannheim and Judith Shklar have argued that the end of revolt and class warfare means an end to utopianism and perhaps the beginning of a general totalitarianism, utopian visions in the present are to be found as one walks across almost any school yard in most parts of the world or sees any proposal for radical changes in the educational process designed to create a different future.[18]

Mannheim's taxonomy of utopian conceptions works to explain the specific educational utopias treated in this book, but his claims of a systematic utopian dialectic going from Chiliasm to liberalism to socialism is too simple. The ideological slices do not fall so neatly or so sequentially. Mannheim finds utopia at work in the mutually antagonistic social movements of: (1) the Chiliasm of the Reformation that endures through various anarchist movements, ending with Bakunin; (2) the liberal humanitarianism that begins with a "bourgeois ideal of reason" and culminates in De Condorcet, Lessing, and Herder; and (3) the socialist/communist movements that began with Marx and culminated in the 1930s movements extant when Mannheim published *Ideology and Utopia*.[19] In dialogue about educational reform, the chiliastic movement corresponds to the seventeenth-century Baconian and Commonwealth educational reform movements; the liberal movement corresponds to the search for compulsory educational reform beginning with Adam Smith and the Utilitarians; and socialistic education begins with Robert Owen. But the movements do not really succeed one another, and clearly Owen and later Marxist educators did not define any terminal kind of education. The "liberal" mode is what we have. Further, what is liberal in one age becomes reactionary in the next—this is certainly the case with nineteenth-century Utilitarian forms of education. To confuse things even more, Mannheim also describes a conservative utopianism that applies to some of the Tory works I treat.[20]

In Chiliasm, what Ricoeur calls "the conjunction between heaven and earth, the preacher and the revolt of the peasants" is decisive in making the absolute seem "the immediate here and now," the inward vision seem the outwardly realizable. In contrast, in liberalism and socialism the notion of human agency is central. However, Chiliasm, liberalism, and socialism all design to create the kingdom of heaven on earth in some sense. They diminish or forgo altogether afterlife arguments and the notion of strict limits on this-worldly action. All depend ultimately on coercive violence; in the case of education, this involved subtle, long-term coercive action designed to shape human nature and the culture's intellectual assumptions. Though educational revolutions may appear to be coercion free, they rest on the coercive power of a state that can use the requirement of compulsory attendance, state-controlled teacher licensing and credentials, state-prescribed curricula and tests, and state taxing authority to create the "optimum" new society.

After More, the most influential utopian visions, in precisely Mannheim's sense that they organize social action, have not concerned political or economic change directly but the sociology and distribution of knowledge (Mannheim's other subject); the organization of society (or societies) for the discovery of knowledge; and use of knowledge for social and natural transformation and for the solution of problems perceived as crucial by the group. Unlike the more directly cataclysmic, often violent, movements that Mannheim assesses, utopian educational movements present themselves more as evolutionary than revolutionary in purpose; but given the power of state coercion, they have often had and do have more permanent and drastic consequences than any outpouring of crowds into the streets of Paris. Utopias of research and knowledge channel revolutionary enthusiasm into a faith in the power of education and science to change things.[21] They serve aspirations to power by presenting a plausible alternative to naive views of the perfectibility of human nature basic to many utopian visions. They do not treat human nature as Robert Owen does—as instantly perfected when the old order disappears—but rather suggest that human action and thought can be drastically improved and shaped by a universal training of it.[22] In this sense they are subtly revolutionary. They ultimately have created vast changes in the earth's population, its flora and fauna, its atmosphere, and in our common conditions of work and life. In the name of Bacon's search for the extension of human empire "to the accomplishing of all things possible," we have gained comforts and lost the ability to live in the stable or sustainable relationship with the natural world that many earlier agriculturalists and hunter-gatherers once had. We have set in motion environmental forces beyond our control.[23]

THE STRUCTURE OF THE BOOK

The argument of the book follows essentially the three movements of Mannheim's structure for the evolution of utopias, tracing the educational and evolutionary alternatives to Mannheim's revolutionary chiliastic, liberal, and socialist systems. However, it does so while taking time out to record the counter-utopias and dystopias that significant writers, such as the Tory wits and later Dickens, place before English-speaking society, giving it some option of choosing possible futures. Chapter 1 treats the benchmark views set forth in More's *Utopia* and Shakespeare's *Tempest*, pictures of an early modern world where teaching through culture is possible and where the changing of nature is perhaps feasible but certainly not desirable. In contrast, the almost contemporaneous subject of chapter 2, Bacon's utopian *New Atlantis*, envisages an earthly paradise founded in a knowledge and technological mastery beyond the reach of sectarian dispute. While Shakespeare's work adumbrates a paradise that assumes a divinely created millennium and a divinely created ruler as foundational to whatever temporary perfection education can make possible in this world, Bacon's work tells of a progressive human conquest of nature by scientists whose collective work has spanned centuries and whose mastery, though it pays tribute to the divine in creation, depends primarily on human agency.[24] The successor pre-Commonwealth and Commonwealth Baconian educational utopias (chapter 3), especially those created by Hartlib, Comenius, and Durie, turn Bacon's ideas into chiliastic proposals so transparently programmatic that they can even come before Parliament. The reaction, the posing of choices for human culture, was not long in coming; chapter 4 looks at the Tory defenses of a semifeudal educational, cultural, and environmental order through a satiric resort to the classical fictions that the new educators purport to replace. Since the older conservative, heroic educational views had been communicated through the allegorized epic, Arbuthnot, Swift, and Pope quite naturally use an inverted version of this epic to critique the new view. As a market economy expands and gradually destroys the static hierarchies of the old order and undermines its canonical texts, Adam Smith (chapter 5) begins a new wave of utopian movement toward Baconian education with his critique of monopolistic guild and university education and his proposal for a universal, compulsory public education that will be freed from the old hierarchies and the old texts. Building on the Smith chapter and centering in Smith's and Bacon's descendants in the Utilitarian/liberal group, the sixth chapter looks at the first burst of energy to create a liberal "school" utopia wholly independent of the classical past. The new educators are the Gradgrinds of Dickens's story. But seen apart from Dickens's filter, they appear as persons of idealism and compassion, certainly not as monsters. They are the systematic rehearsers of the dominant knowledge and motivational modes needed by a developing "market" capitalism, especially as represented in James Mill's proposals for a new school psychology and reform, the

Introduction

Lancastrian monitorial schools that Mill approved, and Bentham's utopian *Chrestomathia*.

At this point, utopia becomes a place on a school ground. The seventh chapter culminates in an account of the realization of the ideas of the Utilitarians in the Birkbeck schools established by William Ellis, in the school founded by George Combe in Edinburgh, and in a number of other working-class schools founded to be models for the new compulsory education and to set the terms of the new industrial order—schools that were to be alternatives to Robert Owen's socialist schools and to stop working class revolt, especially after 1848. These schools and teacher education efforts associated with them found an echo in the work of Horace Mann in the United States. The half-century-long polemic for a compulsory scientific/industrial education carried on by George Combe, Henry Brougham, J. A. Roebuck, and William Ellis in the United Kingdom and by Combe's friend Horace Mann in Massachusetts was successful and created many of the basic forms of modern education in the English-speaking world.

The price of the new order was a working class regimented by the schools intended to help it. But the posing of alternatives arises again at this point. The eighth chapter deals with Dickens's *Hard Times* and its satiric and dystopian treatment of the advancing Utilitarian program of the Ellis/Combe group. While the Utilitarian impulse dominated the movement toward universal compulsory education controlled by the state, the statements in *Hard Times* about childhood, learning, capitalism, and the environment present an antidote to them. The conclusion closes the book with a summary analysis of our educational "progress" and its relation to what has happened to the environment, to human community, and to children. The educational utopias created desire and action, and what they promised was produced, in some measure. They also produced costs that are not counted in their rhetoric of hope, costs that still require payment through changes in educational policy and in our imagination of what we can do.

CHAPTER ONE

Shakespeare's Utopian *Tempest* and Education by the Book

W

HEN WE THINK of early modern groups working to transform the construction and transmission of knowledge, we do not commonly focus initially on educational utopianism promising the transformation of a whole society. Rather we recall the formal educational inventions of the period: compulsory schooling in Protestant Germany and Switzerland and the Jesuits' *ratio studiorum* in Catholic Europe. But sixteenth-century England, in many ways a backwater, saw neither of these institutions. The old grammar school, guild, and university system continued to prevail. Given the country's educational conservatism, we may forget that England toyed with a third way that eventually had radical consequences, a groping toward a culture-wide education communicated through utopian visions, millennialist hopes, alchemical dreams, and the programs of academy-like groups. This third way directs as many of the productions of culture as possible—popular informal learning, art, architecture, music, literature, public guilds, the court, coterie groups, and academies—into educating the social order toward the Edenic. It puts on display for all to see exemplary history, the harmonizing mathematical disciplines, effective artistic persuasion, and ideal social organization. Ultimately, it emerges in the institutions that empower the scientific revolution.

This third way appeared among the fifteenth-century Florentines committed to Plato, and it cropped up in Catholic and Huguenot France in the academies.[1] In the work of such writers as Ficino, the trivium—formerly the grammar, rhetoric, and dialectic studied in academic institutions—becomes the more public grammar, rhetoric, and poetry. The quadrivium, formerly arithmetic, geometry, music, and astronomy, becomes the public arts of music, orphic singing, architecture, and painting.[2] In a similar spirit, in Stuart England, George Buck, Shakespeare's overseer as the Master of the Revels, described London (and by implication, Westminster) with its court, Inns of Court, playhouses, and informal learned groups, as a *third university*.[3] This means that London's educational centers, art, architecture, music, dance, progresses, and drama do much of the work of communicating ideology and learning that formal education was to do in other contexts.[4] The form of education described by the writers from Ficino to Buck promises no progressive alteration of nature and society but examines the possible within a static-state assumption that nature and human nature will not change radically. The subjects of this chapter, *Utopia* and *The Tempest*, also assume this. Though English static-state utopianism was soon to disintegrate under the weight of Bacon's and the Baconians' vision—the "dynamic" scientific/educational vision that is the primary subject of this book—it does exist in differing forms in the work of More and Shakespeare. Such static-state utopianism furnishes the benchmark against which the dynamic-state utopias can be measured.

More and Shakespeare are related in their static-state assumptions, but different premises underlie their views of how utopia is to be evoked. While for More, Utopia is evoked by a *culture* that reinforces natural law, for Shakespeare it emerges because of a sublime monarchic *art* evoking the human capacity for Edenic living. In contrast to More, Shakespeare moves toward a more instrumental vision of the natural world and a more pessimistic and elitist view of culture and the polis. But, though he flirts with the possibility that the natural world can be drastically altered for society's benefit, he ultimately returns to More's static-state view of the natural world and government and, like More, rests his hope for a good society on an I-thou view of nature and supernature rather than I-it assumptions.

More's *Utopia* and Shakespeare's *Tempest* are quite different works. The latter in some areas refutes the former. That is somewhat predictable not only on the basis of the differing religious roots of each but also on the basis of Shakespeare's treatment of More in the play *Sir Thomas More*. If one assumes that Shakespeare's hand is indeed the Hand D of the *Sir Thomas More* play, then one has evidence that he knew a good bit about the author of *Utopia* (one assumes that he read the whole play of which he wrote a part). The detachment and lack of concern for wealth and position that the character More displays in the later scenes of *Sir Thomas More* show him respecting the same norms that the historical More advocates in *Utopia* in regard to contempt for wealth and position.[5] Shakespeare's More is in almost every way the kind of man who could have written *Utopia*. But the character More and the author of *The Tempest* suggest incompatible things about rulership: the character More *mistakenly* asserts the divinity of the king in the Hand D sections that the play itself denies to its wrongheaded monarch. In contrast, *The Tempest* seems to affirm that divinity, on the basis not of birth but of experiences of learning and rapture that unify the ruler with the deity.

Shakespeare's monarch requires the sibylline rapture and the magic that divine powers give him to control the depravity of his subjects. His "divinity" creates a society as close to a good society as is possible, given the terms of the play. While More's Utopian subjects need only to obey the natural law and reason that their nature has given them to create their benign social world, the subjects of Shakespeare's play deny the efficacy of the natural law central to *Utopia*'s construction of the good society. But if Shakespeare denies the rationality of spontaneous social organization, he also does not visualize a permanent Baconian alteration of the natural world to make a good social place for humankind.

Comparing *The Tempest* and *Utopia* is called for because *The Tempest* is intertextually connected both to *Utopia*'s vision of island life in the new world and to Montaigne's version of it projected on the Carib Indians. Shakespeare's Gonzalo would create an island paradise even nicer than More's:[6]

[N]o kind of traffic
Would I admit; no name of magistrate;

Letters should not be known; riches, poverty,
And use of service, none; contract, succession,
Bourn, bound of land, tilth, vineyard, none;
No use of metal, corn or wine, or oil;
No occupation, all men idle, all;
And women too, but innocent and pure;
No sovereignty. (*Tempest* 2.1.139–52)

However, when we encounter the "reality" of Prospero's island, we quickly recognize that Gonzalo's hoped-for utopia could not exist there since most of its inhabitants know nothing of innocence or "natural" feeling.

The difference between More and Shakespeare is the difference between a utopia created by a consultation with natural forces within people and one created by an external combination of coercion and artistic wooing directed by the monarch. When Ferdinand imagines that he is in paradise after the betrothal masque, it is only because court artistic productions have created the good place, not because human nature here is good or potentially good. Most of the denizens of the island are in hell or just outside the gates of Hades (see later discussion). Only Ariel's and Prospero's art gives us hope of a paradise on earth. The humane community at the end of the work is entirely created by Prospero as Eden is won out of the confrontations of art, not out of obedience to natural law. Those who become good are made so by a combination of revels and authority.

The difference between the "nature" of Shakespeare's "natives" and More's has to do with More's confidence that natural law in the medieval sense can make us human enough for society and Shakespeare's confidence that official art can do the making. Both *Utopia* and *The Tempest* depict static-state utopias, but one is based in a general respect for human potential and the power of culture while the other is rooted in the power of monarchic union with God and the efficacy of the art that derives from that union to alter human aspiration. Though differing in their analysis of the sources of the good society, *Utopia* and *The Tempest* represent benchmarks expressing common early modern English legal and sociological assumptions about: (1) the ultimate inviolability of the natural world; (2) the need for stasis in the social order; and (3) the culture-wide character of education that promises to evoke our better angels. These are the assumptions that Bacon and the Baconians ultimately destroy.

To examine the two works in detail: as the first work exemplifying Mannheim's utopian vision transformative of both culture and knowledge, *Utopia* privileges a social construction in which cultural custom reinforces natural law and creates the ideal place. But *Utopia* is, paradoxically, at base a conservative and essentially "medieval" work in that it reposes its hope in the species of static-state society that would have been familiar enough to the Chaucer who wrote "The Former Age" or to the medieval natural law legal theorists who follow in the tradition of Thomas Aquinas. Utopia is not the sort of society that gets better and better. The majority of its people, committing themselves to community benefit, rely on the dispersed authority of a personal culture that educates almost everyone to seek the common benefit as the community climate educates the inhabitants of an ideal monastery or a Hutterite community. Living together in community in everything from work to eating to education teaches Utopia's people duty, community interest, and an empathic ethic. Unlike the somewhat similar dreams set forth by the Anabaptist groups founded by Jacob Hutter about twenty years later, *Utopia*'s dream as announced in 1516 did not become the basis for any mass social reform movement, in my view largely because its precepts were old hat to those who knew natural law political theory.

The governing terms in More's Utopian education and culture are the old ones—nature, right reason, and the common good, terms derived from natural law philosophy, coming down from Aquinas and the scholastics and transmitted to England by Sir John Fortescue. Natural law philosophy makes nature an unchanging and unchangeable entity that requires no alteration. It is organized in static ranks and cycles that model how human culture and education should be ordered. In this view, humankind, with the Fall, shattered its right reason, preferring private good to the common good. Hence, the crucial *fallen* elements in human nature define the remedial need for property, for the care of children, for free choice of a partner in marriage and general free choice, and for discursive assemblies that cultivate education in the sense of right reason.[7] Medieval–early Renaissance philosophy of natural law set forth by Thomas Aquinas's *Summa*, Giles of Rome's *De Regimine Principum*, and (for English readers) Sir John Fortescue's *De Natura Legis Naturae*, written only two generations before More set down *Utopia*, assumes that humankind *can* will to recover *some* of what was lost in the fall. It can do so with the help of good administration by temporal lords. In the lands where natural law rules, neither revelation nor pride or "singular" profit dominates.[8] The benefits of obedience to natural law accrue to righteous pagan as well as to Christian.[9] However, the species that lived spontaneously for the common profit before the Fall must, in postlapsarian times, *strive* to order itself to become natural, and that is what the Utopians do through their natural-law-based educative culture and institutions.[10] If the content of Utopia is old-fashioned, its language is also a Latin read primarily by court lawyers and clerics. When *Utopia* was translated into English by Ralph Robynson in 1551, a Protestant Edward VI ruled, and the Catholic-Protestant struggle probably precluded the emergence of any serious revolutionary hope based on a work from the hand of a Catholic writer—who, in any case, could be seen as stating only what could, without discomfort, be assumed both by Catholic and Protestant working within the natural law tradition. In the sixteenth century, *Utopia* simply could not be made the radical reformers' document that it became in the nineteenth century in English translations—after the death of natural law theory and the triumph of the idea of progress.

As a place where natural law is generally but not always observed, *Utopia* visualizes an education toward conformity to natural law produced by cultural organization and a stable-state society. Like Chaucer's "Former Age," *Utopia* juxtaposes the evils of the present age against what a natural law society might do. More's horrendous pictures of present society under Tudor rule do not foreclose some reaching toward a utopian condition on the part of the contemporary individuals or groups; indeed, natural law theory in medieval culture never precludes reaching toward obedience to natural law. The most responsible character in More's fiction who hears of Utopia's arrangements assumes that some emulation of it would be possible in his culture.[11] Cardinal Morton, as the normative figure in the piece, visualizes the possibility that something approximate to Utopia's obedience to natural law could be developed in England. Through Morton, More insinuates that much Utopian practice could be a goal to which Europe and England should press, as the prefatory remarks attached to the work also make clear.[12] Of course, Hythloday as the messenger from Utopia presents a detached view of this perfect place, assuming no responsibility for the creation of its counterpart in Europe, and Morus, More's fictional counterpart, dismisses all possibility of change. But Hythloday and Morus appear frivolous in their avoidance of responsibility. Much Utopian practice is mistaken and much of it is designed only to satirize European excess, but the main job that the Utopians do in their work of culture construction cannot satirize European and English defects at all unless it creates in readers some sense of responsibility for moving their own social order toward the more "ideal" natural law state that the Utopians have achieved or toward some other alternate, better state. That state would grow out of individual and collective moral decision, not out of changed physical circumstances created by science. Clearly in the Harleyian manuscript, Shakespeare's and the other playwrights' More reaches toward such a condition in his inner heart in the latter part of the play.

For most of the citizens of Utopia, culture is education in natural law—in reaching inward to form a better conscience and not in reaching outward to change nature. Whatever Utopia's later "unstable" readings, it was in its own time framed both by the ancient conservative educational fictions of Plato and the *Odyssey*, and by the slightly destabilizing promise of the new settings in America. Utopia's discoverer, Raphael Hythloday—"his sailing has . . . been like that of Ulysses or, rather, of Plato"—like Vespucci, has reached a newly discovered epic Phaeacian-style paradise epitomizing the best in educative culture.[13] This educative culture is everywhere. The universal Utopian contempt for the adulation of the rich derives partly from "instruction and reading good books."[14] A "large part of the people . . . men and women alike, throughout their lives, devote to learning the hours which are free from manual labor."[15] Though no formal universal compulsory education of the kind soon to emerge in some of the Protestant cities in Germany appears, everyone studies; after "boyhood," however, only those few who show special aptitude devote themselves to formal learning and to the usual medieval disciplines of the quadrivium and logic.[16] They study logic minus its modern scholastic refinements. The elite few also study ethics, taken as the search for pleasure in the sense of Aristotelian eudaemonia.[17] Those who lack special brilliance and a constant hunger for knowledge give themselves an elevated and eclectic education.

Though the ideal of scientific education directed to the transformation of the world was not unknown in More's time (alchemy had from the time of Ramon Lull's period in England promised its few initiates that nature could be transformed), no such education exists in Utopia. Even Greek learning, which contains some "progressive" strands, does not alter Utopia's static character. After Raphael Hythloday has opened up Greek learning, the Utopians add Plato and Aristotle to their reading, and they look at the standard Greek poets including Homer, a mutilated copy of Theophrastus' *On Plants* (their sole Greek scientific treatise), and the usual Greek historians and medical writers. But even after experiencing such a "Renaissance," they undertake no experiments. The few scientific disciplines that exist mandate a study of the natural world that is contemplative, personally religious, and without design to reshape the natural order beyond what agriculture requires. Nature is primarily a model and icon inspiring the worship of the divine: "When by the help of . . . philosophy they explore the secrets of nature, they appear to themselves not only to get great pleasure in doing so but also to win the highest approbation of the Author and Maker of nature. They presume that, like all other artificers, He has set forth the visible mechanism of the world as a spectacle for man, whom alone He has made capable of appreciating such a wonderful thing. Therefore He prefers a careful and diligent beholder and admirer of His work to one who like an unreasoning brute beast passes by so great and so wonderful a spectacle stupidly and stolidly."[18]

If Nature rather than revelation is the Utopian norm for behavior (not that revelation is denied), it is because Nature is seen as a source for right reason in all men, Christian or not. More's letter to Oxford University recalls the traditional ladder going from natural philosophy to metaphysics and the supernatural as the foundation of spiritual truth, and the Utopians, though they appear to know nothing of Christ's incarnation, know and strive to climb this ladder.[19] More extends the striving from the institutions of legal coercion visualized by Thomas Aquinas, Giles of Rome, Sir John Fortescue, and the other great natural law thinkers to the institutions of public works, entertainment, discussion, and education. In this and only this is More new. Clearly the contemplative or aesthetic science central to Utopian worship of, and conformity to, natural law looks back to Origen and Augustine and forward to Kepler while turning away from alchemical or Baconian-style efforts to employ knowledge in the creation of Paradise.[20]

Respect for natural law radiates through the Utopian religious study teaching citizens that virtue is to live according to nature—that they, seeking only such pleasures as are endorsed by "right reason" in addition to the senses, should pursue the common good before private profit. Without a scientific technology that looks to future discovery, they create universal material prosperity and a six-hour work day by recognizing the folly of accumulating wealth and of seeking an absolute right in property. Since they require everyone to work at both agriculture and trade, they prevent divisions of labor or the separation of the city from the country.[21] Utopia appears to be as ordinary as a Breughel painting because it pictures a practical functioning of the medieval sense of the common and of the search for the common profit in education and work that critiques the new solipsism of the enclosure movement and the other forms of pride and privatization attacked in book 1 of *Utopia*.

Shakespeare's Utopian Tempest

The Tempest was probably written in the version that we have for the Protestant 1612 marriage festivities of King James I's daughter, Elizabeth Stuart, and for Frederick, the Palatinate elector who was married to Elizabeth during the festivities. It attacks More's island in the new world with a new island in the old world where the will and revel of the monarch, rather than natural law and common culture, are the sine qua nons of community creation.[22] Peter Greenaway, in his film reconstruction of *The Tempest*, titled *Prospero's Books*, properly has Prospero open his Book of Utopias when Gonzalo speaks of how he would organize Prospero's island as a Moresque commune were he its ruler (2.1.139–52). Gonzalo imagines his islanders to be what More's are in the realm of King Utopus and what Montaigne imagines Caribbean Indians to be when he pictures them wholly obedient to natural law: "The lawes of nature doe yet command them [the Indian nations]. . . . It is a nation, would I answer Plato, that hath no kinde of traffike, no knowledge of Letters, no intelligence of numbers, no name of magistrate, nor of politike superioritie; no use of service, of riches or of povertie; no contracts, no successions, no partitions, no occupation but idle; no respect of kindred . . . no apparell but naturall, no manuring of lands, no use of wine, corne or mettle. The very words that import lying, falshood, treason, dissimulations, covetousness, envie, detraction, and pardon, were never heard of amongst them."[23]

But, as in Greenaway's reconstruction, in Shakespeare's play the Book of Utopias quickly fades to be replaced by other books. In Shakespeare's own play, Gonzalo's form of natural law–based utopian vision disappears because Gonzalo is so wrong about the innocence of the "native" life and its capacity to create communal benefit. If Gonzalo, as a nonce ruler, were to remove from society commerce, rulership, and sovereignty, distinctions of poverty and wealth, mastership and service, hereditary succession, property and conventional agriculture, most labor, and letters, the racially/demonically fearful Calibans from the island and the barbarians from Naples and Milan would rule absolutely and wholly destructively. That is Shakespeare's fiction. In Shakespeare's world, Gonzalo, Montaigne, and the natural law theorists are all wrong. Caliban's nature, that of the lowlife intruders who manipulate him, and that of the Neapolitan and Milanese nobility who act out his depravity in trying to get rid of Prospero, are all "Calvinistically" depraved.[24]

If Shakespeare's utopia owes something at the level of verbal echo to More and to Montaigne, at the level of substance its "debt" appears primarily in its denial of them.[25] The corrupted Caliban, who knows no worship of an "Author and Maker of nature," makes up his own cargo-cult religion directed at the material idol who brings him alcohol. Like Calvin's natural man, he cannot know God. His vices of avarice, rapine, cursing, and attempted murder are also those of his European allies unaccompanied by Swift's *capax rationis* or any conscience that might move him toward utopian community. Whatever community exists in the play emerges entirely from Prospero's and Ariel's construction of an educative culture centering in natural and spiritual showings, monarchic surveillance, and monarchic punishment of the wicked: pinchings, torments, rage, and abuse—the royally constructed answers to Montaigne's conventional and dystopian schools: "verie prison[s] of captivated youth . . . nothing but whipping and brawling, both of children tormented, and masters besotted with anger and chafing."[26] Montaigne's happy reliance on humankind's natural state to empower the pleasant pedagogy of his essay on education cannot work on a Prosperan island where the training and education of Caliban and the Neapolitans requires Ariel's torture, the biting of Prospero's dogs, and all sorts of ghostly appearances that set the boundaries to the permissible while a positive iconic art creates horizons of the possible. Through the manipulation of the permissible and the possible, Prospero becomes what James I imagined himself: "the great schoolmaster of the whole land."[27]

Prospero's education is given directly and tutorially to Miranda and indirectly through his and Ariel's cultural productions to the remainder of the island's people, making the island into Ferdinand's version of paradise and that of the Stuart hegemony (4.1.124). Prospero's education, forgiveness, and withdrawal from magic are all justifications for a static role system in the state and a static preservation of the natural world. They are all mystification, Mannheim's ideology in the cloak of utopia. The historical king has no magical powers beyond brute control of the instruments of propaganda. While the dream of the play is with us, his powers all seem possible because of the power of song, music, and *mis-en-scène* at his control through Ariel. It seems the monarch could educate us toward ideal community; it seems that we all could set aside aspiration and forgive one another, know one another, and grant one another indulgence (epilogue, 1–20; 5.1.205–73). It seems that the monarch could be sybilline, possessing a frenzied prophetic brain, and that he could know what empire could be and what its limits must be in the final dissolution of the cloud-capped towers and the great globe of the material world. But though Shakespeare writes as it were on the edge of Bacon's vision of an alterable natural world and shares Bacon's vision that nature can be changed in some ways, at least temporarily, he has no hope of benign permanent change or progress. He has no Baconian/Democritan belief in the solidity of the material world. His changing nature only gives temporary material form to ancient intertexts in order to reform people and send them back to the old order. Ultimately Prospero abandons the possibility of altering nature by giving up his book and rod (he seems to keep his robe, though he does not appear in it in the epilogue).

Prospero's myth is also a long way from More and Montaigne. It represents the last great burst of persuasive Stuart artistic mystification and its assertion that all true culture, provided by the monarch, can be education. James must have been flattered with a presentation that made him, as he deemed himself, not only the universal schoolmaster but the universal educator and wise spy, controlling everything. While *The Tempest* continues More's tradition that makes education and culture nearly coterminous, More's education is in the hands of the natural law–based community; Shakespeare's is in the hands of the culture-creator extracted from the community, a person whose aesthetic tools and violence conspire together to make what community there is. Prospero as educator-through-culture is like Lenin's vanguard party—the creator through art of the new world.

Shakespeare's Utopian Tempest

Prospero's literary/rhetorical arts are primarily ethical in their effects, having the potential to make us know "each of us ourselves, / When no man was his own" (5.1.215–16), as holy Gonzalo puts it in his beautiful benediction on the action. Yet, seen from an etic perspective, the price of self-knowledge is an absolute educative and coercive power in the hands of the monarch. It is the universal social surveillance to assure good behavior that Foucault attributes to the Utilitarians two centuries later. It is a shape-shifting and unpredictable nature. As compared with More, Shakespeare appears to manifest a great loss of confidence in the possibility of obeying natural law, in the hopeful potential of popular culture, and in the future of cultural self-regulation. No change is envisaged after Prospero's island has been abandoned; no permanent knowledge or institution for the discovery of knowledge emerges.[28]

The ultimate withdrawal from intervention in the natural world in *The Tempest* recapitulates the structures of the old static order rather than rehearsing the new "progressive" one already promised by Bacon in *The Advancement of Learning* (1605) some years before *The Tempest* was performed. Shakespeare, following some of the millennialist claims of alchemists and magicians such as John Dee, makes a gesture in the direction of the new order in scientific education and control of nature in his presentation of the monarch who can control the natural world to construct art, but he ultimately pulls back from this gesture to found his hope on three things: (1) the temporary usefulness to political order of that element of official culture that is sponsored by the monarch, (2) the economy of indulgence and forgiveness at large in the last scene of the play, to which Prospero as actor also appeals in his last speech, and finally (3) the monarch's ultimate detachment from empire, given that he knows that it and the world will vanish. To get to utopian hope, Prospero has to educate his island with showings that make him into a godlike figure and make the material and spiritual worlds into a temporarily malleable clay that embodies canonical texts to instruct the subjects.

Anthony Hecht has argued correctly that "our first view of Prospero is that of an educator, first of his daughter, and then, in delib-

29

erate sequence, of Ariel and of Caliban."[29] He could well have argued that Prospero acts as educator throughout the play, training and wooing with artful showings those whom he finds on his island—including Alonso, Antonio, Sebastian, Ferdinand, Trinculo, and Stephano—until the state of his pupils (or most of them) comes as close as possible in a fallen world to the utopian community Gonzalo thinks he could make it at the beginning (2.2.143–52) or the paradise Ferdinand declares it to be at the end of the betrothal masque (4.1.123–24).

In presenting cultural productions as educative and utopia-creating, *The Tempest* limits them to court-sponsored superstructures—eicastic music, dumb-shows, masques, and showings. These all play with *The Aeneid* and Isaiah reshaped to create a new illumination.[30] Prospero can educate the whole culture because, as king-mage, he is not automatically divine by virtue of birth but is one who has achieved the spiritual discipline to become the mask of God and to access the Virgilian and Isaianic archetypes. The Agrippan magician, with his I-thou control over nature, possesses divine enlightenment from the unitive experience.[31] Likewise Prospero, in his actions as ruler and in his public body, has gone beyond mortality to identify with the divine in his transport and rapture (1.2.66–76; 4.1.146–63)—rather like the figure of Sibilla in Campion's masque for the 1612 marriage of Elizabeth Stuart and the Palatinate elector at which *The Tempest* was also performed.[32] (In his "private body" as an ordinary person without the corporate body of the kingship symbolized by his magic, Prospero displays faults—excessive anger at Caliban, silly vanity in ordering Ariel to become a sea nymph when he could do his next duties in any form [1.2.300–17], and a teasing disposition in playing on Ariel's fears of never achieving freedom [1.2.256–98].) In ascending to a divine role, Prospero has studied all of the liberal arts necessary to the unitive experience. Using the language of rapture customarily used to describe those who have ascended to the Archetype, as Barbara Mowat has shown, he speaks of himself as having been "transported / And rapt in secret studies" (1.2.76–77), and even within the play he can still be transported by a "beating mind" to eschatological scenes (4.1.146–63).[33] Even as the sibyl in her frenzy takes Aeneas on a dream-trip that prophesies the future of Rome and the structure of the afterlife, Prospero makes the disappearance of the spirits rehearsing the future in the betrothal masque fade into a frenzied prophecy of the end-time where "the cloud-capped towers, the gorgeous palaces, / The solemn temples, the great globe itself, / Yea, all which it inherit, shall dissolve . . . / Leave not a rack behind" (4.2.152–56).[34] What he has ordered, Ariel can describe as "Destiny," and Ariel describes himself and his troupe as "ministers of Fate" (3.3.53–56). In the battle over whether the monarch should be more the contemplative or the active person, Shakespeare argues for the monarch's simultaneous possession of both—both mystical and political power, each dependent on the other.[35]

Because of this, Prospero's illumination-based, image-based education gives each cluster of characters the opportunity to discover themselves through art and to move a step closer to enlightenment. Prospero—the Solomon figure, the knower of divine Wisdom, according to the image that many of the masques used to flatter James— goes beyond Solomon to become the mage, sibyl, prophet, and the prophetic fury, an analogy to the fury that appears in Campion's masque.[36] He can make what he foresees come about in tempests, ghostly banquets for the Milanese-Neapolitan groups on his island, dog chases for Caliban and his crew, and marriage masques for his daughter and future son-in-law. Prospero can perform these feats because his natural world, like the Neoplatonic one described by Stephen Jay Gould, is finally a matrix of metaphors—a ghostly spume, the mineral, vegetable, and animal all organized in metaphoric correspondences.[37] Prospero's human/divine alteration of one term of a correspondence changes the corresponding terms in parallel worlds. In the mineral world, a most "auspicious star" (1.2.182) allows him to reach his "zenith" (1.2.181) so that he can focus metaphysical, animal, and vegetative forces to make nature conform to Virgilian and Isaianic story to reform the island in utopian directions. As contrasted with the solid world of motion and matter that Bacon was soon to posit, nature in Shakespeare's play is no solid, material substance but a mysterious Thou, a temporarily manipulable symbol that can be made to speak the language of an art that transforms people. Like art, it will disappear in the coming eschaton.

Prospero's and Ariel's apocalyptic showings that fuse Virgil and Isaiah make literary texts become natural and supernatural tranformations that construct the promise of a better world. Shakespeare, as Donna Hamilton has documented brilliantly, invites his audience to see portions of the *Aeneid* as a controlling intertext behind his spectacle.[38] But through his use of Isaiah's Ariel and a series of Isaiah's episodes paralleling Virgil, he also invites us to see Isaiah fusing with and superseding Virgil.[39] It is as if the monarch can materialize an apocalyptic and millennialist archetype present in both works to make storm, banquet, fury-dog rout, betrothal masque, and ultimate promise of eschaton reform his subjects and enemies.

This combination of the Virgilian and the Isaianic in *The Tempest* would not have surprised any reasonably literate person in Shakespeare's time. The intertexts were readily available and conventionally related. Lancelot Andrewes, in a 1622 sermon, calls attention to the similarity between Virgil's cognizance of prophecy and the magi's understanding of Isaiah. As he puts it, toward "the end of Augustus' reign, . . . a star was seen" and Virgil "would needs take upon him to set down" whose star it was: "verily there is no man that can without admiration read his sixth Eclogue [error for fourth eclogue] of a birth at that time expected, that should be the offspring of the gods, and that should take away their sins."[40] Andrewes's Virgil, however, made the mistake of attributing the star to Caesar—to little Salonine—when he should have attributed it to Christ. On the other hand, Andrewes's magi, followers of Isaiah, knew whom the star announced, came to worship Christ, and found their world transformed.[41]

A little ingenuity on the part of Andrewes or Shakespeare can make Virgilian work become Isaianic because of the affinity of Virgil's hope for a new age with Isaiah's similar hope.[42] Virgil's *Aeneid* parallels Isaiah's prophecy in its supposed general assumptions and in specific scenes. Both the *Aeneid*'s sibyl and Isaiah were thought to have foreseen Christ. (It is not accidental that both Isaiah and Virgil's Cumaean sibyl sit among the prophets of the new dispensation in the Sistine chapel—though Michelangelo saw fit to pair Isaiah most closely with the Erythraean sibyl.) In imitating Isaiah, Shakespeare is telling his audience what kind of new age is coming—what kind of messianic "millennium" the monarch will provide. In imitating and inverting Virgil, he tells us that the new age will not come from the old Roman imperialism or from all that Rome stood for in the seventeenth century, even though the divine events constructing the prospect of a new age in the *Aeneid* and those presented in *The Tempest* are similar. The new Protestant empire will provide for a limited imperialism and an educative monarchy in which the educable are trained to forgiveness and reconciliation, the evil are contained, self-knowledge abounds, and the old dynasty is restored.

Initially, Shakespeare seems to present human control of nature as a desideratum, as Bacon was doing at the same time. But Shakespeare's godlike king replaces Virgil's Jupiter and Isaiah's God as the controller of storms, and the storm that begins and names *The Tempest* is itself a "prescientific" event created by the personal whim of the magician ruler who commands esoteric, rather than scientific, rules controlling the universe and creates literary storms. The destabilizing frenzy of his storm comes from both Isaiah and Virgil. Ariel creates the storm in both *The Tempest* and Isaiah. He, as the spirit of air, plays the role of the Juno whose tempest made Aeneas go ashore near Carthage and whom the Renaissance made into Virgil's spirit of air and marriage.[43] But Shakespeare also inverts Virgil: he makes Ariel—who sponsors the love of Miranda and Ferdinand and puts on the masque in praise of marriage for the two—a marriage-making equivalent of Aeneas' adultery-creating Venus.[44] As Prospero's familiar, Ariel also teaches what monarchy requires even as the biblical Ariel, identified with monarchy's center—"the city where David dwelt" (Isaiah 29:1)—speaks to Zion with a "voice [that] shall be, as of one that hath a familiar spirit" (29:4).[45] In the Geneva Bible, he is "the lyon of God"—God's agent. In *The Tempest* he is the agent of the godlike ruler.[46] As the Isaianic Ariel mingles with thunder, earthquake, whirlwind, tempest, and "the flame of devouring fire" (Isaiah 29:6),

Shakespeare's mingles with the same elements in performing his educative errands for Prospero.[47] Isaiah's figure's voice comes from the ground (Isaiah 29:4), as must Shakespeare's sprite's when he performs Prospero's "business in the veins o' th' earth / When it is baked with frost" (1.2.253) or when he speaks from the earth to bewilder the villains (1.2.387).[48] Finally Isaiah's Ariel defends Zion, the monarch's physical place, as Shakespeare's defends his hierarchical place. Emphatically, the biblical Ariel, as the lion of God, is not different from the one found in the lore of the magicians.[49] This is the Ariel who summons Juno's masque—her counterpart's showing—and creates the conditions for the contract of true love in *The Tempest* as Venus creates the circumstances that make possible the contract between Dido and Aeneas in the *Aeneid*.[50]

After the *Tempest*'s Isaianic-Virgilian storm has destabilized standard political relationships, in the same way that the storms in Virgil and Isaiah destabilize the regimes that are destined to be tested in those works, education through further showings derived from those works shapes the specific subgroups that are Prospero's enemies and allies and advances their faculty development so that they can be part of a more utopian social condition. Ellen R. Belton argues that Shakespeare arranges his *Tempest* characters according to the faculties in standard Renaissance faculty psychology. He makes the fools, Caliban and his followers, live by their senses alone. He has the Neapolitans live by a debased reason detached from conscience. And he presents Prospero and those closest to him as potentially guided by a God-illuminated mind.[51] The artistic construction of utopia in *The Tempest* proceeds through an artistic appeal to the same ruling faculties, inviting each character through art to subordinate his ruling passion to the next higher faculty stage. Prospero uses the superstructural tools drawn from Isaiah and Virgil—the harpy banquet for those who detach reason from conscience, the clothesline for those dominated by their senses, and the masque of Juno for those seeking divine illumination—to educate his pupils to their proper next stage of development. He does so through a material or apparently material artistic manifestation showing, first, the power of religion's Isaianic utopian hope and, second, both the power and the limitations of Virgil's and Rome's political hope of utopia won through imperial power.

Ariel's first educational showing to a subgroup, the harpy banquet presented to Alonso, Sebastian, Antonio, and Gonzalo, summons a fused Virgilian-Isaianic repast in order to rejoin conscience and reason in the Neapolitans and Antonio (see act 3, scene 3). The whole scene is a page from an imaginary emblem book drawing on Isaiah and Virgil with a motto inviting conscience and reason to meet again in that realm where pictures and mottoes open possibilities for changes in the will and imagination. When Ariel shapes nature and supernature to conform to the educational designs of a duke who has grown into a demigod, he changes only Alonso, perhaps in deference to some idea that monarchs are particularly open to grace, but thereafter Antonio and Sebastian are impotent to contemplate regicide.[52] The harpy banquet in act 3, scene 3 reverses act 2, scene 1, where Antonio and Sebastian draw their swords on the sleeping Alonso with intent to pluck his Neapolitan throne.[53] Ariel seems to protect him because he is an anointed king, but he does nothing to punish the would-be regicides at the time (3.3.10–16).[54] The mirror banquet scene that follows (3.3) has the conspirators attempting to pluck an evanescent banquet's foods whose disappearance makes them witness the futility of their regicidal designs.[55] Shakespeare's harpy banquet accurately mirrors the details of a Hades banquet in the Aeneid where the dangers of usurpation and familial murder are also clear (cf. Aeneid 6, 601–13).[56] The *Aeneid*'s Hades scene presents a fury/harpy banquet where the couches gleam with golden legs and a rich repast appears before the damned until the fury/harpy stands nearby to threaten those who stretch out their hands for food. She shouts with a thunderous voice that those who frustratedly reach had, in the temporal world, hated their brothers, attacked their parents, involved their families in fraud, provided no wealth for their kin, killed for adultery, and participated in treason against their masters. Shakespeare's similar banquet has the Ariel/harpy come in a gleam of light with thunder ("thunder and lightening"), leap up to "clap his wings upon the table" (3.3.52), and furiously forbid food to the Neapolitan and Milanese usurpers who have hated their own brothers and treasonably tried to betray them (3.3.68–82). He sermonizes the group for its betrayal of relatives and promises "lingering perdition" unless the group repents and leads "clear lives" (3.3.82).[57]

Isaiah is also at the banquet. It is not just a reaching and a taking away but a kind of trance. Gonzalo speaks of those who have seen the banquet as in a "strange stare," while Alonso tells of a dreamlike experience in which the winds and thunder bespeak his sins and the doom of his son. Both trancelike descriptions follow the King James version of the narrative that introduces Ariel, which renders a banquet where a sleeping/waking illusion dominates: "It shall even be as when an hungry man dreameth and, behold, he eateth; but he awaketh, and his soul is empty: or as when a thirsty man dreameth, and behold, he drinketh, but he awaketh, and, behold, he is faint, and his soul both hath appetite: so shall the multitude of all nations be, that fight against mount Zion (Isaiah 29:8)."[58]

The Geneva Bible's commentary makes Isaiah's waking/sleeping banquet the repast of those who have waged war against Zion (i.e., the Davidic king's dwelling). Similarly, *The Tempest*'s banquet plays with Virgilian and biblical intertexts to make a penitential Tartarus of this portion of the island after Virgil and a picture of the war against messianic kingship after Isaiah.[59]

An I-thou nature and supernature, using sensate punishment that topples those dominated by the senses, also works in the clothesline scene. Shakespeare doubles the sins of Alonso, Sebastian, and Antonio by creating another set of usurpers in the play's gargoyles: Caliban and his drinking companions. Kermode properly compares Caliban to Polyphemous in the *Aeneid*; but the grotesques should also be compared to their counterparts in Isaiah, the drunkards of Ephraim, who are filled with vomit and filthiness (Isaiah 28:1–9) and reel drunkenly while confusing alcohol with vision.[60] Renaissance commentary makes the drunkards of Ephraim into those who are drunk with power and pride, the equivalents of Antonio, Sebastian, and Alonso, but also into those literally drunk on wine and/or hypocritically drunk on would-be "new age" religious vision (28:7), the situations of Caliban, Trinculo, and Stephano (2.2).[61] This latter drunkenness may refer to the chiliasts and enthusiasts who will later lead to the Commonwealth. As Isaiah's drunkards think they are prophets, so also the drunken Stephano, Trinculo, and Caliban think that they act out the roles of God/King, minister, and worshiping servant (2.2; 3.2, 4.1; cf. 5.1.295ff.).

To cure these drunkards of Ephraim controlled by their appetites, the Virgilian-Isaianic showing in the glittering apparel episode punishes the three grotesques in their sensory faculties by countering planned pain with real pain and planned violence with real hurt. Hamilton has shown how much of that episode plays against the *Aeneid* scenes of the glittering golden bough, the stinking Avernus, and the lime tree or linden tree of false dreams outside the opening to Hades emblemized by the clothing that Ariel hangs.[62] Near the place of false dreams, Caliban and his league create their cargo-cult religion dedicated to Stephano-the-butler-god and his booze, then plan to murder Prospero and, in satiric imitation of Montaigne's Carib Indians, end all "legitimate" lordship. However, ending sovereignty does not create utopia as Gonzalo has proposed. Like mad Lear, the gargoyles identify the satiric "golden bough" of the robes with authority, reaching for that authority by dressing in the fripperies Ariel has left on the line (4.1.193). Trinculo, seeing Stephano in his new robes of office, calls him "King Stephano," "worthy Stephano," and "Thy grace" (4.1.221–29). Then the fury-dogs that belong to the same *Aeneid* scene as the lime tree come on:

> *Enter divers Spirits in shape of dogs and hounds hunting them* [i.e., Stephano, Trinculo, and Caliban] *about, Prospero and Ariel setting them on:*
> PROS: Hey, Mountain, hey!
> ARI: Silver, there it goes, Silver!
> PROS: Fury, Fury! There Tyrant, there! hark! hark! (4.1.253–61)

The harpy/fury-dog destroys the tyranny to which Caliban, Trinculo, and Stephano aspire as she disintegrates the hegemony sought by Antonio and the Neapolitans at the banquet scene. The harpy/fury at the pit of Virgil's Hades who controls the banquet of unnatural kin is, in Renaissance mythology, one with the fury-dogs heard at the mouth of Virgil's Hades (*Aeneid* 6, 255–60). As Aeneas and the Sibyl approach Hades, the Sibyl is about to enter into prophetic ecstasy as the dawn comes on, the ground gives forth sounds, and the woodlands shake. Then the hell-dogs begin to howl in the dawn light. Fabricius's popular Renaissance commentary makes these hounds of hell into the fury/harpy of the banqueting scene and also into the furies/harpies of the Strophades islands in the *Aeneid*, book 3.[63] The wonder dogs—"Mountain . . . Silver . . . Fury . . . Tyrant"—evoke the total scene in Virgil and then punish Caliban, Trinculo and Stephano, running outside Prospero's cave, a place like the Sibyl's cave in Virgil (6, 236 ff.), as the grotesques reach for the habiliments of power.

Isaiah, who comes as close as Virgil to being a source for the play, reinforces the same idea when he promises to the drunkards of Ephraim that they will be trodden under foot—presumably what the fury-dogs do (Isaiah 28:3). Prospero's cavern appears at the gateway to the other world where the spirits come and go as does rulership itself in Renaissance royal mythology, hedged round as it was supposed to be by flights of angels. To put the matter in other terms: Virgil's poetry of empire and of the rise of the Julian house becomes, by a combination of intertextual imitation, inversion, and combination with Isaiah, educative as to the value of respect for Protestant empire: for authority and family, for individual conscience and its emblemology.

But this poetry of empire also speaks to the limits of empire and material possession. Ferdinand and Miranda's betrothal masque also connects conscience to reason and urges control of the senses, but it further suggests what illumination and union in the world of the spirit are about.[64] As Prospero has been unified with the One in the rapture of which he speaks at the beginning of the play, so now his successors need to follow him. Prospero and Ariel's formal play for the lovers is directed toward illumination by Iris and unification with the One by the spirit of Juno ("Uno").[65] Juno is the figure for the unitive mystical experience that dominates much masque iconology, including Ben Jonson's *Hymenaei*. Prospero and Ariel's masque is directed at Miranda and Ferdinand, the figures closest to illumination.[66] To help control sense and to keep conscience joined to reason, Miranda and Ferdinand receive the usual warnings against copulation prior to marriage. As a prelude to their unitive marriage, the Venus Vulgaris, who is "Mars hot minion" (4.1.98), and her son, the Cupid that enabled Aeneas' seduction by Dido, return to Paphos, where they cannot use their wanton powers on the lovers. Cupid, in token of Ferdinand and Miranda's constraint of lust, has broken his arrows and goes to play with sparrows (4.1.99). The betrothal commitment apparently transforms private libido into a desire that has the common good as its benefit, and Shakespeare both echoes and reverses Virgil in his depiction of illumination and transport. Read literally, the Venus of the *Aeneid* is the patron of the Roman empire and of that Christian Rome that is the successor to the pagan empire. Her enemies, Juno and Iris in books 9 and 10 of the work, try to prevent her from founding Rome as a new Troy. To Renaissance commentators, Juno is not only the enemy of Rome but also the power of marriage union, of air, and the companion of Iris, the goddess of rainbows and faithfulness. Hence while *The Tempest* masque's primary female gods, Juno, Iris, and Ceres, derive from the *Aeneid*, they reverse their Virgilian roles in relation to the cause of empire. This is Protestant empire and it will dissolve, with the cloud-capped towers, in the eschaton. What creates dynastic strength and a good marriage in *The Tempest* is not the Venus who secures Aeneas' relationship first with Dido and then with Lavinia. Strength and marriage come from Juno, Aeneas' enemy, Iris, Juno's ally, and Ceres, the goddess of the harvest. If these figurative nuances are correct, then the masque of Juno asserts humankind's or the Protestant world's unitive marriage with the power of the divine One ("Iuno") that leads sky ("Iris") and earth ("Ceres") to produce fruition.

What Prospero's and Ariel's use of Isaiah adds to the Virgilian dimension of this scene is precisely what Lancelot Andrewes claims Isaiah's followers, the magi, add to Virgil in reference to the signs of the

nativity. They add revelation-signs understood—products of the reconciliation that occurs when the illuminated intellect leads reason and
conscience so that these control the senses. Isaiah is ultimately an eschatological writer who regards the material world as a veil, as does
Prospero when he returns from his sibylline moment to announce
that the world will dissolve as dreams do into a sleep (4.1.146 ff.). The
insignificance of the world may empower Prospero's forgiveness.
Some members of the group apparently incorporated into the social
body in this last scene, especially Sebastian and Antonio, remain basically unchanged, and poor Caliban at this point can only say that he
will do his assigned job and seek for wisdom and grace hereafter
(5.1.295–96). Still all are allowed at least to live. Empire's transient
prospect may be what leads Prospero ultimately to the forgiveness
and incorporation scene that ends the play (5.1.172–epilogue, 20). In
any case, the play ends in a mode wholly inconsistent with Virgil's
Roman mythos of justice and might.

More and Shakespeare have their differences. Even given the injustices that he saw in the early Tudor world, More is a far more optimistic writer than the later Shakespeare. More believes that we can
create a common culture of nature and right reason (and not of Bacon's altered nature), while Shakespeare believes fundamentally in the
reforming and educative power of the archetypes reached by canonical literature as represented in monarchic art. But when we look at the
global assumptions of More's and Shakespeare's two worlds, it is clear
that they both assume a stable-state relation to the natural world and
the possibility of a more Edenic social order without progressive or
dynamic change. Neither places any final hope for a new age based on
changing the material world in permanent ways. Hardly a decade
later, Bacon, in writing his utopian *New Atlantis*, alters their vision
entirely—toward the assumption of the possibility of a permanently
changed nature, a material progress that will never end, and a society that will live to extend human empire to the maximum degree
possible.

CHAPTER TWO

New Atlantis and the Chiliastic Utopias

B EFORE A NEW education could come into being, the human race had to create the vision of a natural world that
could be permanently transformed and had to imagine a research society capable of accomplishing the transformation. That was
being done even as the 1612 *Tempest* was looking backward to a neomedieval stable-state world. Written for the same festivities for which
the 1612 *Tempest* was performed, Bacon's masque *The Marriage of the
Thames and Rhine* proposes social mobilization toward a technological society that will accept few limits to the transformation of the
natural world. Just a few years later, Bacon's *New Atlantis* elaborates
his masque and answers More's *Utopia* by proposing a world where
utopia comes from science and technology. *New Atlantis* does not
promise all of the social dynamism promised by the later prophets of
brave new scientific/industrial worlds, but it does envisage human
social groups who, having created the correct advanced educational
and research institutions and the correct discovery procedures, can
change the face of nature to make it offer a comfortable smile. In
short, Bacon's *New Atlantis*, following in the footsteps of *The Marriage of the Thames and Rhine*, represents the first widely circulated
utopian fiction that is a tool for the construction of transformative scientific research communities. *New Atlantis* makes conceivable the assumption that "progressive" societies can alter the face of nature for
the better.

In some ways Bacon's vision is a chiliastic one, depending as it does
on the gradual realization of a human empire over a nonhuman nature that would make for the best possible world.[1] Besides the 1612
Marriage of the Thames and Rhine, Bacon's *New Atlantis* was preceded
in 1605 by discursive gestures in the direction of the assumption of dy-

namism in *The Advancement of Learning*. It was also anticipated by the chiliastic assumptions that seemed to undergird the 1612 marriage festivities associated with the union of Elizabeth Stuart and Frederick of the Palatinate. The marriage created a new alliance linking Protestant England and its sea empire with the Protestant Palatinate's land-based state at the heart of the Hapsburg Catholic possessions.[2] England had recently embarked on a policy of plantation and seeking empire in the New World and in Asia, and the wedding appeared to cement a solid Protestant empire on the Continent, the British Isles, and across the world—a policy that is partially "celebrated" in the 1612 *Tempest*. Not long before the marriage, the Protestant Rosicrucian movement had revived the Apocalyptism and millennialism that were staples of much of earlier Protestantism—not only of the chiliasts—from the time of Luther, and it came to associate its millennialism with the wedding time.[3] The Rosicrucian Simon Studion's *Naometria*, dedicated to the Duke of Württemberg, and Johann Valentin Andreae's related *Turris Babel* had forecast millennial events in which the English monarchy and the Protestant continental forces would have a role. Further, the Rosicrucian manifesto called the *Fama*, circulated by 1612, promised a "Universal and General Reformation of the whole wide world," partially based on what humankind can magically collect from the book of nature.[4] The end-time and millennialist rhetoric continued in events surrounding the Stuart-Palatine marriage. Much of the ceremonial entertainment given during the betrothal and marriage period cast England's Palatinate alliance as the victory of fairy tale good over a diabolic evil that justified Protestant England's conquering and "civilizing" destiny. This was especially the case in the run-up ceremonies that gave Frederick the Order of the Garter and the cross of St. George, and in the celebration fireworks that showed St. George delivering a queen from a wicked magician.[5] The fireworks at the wedding seem to have recalled Spenser's apocalyptic picture of the Red Cross Knight rescuing Una/Protestantism from the necromancer Archimago/Catholicism.[6] In the same vein, a mock battle showed the English delivering the Venetians from the

Turks and cast the English—not the Catholic Empire that was actually fighting the Turks—in the role of Christendom's protector.[7]

There were also civilizing and imperial themes. Inigo Jones produced a masque by Thomas Campion in which the furies of poetry, religion, prophecy, and love (Orpheus, Prometheus, Sibilla (or the sibyl), and the lovers, respectively), drawn from Pontus du Tyard's mythology, appear to civilize the culture. King James acted as Jove's representative in the civilizing process. Campion's contrasting antimasque figures come from the world of Jacobean comedy, where figures for love, self-love, melancholy and fantastical schoolmen, and usurers mingle and seem harmless enough.[8] On the evening after the wedding, the new age begins in the new world in George Chapman's work *The Memorable Maske of Two Honorable Houses*, which included an antimasque composed of baboons and American Indians and which continued the "civilizing" and racist themes developed in *The Tempest*.[9] In this context, before Frederick's ill-fated effort to relieve the Bohemian Protestants, before the outbreak of the Thirty Years War in which he was disastrously defeated, and before James attempted his alliance with Catholic Spain, the 1612 *Tempest* and Bacon's *Marriage of the Thames and Rhine* mark a watershed between the world as a "thou," a veil over a divine speaking, and the world as an "it," a thing made only of matter following fixed rules.[10]

If, as we have demonstrated, *The Tempest* looks back to a stable-state nature and social order, Bacon's masque for the Palatinate marriage occasion promises a dynamic, evolving control of nature. Bacon rejected the idea of the divine right and power of kings, and his masque for the Palatinate-English marriage, *The Marriage of the Thames and Rhine* (otherwise known as *The Masque of the Inner Temple and Grayes Inne*), proposes an analytic view of nature and education that contrasts starkly with the metaphoric view in *The Tempest*.[11] Bacon's view of power includes no reticence before permanent temporal empire, none of the stuff of Prospero's eschatological speech and his forgoing of his staff after his regime's restoration.

The masque's cost in money and court time suggests its ideological importance. The great legal powers of the realm, the two Inns of Court, were its presenters. It symbolized the full potential might of the new Palatinate alliance and more.[12] On the evening when the masque was first to be performed, the Inns' masquers traveled up the Thames on the royal barge in full costume, with musicians and guns, elaborate lighting, and gentlemanly attendants, including the two admirals who were their "guides." They were greeted at the end of their trip by King James, by Prince Frederick and the Lady Elizabeth, and by other court greats assembled to meet the Inns' people at the windows of the king's "privy gallerie" on the Thames riverfront.[13] However, after the masquers had presented themselves before King James in full costume, they and Bacon found that he was tired from two nights of nuptial celebrating. He said that he "could last no longer."[14] The masque was postponed from Tuesday until Saturday, and the Saturday performance proved anticlimatic since the masquers' costumes had already been displayed.

However ill-fated as a performance piece, the delayed masque presents the alternative to Shakespeare's *mythos* of the mystical educator and ruler as utopia maker. Bacon's good rule can be created *in this world* through pure power and the right use of the technology symbolized by Vulcan. The "arguement" of the masque as described in the printed text is that Jupiter and Juno, wishing to honor the marriage of the Thames and Rhine (England and Palatinate), call upon their messengers, Mercury and Iris, to do the honoring. Thereupon Mercury presents his antimasque dance made up of female Naiades and Hyades and of male blind Cupids and Vulcan's dancing robots: silver and golden statues. Iris then presents a second antimasque on behalf of Juno, in which Flora, as Iris's ally, calls in a May-dance group. This group, according to the argument, symbolizes that the marriage will be "blessed with the love of the Common People."[15] After this, Mercury, in the main masque, brings in the knights of Olympus to symbolize that Jupiter is reviving the Olympic games to celebrate the English-Palatinate dynastic union.

In the initial dance, the English-Palatinate marriage is blessed by natural forces in the form of the deities of springs and rain clouds as well as by the blind Cupid of the *Venus Vulgaris*, who is also a natural force. More important, the marriage is blessed by a technology symbolized by the mechanical force of Vulcan's golden and silver statues. Since Vulcan is as close as classical myth comes to a god of technology, the robotic dance of the gold and silver statues presumably symbolizes the increase of the natural wealth of the two realms uniting in the marriage through the force of the fertile Cupids combining with technology. Nature is enhanced by technology when the robots dance with the female spirits of the springs and rains that feed the two rivers. The two rivers or two realms Iris affirms to be destined to "grow / Into a thousand streames, great as themselves." Dynastic empire is promised to a realm in which nature is recreated by technology.[16]

In the end, the work touches the hope for a timeless realm such as the complete conquest of nature promised in *New Atlantis* will accomplish.[17] Unlike Shakespeare's *Tempest*, Bacon's masque has no teacher and ruler and no eschatological bang at the end since Bacon, by this point, had already detached himself from theories of the divinity of kings. And, as a Democritan atomist, he could not logically represent the seen world as a dream. His main motif is the marriage of the Thames and Rhine, a simple metaphor for a new power relationship, but that marriage will also be supported by natural riches complemented by technological innovation. All levels of society celebrate this new power structure fearing no eschaton because Bacon (who in 1605 had already published *The Advancement of Learning*) did not believe earthly reality to be a ghostly spume covering the architecture of the divine ideas.

In *The Advancement of Learning*, Bacon had set forth his principles for the construction of a knowledge-finding society—one considerably different from Shakespeare's—that would deserve political and intellectual authority. In *The Marriage of the Thames and Rhine*, he tried to attach that dream to a dynastic hope. Finally, in *New Atlantis*, he gives that society body and patronage from a Solomon-like king, like Prospero.

The vision expressed in *The Marriage* was to fail. Frederick's efforts to become the great Protestant leader of the rebel Bohemian lords ended in failure at White Mountain in 1620, and the promise of the marriage went nowhere. But the dream of permanent empire that went beyond dynastic failures and political vicissitudes did not die in Bacon with Frederick's defeat. Though in April of 1621, about three years after the beginning of the Thirty Years War, Bacon confessed to several charges of accepting bribes in chancery suits and resigned as James's chancellor, between 1624 and 1627 he wrote what we have of *New Atlantis*, obviously a continuation of the thrust of the marriage masque and an answer to More's utopian education toward constraint of consumer desire. It is possibly also a riposte to Shakespeare's kind of education returning one to the old order. *New Atlantis* subverts Timaean assumptions about how knowledge is discovered that are as old as Plato, and it also challenges Judeo-Christian assumptions about how Wisdom manifests itself that go back to the Solomonic books. As opposed to the sybilline Prospero's venting about how we and the world are a dream that will pass, Bacon presents us with a monarchy that can create research allowing us to dominate the natural order permanently. We can have our desires in all matters save the sexual. And the ex-chancellor creates this mythos not with an epic subcreation like Shakespeare but with subcreation attached to the great epistemological myths of the Western world: namely, the aforementioned *Timaeus* and the Wisdom books attached apocryphally to Solomon's life.

New Atlantis is a deliberately incomplete work, to all appearances. William Rawley, Bacon's literary executor, says his master had planned to complete the work with a picture of "a frame of Laws, or the best state or mould of a commonwealth," but this part of the work was never finished.[18] However, what we have contains implications concerning the kind of political authority that derives from societies for the construction and/or discovery of knowledge. The vision of such societies and related educational institutions became especially powerful when read in the context of Bacon's other works on the promise of the inductive method and in the Stuart political context. Rawley examined *New Atlantis* as a "model . . . more vast and high than can possibly be imitated in all things; [but in which] most things . . . are within men's power to effect," and Rawley's remark is not surprising.[19] The regime in *New Atlantis*, centering in an oligarchy of scientific philosopher-kings gathering physical evidence so as to control weather, wind, food supplies, and/or industrial military machinery, must have appealed to a century drunk on religious wars over matters beyond evidentiary proof.[20] In consequence of its call for a society dedicated to a brand of knowledge beyond controversy, *New Atlantis* attracted followers from controversially opposed groups: continental chiliasts such as Comenius, the leftist Commonwealth educational theorists, and the Royalist thinkers who promoted the Royal Society. Comenius's Pansophia, Plattes's and Hartlib's Macaria, and ultimately the designs of the promoters whose work led to the Royal Society—each group significant in the reshaping of Western education to what we know now—are hardly conceivable apart from the focus and the legitimizing rhetoric provided by *New Atlantis*.[21] That Bacon, the Stuart absolutist, could inspire Commonwealth education/research designs suggests that his rhetoric works with enough force to inspire action and enough duck-rabbit ambiguity to allow radically variant factions to claim him.

However, the myth of Bacon as the Moses or prophet or Adam of the new scientific world, as developed by Abraham Cowley and other leaders of the Royal Society later in the century, is a slightly inaccurate one.[22] Unlike the Moses whom the biblical narrative represents as alone seeing the Pisgah prospect, Bacon had models for the new world order he proposed—the experiments with ordnance carried out by the Royal Office of Ordnance; the experiments with mine pumping common both on the Continent and in England; the introduction of new fruits and vegetables from the western hemisphere; the menageries and cabinets of curiosities kept by many noble houses; Tycho of Brahe's observatory; and the Emperor Rudolph's scientific group.[23] The new foods introduced in consequence of plant breeding by Native American groups seem particularly important to Bacon in that he locates his utopian realm in a fictive Native American realm.[24] The fact that New World foods did alleviate, at least temporarily, the threat of severe protein and complex carbohydrate shortages in Europe must have contributed to the plausibility of Bacon's island world. But the historic formations on which Bacon relies, save for the Native American one, resemble the dilettantish attachments to a court that Bacon proposes in his masque for Grey's Inn.[25] There, he says, the monarch, as part of the cultivation of philosophy at this court, should have complex gardens, a zoo, an aquarium, and a collection of products of technology and manufacturing devices. It is as if Bacon himself in earlier works, and a variety of other writers and projectors in their pre-*New Atlantis* writings or activities, saw one aspect or another of the Pisgah sight. What makes the proposal in *New Atlantis* compelling beyond these other writings is its comprehensive view of how institutions for the pursuit of normal science and related technology, for collaborative research and education, and ultimately for "progress" can be created.

The *New Atlantis* institution for scientific study, Solomon's House, is a place supported by the state for the exclusive collaborative pursuit of normal science across hundred of years. Yet it is, to some degree, autonomous from the state: a society for the production of knowledge and thus a proposal as to how the "sociology of knowledge" is to develop. *New Atlantis* is the progenitor of thousands of think tanks, land grant universities, and centers for the study of specialized subjects across the world. But the work assumes a static oligarchy. Of course, no major technological change can occur without altering how human beings organize themselves into communities and how they govern themselves or are governed. But the paradox of changing technology and unchanging government is only one of the paradoxes leading to the power of *New Atlantis* and its generation of varied educational offspring among the revolutionaries and royalists of the next few generations. In advocating a search for knowledge in Solomon's House that will lead to technological change, Bacon advocates a study distinct from that characteristic of the acknowledged quadrivium sciences in the Middle Ages and the new astronomical/physical sciences of the Renaissance (called the Wisdom sciences later in this chapter), both of these consistent with More's religion of a "careful observation of nature and . . . reflection on it and the reverence that arises from this" as "a kind of worship . . . pleasing to God." When Bacon says humankind can only master the natural world by being its slave ("For nature is not conquered except by being obeyed"), he means a physical domination of nature, not Prospero's spirit-winged domination based on metaphoric correspondences.[26] Obedience to Nature refers to an intellectual study that permits systematic natural manipulation. His version of the idea of progress, therefore, paradoxically provides for significant human alteration of the material universe that will sustain an unchanging authoritarian government.[27]

Renaissance science in the quadrivium and the Platonic tradition of astronomers and physicists are essentially science as worship. A by-product of the application of mensuration and musical analogies to the natural world, such science has an aesthetic component at its base; on the other hand, the schoolmen espoused the more Aristotelian notion of science-as-collection. However, as Bacon knew well, they did little serious collecting of specimens or investigation of the kind that their master practiced in his more observation-based treatises on natural history.[28] The observations of plants and animals and of other natural phenomena in the standard schoolmen's works on these subjects, extending from Albertus Magnus through Bartholomaeus Anglicus through Renaissance bestiaries, herbals, and encyclopedias, show little observation that goes beyond Aristotle and a superficial glancing at the phenomena.[29] Bacon's scientists have also been compared with Prospero-style magicians or alchemists, but they are not magicians; they are not secretive to the other members of their academy about how they produce their results, as the alchemists commonly were and as Prospero is in relation to his subjects. They do not work alone like Prospero, and they make no theurgic claims.[30] Their closest Renaissance semblances may be practical experimenters in such areas as mining and ordnance and the few inquisitive explorer-collectors who were returning from Asia, Africa, and the Western Hemisphere. But few of these figures had long-term government support in systematic centers for research, publication, setting research priorities, and critiquing what they had done.

The scale of Bacon's vision of what can be done is unique. The illumination his "philosopher-kings" seek through their experiments of light leads to fruit in the "enlarging of the bounds of Human empire to the effecting of all things possible," the "possible" including "coagulations, indurations, refrigerations, and conservations for producing artificial meters."[31] The possible embraces the creation of composts and experimental soils, the development of processes for making fresh water out of salt water, the establishment of chambers for creating artificial weather, agricultural experiments to create new species of plants and animals, the discovery of a new pharmacopeia, and provisions for the experimental creation of new war machines. The Father of Solomon's House claims all these for his institution in his ultimate piece of science fiction:

—caves . . . for . . . the producing also of new artificial metals, by compositions which we use.
—engines for multiplying and enforcing of winds, to set also on going divers motions.
—Water of Paradise . . . [for] prolongation of life.
—means . . . to make one tree or plant turn into another.
—a number of kinds of serpents, worms, flies, fishes, of putrefaction; whereof some are advanced . . . to be perfect creatures, like beasts or birds; and have sexes, and do propagate.
—swifter motions than any you [Europeans] have, either out of your muskets or any other engine that you have . . . stronger, and more violent than yours are, exceeding your greatest cannons and basilisks.
—ordnance and instruments of war . . . compositions of gun-powder, wildfires burning in water and unquenchable.[32]

The power of nineteenth- and twentieth-century science and its capacity for domination are witnessed here, in a dream that is the polar opposite of More's vision of universal constraint.

This new scientific world will fulfill human biological need better, and its heroes will be the conquistadors of technological evolution without regard to moral considerations. The dwelling houses of the scientists include an iconic storehouse made up of two "long and fair galleries," filled like the Smithsonian Institution with the best inventions or their representations, among these gunpowder and ordnance, presented as divine blessings.[33] In *The Advancement of Learning*, Bacon cites the discovery of gunpowder as evidence of the need for systematic inductive research: "All the discoveries which take rank among the nobles of their kind, have . . . been brought to light, not by small elaborations and extensions of art, but entirely by accident."[34] Though Baconian progress is to culminate in "experiments of fruit" that will make life more comfortable, though its purpose is to recover humankind from the effects of the Fall, its most palpable "fruit" is weaponry of the kind that Gulliver offers to the king of Brobdingnag—which offering leads the king to refuse all the benefits of Gulliver's civilization, calling him for his proffer a member of the "most despicable race of little odious vermin that nature ever suffered to walk upon the face of the earth" (see chapter 4).[35]

The absence of a cost-benefit agenda or analysis of the cost of constructing paradise is evident not only in the treatment of gunpowder. The scientists in Solomon's House do not study the manner in which the alteration of entities in the natural process by human manipulation in turn affects other parts of the natural world. None of the House's feats creates any disturbance in other parts of the natural or human system or requires any analysis of its disadvantages. Though the college may suppress knowledge, publishing only "such new profitable inventions as [it] think[s] good," none of the proud changes listed has been treated as "not good" by the college, nor has it wondered what else has happened by virtue of what it has done.[36] The rhetoric is that of pure fairy-tale happy endings.

THE TRANSFORMATION OF WISDOM AND OF SOLOMON

To give power to this vision of progress without pain, Bacon has to go back to the epistemological sources of Western science, Plato and the Jewish-Christian Wisdom tradition, and reconstruct them to make a new investigative mythology and pattern for a support system for research. Bacon transforms Solomon away from the ancient images in his picture of Solomon's House. In addition, he is at pains to pull in, beyond Solomon, a great many other references to Christianity.[37] He gives us St. Bartholomew's miracle of the letter and Bible in his bibliographical ark, the pillar of fire and the cross that accompany it, the conversion subsequent to this miracle, the Christian priest with the red cross hat that governs the House of Strangers, the prayers, hymns and references to "our Savior," and the pastoral staffs and crosiers. But all seem like marginal decoration designed to sanctify the transformation of wisdom's countenance implicit in Bacon's transformation of Wisdom and Solomon.[38] To change the world, Bacon changes Solomon and Solomon's God.

Since Origen's time, Solomon had been regarded as the architect of the academic disciplines through which human beings could apprehend the divine ideas contained in Wisdom, especially of the disciplines Bacon wants to change or to replace. Since Plato and the Greek theorists of the disciplines were Solomon's analogue, Origen says Solomon described physics or natural philosophy in the book of *Ecclesiastes*, ethics in *Proverbs*, and metaphysics/theology in the *Canticle of Canticles*—the disciplines covered by Plato in the *Timaeus*, *Republic*, and *Parmenides*, respectively (the *Timaeus* was also thought to include mathematics).[39] These are also, if Agrippa is to be believed, the disciplines through which the mage, like Prospero, rises to the One.[40] Bacon need not have read Origen to have come to the conclusion that Plato's primary disciplines and Solomon's were one. Solomon, as the wisest of men, by logical inference had to be the author of the disciplines of study, and Plato was thought to have done a similar kind of work. Furnished with a precedent for fusing Solomon with Plato, Bacon creates a new *Timaeus/Republic* where once lived a new Solomon who set the research agenda thousands of years earlier. Though this fiction is a poet's lying idol (or eidolon), Bacon could hardly afford to protest against his own lie as he elsewhere protests against other false idols, especially in his *Advancement of Learning*. *New Atlantis* puts him in the position of the eidolon maker who answers idols with other idols to inspire "truth" seeking that will create the new world years hence, as Solomon's fictive endowment has made it thousands of years earlier.[41]

Since Solomon's House is named after King Solomon and/or his

Bensalemite equivalent, Salomona, it should pursue the divine Wisdom of whom "Solomon" rhapsodizes in Proverbs 8, Ecclesiasticus 24, and Wisdom of Solomon 6 (or Proverbs 8 alone if one eliminates the apocryphal books). However, though the Solomon of *New Atlantis* is a scientist of sorts, he is never explicitly made the author of the Wisdom books. He does not rehearse an ascent to Wisdom through number or mathematical study, as the traditional Solomon was thought to have done in the Middle Ages and early Renaissance. Rather, he writes a book of inductions and/or natural observations, a "Natural History . . . of all plants from the 'cedar of Libanus [Lebanon]' to the 'moss that groweth out of the wall,' and of all 'things that have life and motion.'"[42] Based on a misreading of I Kings 4:33, Bacon makes him become an inductive encyclopedist who can create the foundations for empirical research (Virgil Whitaker believes Bacon himself tried to be an encyclopedist under the influence of Vincent of Beauvais and Barthlomaeus Anglicus).[43]

Bacon was aware of the other Solomon. He writes of the traditional Solomon in an explanation of Ecclesiastes 3:11 in *The Advancement of Learning*:

> [Solomon] concludeth thus: '*God hath made all things beautiful, or decent, in the true return of their seasons: Also he hath placed the world in man's heart, yet cannot man find out the work which God worketh from the beginning to the end*': declaring not obscurely that God hath framed the mind of man as a mirror . . . capable of the image of the universal world . . . delighting in beholding the variety of things and vicissitude of times, but raised also to find out and discern the ordinances and decrees which throughout all those changes are infallibly observed. And although he doth insinuate that the supreme or summary law of nature, which he called '*the work which God worketh from the beginning to the end*' is not possible to be found out by man; yet that doth not derogate from the capacity of the mind, but may be referred to the impediments, as of shortness of life, ill conjunction of labours, ill tradition of knowledge over from hand to hand and many other inconveniences whereunto the condition of man is subject.[44]

This passage echoes Ecclesiastes 3:11 and correlates closely with parts of Solomon's prayer in the Wisdom of Solomon 8:1, where the figure of Wisdom is said to work "mightily from one end of the earth to the other" and to order "all things well." Traditionally, this Wisdom was the source of astronomy and the more mathematical or "deductive" sciences through her association with number and mathematics. Neither she nor Solomon as her hymnist was an originator of the kind of inductive work that *New Atlantis* attributes to the Solomonic encyclopedia. The old pre-Baconian Wisdom furnishes humankind with sets of ideal proportions that act as a heuristic in guiding mathematical and mathematically based investigations that might terminate in empirical observation. She relates to the Timaean and Neoplatonic intermediary figures, containing within herself as a gift from God the architectural, musical, or Pythagorean divine proportions for all species and natural relations. Her function is to receive them from God and impose them on the natural world. She is, in patristic and some Renaissance thought, identical with the Logos of John 1, which justifies the Christian study of the natural world: "summary law," in Bacon's parlance. But she is not centrally an encyclopedist.

In contrast, Bacon's Solomon, unlike Shakespeare's recidivist Prospero/Solomon as mage and philosopher-king, is a foundational figure for a new beginning that promises to destabilize the natural world. Much of the old science that produced the amazing discoveries in astronomy and physics in the sixteenth and early seventeenth centuries depended on the old construction of Solomon and his divine lady. In Bacon's own centuries, Copernicus's discoveries depend on his alliance with a Florentine Neoplatonism that emphasizes the systematic control of things by Wisdom and number, and Kepler assumed that "God created the world in accordance with the principle of perfect numbers."[45] Harmonies in the mind of the Creator furnish the reason "why the number, the size, and the motion of the orbits are as they are and not otherwise."[46] Galileo's idea of a systemic planet world, mathematically and sapiently ordered, gives, in his view, a more direct picture of God than do the scriptures because it is not open to subjective and diverse exegetical interpretation: "The truth of mathematical demonstration gives us [discursively], the knowledge . . . which the Divine Wisdom knoweth" directly. (A mathematical understanding of what divine Wisdom has imposed on matter reveals the whole mind of God "written in that great book which ever lies open before our eyes . . . the universe" a book which "we cannot understand if we do not first learn the language and grasp the symbols" written "in the mathematical language.") [47] Clearly Galileo's cosmic book devised by Wisdom is not Bacon's Solomon's "natural History . . . of all plants from the 'cedar of Libanus' to the 'moss that groweth out of the wall.'" [48]

Bacon supports his turn away from the old Wisdom's emphasis on the systemic and mathematical with redefinitions that make Wisdom residual within the individual motions of the natural system rather than the systemic itself. Solomon's House may not investigate summary law or systemic relations because Bacon thought, on the basis of the Ecclesiastes 3 : 11 quote already given, that such law cannot "possibl[y] be found out by man." In contrast, the experimental/technological mode, centering in "light" and "fruit," could produce small but useful findings. Though Solomon's House includes a great repertoire of tools for the manipulation of individual variables—coagulations, indurations, refrigerations, conservations, distillations, separations, diversity of [furnace] heats, sound experiments manipulating echoes, harmonies, sounds of all sorts, and demonstrations—it includes no tools for or emphasis on systemic study such as the astronomers and physicists of the time carried ahead. [49]

The privileging of the isolation and manipulation of the particular variable as opposed to systemic study shows in Bacon's foundational redefinitions of divine Wisdom, making her less the systemic structure in the divine mind and more the matter and motion of individual atoms. [50] His works other than *New Atlantis* evince confidence that a knowledge of the new Wisdom/wisdom will lead to a technological transformation wholly foreign to earlier Wisdom: "wisdom . . . anciently defined as the knowledge of things human and divine" has "variety of means," so that "physical causes give light and direction to inventors in similar matter." In Bacon's view, the conventional study of sapience, done with "a certain rhapsody," lacks "sobriety" and combines an "incongruous mass of Natural Theology, of Logic, and of some part of Natural Philosophy." It should be replaced, in his view, by the superior study of forms or laws, formulations concerning the *behavior* of matter that speak of the divine power and concerning a "beauty of the form" that speaks of divine wisdom.[51] These "Forms" or natural laws do not easily form themselves into a synthesis—systemic or summary laws that give access to Wisdom in the traditional sense:

> Nothing really exists beside individual bodies, performing pure individual acts according to a fixed law, yet in philosophy this very law, and the investigation, discovery and explanation of it, is the foundation as well of knowledge as of operation. And it is this law, with its clauses, that I mean when I speak of *Forms*.[52]

In Bacon's world, the study of these essences, forms, or laws (not to be confused with Plato's "forms," which are mere thoughts, or with Aristotle's, which are mere words) requires experimentation and a laboratory formulation of the constitutive laws.[53] Indeed, by the end of his career, Bacon is announcing to Father Baronzon that "true physics will eliminate metaphysics."[54]

In a Baconian/Solomonic world, to know individual things aright—"individual bodies, performing pure individual acts"— means to name them "correctly." This requires a picture theory of meaning and a language of simples, as Wittgenstein would call it. In other writings, Bacon argues for the invention of a "real character and philosophic language" where words will name things directly and confusion will fade before the light of a new language.[55] In *The Advancement of Learning* Bacon frets about "idols of the human mind": dogmas, superstitions, subjective discoveries of order, and subjectivity itself—about the tendency of philosophers to invent terms to cover their incapacity to come up with scientific explanations: "Substance, Quality, . . . Passion, Essence, . . . Heavy, Light, Dense, Rare, Moist, Dry, Generation, Corruption, Attraction, Repulsion,

Element, Matter, Form . . . all . . . fantastical."[56] To prevent such linguistic libertinism, the earlier Bacon had called for "Characters Real" such as Chinese ideograms as he understood them: written signs that attach to real things rather than to the phonology of a particular word and that therefore are understandable across several languages. Some of this by implication appears in *New Atlantis*; for example, the Bible and the letter from St. Bartholomew seem to be cast in a Pentecostal language everyone understands and in the same way. The sound experiments of Solomon's House can produce "all articulate sounds and letters," as if in a universal phonology for a universal language. And the fellows of Solomon's House "hate all impostures and lies," perhaps including both magical illusions and fictions created by the abuse of language.[57]

Bacon's new theory of Wisdom is emphatically present in his rejection of Copernicus's mathematically based deductions about distant planets, which he calls "mere hypotheses."[58] He also ignores Kepler's and Galileo's related work, and he always seems uninterested in efforts to explore the holistic and systemic in the science of his own time. Though he includes synthesizers among the personnel in Solomon's House, one cannot know what they do. Bacon knew science and induction and the role of mathematics in the development of experimental procedures. He had a good grasp of the need for the collection and classifying of arrays of natural objects on the basis of "real" resemblances that went deeper than any surface similarity. He knew of the importance of mathematics in laboratory inductive science that might discover these similarities. He understood the significance of the formulation of hypotheses and the usefulness of literary and mathematical models to such formulation. He also understood how the manipulation of variables might work and the establishment of probabilities through the observation of samples within a class.[59] What his method lacks is a procedure whereby scientists can go from experiments on individual variables to an examination of systemic effects—for example, the effects that astronomers watch or that a traditional farmer with an eye for relationships captures. Focusing on individual variables and single outcomes means that one does not

ask the future to look back from the individual outcome to the systemic effects in contingent arenas of an intervention—for example,
what new metals will do to the system of metals or to the social system, what altering the weather will do to crops and systems of plants
and animals, what prolongation of life will do to population levels,
what creating new animals will do to the rest of the animal kingdom,
or what more violent ordnance will do to political relations.[60]

One may argue that it is too much to ask of a thinker that he legitimize new knowledge as well as create a plan for examining the hazards of his approach. However, many thinkers express a concern in
Bacon's period about the diabolic dangers of alchemical and magical
action, about Faustian bargains, and about the hazards to humankind
of new weaponry. He was not without examples from others who
considered the costs. Indeed, Prospero's retreat from natural domination is partly impelled by a consciousness that Bacon lacks; Prospero knows that destabilizing the natural world overmuch or over-
long is an unnatural enslaving of the elements and the elemental
spirits (5.1.316ff.).

WISDOM'S MYTHS: THE *TIMAEUS* AND SOLOMON

Placing its locus and history in a Timaean landscape, *New Atlantis* attacks and alters *The Timaeus* as it alters Solomonic ideology. Bacon's
earlier *On the Wisdom of the Ancients* (*De Sapientia Veterum*), dealing
with conventional classical mythology, forecasts the counter-creation
apparent in the reshaping of the *Timaeus* in *New Atlantis*. For example, in the revision in *On the Wisdom of the Ancients* of the conventional allegorized version of the myths of the ancient world, the creative Cupid is the natural motion of atoms.[61] Though he is perhaps
derived from the benign form of the Venus Vulgaris who is the external force creating natural order in things, Bacon's Cupid/Venus
force is internal to the simples and inductively investigatable.[62] In the
same work, the Logos of John 1 that had been traditionally Wisdom
as the font of ideas imposed on matter becomes Mercury or a law ordering confused matter from within. From Martianus Capella on
down, Mercury had been the eloquence associated with wisdom, in-

stead of wisdom itself. He now becomes something that can be inspected, not by looking holistically but by altering the motions of individual atoms. Following the selfsame system of reinterpreting old myths as props to Democritan materialism, Bacon totally alters the mythic underpinnings of the Timaean scientific project.[63]

In doing this, *New Atlantis* latches onto the central mathematically based epistemic myths in the *Timaeus* and related Platonic works and converts them from myths arguing for the analysis of full systems to justifications for both the empirical study of individual variables and permanent interventions in the natural process.[64] That Bacon saw Plato's central works somewhat as Origen saw them, as an ascent through the disciplines or at least a commingling of them, is suggested by his assertion that "Plato intermingled his philosophy with theology . . . and the second school of Plato, Proclus and the rest, with mathematics."[65] The intermingling that had been Plato's strength in patristic and Neoplatonic times becomes his Baconian fault. *New Atlantis* recreates the *Timaeus* and *Republic* by keeping natural philosophy (physics and chemistry) and mathematics apart and keeping both busy with the examination of the detail of individual things in Solomon's House. The mathematical house, containing mathematical instruments of geometry and astronomy, is kept separate from the houses where experiments involving material objects or technology go ahead.[66] As Plato's utopia served the cause of the mathematical contemplative activity, Bacon's serves the cause of the empirical inductive work that becomes the norm in institutions of applied science in the eighteenth through the twentieth centuries.

Bacon undermines the Timaean myth by combining it with stories that grew, or could grow, out of the exploration of the New World and the ethnoscientific discoveries of the inhabitants of the Western Hemisphere. Though the New World of the Western Hemisphere could easily have been regarded as forecast in Plato's Atlantis, the future world of advanced intellectual discovery was not perceived as having New World origins. Most writers either followed Montaigne in attributing noble savagery, or followed Shakespeare in attributing a diabolic criminality, to post-Columbian New World cultures.[67]

New Atlantis

Though More's Utopia comes into the traveler's vision after he has gone beyond the new world, and though he calls his traveler one of the kind who followed in Plato's wake, his world is one where nature is followed, not changed. Clearly the little-known New World that could be reached only by sea voyages was as easy a place to locate utopias and special imaginary social states as Homer's Mediterranean had been for his time. However, Bacon's use of an offshoot of the New World for a sophisticated utopian, scientific state to outrival the Athenian republic of advanced cosmological exploration in the *Timaeus* and *Republic* has no evident precedent.

The governor of Atlantis's main city, Bensalem ("Son of Jerusalem"), asserts that his country's history began about three thousand years before (i.e., 1500 B.C.) when, in his account, exploration of the world by ship flourished as in Renaissance Europe. Each nation, including the Indians of Atlantis, visited every other. The Western Hemisphere Indians once had a "high culture" (they are primitive only in consequence of their great wars and the subsequent flood that took away their culture, forcing them to make the simplest of adaptations to nature). The governor of New Atlantis argues that the representation of Atlantis in Plato's *Critias* as "planted" by the "descendants of Neptune" and having a temple, palace, city, and hill with many "goodly navigable rivers" surrounding the *scala coeli* of the site is "all poetical and fabulous."[68]

But a real Atlantis existed—great Atlantis, powerful before Bensalem became important (the "real" Atlantis "that you call America"). According to Bacon's myth, both of the parts of the real Atlantis chose to launch important military expeditions at the same time; the Aztecan or Tyrambel group against Europe in the war between Atlantis and Athens described by the *Timaeus*; and the Inca Peruvians or Coyans against Bensalem.[69] Having traded with the Atlantis powers and still carrying on the seafaring tradition of the ancient Atlantis, Bensalem had adopted the high culture of the Incas prior to their fall. It became, thereby, a *new* Atlantis that rose to its present strength when its military forces outwitted the Incas. Whereas the defeated Aztecs were killed by a cruel Greece, Peru's soldiers, losing to Bensalem, were forgiven by the conquerors who defeated them "without striking stroke." It was then that the Incas encountered an avenging flood that reduced their remaining populations to a primitive state (Bacon believed this part of his fable to be historical).[70] But the new Atlantis, possessing all of the scientific skills of old Atlantis and more, the civilization that could rival the Athens of the *Timaeus*, remained. Bacon's Bensalem, then, is a place for the manufacturing of knowledge from the new world perspective as Plato's ancient Athens was the place for the manufacture of Pythagorean knowledge. To Bensalem's high culture have been added the innovations of Solomon's House and the clemency of Christianity.

Atlantis's holocaust, the equivalent of Plato's earthquake and flood, reminds us that Bacon's version of the idea of progress has a Platonic equivalent in Plato's theory of the cycles of civilizations. The discussion in the *Timaeus* of the ancient battle between Athens and Atlantis and then of the Demiurge, the world soul, the world body, and the planets, of reason and necessity, was to serve as an introduction to the description in the *Critias* of developments prior to the flood that destroyed Atlantis, and also to the unfinished and lost *Hermocrates* that was to "reinvent" civilization after the postdiluvian simplicity. (This material also appears in the discussion in Plato's *Laws* of how a state based on the laws of nature would function.) Simulating a new progress and following a roughly parallel logic, Bacon shows how his original Indian states of Tyrambel and Coya returned to simplicity after the flood, while a land derivative from old Atlantis, "New Atlantis," continued to progress. Fictively, a part of Plato's lost design from the *Hermocrates* is fulfilled in Bensalem.[71] Like the prayerful Timaeus of Plato's dialogue, the community in Solomon's House gives voice to "certain hymns and services" thanking God for scientific illumination. And reversing the journey of the philosophers who escape from Plato's cave in *The Republic*, the "Speculative and Operative" scientists of Solomon's House make "missionary" trips to the citizens below to spread the light of the newly discovered to the unenlightened.[72] Of course, their message is very different and is the essence of Bacon's counter-creation.

Bacon's scientists, like Prospero, outrival Plato's philosopher-kings in power over nature. They are new magi, though one never knows exactly what their political powers are (see later discussion). Part of the basis for making the guardians into magi as well comes from Bacon's understanding of the principle basing a civilization on natural law in a fashion different from how More does this.[73] In Bacon, civilization, through knowing the laws of nature, becomes Nature's maker, not its servant; civilization becomes the satisfier of desire, not its constraint. Bacon's scientists are transformers like Prospero, but they are permanent transformers of the natural process, and they operate in a systematic and public mode *within a community* for the construction of knowledge and closed off from the rest of the world. Metaphorically we see Plato's guardians become the biblical magi as Bacon and the Renaissance understood them. In *The Advancement of Learning* (1605), Bacon speaks of the Persian magi whose chief business was "to note the correspondence between the architecture and fabric of things natural and civil," and the imagery of the mage pervades Bensalem's secret rooms.[74] The first person to greet the visitor to Bensalem, a man with a revered appearance, is clad in garb reminiscent of a Renaissance magi painting: wide-sleeved gown, blue silk and blue "watered chamolet," and green turban.[75] His first words to the visitors are "Are ye Christians?"—as if to ask if they have sought the right god. The father of Solomon's House, when he comes to town, wears Eastern garb of "fine black cloth, with white sleeves and a cape." He has a girdle of white linen and a hat "like a helmet or Spanish Mantera." He is carried in a "cedar, gilt, and . . . crystal" chariot decorated with the sun and a cross of gold. Under his feet and associating him further with the magi are "carpets of divers colours, like the Persian," and he sits like an Eastern king "upon a low throne richly adorned," with a rich blue satin cloth of state over his head.[76]

However, the job of the mage in Bensalem is not that of Plato's guardians, or of a Renaissance magician, or even of the traditional biblical magi. The guardians and mages know nature through some sort of illumination. The biblical magi not only knew nature but saw the coming of a new age in the first appearance of Christ. The job of the members of Solomon's House is not to note the correspondences either within the natural world or between the natural and civil worlds. Instead, it is to destabilize nature and create it afresh after the fashion of human desire.[77] *New Atlantis* simply transforms the culture of the mage that appears in fifteenth-century Florence, continues in the continental Platonic academies, and crops up in England in such presences as Giordano Bruno, John Dee, and the English translations of Agrippa.[78] It makes the traditional culture of the mage into that of the Platonic guardian-as-scientist having government support and a research institution for collaborative science.

Utopia comes down from above—the above of the think tank—in *New Atlantis*. As previous scholars have noted, *New Atlantis* gives us almost nothing about Bensalem's character, size, population, number of cities, governmental institutions, or social gradations exterior to Solomon's House. It does not tell us of Bensalem's laws, economic system, land settlement patterns, provisions for the poor, or educational institutions. More treats all of these items at length, and Shakespeare dramatizes most in some measure in the *Tempest*, to the degree that the island setting allows. What we know in Bacon are "the Strangers' House, the Infirmary, Solomon's House, the City Companies, and the municipal government."[79] Though the island clearly once had a king, he does not appear or come into the discourse even by name. A hidden bureaucracy governs without identifiable civil laws or law-bound allocations of power, a substitute for the hidden Ariel who governs Prospero's island by an invisibility that obviously appealed to James.[80] Of course, one might say that had Bacon been able to add "a frame of Laws, or the best mold of a commonwealth" as he planned, all of this would have been supplied.[81] But it was not supplied, probably because the contradictions between universally used objective knowledge and a closed elite would have become obvious. On the island, the members of Solomon's House know best what knowledge to give out and what to withhold. In the presence of authority, the strangers offer much kissing of skirts, humble beseeching, bowing, and self-abnegation. We are in the presence of a liturgically ordered civil society governed by benevolent and powerful scientific wizards.[82]

The promised transformation of nature makes revolutionary alterations in the natural process appear to serve conservative ends. Beyond the mysterious wisdom of the monarchy, dead or alive, beneath the wizards of Solomon's House, Bensalem has the extended family that replicates the invisible system of paternalistic authority practiced by the scientists and extends it to the populace; the father exists in relationship to the family as the scientists to the realm. We especially have the "revered custom" of the Feast of the Family. In the *Advancement of Learning*, Bacon writes: "Aristotle noteth well, that 'the nature of every thing is best seen in his smallest portions,' and for that cause . . . the nature of a commonwealth, first in a family, and the simple conjugation of man and wife, parent and child, master and servant, which are in every cottage." The feast gives one a sense of a commonwealth all made up of Bensalemite families ordered by the worship of an invisible patriarch who is the vine to the iconic golden grapes of offspring whom he blesses from his invisible seat, conferring on them the blessings of the trinity from a kind of Yeatsian Byzantium completely out of nature, beyond all libertinism. Worshiped in rituals as hieratic as Egyptian statuary, all of the family father's authority ironically issues from his copulative potency as the authority of the scientists issues from their manipulative potency.[83] By king's charter, the family controls the revenues that it derives from its properties, may be exempted from taxes, and receives special royal honors. If, as Denise Albanese has argued, "the occultation of the current ruler of Bensalem . . . removing the king from sight of his subjects, dispersing his gaze, and hence calling his existence into doubt . . . inserts the philosophers of nature into the space of the authority," that space is also filled by the "occultated" family patriarch, who is a philosopher of nature only in his fecundity of body. This fecundity, in turn, leads to large private properties, royal honors, tax exemptions, and magnificent ceremony in a large room. The hieratic presentation of the family reassures us that this is a powerfully conservative social order (Stuart to the extreme), a place where private property is secure and the mysteries of power remain as retired from public view as the Tirsan of Bensalemite families going to his private prayers. Bensalem is a society in which radical natural change can be ordered from the elite think tanks of Solomon's House without its having a derivative effect on other social arrangements. These are as impermeable to change as the Tridentine mass before Vatican II.

The dialogue over education, research, and the construction of utopia changes with Bacon's *Advancement of Learning*, his masques, his *New Atlantis*, and their progeny. The proposal that humankind attempt a permanent makeover of the natural world to accomplish the "enlarging of the bounds of Human Empire to the effecting of all things possible" leads to the creation of institutions of education and research that could conduct the makeover.[84] Bacon's utopia, unlike Shakespeare's, has social and environmental consequences, because it does not depend primarily on miracle as the engine of its perfective process. It is not accidental that it was used to organize social energy toward the creation of real institutions on the Protestant left in the middle of the seventeenth century and within the royalist center in the latter part of the century, especially to furnish legitimization for the Royal Society. The souls in Virgil's Elysium know a miraculous perfection for a thousand years before they must return to be reborn in a body (*Aeneid* 6, 724–51) to make Roman violence and peace. Prospero, who depends on violence, emblem, and miracle, turns sibylline to announce the wondrous future dissolution of the cloud-capped towers and the great globe. On the other hand, Bacon's *New Atlantis* utopia is in process and has no end. It is a place that started its slow reconstruction of the natural world centuries ago and continues conquering nature to this day. It is a place of habit and routine.

It was easy for the Commonwealth reformers to seize Bacon as an ally, particularly as Chiliasm had by this time acquired a distinctly this-worldly beat. It was also easy to see Bacon's program, however inspired by Stuart absolutism and imperialism, as an alternative to the violent revolutions and confrontations that had not worked for the chiliasts through the period of the Thirty Years War. Because of Bacon, the future kingdom was to be the kingdom of science and technology, constantly changing and controlling the natural process with new inventions as Bensalem had changed with the scientific progress that it had made. Bacon's advocacy of the Palatinate-English alliance and of colonialism in Ireland and America and his interest in enlarging the "bounds of human empire to the effecting of all things possible" are similar. The colonizing of nature is a far more powerful project than the colonizing of Europe, Asia, or the Americas.[85] It involves everything tangible. To put matters in other terms: Bacon saw the scientific project, the educational project, and the colonizing projects carried out by distant guardians of the good to be one. While Caliban seems savage to a Prospero thrown up on his island, the ruler readily leaves Caliban's island when he has reestablished his European order. He apparently allows Caliban and the old natural order in which Caliban is at home to revert to form. Bacon's plans for the colonization of nature using the skills of the new world and the colonized subjects are permanent and permanently destabilizing.[86] They have changed how we live.

CHAPTER THREE

Bacon's Commonwealth Offspring

BACON DIED IN 1626 before the storm that was to come down on England near midcentury had fully gathered. Since much of his political effort had gone to keeping its clouds from appearing at all, and then temporizing when they did, he died a "political failure." But, though a failure in the short run, he succeeded magnificently in the long—in setting the foundations for the construction of the utopian movement that was to create the scientific/industrial transformation of the natural world. Paradoxically, the first generation of the movement after his death attached itself to distant chiliastic and utopian religious impulses coming from the Continent that matured in England when the kind of government that he served was wobbling or had been removed. This generation also invented the idea of a possible utopian mode of education to serve the coming New Atlantis, education that was to be graded, systematic, and compulsory.

By the 1630s and early 1640s, the intellectual and political divide that was to result in the Commonwealth had opened between the monarchy and dissenters. The Battle of the White Hill that destroyed Frederick and Elizabeth had assured the imperial title to a Catholic emperor since the new Bohemian ruler's Catholic commitment meant that the emperor would also be a Catholic. Since the German Protestant principalities were no match for the imperial army, and the only non-German Protestant forces facing this army, under the formidable command of Wallenstein early in the Thirty Years War, were the Danes, it appeared by the late 1620s that the Protestant cause would fail. But it revived with the intervention of Sweden and Gustavus Adolphus on July 4, 1630. His diplomatic, administrative, and military/strategic skills and his financing by French Catholic funds until his death at the battle of Lützen (1630) rescued the Protestant cause. Thereafter until its ending in 1648, the war degenerated into the endless bloodbath created by the imperial army and the allied intervening French and Protestants. The war decimated the population of Europe. At the end, circumstances were little changed: Frederick's son was restored to the Palatinate throne, Sweden expanded its territory in the Balkan region, and Protestant hegemony in northern Germany was guaranteed.

Meanwhile, the British Isles, though not directly involved in the continental war, saw their civil society torn apart by the same forces tearing the Continent asunder, though somewhat later. On the right, Charles I (1625–49) asserted the divine Prospero-like grandeur of the monarchy, in more substantial terms than had James, and refused to call new 1630s Parliaments. In the religious area, Charles permitted his Archbishop of Canterbury, William Laud, to push for Anglo-Catholic liturgical conformity. He married a Catholic queen, persecuted the Protestant left, and imposed on Scotland an English-style prayer book and episcopal system. When in 1638 the Scots rebelled against this imposition of episcopacy, Charles responded weakly, using his own royal resources. He was eventually obligated to go to Parliament to gain funds to support his northern campaigns, and he had to do so under a system governed by the requirement in the 1628 Petition of Right that Parliament approve all taxes and that all garrisoning of troops in private homes be done with the homeowner's permission. The reconvened parliament not only reasserted its control over the raising of taxes but impeached and executed Laud, abolished much of Charles's government bureaucracy, and mandated that Parliament alone, meeting at least every three years, could dismiss itself.

When Parliament declared that the army would henceforth be under its control, its action precipitated the 1642–48 English Civil War. In response, Charles came at Parliament with his army, but the parliamentary forces, eventually commanded by Cromwell, captured the king in 1646, executing him in 1649. The execution of the monarch, the creation of the Commonwealth, and then later (1653) the establishment of the Cromwellian protectorate announced the beginning of the end of Prospero's old order and opened vistas of possible brave new worlds: those being settled in the Americas, those developed by the colonialist East India Company, those promised by Cromwell's conquests in Scotland and Ireland, and most of all those utopian educational ones, partly imported from the Continent, and glimpsed by religious independents in both the pre-Commonwealth and the Commonwealth periods. The appearance of opportunity for social experimentation as the monarchy weakened and the Commonwealth was set up meant a new proposing of utopias, not as grand dreams but as actualizable blueprints, plans, and legislative proposals.

The blueprints, plans, and legislative proposals divide into two general groups: those that look to the *immediate* reorganization of all property rights and social institutions and those that anticipate a *long-term* restructuring of society through the educational re-creation of human beings. To the former group belong the prominent visionary pieces of James Harrington and Gerrard Winstanley, and their pictures of what should be had some immediate impact on social organization in some places. James Harrington's *Oceana*, dedicated to Cromwell and generally distributed in 1656, would restrict the amount of property that any one person could own, extend the electorate to all property holders, impose a republican form of government in which all offices would be elected ones, and create a two-house legislature, one designed for debating and one for voting.[1] It inspired constitutional action, especially in Pennsylvania. In contrast, Gerrard Winstanley's more communitarian *New Law of Righteousness* (1649) advocates the end of private property accumulation and the restriction of holdings in land to what one person could himself cultivate. It inspired the Digger movement.[2] Winstanley's later *Law of Freedom* (1652), less significant for seventeenth-century political action, calls for the abolition of private property in productive means and for a government of neighborly aid a little like that Gonzalo envisages for Prospero's island (one in which new officers of government would be elected every year and where most of the tasks of government, including education, would be carried out in a decentralized system by local citizenry untrammeled by a professional bureaucracy).[3] In this Commonwealth-era period of revolutionary ferment, other pictures of a society changed by the radical restructuring of social institutions developed, but these are not our central concern.

Our concern is the more influential educational utopias proposed by the Protestant left in the period just before and during the Commonwealth that had to do with a reorganization of society through education—always the cautious response in periods of ferment. In this educational thrust, Bacon's ideas (sometimes extended into Protestant reinterpretations of medieval Wisdom theories) formed the central strand in the intellectually powerful Hartlib circle. The circle included Comenius, Durie, Plattes, Petty, Milton, and Boyle, and many other lesser figures. Part of the group's power came from its inclusion of Comenius himself in 1641–42, the period when the Civil War was just breaking out and when ferment was vigorous.[4] Much of it came from Hartlib's long-term organization from the 1630s to the 1650s of a network of influential people capable of political action, interested in establishing the kingdom of God on earth, and committed to universal "scientific" education and research.[5] The third factor, the influence of books, especially of those by Comenius, was longer lived. Though all the principals in the Hartlib group wrote influential pieces on education, as later discussion makes clear, Comenius's books offered *the* important theoretical basis and textbook exemplifications of this basis to the underground of English educational thinking in the late seventeenth and eighteenth centuries. Comenius's publications in England cover a long span of years: 1637 for the *Conatuum Comenianorum Praeludia*; 1639 for the *Linguarum Reserata*, with another two editions after 1700; 1657–1700 for six editions of the *Orbis Sensualism Pictus*; 1639 and 1642 for the *Pansophiae Prodromus*; 1668 for the *Via Lucis*; and 1641–1700 for the twenty-three editions of *Janua Linguarum* (seven editions after 1700). Like the books of theory, the textbooks emblemize what education should be while also mediating a utopian vision to the young and their teachers.

The new Baconian dialogue came in the wake of the seventeenth century's ancients-moderns dialogue. The new Baconians appeared after George Hakewill's and John Jonston's 1627–35 attack on ancient learning and their defense of modernism, including Jonston's defense of the new science.[6] In pursuing the ancient-modern dialogue, the Hartlib group, aside from Milton, does not so much attack as ignore ancient learning. The ancient eidola with their ideal islands set in a distant sea, teeming with monarchist and imperialist associations, disappear in an abandonment of classical intertexts such as Bacon's Plato or Shakespeare's Virgil.[7] Bacon himself and *New Atlantis* become the replacement myths. And what Bacon's 1630s–50s followers do with his myth is more important (and more illuminating for Mannheim's unstated question of how the literary becomes the visionary) than what Bacon actually was and said.

Bacon becomes a prophet. Most of the central figures in Hartlib's group have connections to a central European chiliastic Protestantism decimated both by the Thirty Years War and by the Counter-Reformation. They try to connect to the new dreams of pre-Commonwealth and Commonwealth England, and all work at legislative ferment and school experimentation.[8] Having left behind the collapsed continental dream of the goodly society, they collectively and individually take up Bacon's mythos of the transformation of nature through research and education and convert it to a project that can serve dissenting purposes—and do so even after the Commonwealth dies. The dissenters' choice of Bacon, the most powerful administrator in an earlier Stuart monarchy, as their approved millennialist altered the later politics of scientific and educational change. Bacon historically belonged to the religious and political "right," but he became the iconic Moses of the left. The Hartlib circle uses him to propose its form of popular educational reform in the direction of science and utility in the schools, and the Restoration center-right uses him to promote its new research structures. While the Hartlib group's Bacon looks forward to an educated citizenry, the post-Restoration Royalists' Bacon stirs the elite hearts of the court and the Royal Society's Solomon's House members and philosopher-kings. And when this other Bacon promoted by the Royal Society appeared, few people attacked him or the Royal Society since the latter was formed with the royal sanction of an autocratic king. But two decades after the Restoration, after the appearance of a Restoration consensus was no longer such a desideratum, the Tory wits, especially Swift, Pope, and Arbuthnot, could take out after Bacon, Baconian educators like Comenius, and Baconian scientists like Boyle in defense of a Jacobean stratified society that would educate through cultural productions and would confine the production of abstract verbal and mathematical knowledge to elites.[9] At the same time, the dissenting academies continue to use Comenius's work for texts and for theory.[10] Though sometimes the same names turn up on the roster of Commonwealth educational utopians and Restoration scientific advocates, the movement toward a new education and that toward a new research are quite different, and predictably the two Baconian movements converge only when the old feuds are forgotten in the Utilitarianism of the nineteenth century and the new research-and-education consensus foundational to the industrial/scientific order appears.[11]

Hartlib, Comenius, and Durie in the 1630s–50s added Baconianism to Bartholomaeus Keckermann's and Johann Heinrich Alsted's early seventeenth-century central European efforts to create an urban Protestant compulsory education.[12] Each of the three knew of continental compulsory education and of its role in the frustrated Thirty Years War Protestant cause in central and northern Europe: Comenius as the last bishop of the Hussite Bohemian Brethren slaughtered by the Hapsburgs, Durie as minister to the English Company of Merchants at Elbing in West Prussia (and negotiator in the Protestant Continent for Protestant unity in the 1630s–50s), and Hartlib from his birth in Protestant Elbing, West Prussia, and his upbringing in Danzig (Gdansk). The three turned in the 1630s–40s from the destruction of the Thirty Years War on the continent to a hoped-for reconstruction of society in England, interacting in the invention of educational utopias and pedagogical means to realize them.[13] They did so to answer the primary chiliastic question—Winstanley's "Why may we not have our Heaven here (that is a comfortable livelihood in the Earth) and Heaven hereafter too?"[14] Despite his Stuart service, Bacon's anti-authoritarian attitude, contempt for scholasticism and

Aristotle, and trust in the direct investigation of the truth went with Protestant values.[15] Bacon had promised, in *Novum Organum*, that science could recover humankind's paradisal dominion over nature.[16] Now with the revolution about to happen or in progress, the time for action for a millennial recovery was ripe.[17] In the hands of the Protestant left, the metaphor for organized research, Solomon's House, alters into one for a general and often compulsory education that promises to create the new society called Pansophia or Macaria or Antilia.[18] As Charles I's administration begins to fall apart and the tensions basic to the coming civil war begin to appear, Hartlib becomes the organizer for the group and attaches his wagon to Comenius's 1630s educational proposals and Plattes's utopian *Description of the Famous Kingdom of Macaria* (1641). At the same time, he enters into a conversation, face to face and by letter, with Boyle, Milton, Petty, and dozens of other Protestants interested in education reform.[19] Though Comenius was not long in England (1641–42), his English translations center Hartlib's development and disseminate a plausible notion of a Baconian and compulsory scientific/technological education.

Among the first educational books that Hartlib published in the 1630s was Comenius's *Conatuum Comenianorum Praeludia*, printed in 1637 without the latter's knowledge and distributed to hundreds of leading European thinkers.[20] An elaboration of this work entitled *Pansophiae Prodromus* came out under Hartlib's auspices in 1639.[21] In 1642, Hartlib published his own English translation of both of these works, in connection with Comenius's 1641–42 English stay, under the title *A Reformation of the Schooles*.[22] (In 1651, an unknown translator put out Comenius's *Naturall Philosophie Reformed by Divine Light*, and in the same year Jeremy Collier translated his *A Patterne of Universall Knowledge* for Hartlib).[23]

The publication of some of Comenius's works in England, the Hartlib circle's utopian work, and all of its later lobbying and energy to create new institutions testify to the power of Comenius's vision at the time that the Civil War was about to break out (1641–42). Hartlib's publication of his *Reformation of the Schooles* (1642) gave the foundational statement. There Comenius—in a summary of his whole

73

educational position—argues that a new society can be created by a graded, cognitively sophisticated, and compulsory scientific/industrial education for both sexes. This turn to social reconstruction through education in the 1630s is new for Comenius. At first, after Frederick's 1623 defeat and the Hapsburg Catholic slaughter of the Hussite forces in Czechoslovakia, Comenius wrote in his *Labyrinth of the World and Paradise of the Heart* of a pilgrim-hero who turns to private mystical experience, essentially "inner light" Christianity, after viewing the various abuses in learning and society.[24] When, shortly afterward, he comes under the influence of Bacon, he suddenly turns back to the social world to advocate an all-embracing educational reform, based in science and divine Wisdom, an education that will transform the world and produce the new millennium. Indeed, the most obviously chiliastic of the three writers treated in this chapter is Comenius, who, in his 1657 *Lux ex Tenebris* (later *Lux in Tenebris*), prophesied, on the basis of other central European prophecies, the destruction of the Hapsburgs and of the papacy and the creation of a new social and religious order.[25] Webster has characterized how millennialism entered into Comenius's educational utopianism:

> The age of light was not yet realized, but its appearance was guaranteed: "for it is necessary that what has been pre-determined by the counsel of God and foretold by his word must first be fulfilled and brought to completion." Positive policies for this situation were explained by Comenius in terms of the imagery of light. This metaphor was of course a Christian commonplace, but the millenarians made it peculiarly their own. Since God reserved his greatest gifts for the last age, this was the age of the greatest light, and most profound enlightenment. The emergence of the age of light out of unsettled conditions was both described and given emblematic expression by Comenius:
>
> "But it sometimes happens that rain or mist comes on in the morning, and then the sun dispels the darkness of the clouds with more difficulty and more slowly, and only succeeds at last toward the evening in pushing forth its conquering rays, and rejoicing the

inhabitants of the world with its full vision. And it is not otherwise with the intellectual light of the soul, namely, Wisdome."[26]

The kingdom of this Wisdom is Pansophia, rooted ironically in medieval theories of Wisdom education given a Baconian twist, a kingdom constructed through universal education that lays hold on the laws of nature and constructs out of that seizing both a holier and a more comfortable kingdom. Comenius's political Chiliasm complements that of his educational works in that the kingdom of God (or Pansophia) comes both through the fall of the great Catholic powers and through a Baconian gradual systematic investigation of the Wisdom of God that will permit human beings to transform the Creation.[27] By the time Comenius writes the *Praeludia* in the 1630s, he has acquired the main outlines of his educational and social vision, and by 1633, he is hymning Bacon as the herald of the new philosophy.[28] Unlike many Protestants of the time but like Bacon, he retains a considerable interest in the idea of a Wisdom that somehow announces the structure of nature and in an educational and research program to lay hold on that Wisdom.[29]

Comenius's Wisdom, as described in *Reformation of the Schooles*, includes the traditional pre-Baconian notion that all things have a structure imposed by Wisdom and that all human beings have an inner wisdom that seeks the outer Wisdom through experience and scientific study. He avoids Bacon's idea that everything one knows about Wisdom is to be found in isolated atomic actions and also avoids the elitism of Bacon's restriction of important scientific learning to the secret society of Solomon's House.[30] Comenius's philosophic and theological proposals are often fuzzy, drawn as they are from Aristotle and Cicero as well as sapiential biblical texts, but they do contain three consistent theses: (1) following Proverbs, that Wisdom reconstructs the young person's mind according to the "light" and the image of God; (2) that Wisdom's happy character, exhibited in its playing before God at the creation (Prov. 8:30–31), means that the school seeking sapiential knowledge should be a place of play, a *ludus literar-*

ius; and (3) that, contrary to the sectarianism of the day, Wisdom reveals a true and universal philosophy *PhiloSophia*—relieved of all ancient partisanship. This philosophy displays itself with a certitude "like unto Mathematicall demonstration," Euclidean geometry, the chemist's experiments, or Bacon's science. The methods for finding Wisdom are like Bacon's: "an accurate Anatomizing of the whole universe," a definition of all words so that they are used accurately and without ambiguity, and a formulation of the laws governing things, especially atomistic research.[31]

Wisdom's transformative revelation, designed to create the good society, will come through the graded compulsory school. There all knowledge will be taught and Pansophia, or utopia, created. Comenius uses differing levels of Ezekiel's Jewish temple, from the outer court to the holy of holies, to speak of an individual's cognitive development moving from the concrete to the abstract to the "systemic" to God himself.[32] This developmental scheme owes a great deal to an old Wisdom tradition extending back to Boethius but also, as Jean Piaget argued, a precedent to modern cognitive psychology.[33] In recognition of the exigencies of natural cognitive development, Comenius' education manipulates concrete objects (or pictures) to teach children and encourages observations of these which go from the general to the special, the obvious to the obscure, and the academic to the practical. Given the nature of human cognition, effective schools must be predicated on an understanding of the total structure of knowledge and conducted according to an understanding based in the laws of cognitive growth. So organized, they can do without the coercion of "fist . . . ferula, roddes and scourges" or any other brutalization. In a very unusual argument for education based in concrete objects and utilitarian ends, Comenius states that brutalization is presently absent in the guilds' apprenticeships—their "learning in any mechanick art"—because they come closer to understanding what learning truly is and how it ought to be taught.[34] The coercion would come in the state requirement of school attendance.

A Reformation of the Schooles ends with a summary of a preliminary version of the *Great Didactic* (written in the 1630s but not published at all until 1657 and not published in Great Britain until the nineteenth century) that details how the new school and society are to be built—the new school to be ordered according to cognitive levels, compulsory for both sexes, and dedicated to the study of Sophia or the scientific exploration of nature and the technological offspring of this exploring. Comenius promises that his forthcoming larger book will assign "taskes to Yeares, Months, Dayes, and Houres," providing a pedagogical method for each level, and that it will show patterns for the improvement of schools leading the Christian state to "lesse darkness, confusion and dissentions, but more light, order, peace and tranquillity." He specifies that "youth of both sexes should be put to Schoole" and "instruction . . . be universall." The pattern of the school should follow the pattern of nature discovered by encyclopedic research and cognitive development, and schooling should be divided into four levels: the Mother School (Comenius's equivalent of kindergarten), the "nexte Schoole" (i.e., elementary or vernacular school), the "Latine Schoole" (his equivalent of grammar school or high school), and "the University."[35] Thus, Comenius's fundamental scheme, later expanded in the *Great Didactic*, was laid down fifteen years earlier for English audiences.[36]

At the same time as Comenius was writing works of pedagogical theory, he was writing texts adumbrating how a school should be organized, and these had wide circulation in England and elsewhere. The many English editions of *Janua Linguarum* and *Orbis Pictus* in the late seventeenth century and early eighteenth propagandize for essential Comenian convictions. For example, *Orbis Pictus* shows the school to be an orderly place having clear grades or forms and a strict routine. The study shows the student pursuing knowledge diligently alone. Comenius's sense of the scientific appears, for example, in his presentation of birds according to habitat and species and in his maps that show the Western Hemisphere. *Orbis Pictus* closes with an encouragement to the child to fear God and to pray that He will bestow on him or her the spirit of wisdom.[37]

Nothing so sophisticated as the idea of Pansophia appears in the writings of Hartlib and Durie, save when they are advancing Comenian proposals.[38] But their plans for a new education and new communities ultimately articulate common kitchen cookery versions of Comenian Chiliasm.[39] In introducing Comenius's proposals, Hartlib builds on the logic of his own utopian lands, Antilia and Macaria, making the reform of schools and schoolmasters mean the reform of the land itself.[40] Indeed, the second related utopia to come from the Hartlib circle, Durie's *The Reformed School*, is Baconian by implication. Its requirements for learning are utilitarian, and Durie himself was a committed Baconian.[41] Since Max Weber and R. H. Tawney, Protestantism of the Commonwealth variety has been associated with the furthering of an individualistic capitalistic ethic.[42] Durie's utopia, however, includes a communal group living together to worship and to provide education for its young via a common treasury governed by a steward. The community is to manifest a complete commitment to the religious functions of education, but it also has a kind of humdrum sense of utility about it. For Bacon's Faustian science, Durie substitutes education in agriculture, trades, administration, military skills, and economics, especially family economics. The pedagogy in the school is to be calculated on the basis of the ends of learning, the development of means to the ends, and the subdividing of the parts, all to be figured in terms of an understanding of religious utility: "The Encyclopedia of Sciences must answer the wheel of humane faculties, and this wheel must answer the Circle of the Creatures whence man is to supply his defects. As then in a watch, one wheel rightly set doth with its teeth take hold of another, and sets that toward a third and so all move one by another, when they are in their right places for the end for which the watch is made: so is it with the Faculties of the human nature, being rightly ordered to the ends for which God created them." As in Comenius, Durie's pedagogy begins with concrete objects where possible and climbs the traditional faculty ladder through imagination, memory, and reason. Durie's "reformed school" is to "supply . . . these defects which deprive us of some part of our natural happiness" by proceeding from the concrete to the abstract and the thing to the word. And the education is to have specific goals for specific age levels, beginning in infancy. The curriculum is a brief but articulated program in reading, nomenclature, mathematics, and scientific observation, including classical (and perhaps modern) authors, dealing with agriculture, natural history, architecture, ethics, economics, mathematics, chemistry and pharmacy, chirurgery, and "Logick, Rhetorick, and Poesie."[43]

Whereas Durie's utopia is confined to the commune that creates an education for the voluntary group, Hartlib's own educational vision is attached to that of Gabriel Plattes, to whose work he also attaches his name and his considerable reputation. Plattes's Macarian proposal (1641)—published and promoted by Hartlib at almost the same time as he promotes Comenius's *Reformation*—concerns a whole colony or nation.[44] Macaria derives its name from a country More locates near Utopia where, when he begins to rule, the king takes an oath never to have more than a thousand pounds in his treasury, so that his country has enough to defend itself against invaders but not so much as to seek to invade other lands. Whatever more comes into the royal treasury goes back to the people. Plattes reminds us early in his work that Macaria has for its pattern "Sir *Thomas Moore*, and Sir *Francis Bacon* once Lord Chancellour of *England*."[45] By making the king a populist and fusing More's Macaria with Bacon's Bensalem, Plattes creates a Commonwealth Bacon who is more nearly the people's—the English people's—man. And Macaria is a distinctly Protestant land; its proposals contain no hint of Bacon's elaborate ritualization of life, no new Solomons and Platos, and little of the legitimizing intertextual reference to ancient precedents that Bacon uses to appeal to his learned court or university audience. Though the dialogue between the Traveler and Scholar that makes up the discourse relates Macaria to three utopian predecessors (Bensalem, Utopia, and Plato's old Atlantis), it does so cursorily.[46]

Plattes's Macarian reforms breach the line between fiction and action. They are addressed to the Long Parliament and concern education, science, democracy, and, significantly, the plantation of new colonies. They argue that an ideal Parliament would have to rule through five subcouncils concerned with (1) husbandry; (2) fishing; (3) land trade, including the supply of guild craftsmen and apprentices; (4) sea trade; and (5) plantations and colonies sent out at public cost. As part of the populism of the proposal, the husbandry subcouncil is to watch development policy and land reform, preventing any man from holding "more land than he is able to improve to the utmost."[47] (Unlike More's wholly defensive Macaria, this land has a colonization policy in which each year "a certain number [are] sent out, strongly fortified" at public expense to settle new worlds.) For its intellectual leadership, Macaria has a Solomon's House–like "college of experience [i.e. experiments]," but its scope is less grandiose than Bacon's, confined to medicines and improvements enhancing the wealth of the nation in "Husbandry, Physick, and Surgerie." In contrast to the elitist practice of Bacon's Solomon's House, everything done at Plattes's proposed house is public: "All such as shall be able to demonstrate any experiment for the health or wealth of men, are honorably rewarded at the publicke charge." A kind of social cost-benefit calculus exists in that the Society of Experimenters is "liable to an action" if it "deliver[s] out any false receit" (clergy are also physicians in Macaria).[48] Since all Macarian officers of state are subject to annual review by the Parliament or Great Council on the complaint of any citizen, the fictive government is honest. Any opinion may be brought before the Parliament for a disputation in order to prevent dispute elsewhere.[49] Finally, Macaria is millennialist. When the Scholar proposes that no such utopia can exist before judgment day, the Traveller says that he knows a hundred scriptural texts promising such places in *this* world.

Hartlib and Plattes name their Baconian utopias Macaria or Antilia, and the evidence that they did not intend these to remain fiction comes not only from their text addressing the Long Parliament but also from actions they undertook. In 1648 they made themselves trustees for a Baconian scheme to receive money for "The Advancement of Universal Learning," a forerunner of the Royal Society. Setting up this foundation, they call it Antlantis, after Bacon's Atlantis and Hartlib's Antilia-Macaria.[50] That the new foundation, while not a country or colony, includes Antilia in its title follows from the fact that Antilia is sometimes a colony and sometimes a think tank and

network of scholars and educators working together on the advancement of knowledge. As a place, Hartlib visualized it as a colony that
someone might establish in Virginia or Scandinavia, a structure that
he labored to create from 1628 to 1661.[51] Ultimately, the think tank
idea triumphed. Even as the Commonwealth was ending and the
Restoration coming on, Hartlib still believed that "the fire" of Macaria was "not altogether extinct but may flame."[52] As late as 1660, he
saw the Royal Society as a manifestation of Macaria.[53]

Following the practical utopian bent of Hartlib's circle, in 1647
Hartlib and Durie made a proposal "Tending to the Happy Accom-
plishment of England's Reformation," in which they propose for England a post of warden in the humane sciences, designed to advance
"Divine and Humane Wisdom."[54] Its holder is to assist advanced re-
searchers to "put in Practice the Lord *Verulam's* Designations, *De
Augmentis Scientiarum*" and to help less advanced scholars to perfect
"Mr. *Comenius* Undertakings, chiefly in the Method of Teaching,
Languages, Sciences, and of Ordering Schooles for all Ages and Qualities of Scholars."[55] What Bacon is to do for advanced research, Comenius is to do for schooling.[56] Hartlib and Durie's replacement
of Bacon with Comenius in the schooling pantheon may be a reaction
to Bacon's admiration for the Jesuitical elite schools of the *ratio
studiorum*, hardly the stuff of Chiliasm.[57] Bacon had little respect
for popular education or for the increase of grammar schools at the
lower levels since the education of excessive numbers of grammar school scholars would fill the realm with "indigent, idle and wanton people."[58] In contrast, Comenius wanted universal compulsory
education.

In 1653, at the height of the Commonwealth and following up on
Comenius's proposals, Durie and Hartlib sent Parliament another
proposal, bearing the Baconian title of "Some Proposals for the Advancement of Learning." Again, the new proposal contains a rubric
providing for the compulsory scientific industrial education for all
children, including girls, and a proposition for an advanced level
made up of trade schools and ruling schools for "teachers or . . .
Prophets."[59] The school for rulers, including education in the "Pan-

sophicall" use of reason, again betrays Durie's indebtedness to Comenius's 1641–42 stay in England.[60] This vocational plan anticipates the Utilitarian emphasis on vocational education, although it contradicts the later Utilitarian push for the elimination of explicitly Christian teaching from the curriculum. Moreover, the plan includes provision for adult education. All of the required public education for children and youth is to be supplemented by resources for voluntary use: an encyclopedia of divinity, open public libraries, and a learned press. The two authors even include a step-by-step process for Parliament to implement their plan.[61]

Beyond these activities, the Hartlib manuscripts contained in the University of Sheffield Library show his circle at work trying to raise money for Comenius's "didacticall and Pansophicall undertakings," costing no more than "one hundred and fifty pounds in all."[62] They gathered letters in support, or partial support, of Comenius's, Hartlib's, or Durie's scheme and made proposals to create "Pansophicall" institutions that would endure after Comenius's death and deliver a Baconian light to the world.[63] The manuscripts contain arguments concerning the necessity to use material objects and pictures in the initial teaching of children, arguments in favor of the experimental method in science, a defense of the prudence of William Petty's design for an institution for the advancement of knowledge, and what appears to be an extensive treatise by Petty concerning an "Office of Address" to communicate matters concerning the "Advancement of Divine and Humane Learning."[64] This treatise, chiliastic throughout, argues for the communication of accurate knowledge of a spiritual, rational, or experimental kind as basic in the journey to God.[65] It advocates that the communication of scientific knowledge ("Reall Knowledge") is crucial to a Christian acknowledgment of the glory of God and urges a listing of all of the objects of human knowledge, as well as a "reall" way of knowing these; a set of rules for referring them to "the manifestation of Christ in his glory"; and a series of rules or techniques for obtaining a sense-based knowledge of all things and all causes and effects.[66] This effort would then conform to Bacon's divisions of learning and science, produce a group of rules or observations for ordering the world of real objects and communication about them, and produce applied techniques for determining the properties and utility of each object. The collection also contains letters and proposals concerning an effort to found an institution of learning, funded through public or private benefactions, to be based on the efforts of Boyle, Durie, Sadler, and others.[67]

The three utopian proposals that come from Comenius, Durie, and Plattes are the central Commonwealth footnotes to Bacon, and though none of the three is successful in creating government action (partly because of the short life of the Commonwealth), they have an energizing effect. Going beyond Comenius's sphere of influence, Hartlib systematically sets out to create a national dialogue among leading intellectuals concerning how to improve life through education. The proposals he receives and disseminates testify to his power in raising the question with important people beyond Plattes, Comenius, and Durie: Milton's plan in *Of Education* (1644) for a revived classicism, which is beyond the scope of this book and in many ways the least interesting of the lot; William Petty's proposal for a "literary workhouse" (1648) to provide compulsory education for all children aged seven to ten or twelve and vocational, scientific, or medical specializations for older ones; Petty's critics' suggestions for using the proceeds of children's work in the "literary work house" to pay for their education; and their similar advocacy of funding advanced training in the schools and guilds through the sale of guild masterpieces and through tax relief.[68] Though Mannheim, in his Marxist manner, presents a picture of linear utopian movements succeeded by equally linear movements in the dialectic of history, Hartlib, Durie, and Comenius turn to Bacon, a 1620s spokesperson for Stuart conservatism, as their model. In the 1630s–40s, they appropriate his royalist/elitist meaning to a republican and populist vision of where education and research should go, simultaneously embracing his notions that humanity's comfort can be enhanced by technology and that the scientific method can lead humanity out of the sectarian trap. Hence, they advocate a universal compulsory education in science and technology. For Bacon's approval of the intellectually elitist *ratio studiorum* combined with a general indifference to lower school education, they substitute a powerful interest in effective pedagogy for all children. And, in contrast with Bacon's state controlled by secretive, scientific elites who know what is best for everyone else, they advocate something close to civil rights. In the process of modifying Bacon, the three reformers also build on his concerns: for example, both Hartlib and Comenius want the invention of a "real character" and philosophic language along the lines advocated by Bacon, and both either invent or encourage the creation of textbooks in which words are labels for things.[69] The study of the relationship between words and things leads to the picture books through which Comenius created some of the most effective and earliest school texts written for children. All three reformers, two of them reacting to continental school practice that emphasized language-based subjects for theological reasons, privilege the study of science and technology. Though Bacon visualized an institution somewhat like the Royal Society in the form of his Solomon's House, these three took steps toward establishing a Solomon's House without a monarchic Solomon. They did so to realize modest improvements in the quality of life.

The Hartlib manuscripts deposited at the University of Sheffield also give one some idea of how broad the discussions that Hartlib prompted became. Religiously conservative criticism of the movement developed by the three figures on the Protestant left appeared in the 1630s responses to Hartlib's sending out of Comenius's *Praeludia*. One of particular importance is that of the Polish Brethren aristocrat Jerome Broniewski, who argues that Comenius confuses divine and human wisdom, God and Belial, revelation and reason.[70] Further, he says Comenius confounds Christian, Arab, Jewish, and pagan learning while ignoring Christ as the source of true Wisdom and of salvation. Comenius, by his faith in human effort, detracts from the unique authority of scripture and commingles the states of innocence, sin, and grace. In short, he argues that Comenius proposes that human beings can perfect themselves through education, an essentially Socinian doctrine.[71] This charge Comenius tries to answer (none too successfully) both in the *Pansophiae Prodromus* and in *A Reformation of the*

Schooles by simply asserting that he understands Broniewski's distinctions. The quarrel is understandable. Broniewski, while a member of the Unity of the Brethren, places a kind of Lutheran emphasis on the text of the scriptures and deemphasizes the efficacy of revelation through the book of creation. Further he places a Pauline, Lutheran, or Calvinistic emphasis on the absolute significance of divine action or grace in the salvific scheme. Comenius, on the other hand, follows a path that derives from the Old Testament and New Testament Wisdom writings as well as from Origen, early Augustine, and the medieval and Renaissance Neoplatonic writers. These writers emphasize that the Logos or Wisdom in the godhead is answered by a logos or wisdom within that seeks to understand the divine mind and the structures it initiates. Another probably related critic treats Comenius as a destructive blasphemer who mixes Christian with pagan wisdom, biblical with classical authorities, and the Word of God with human wisdom; in short, he is a person who (unlike the apostles in their use of pagan authorities) does not always begin with Christ but instead with the pagan authority or with the book of nature uninformed by the study of Christ and the realization that the book of nature is created to glorify God. Comenius does not begin with a solid grounding in theology (by which the author appears to mean some species of conservative Augustinian theology); he is a man who proposes impossible dreams.[72] From a strict Lutheran or Calvinistic perspective, from the perspective of the late Augustine who was definitive for the reformers, Broniewski and the others correctly identify the Comenius of the period after his Baconian conversion: the Comenius of the educational works. He is essentially an Enlightenment figure looking forward to the world of "progress" and a Neoplatonic figure looking back to a Pelagian world without the old Protestant or Augustinian furies, the hard-edged religious view where sin, grace, and unique God-initiated redemption are central.[73]

Comenius is a revolutionary in a revolutionary time—a halfway station on the road to the complete secularization of education. The quest for a good world is to be laid on education's back—admittedly, education created by Wisdom and inspired by a sense of awe before a divine creation. But this Wisdom manifests itself by creating a new ideal state *in this world*, instead of Sophia's other worldly apocalypses.[74] If the group leaves behind the clearly defined world of sin and grace, dogma, and transcendent divinity, it also leaves behind Bacon's legitimating classical metaphors while turning wholeheartedly to his ideas that: (1) some sort of atomical wisdom or regularity worthy of study exists in the material universe; (2) practical *and* experimental education are both needed; and (3) the technological transformation of the world through science and education is possible. To this it adds the dimension of government compulsion.[75]

The Comenius-Hartlib-Durie-Plattes group counted for something beyond a few discussions and a few unsuccessful proposals laid before Parliament. Robert Fitzgibbon Young has claimed that the ferment Comenius excited in 1641–42 led to the founding of the Royal Society, but Turnbull has disputed this.[76] I am inclined to Webster's view that the influence of the Hartlib group through Boyle and Oldenburg, Durie's son-in-law, was important, though "it is difficult to assess Hartlib's (or Comenius's) direct influence" on the founding of the Royal Society because of the discontinuities created by the Restoration.[77] Many figures important in its early history are also important in the Commonwealth period ferment over the prospect of science.[78] Certainly Webster has provided powerful evidence both for a continuity between the Commonwealth and the Restoration stances toward the creation of fundamental institutions to support scientific research and for technological innovation leading to a more comfortable life.[79] What is perhaps most important about the group is that they created a network of individuals endeavoring to make institutions and patterns reflecting their programmatic writing. They communicated to educational centers the idea that utopia is not a dream but a bill to be laid before Parliament. The group began the patient, difficult work of creating the institutions of collaborative, normal scientific research *and of education* at the elementary and secondary level that would support these research centers. Religion and science are intertwined in medieval and Renaissance Wisdom science and education, in Commonwealth scientific and educational theory, and in the Restoration scientific efforts of people like Boyle.[80]

What happens in the Restoration is that universal education, and the Chiliasm that goes with it, essentially drops from the agenda of the establishment research leaders but survives in the dissenting academies.[81] As Irene Parker has observed, "in this respect as in others, they [the dissenting academies] may be compared with the schools of the Pietists in Germany . . . for there can be no doubt that just as the Pietists carried on the work of Comenius in Germany, so the Dissenters put into practice the theories of Comenius' English followers, Hartlib, Milton and Petty."[82] The dissenting academies generally addressed what we would think of as university and college students, but the continued republication of Comenius's introductory works for lower school students suggests that dissenting elementary education was also influenced by his utopian ideologies. After Locke had written his essay on education, his influence mingled with Comenius's in the schools. Parliament excluded dissenters from the universities in the 1662–65 Conformity Legislation requiring university teachers to conform to the liturgy of the Church of England, though late in the seventeenth century dissenting academies were exempted from the Conformity Legislation.

It was in the dissenting academies that scientific education first made its way beyond the elites of the Royal Society, and their presence bothered at least some of the clergy of the Church of England. David Ferch quotes an Anglican clergyman who asks his parishioners to "suppress utterly and extinguish, those private . . . academies of grammar and philosophy set up and taught secretly by Fanatics here and there all the kingdom over."[83] It is no surprise, then, that the Tory wits—Swift, Pope, and Arbuthnot—spent a good deal of time attacking the kind of education and the kind of content communicated by the descendants of Comenius, Hartlib, and Durie. But the hopes did not end. France Condorcet, in his *Fragment sur L'Atlantide*, projects a New Atlantis–style utopia in which the whole society is directed by a scientific group that perpetually creates and recreates both knowledge and society as "progress" unfolds.[84] Adam Smith and the Utilitarians propose their Baconian paradises. The chiliastic notion of a kingdom of heaven on earth founded in knowledge and experimental innovation is indistinguishable from the notion of progress. But even in its own time and in Hartlib's circle, the vision of a better life created through technological innovation was not universally shared. Henry More argued that what humankind needed was not such innovation but a fundamental effort to achieve a deeper moral discipline, a fuller innocence:

> There are so many wholesome provisions already found out by the industry and art of our Ancestors, besydes what Natures full breastes unforcedly spurt upon us without any squeezing or straining, that, could either the Heavenly Powers force us, or our selves Persuade our selves to become temperate, just, loving, and modest, innocent mankinde, in these Ages of the world, need not value these strains, that so highly valued and eagerly persu'd invention. . . . Till men as eagerly seek after this after their naturall accommodations, great projects seem to me, like the building of a Babell against a second expected deluge, and the highest heaps of Luciferous experiments as he [i.e., William Petty] called them, but the ground work of Luciferian knowledge, w[hi]ch the divine light in just indignation may well thunderstrike and confound.[85]

CHAPTER FOUR

The Scribleran Revolt against Education to Extend Human Empire

W ESTERN—PARTICULARLY ENGLISH—civilization could have taken "a road not taken," a route
other than the extension of human empire through
research and education. As late as the mid-eighteenth century, Scribleran thinkers (Swift, Pope, Gay, Arbuthnot, Parnell), having a full
awareness of the dangers of the Baconian educational and environmental project, use satire to point to alternate roads. Demythologizing the moderns who prefer their own learning to that of the pre-
empirical ancients, they endeavor to reduce to moral midgets those
scientists and scholars who prefer accurate pedantry in minutiae to
analyses of whole systems in science and of whole ancient texts, making them models and allegories for present civic action. It is not accidental that they admire Homer, Boethius, and More.

The *Dunciad* summarizes this satiric knowledge in the last book of
its final version. The culmination of its educational holocaust comes
with the new science produced by the *virtuosi*. The *Dunciad*'s comic
annotator, Scriblerus, notes that they "devour and lay waste every
tree, shrub, and green leaf in their *Course*, i.e. of experiments; but suffer neither a moss nor fungus to escape untouched": [1]

> Then thick as Locusts black'ning all the ground
> A tribe, with weeds and shells fantastic crown'd,
> Each with some wond'rous gift approach'd the Pow'r,
> A Nest, a Toad, a Fungus, or a Flow'r. (Bk. 4, ll. 397–400) [2]

Among these virtuosi appear the breeders of flowers, the collectors
of winged creatures, the lovers of cockle shells, and the Bishop John

Wilkins types hell-bent on moon travel. All are merely curious after detail in the presence of nature's and Wisdom's awesome system, all nitpickers who follow one or another version of a corpuscular or mechanical philosophy that refuses to look holistically at natural systems or at their source.[3] A corpuscular spokesperson summarizes the educative implications of his school of thought ("a gloomy Clerk," bk. 4, l. 459):[4]

> Let others creep by timid steps, and slow,
> On plain Experience lay foundations low,
> By common sense to common knowledge bred,
> And last, to Nature's Cause thro' Nature led.
> Allseeing in thy mists, we want no guide,
> Mother of Arrogance and Source of Pride! [i.e. Dulness]
> We nobly take the high Priori Road
> And reason downward, till we doubt of God:
> Make Nature still incroach upon his plan;
> And shove him off as far as e'er we can:
> Thrust some Mechanic Cause into his place;
> Or bind in Matter, or diffuse in Space.
> Or, at one bound o'erleaping all his laws,
> Make God Man's Image, Man the final Cause . . . (Bk. 4, ll. 465–78)"[5]

The final commendation of shrunken education before Pope's great apotheosizing of Dulness at the end of his work displays, as Warburton puts it, "the whole Course of Modern education . . . the study of *Words* only in Schools . . . the authority of *Systems* in the Universities . . . [the delusions of the] names of *Party-distinctions* in the world."[6]

Although the comic *Odyssey*- or *Aeneid*-style epic usually ends with a reconciliation scene in which the primary tensions of the work are resolved and the deity who has superintended the progress of the hero triumphs *through* him, the *Dunciad* offers no such prospect because the presiding deity and the hero of the poem are both cosmic Dulness, Cibber being merely her helpful acolyte. *The Dunciad*'s conclusion merely ironically ritualizes and apotheosizes the materialism that Dulness's followers have pursued throughout, declaring the triumph of materialistic education over the disciplines that scale Wisdom's ladder.[7] In the ritual, after a cook's feast of exotic *flesh*, Dulness grants titles to Fellows of the Royal Society, Free-Masons, Botanists, and Florists and then imitates some versions of the allegorized epic that say it returns to the active life in its concluding sections.[8] Dulness charges her followers to trivialize the active life with the gamesmanship of making legwear from spiderwebs, fiddlers of kings, dancers of senators, kings of first ministers, and a dunciad of all three estates. After such grand Gantry evangelism, the schools, the courts, Westminster, the church convocation—the whole educational apparatus—and the realm yawn and doze.

While sleep overtakes the land, Dulness restores Chaos and Night to control of the land's intellectual culture by destroying disciplined learning and the disciplinary ladder to Wisdom. *"Art* after *Art"* (bk. 4, l. 640) darkens in the shadow of the heaped mountains of casuistry as the "sick'ning stars" of the light of Divine Wisdom hymned by Boethius give way to Medea's darkening witchcraft:

> *Philosophy*, that lean'd on Heav'n before,
> Shrinks to her second cause, and is no more.
> *Physic* of *Metaphysic* begs defence,
> And *Metaphysic* calls for aid on *Sense*!
> See *Mystery* to *Mathematics* fly!
> In vain! they gaze, turn giddy, rave and die.
> *Religion* blushing veils her sacred fires
> And unawares *Morality* expires.
> Nor *public* Flame, nor *private*, dares *to* shine;
> Nor *human* Spark is left, nor Glimpse *divine*!
> Lo! Thy dread Empire, CHAOS! Is restor'd;
> Light dies before thy uncreating word:
> Thy hand, great Anarch! lets the curtain fall;
> And Universal Darkness buries All. (Bk. 4, ll. 643–56)[9]

Anti-Wisdom, the Anti-Logos that comes through lifted gates like a false messiah and an eighteenth-century version of the modern physicists' antimatter, triumphs.[10] The whole of the wisdom tradition in education is discarded.[11] Pope's Dulness is the playless daughter of Chaos and Night (her games are not fun) as Wisdom in Proverbs 8 is God's playful daughter.[12] She it is who destroys the Wisdom/Word that is the light coming into the world of John 1:19.[13] She reconstructs the primordial empire of Chaos: "Light dies before [her] uncreating *word*" (italics mine, bk. 4, l. 654).[14] She is the antithesis of the Wisdom/Reason concerning whom Pope writes in translating Boethius, *Consolation of Philosophy*, book 3, meter 9:

> O thou, whose all-creating hands sustain
> The radiant Heav'ns, and Earth, and ambient main!
> Eternal Reason! Whose presiding soul
> Informs great nature and directs the whole!
> Who wert, e're time his rapid race begun,
> And bad'st the years in long procession run:
> Who fix't thy self amidst the rowling frame,
> Gav'st all things to be chang'd, yet ever art the same!
> Oh teach the mind t' aetherial heights to rise,
> And view familiar, in its native skies,
> The source of good; thy splendor to descry,
> And on thy self, undazled, fix her eye.
> Oh quicken this dull mass of mortal clay;
> Shine through the soul, and drive its clouds away!
> For thou art Light. In thee the righteous find
> Calm rest, and soft serenity of mind;
> Thee they regard alone; to thee they tend;
> At once our great original and end,
> At once our means, our end, our guide, our way,
> Our utmost bound, and our eternal stay![15]

The opposite of Dulness ("the dull mass") is Messianic Wisdom through whom the world was created and that invades and teaches the mind of the seeker.[16] As Wisdom has an existence both as a cosmic principle and as a feature of the minds of her followers, so Dulness has her external existence as an uncreating Word and her internal being in "Slowness of Apprehension, Shortness of Sight, or imperfect sense of things," as one of the pseudo-Bentleyan notes puts it.[17] Since Dulness, like Divine Wisdom, exists both as a cosmic principle and as a principle in the human mind, how the human mind collaborates with her determines the structure and meaning of humankind's cultural productions and the structure and meaning of its perception of the natural world. If Pope's Wisdom in the *Essay on Man* reinstates a "scientific" version of the Wisdom eulogized in Proverbs, the Wisdom of Solomon, and Ecclesiasticus—one that creates the structures of things and imposes them on original chaos—then her followers are appropriately contrasted with the "fools." They are so contrasted in the Wisdom books (e.g. Prov.1:7, 9:6–13, 10:1–14, 12:15–23). Concomitantly, in Pope's *Essay on Man*, when the fool figure endeavors to teach eternal Wisdom how to rule, he is told to "drop into himself" and be a fool (epistle 2, 29–30). For the epithet "fool" in the Wisdom works, the *Dunciad* substitutes "dunce." The frontispiece of the *Dunciad*'s 1729 edition portrays the ass—symbol of foolery—with the books of the dunces on its back. As the *Essay on Man* makes clear, though Wisdom's order is independent of human perception, *it can only be imitated if people see it*. So far as the *Dunciad* is concerned, all human incapacity to perceive Nature's and Wisdom's system, especially that derived from empiricism's concentration on minutiae, empties the grand design of nature of meaning for human culture.

The dystopian eschatology of the *Dunciad*'s ending comes after Pope has shown how learning corrupts with advances in scientific and linguistic empiricism, the latter promoted by Bentley. Dulness's conquests will be wrought through the destruction of Wisdom's consorts and through turning learning into play, as Martinus's father endeavored to do. As Settle prophesies:

> Proceed, great days! 'till Learning fly the shore,
> 'Till Birch shall blush with noble blood no more,
> 'Till Thames see Eaton's sons for ever play,
> 'Till Westminster's whole year be holiday,

'Till Isis' Elders reel, their pupils' sport,
And Alma mater lie dissolv'd in Port! (Bk. 3, ll. 333–38) [18]

Dulness destroys education in book 4. In the 1743 edition, Pope shows the goddess Dulness enthroned in an allegorical wonderland at Westminster. There she adjudicates concerning order in the nation's arts and learning so as to destroy all discipline in learning, all order and meaning in the observation of the natural world. She *has* to reverse the processes of the ascent to Wisdom usually described as a movement from the subjects based in language (rhetoric and logic) to the study of Ethics and Physics and on to the Mathematicals and finally to Metaphysics and Theology. She does so at Westminster in connection with its school but, by indirection, she includes in her destruction all that city's culture connotes when attached to an enthronement. She destroys a whole culture. She promotes, first, the destruction of the verbal disciplines: Logic lies gagged and Rhetoric "on the ground" (bk. 4, l. 24). Then she destroys Ethics ("morality," bk. 4, l. 27) by arranging for it to be orphaned and in the care of an abusive law and clergy ("*Chicane* in Furs, and *Casuistry* in Lawn," bk. 4, l. 28). Third, she makes certain to separate the Mathematical subjects from rational use ("Mad *Mathesis*," bk. 4, l. 3l). And finally she sweeps away the fine arts that synthesize these disciplines, the bound muses of all of the disciplines in literature, music, and art, which now give way to the Doll Commons of the contemporary stage, Italian opera and Italianate music (bk. 4, l. 4570). The disciplines that usually make up the ascent to Wisdom are now bound or rendered crazy by Dulness, only Physics escaping, perhaps because of Pope's respect for Newton and his relating of Newton to Wisdom. Theology and Metaphysics are absent until the end of the poem, when they too are bound by materialism.[19] Dulness's triumph culminates the Scribleran's four-decade reaction to the extension of human empire begun with Pope's Homeric utopia and the Scribleran's two dystopian works, *The Memoirs of Martius Scriblerus* and *Gulliver's Travels*. The rest of this chapter explains how we got to Dulness's apotheosis and the vision of a road not taken.

The Scribleran Revolt

SOME BACKGROUND TO THE REACTION:
STRAIGHTFORWARD SCRIBLERAN
EDUCATIONAL ADVOCACY

In this discussion I am skirting a chasm bridged elsewhere, the territory covered by the history of the founding of the Royal Society established for the systematic construction of knowledge and the extension of human empire.[20] As the restored monarchy realized the need for consensus projects, the Royal Society gradually gained support with its emphasis on verification, inductive investigation, and objectivity.[21] Newtonian politics was Anglican and establishment in orientation, designed to answer the radical pantheists and enthusiasts who survived from the Commonwealth, but that emphasis was quite subtle.[22] For the Chiliasm, pantheism, and "inner light" theories of the Commonwealth radicals that seemed to authorize rebellion against authority and a radical reshaping of nature, the Latitudinarians who dominated the Royal Society substituted a rejection of millenarianism (or the adoption of a very private version of it) and made a clear separation of the spirit or "forces" in things (such as gravity) from the matter of things. While their theories allowed for God as the sustainer of the forces in things, they generally adopted a hierarchical view of the natural world that, by analogy, legitimized political hierarchy. Since the majority of Royal Society thinkers were not serious chiliasts, they did not expect a sudden scientific transformation of nature but envisaged a slow research project to master the physical domains. However, the presence in the society (or among its early defenders) of Hartlib, Wilkins, and Boyle who *did have* a role in the chiliastic Baconianism of the Commonwealth generation meant that many political factions in Restoration England felt they were part of the grand design, and though some conservative theologians were not happy with the new science, attack found little place among first generation Restoration intellectuals.[23]

The next generation, with its new ancient-modern controversy, was different (see chapter 3 for the first generation). While the surface of the 1696–1742 controversy over the new empiricism of the Royal Society and the privileging of ancient over modern learning superficially concerns whether the ancient or modern period can claim the weightier poets, scholars, scientists, and philosophers, the deeper controversy concerns the consensus during the Restoration and early eighteenth century about practical scientific research and education, a monotonous chorus that contained efforts to disrupt it from the right or left. After 1696–1704, with the writing and the publication of Swift's *Battle of the Books*, the ancient-modern controversy again opened the gates for a Tory confrontation with the new scientific mythos. The extensions of that controversy beyond research to all education in the Comenian mode practiced in the dissenting academies or in tutorials for scientifically inclined children were as significant as the attacks on the new empirical research. Both the research and the educational extension say that the use of mechanistic and experimental science to promote human imperialism in the natural world denies the strengths and limitations of nature and human nature, especially those described in the ancient epic.[24]

Scribleran writing began during the first true reaction against the Commonwealth, the Tory ministry of Bolingbroke and Harley (1710–14), when the memory of Commonwealth visions and revisions was still fresh. It ended shortly after 1742 when Walpole ceased to rule, also the terminus of the Scribleran period. At the beginning, the Scribleran group even included Robert Harley, the chancellor of the exchequer, among its members, though Harley participated only casually in the group's collective efforts. Immediately after the Tories fell and at the beginning of the Whig hegemony (1715), both Harley and Bolingbroke were impeached for treason; Harley was found not guilty in 1717 and Bolingbroke left for France in 1715, only returning in 1723 when he was no longer in danger. The decade of the twenties brought the prime ministership of Robert Walpole and the 1722 Atterbury plot that made Toryism almost synonymous with Jacobite treason. Thus the forces that had made the Commonwealth, now somewhat transfigured, had reascended to power. In religion, these new classes were initially the Protestant Latitudinarian merchant classes and later the Methodists. In the 1730s and later, the Methodists appealed both to the urban masses and to the rural poor. In business, the new classes appeared in the urban financial centers and interested themselves in the development of colonial empire and in the joint stock company, which became predominant after 1720.[25] In science, the intellectual members of the new classes created the science that offered an extension of human empire to new industrial landscapes through the Newcomen steam engine draining mines and turning mills. In manufacture, the iron industry appeared. In the growing industrial centers, masses of poor people—many of them forced off the land by the wave of enclosures—congregated to find work and, in many cases, depended for survival on the ministrations of the new dissenters, the followers of the Wesleys.

This group, the new "rabble" in Marxist terms, fed the presses and the hunger for popular culture against which Pope rebels in *The Dunciad*. The first two Hanoverian rulers, George I and George II, either ignored their adopted land or concentrated on its military efforts while their prime minister, Walpole, ruled at home through a combination of cynicism, manipulation, peculation, and support for the rising forces of business and empire. Britain seemed to be prospering in commercial or material terms. It was now a world power. But the Scriblerans saw it as lacking all cultural leadership, all heroic virtue, all capacity for constructing an educative culture, and all interest in a wisdom emulative of divine Wisdom. With a courage more notable than their persuasive success they set out to say what was wrong.

The Scriblerans' polemical papers and poems on education, their translations of epic material, and their mock-epic works purport to answer the enthusiasts who had built the Commonwealth and had created ideas still threatening in the late seventeenth and early eighteenth centuries. Their more likely target is the new order itself, which inherited the Commonwealth's mantle. As I argue in chapter 3, Comenian and Hartlibian education theories still flourished in the dissenting academies, and the Baconian and Cartesian approaches to the winning of knowledge dominated the research agenda.[26] For this new world, the Scriblerans construct speaking pictures mandating that the environment remain largely unaltered, that scientific/industrial culture cease wasting nature and humankind, and that education provide reading, writing, and arithmetic to all people and governing knowledge to elites.

To provide for changes in the masses of humankind, cultural productions—art, architecture, music, poetry—should speak of the civility, grace, and responsibility visualized by More in his *Utopia*.[27] That is why Pope is so concerned in *The Dunciad* at the failure of the court to lead in the matter of education, poetry, and cultural productions. This concern, of course, goes with a "reactionary" political agenda. Swift, the earliest and most prolific of the Scribleran writers, supported a political regime that looked to vesting responsibility in a careful landed aristocracy, expected the church to be headed by an anti-enthusiastic and meticulous clergy, and desired the continuation of the steady-state social arrangements that the Restoration appeared to have brought back. Yet, although it is easy to project the categories of the twentieth-century left and right back onto earlier times, in many matters the Tories of the eighteenth century take stances that suggest the left of the twentieth century, especially in matters of the environment, science and public responsibility, and education. There is no hope for progress or for the conquest of nature in Swift or in the other Scriblerans, no narrative of continuous upward movement. Swift puts the basic sentiment of Scribleran writing about humankind and its improvement into an animal comparison: "Lions, bears, elephants, and some other animals, are strong or valiant, and their species never degenerates in their native soil, except they happen to be enslaved or destroyed by human fraud." In contrast, "men degenerate every day, merely by the folly, the perverseness, the avarice, the tyranny, the pride, the treachery, or inhumanity of their own kind."[28] The Scriblerans' dream attached only to improvements in human fulfillment of responsibility in a steady-state society in which people did their jobs. Perhaps Swift admired Sir Thomas More not only because of his satiric side or his religious courage but because he based his utopia on obedience to natural law and the construction of stable, no-growth communities.

The Scribleran Revolt

The Scriblerans produced some straightforward educational writing complementing their social view and setting the stage for their educational fictions: several essays and fragments by Swift, Gay's fables (so transparent as to be "straightforward"), the fragments of what Pope planned to write about education in his *magnum opus*, and Arbuthnot's address to Oxford on the study of mathematics.

Swift directs almost all of his educational analysis to the effects of education on elites. His *Intelligencer IX* argues for the reform of the aristocracy from corrupt French ways (from the French tutors fashionable during the Commonwealth exile and the "dissolute" Francophile Restoration ways that have led to the nobility's disintegration).[29] The reform must come in the form of a return to old-fashioned grammar school and university courses in Greek and Latin books that are "incitements to Virtue, and Discouragements from Vice." These will lead to a continued use of the classics to inform policy in later life. The no-nonsense classical grammar school formation of young aristocrats should be replete with whippings and a training of aristocrats as administrators: "The very Maxims set up to direct *modern* Education are enough to destroy all the Seeds of Knowledge, Honor, Wisdom, and Virtue among us. The current Opinion prevails, that the Study of *Greek* and *Latin* is Loss of Time; that the publick Schools by mingling the Sons of Noblemen with those of the Vulgar, engage the former in bad Company; that Whipping breaks the spirits of Lads well born; that Universities make young Men Pedants; that to dance, fence, speak *French*, and know how to behave yourself among great Persons of both Sexes, comprehends *the whole Duty of a Gentleman*."[30]

While visualizing an aristocracy restored to responsibility through Greek and Latin education, Swift also proposes better charity schools to teach the poor obedience, cleanliness, honesty, industry, craft, reading and writing, basic accounting, and religion, since poor children and servants, deprived of education, will infect aristocratic children with "Folly, Malice, Pride, Cruelty, Revenge, Undutifulness in their Words and Actions."[31] Even the fragmentary notes in Swift's "Hints: Education of Ladyes" idealize a women's education directed toward preparing them to be companions and administrators in aristocratic households.[32] Swift's whole direction is to construct an aristocracy competent to rule on the model of the aristocracy of epic poetry.

The other Scriblerans develop Swift's position and, in contrast to the Pansophists, valorize individual limits and a social order based on differentiated class and role. John Gay's fable of "The Owl, the Swan, the Cock, the Ass and the Spider" tells of a man who "educated" his son beyond his abilities, so that he became a worthless lawyer, warrior, doctor, and preacher. The man is like an Owl/pedagogue who advised a Swan to soldier, a Cock to go sailing, a Spider to seek the court, and an Ass to make music. The animals' owner-farmer accuses the Owl of teaching by using a stupid pedagogy that consulted "nor parts nor [the] turn of mind" of the students: the Swan should have been told to go sailing, the Cock soldiering, the Spider weaving, and the Ass blockheading.[33] Gay's fable of "The Shepherd and the Philosopher" reinforces the same moral through a fictive philosopher who asks a shepherd if he has studied Greece and Rome, Plato and Socrates, Cicero and Ulysses. The shepherd replies that he has had neither formal learning nor grand tour experience but has gathered from "simple nature" a hatred of vice, the industry of the bee and ant, the gratitude of the dog, the care of family of the hen, and the sobriety of the owl.[34]

The model for a differentiated education for a class-based society is a differentiated Nature extending from dull matter to the Wisdom that designed things, a ladder to the ultimate. Pope celebrates this vision of Nature in his *Essay on Man* and his Boethius translation.[35] His planned related essay on education, summarized in book 4 of the *Dunciad*, and uncertainly reconstructed by various scholars, almost certainly would have told us how education for role would work.[36] In the 1734 scheme for this magnum opus that was to develop from the *Essay on Man*, Pope speaks of a second set of epistles extending the *Essay on Man* to educational issues, including one concerning the limits of human reason, learning, and wit, and one discussing civil and ecclesiastical polity in relation to education.[37] In 1736, Pope writes to Swift that additional verse epistles he might write will examine, among other things, the limits of reason and science, the useful and unattainable arts, and the uses of learning.[38] And in 1743, he tells Spence that he has included his essay on education in the fourth book of the revised *Dunciad*.[39] This suggests that his proposed essay on education would have related to Wisdom theories of education since perverse education in the *Dunciad* is so insistently related to Wisdom's obverse, Dulness. It may not be too much to suppose that the essay would have expanded his reservations in the *Essay on Man* about looking beyond humankind and would have approved holistic examinations of the natural system. (Unlike Swift, Pope gives some support to Lockean principles that might eliminate the necessity for fierce school corporal punishment, but in general, Pope's plans reinforce the Swiftian approach.)[40]

In the sciences and the description of nature, the Scriblerans look to holistic mathematical science, to Newton (except for Swift), and generally to pre-Baconian versions of science.[41] Arbuthnot, the one scientist of the group and a member of the Royal Society, called in his *Essay on the Usefulness of Mathematical Learning* for the resurrection at Oxford of the quadrivium arts that allay credulity and strengthen reason.[42] He argues that students should examine Newton's physics and optics, Kepler's geometric and optical studies, mathematically based hydraulic engines, and pendulum clocks, all of these commending the notion in the *Republic* that magistrates ought to be educated in the mathematical arts. Students should study the ideas of Wisdom and number as the mediators, to the creation, of the mathematical ideas in the mind of the Creator: for example, Newton discovered the "grand secret of the whole Machine; which, now it is discovered, proves to be (like other contrivances of infinite Wisdom) simple and natural."[43] All the "visible works of God Almighty are made in number weight, and measure" and their understanding in turn requires the study of "arithmetic, geometry, and statics."[44] Studies of the animal kingdom and of medicine require mathematics and geometry as controls if they are to avoid the "nonsensical, unintelligible stuff" of these areas' ordinary writers, presumably minor Royal Society–style pseudoscientists.[45] Enlightened mathematical pedagogy, avoiding all compendia and abbreviated books, requires that no mathematical rule be taught apart from a demonstration of its rational support and that the whole sequence of mathematics form an integrated curriculum, taking account of the probable future career of the student. Thus merchant accounting should be given as an example of applied arithmetic to the student likely to have a career as a merchant.[46]

Baconian inductive science, on the other hand, receives consistent abuse from the Scriblerans, Pope calling Bacon "the wisest, brightest, meanest of mankind."[47] The total emphasis of Scribleran educational writing then goes to education for role, education based on ancient models, education in mathematics and related holistic sciences, and education promising limited change in the human condition save for that created by fidelity to duty in role.

SCRIBLERAN EDUCATION IN TRANSLATION
OF AND COMMENTARY ON ANCIENT EPIC

If the Commonwealth educational advocates turn away from the classical intertexts provided by the epic, the Scriblerans turn back to them. Through the translation of epics and through criticism of and commentary on epics, they mediate their hierarchical, role-differentiated educational theory and their distrust of promises about the distant future. The epic of the educational journey that begins with Neoplatonic commentary on Homer and Servius or Virgil, set as it is in the context of both the testing of individual leadership and the testing of the group against the natural world, was the preferred intertext that the Scriblerans used to set forth their diagram of an education for social hierarchy that might be responsible and reflective of natural hierarchy. It also forms the basis of their subversive manipulations of epic styles and episodes.

To show how Greek and Latin books could be "incitements to Virtue, and Discouragements from Vice," the Scriblerans reassert the medieval/Renaissance-style commented, allegorical epic as a vehicle for educational thought. (In the discussions of More and Shakespeare, we have already seen reflections of Homer's and Virgil's epics, especially the *Odyssey* and the *Aeneid* journeys containing utopian and dystopian lands.) As everyone knows, in late classical times the *Odyssey* was transformed in the works of Porphyry, Plotinus, and Proclus into a theological, philosophic, and educational document that pointed the way to the good life. It continued to be so transformed in the Eustathius, Spondanus, and Madame Dacier comments on the *Odyssey* used by Pope for his *Odyssey* translation and by Pope and William Broome for their notes. With its commentary, Pope's *Odyssey* translation elaborates the Scribleran straightforward pictures of education, and the Eustathius-Spondanus-Dacier-Pope version of the *Odyssey* undergirds both *Gulliver's Travels* and much of *The Dunciad*.[48] The commented *Aeneid* also contributed since seventeenth- and eighteenth-century editions of the *Aeneid* continued to carry the commentaries of Servius, Fulgentius, and Fabricius (the last was the commentary Shakespeare used for *The Tempest*).[49]

The hermeneutics of epic poetry had redoubled in complication from the days of Petrarch or even of Shakespeare. After early eighteenth-century philological, archeological, and historical criticism had appeared, the appropriation of Homer's words to Christian-classical morality was no longer quite so easy.[50] At almost any point in Pope's translation and commentary, Pope and Broome offer several hypotheses for a mythic event, dissolving the myth into one or more natural phenomena, into a historical occasion or pattern covered by metaphor, into a moral allegory, or into the possibility of several of these simultaneously. At the same time, the commentary may dismiss *some* allegories, an example being Porphyry's interpretation of the grotto of the nymph in book 13 of *De Antro Nympharum*. And Pope's Homer was no private creation. It was, instead, helped along by several Scriblerans. For example, Swift knew of the Pope translation of the *Odyssey* and Parnell assisted with the *Iliad* translation and commentary.[51] As Swift and Pope use Homer, and to a lesser degree Virgil, in their own works, the variety and uncertainty of epic interpretations become a source for horseplay and intertextual meaning taken from the *Odyssey* and, to a less significant extent, from the *Iliad* and *Aeneid*.

To speak to educational issues: the Pope-Broome commentary on the *Odyssey* makes Odysseus take on the role of the wise statesman or aristocrat educating himself in the realms of fable to find yet more wisdom. He possesses the dissimulative gift required of all leaders who serve the interests of their group. As the commentary puts it, the quality a statesman requires is *"Wisdom,"* the foremost component of which is "the great art of Kings . . . the mystery of *Dissimulation."*[52] Ulysses is called αυδραπολυτροπου to denote the dissimulative skill that disguises him, allowing him to take so "many shapes" in the realms that represent useful and perverse education.[53] The issue for Ulysses throughout the *Odyssey* is not whether he tells the truth or not but *how* he tells it, in whose interest and on whose behalf. Thus, his lying to Polyphemus about his name saves him and his crew. His concealing of his grief when he hears the story of Troy's sack from the mouth of the Phaeacian singer, Demodocus (b. 8, ll. 58ff.), permits Phaeacia to see him as a modest man. He creates false and fabled pasts for himself when he returns to Ithaca to protect his identity until he can punish the suitors. Odysseus is the teller of the noble lie mentioned in the quotation from Horace's *Odes*, book 3, ode 11, line 35, that was placed under the frontispiece to the 1735 version of the work, a quotation referring to the lie through which a good Danaid bride preserved her spouse from the anger of her father. Her dissimulation to save her family resembles that which Ulysses practiced to save his sailors en route and his family at home from the lust of the treacherous suitors. It is, of course, the opposite of the kind of opportunistic lying that Gulliver practices when driven into a corner.

Taken in their narrative (as opposed to their temporal) order, the fabulous episodes as interpreted by Pope and Broome demonstrate, first, the need for dissimulative affective control in the leader (items 1–2 in the following series) and, then, the need for a proper use of reason and of the disciplines of astronomy, rhetoric, history, and strategic reading that understands the limits of the possible (items 3–6):

1. Calypso, whose name—in fact and in commentary—means *"concealment"* or *"secret,"* teaches Ulysses to do nothing "without disguise."[54]

2. The Cyclops, a people remarkable for "savageness and cruelty" (9:233) to whom Ulysses appears a dwarf (9:331), have but one eye which is, "an allegory, to represent that in anger, or other violent passions, men see but one single object."[55]

3. Aeolus represents the astronomical sciences since he is "an Astronomer" who "studied chiefly the nature of the Winds." His floating island walled with brass represents the unstable volcanic island, troubled by earthquakes, the brass standing for the reflection of its volcanic fires on the water. Aeolus' six sons and six daughters relate to the heavens and mean the winds of the winter and summer months, while the harsh effects that come from Ulysses' sailors' unbinding of the winds represent the "vain curiosity" of those who endeavor to understand state secrets, or the consequences of avarice and of inappropriate "unseasonable curiosity."[56]

4. Circe's locus teaches the necessity that one learn to make reason triumph over passion since she is a "famous Courtezan" or "Pleasure," her wolves and lions imaging "the attendants of . . . houses of debauchery, which appear gentle and courteous, but are in reality of a brutal disposition." Mercury, teaching Ulysses to liberate himself from Circe, bodies forth "Reason . . . the God of Science" while the moly he provides for Ulysses' liberation is "instruction," bitter in the beginning but full of "pleasure and utility . . . in the end." To explain Circe's seduction of Ulysses, the commentary tells us that Ulysses briefly tastes of her attractions but only to liberate his associates from addiction to pleasure, as dreadful an enemy to humanity as Polyphemus/Danger.[57]

5. The Sirens—queens of the islands named Sirenusae near Capri, where Minerva had a temple and where there also existed a great academy famous for its study of eloquence and the liberal sciences—ruled over this academy's students. As they became intellectual monsters, they "abus'd their knowledge, to the colouring of wrong, the corruption of manners and subversion of government."

The Sirens "promise Knowledge" based only on curiosity rather than on contemplation. They illustrate the maxim that "to desire to know all things, whether useful or trifles, is a faulty curiosity; but to be led from the contemplation of things great and noble, to a thirst of knowledge is an instance of greatness of soul." Because the Sirens' academicians are governed by idle curiosity, the bones and desolation that lie near the siren dwelling are the product of the academy, the abuses of which "consum'd [the members'] patrimonies, and poison'd their virtues with riot and effeminacy."[58]

6. Ulysses' descent into Hades "calls up the Heroes of former ages from a state of inexistence" and opens "ancient History and fables," letting us into "a variety of different characters of the most famous personages recorded in ancient story."[59]

7. The Phaeacians were "a people wholly given up to luxury and pleasures," so "puffed up with their constant felicity and the protection of the Gods, they thought nothing impossible." They were a "credulous people" given to "ignorant credulity" who mistake Ulysses' fables as telling of literal realities.[60] In short, they are literalistic literary critics.

Taken in relationship to the role of the statesman, the episodes on Ulysses' journey in the order of their appearance first teach the concealment and dissimulation necessary to leadership (Calypso) and the need for a mastery of violent passion and brutality (Polyphemus). Then, moving to learning and education, they teach the uses of astronomy (Aeolus) and by implication of the mathematical sciences, the uses of bittersweet instruction in the control of passions and the development of reasonable control over one's subjects (Circe), the dangers of false and corrupt academic learning (the sirens), the functions of historical study (Hades), and the difference between reality and fable, the possible and impossible (the Phaeacians).[61] The journey of Ulysses, in short, takes him through episodes that educate him for rule.

The final action of the *Odyssey* when the hero has to rule—the episodes of the return of the hero, his cleansing of his household, and his reconciliation with his wife—represents the idea that "the Absence of a person from his own home, or his neglect of his own affairs, is the cause of great disorders." Properly, when the absence of the hero has ended, he does not immediately "discover himself" but provides himself with a "prudent disguise" so that his presence "has the same effect on the Authors of the disorders, and all others who knew him not, as his real absence had before . . . 'till the very moment of their punishment."[62] His return under the guidance of Minerva signifies that he is tutored by Wisdom, and his wife Penelope, possessing the same wisdom, is "the favourite of *Minerva*."[63] In short, by studying Ulysses as the archetype of statesmanship, the leader learns from his journey how to educate himself and from his return how to rule with full Wisdom apart from all Dulness.

The similar view of Homer set forth by Thomas Parnell in his "Essay on the Life, Writings, and Learning of Homer," an introduction to Pope's translation of the *Iliad*, again asserts Homer's timeless value, powerful ethical sense, allegorical content, and his acting as the "Father of Learning."[64] Though Swift made no extended commentary on Homer as did Pope and Broome, he presents his Homer indirectly through a fictional defender of the ancients whose Homer, in the *Tale of a Tub*, is an educator who "designed his Work for a compleat Body of all Knowledge Human, Divine, Political, and Mechanik," all forms of knowledge represented in the Pope-Broome commentary.[65] But Swift never becomes too pompous. The persona in *Tale of a Tub* also says, ironically, that Homer has been found deficient by his modern detractors in many contemporary kinds of knowing—political spleen, Cabalistic knowledge, Cartesian "Mechanicks," the "Common Law," and church law in England. The defender further notes (Swift's gift for horseplay showing) that even Homer's detractors recognize his invention of such other great modern accomplishments as "the *Compass* . . . *Gun-powder* and the *Circulation of the Blood*," inventions claimed by the moderns.[66] Finally, it is impossible to say what Gay's view of the emblematic Homer is since his *Achilles* treats a non-

Homeric episode in the life of its hero.[67] His comic persona Esdras Barnivelt speculates that no such person as Homer existed.[68] However, the *Achilles* does end with a little chorus or moral that, though applied to issues of gender, appears to deny all Pansophic hopes that education will completely restructure human nature:

> Nature breaks forth at the moment unguarded;
> Through all Disguise she herself must betray.
> Heav'n with Success hath our Labours rewarded:
> Let's with *Achilles* our Genius obey.[69]

Homer's successor in epic, Virgil, had also been made to write of a progress through education in the writings of Servius in classical times; of Fulgentius, Bernard Sylvestris, and Petrarch in medieval ones; and of Landino and Fabricius in the Renaissance. And Pope at least appears to believe in this Virgil. Following a medieval interpretive myth referenced by Lancelot Andrewes in Shakespeare's time, he notes how Virgil took his messianic message from Isaiah and builds his *Messiah* around this myth. Furthermore, all of the versions of the *Dunciad*, with its constant mock-epic imitation of the *Aeneid*, invert Isaianic prophecy to celebrate Dulness's messianic reign and the triumph of her chosen court under George II.[70]

The emphasis of the Scriblerans on the capacity of ancient literature to produce sweetness and light—the concern of Swift, Arbuthnot, and Pope with the pedantry of Bentley—is no mere quibble in the politics of the debate over ancients and moderns. It derives from the Scribleran sense that Bentley's editions, based on a variety of Baconian scientific empiricism in the handling of texts, load them with detracting information to the detriment of their civilizing function. The notes to the *Dunciad* and the emendations in Arbuthnot's *Virgilius Restauratus* carry the same loading in parodic form. For Pope, Swift, and the Scriblerans, the paramount function of the epic is to tell the leader how to live and how to lead. From the rhetorical surface of Homer, the fabled bee of the *Battle of the Books* gathers sweetness; from its mediated symbolic core, it captures light.[71]

The Scribleran Revolt

The first dystopian work the Scribleran group created is *The Memoirs of Martinus Scriblerus*, originally designed in 1713–14 but published, perhaps amended by Pope, in the 1740s. The Scriblerans needed to give the Commonwealth its comeuppance—not the Commonwealth that died with Richard Cromwell's removal but that which lived in textbooks, dissenting schools, enthusiastic religion, and utopian hopes. The Martinus Scriblerus sequences represent the dangers of modern learning in the Comenian-Baconian style and the devastations and dilettantism of Montaignian or Comenian ancient learning. Nothing about the productions of the Scriblerus Club is easy. One finds no consistent place such as Yoknapatapha County binding the various works together, no consistent set of characters save for Martinus (and he is a chameleon persona), and no consistent generic clustering. None of this should come as a surprise. The Scriblerus Club, composed of Swift, Pope, Arbuthnot, Gay, and Parnell, met for a short time in the autumn of 1713 and the spring of 1714 during the height of the Tory power and occasionally, according to Pope, with Sir Robert Harley, the queen's chief.[72] The collective work of the group, *The Memoirs of Martinus Scriblerus*, came out only in 1741, nearly thirty years later, under Pope's imprimatur. One cannot know who wrote what or how much Pope edited the work immediately prior to publication.

However, between 1726 and 1741, a quantity of other works related to Scriblerus emerged. First came Parnell's *Life of Zoilus and His Remarks* (1717), a satiric attack on the critics of Pope's Homer and the first of the Scriblerus-related works to contain mock footnotes.[73] There followed Swift's *Gulliver's Travels* (1726); Pope's *Peri Bathous; or, Martinus Scriblerus: His Treatise of the Art of Sinking in Poetry* (1728); Pope's *Dunciad Variorum* of 1729, followed by its numerous revisions up until 1742; and then Arbuthnot's *Virgilius Restauratus* (1729) and his *Essay of the Learned Martinus Scriblerus concerning the Origin of the Sciences* (1732).[74]

In the assembled Martinus works, a montage of authors creates the voice of a single fictive satiric persona, Martinus, who often speaks through another persona, the narrator of the memoirs or of the framing introductions and notes. Though diverse hands published works over decades and cannot be expected to be wholly consistent in their mythos or satiric slant (for example, the attitude toward Locke varies somewhat from Scribleran to Scribleran), taken together the works collect most modern and ancient education-gone-wrong into the stuffed ragdoll of the satiric persona Martinus—at once prodigy, fool, savant, madman and cultural straw. Pope correctly described the design of the project as one intended to ridicule "all of the false taste in learning, under the character of a man of capacity enough that had dipped in every art and science but injudiciously in each."[75] Martinus is a Quixote (Warburton originally argued that the Scriblerans conceptualized their production "in the manner of Cervantes").[76] He is "tall" with a "visage long . . . complexion olive, eyes hollow, yet piercing . . . beard neglected and mix'd with grey . . . Melancholy of his countenance," a doll or puppet whose cloak so covers his person that no one can determine whether he has clothes or a body beneath.[77] His oversized sword drags a yard behind him. Like a Quixote unrecognized for his greatness, he haunts St. James Palace, waiting for destiny to manifest him to the world through the papers he gives to the narrator and which the narrator converts, along with his conversation with Scriblerus, into the *Memoirs*.

But Martinus is a flatter character than the hero from La Mancha or his semblances, Parson Adams and Joseph Andrews, whose eponymous novel appears at about the same time as Martinus's work was published. Martinus has none of the coherent inner vision that madness and naiveté abuse in Quixote and Andrews.[78] Martinus dreams no coherent dream of a classical, romance, or Christian order against which the modern is judged. Indeed, the madness of any coherent dream such as that of chivalry or Old Testament patriarchy has been *educated out* of him by a madder yet modernist education that spoils all it touches, whether ancient or modern. And unlike Quixote or Andrews, Martinus possesses no transcendent virtue or power that reaches beyond the foolishness of immediate circumstances with the abuse and self-abuse that these bring.

Martinus is the product of the educational theory emerging from the Commonwealth chiliasts, specifically Comenius. Kerby-Miller, in his magisterial edition of the *Memoirs*, argues that the "more general and important method that is burlesqued is the pedagogical approach which was first introduced by John Amos Comenius" and further cites a complaint from the 1728 edition of Comenius's *Orbis Pictus* that the effects of Comenius's reforms had been spoiled by an "indiscreet use of them, and want of a thorow acquaintance with his Method."[79] But the method of satire is not to attack the abuses of a position just to attack abuses. The Scriblerans present abuses as if they represented the essence of the opponent's view. As the product of Montaignian and Comenian educational theory, Martinus is not infected by books he reads *voluntarily*. His father trains—educates—him from childhood to the madness of his incoherent dream. He comes to his later dizziness by a learning and a pedagogy chosen for him by men as mad as he becomes: his father, Cornelius, and his tutor, Crambe. Though the Martinus myth begins as an indictment of the classical educational culture produced by the modern pedagogical theorists such as Montaigne or Montaigne's father—for whom learning is all motion and no meaning—it ends as an indictment of a Comenius-style scientific, educational, and philological culture inherited from the Commonwealth.

Martinus's bloodline begins with Bacon's and Comenius's predecessors, scientific pedants extending from Albertus Magnus through Paracelsus. Martinus comes into the world after having been conceived by his parents' adherence to classical formulae of unimaginable stupidity, and his father anticipates the birth by writing two Dr. Spock–style treatises, one for a boy, one for a girl. He is born, as are all epic heroes and great men, among the signs of his future learned magnificence—the dream of an inkhorn, wasps about his crib that do not sting, the fruiting of a crabtree, and a manure pile that sprouts mushrooms. Martinus's birth also comes with the modernist augury of a bird/paper kite that drops, embellished with the symbols of his future learning of the military skills, accompanied by bad poetry and tail knots of "Logick . . . Metaphysick . . . Casuistry . . . Polemical Divinity . . . Common Law" and a "Lanthorn of Jacob Behmen."[80] The signs of his time combine the worst of misplaced classicisms, scholasticisms, Whiggisms, and mysticisms of the new age. At his birth, Martinus's parents argue about his education, and his triumphant father asserts that he must be uprooted and know and see everything possible about science and learning, including an apparently Pansophic "Tour of the whole system of the Sun."[81]

Under this father's care, Martinus's early education involves Montaigne's pleasure and Comenius's manipulable solid objects divorced from any pragmatic context. Each satiric object calls attention to supposed abuses in the new pedagogy: clothes as a geography of Europe, bread carved in mathematical figures, conversation only in Latin and Greek (to master the verbal subjects, Martinus, like Montaigne, speaks Greek and Latin from gingerbread time, as Hartlib and Montaigne had proposed), a rote catechism taught by a puppet show, and music from the ancient lyre unaccompanied by any theory teaching of the cosmic music and its proportions. The father constructs toys and games modeled after the ancient ones, excluding only that "invented by a people among the Thracians, who hung up one of their Companions in a Rope, and gave him a Knife to cut himself down; which if he fail'd in, he was suffer'd to hang till he was dead."[82] That the Scriblerus Club in 1713–14 should mock Montaignian- and Comenian-style educational theory current in the dissenting academies should not surprise one. As noted in chapter 3, the Commonwealth educators and their favorites from earlier times were republished long after the Commonwealth failed.[83]

After attacking the misplaced concretism in Comenian early education, the *Memoirs* mock the pure verbalism of later follow-ups that divorce teaching from all practical objects and situations, part and parcel both of scholasticism and of Comenius's misty prose dealing with later education (in this the *Memoirs* anticipate the criticisms of the new education found in *Gulliver's Travels* and the *Dunciad*). Martinus goes to grammar school, university, and post-baccalaureate-level work in grammar, rhetoric, logic, and metaphysics under Crambe, who has dedicated himself to reversing the process of the association of word with thing that characterized Martinus's early learning. In teaching Logic, Crambe reverses the traditional movement from the particular to the abstract and demands that every abstraction be fleshed out with "examples from material things," following a technique recommended by Comenius. However, in this brave new world, what Martinus learns as a logician, he forgets as a philosopher and scientist.[84] All coherence gone from his studies, he advances to Metaphysics, where he encounters the verbiage of Aristotelian scholasticism after it has had its day as a tool of intellectual discovery and exercises his worthless skills in medieval-style disputations with Crambe.[85]

Just as the grand tour was the active-life equivalent of school study for eighteenth-century educated males, so the active life also makes its claim in Martinus's educational journey. Here, activity exposes the pedagogical tomfoolery that demands ridiculous concrete action in the manner of Comenius, Durie, and Hartlib. His inquiries into practical knowledge involve impractical studies in anatomy based on body snatching; textual emendation in the form of spoiling texts à la Bentley; and examining mind-body relationships via castration to cut off a body part in which an offending passion has expressed itself, following literally the biblical injunction to get rid of those members that offend one.

Having been guided into modernism by a father and a tutor after the fashion of Aeneas being guided by Anchises and Venus, Martinus goes into the world to practice his skills in science. He tries to cure a narcissistic courtier by finding the soul of humankind in its pineal gland—after Descartes. During pineal discovery time, he learns that animals and human beings having like temperaments have like-shaped pineal glands; for example, peacocks and fops have the same style of pineal. Becoming a lover himself, he begins his epic journey into adulthood by finding his Dido and Lavinia in one of two Siamese twins sharing the same sexual organ and engages in his Aeneas-Turnus battle for her with a "Manteger," ending up in a court of law to fight the final phases of his great war with the beast. After losing this struggle, he undertakes the journeys Swift was later to flesh out in *Gulliver* as an epic journey in the style of those by Odysseus or Aeneas (see later discussion): journeys to the Pygmaen Empire, the Land of the Giants, the Kingdom of Mathematicians and Projectors, and the place where he discovers "a Vein of Melancholy" proceeding almost to a "Disgust of his Species."[86] Unlike the empire-founding epic heroes of old, he forgoes "any Memorial to the Secretary of State" that might lead the government to subject the lands he has discovered to the imperial crown of Great Britain. He finishes his career by casting the bulk of his useless treatises on poetry, architecture, music, and politics "into a Boghouse near St. James."[87] No wonder he is melancholy.

The academic education given by Cornelius and Crambe and the active life training pursued by Martinus represent a severing of learning from practical civic objects and situations, from apprenticeships, from the forum, and from all of the other places where citizens practice their skills. Indeed, no *civium* appears in the memoirs, only one crazy "idealistic" or "utopian" pursuit after another. Martinus's journeys, if they were planned to be like Gulliver's journeys, probably would have represented a similar severing of modern learning from the civium to the contempt of both Nature and the human species. Indeed, Martinus's occasional epic grandiosity and Quixotic craziness do not attack either classical or modern learning that teaches responsibility, virtue, and vice, instead frolicking with the destruction of meaning in learning that mechanical and overly ambitious pedagogy creates. The Faustian or Promethean mode in education cultivated both by oversolicitous parents and overly ambitious educators, the Comenian hopes that anyone can learn everything, end in a bog near St. James.

GULLIVER'S TRAVELS, THE MARTINUS MATERIALS, AND POPE'S ODYSSEY

The Scriblerus conclusion outlines the four voyages that in 1726 appeared as the voyages of Gulliver. Whether Martinus's list of voyages was part of the original creation or was added by Pope or another Scribleran does not matter, since the outline clearly indicates that *some* Scribleran saw a continuity between Martinus and Gulliver. Gulliver *is* Martinus reborn as a traveling miseducated fool, a modern empiricist and literalist who visits Homer's realms and "misreads" them as Martinus and his father misread the texts to which his Comenian education exposes him. Gulliver-the-modernist sails through the ancient, Homeric realms discovered to us in the translation and notes of Pope's 1725–26 *Odyssey* and, gull that he is, never recognizes the ancient landscape mocking his enterprise. That Swift, publishing in 1726, uses the commented Homer as his intertext to dismiss the new empiricisms in education, research, and philology derives from his knowing Pope's *Odyssey* as Pope composed it.[88] The intertextual connections appear, first, in Gulliver's trip through an education and learning that reflect indebtedness to Homer in the hero's very name and in his fantastic mode; second, in Gulliver's visits to Odyssean places in the episodic part 3; third, in his visits to the lands of pygmies and giants in parts 1 and 2; and, finally, in his return to his wife in part 4.

◀§Gulliver's Name and His "Journeying-through-the-Fantastic" Mode

Gulliver's name obviously includes a part of Ulysses' name: *Gulli*ver. But whereas Ulysses' name and epithets always present him as the wisest of men because of his dissimulation in behalf of his group, Gulliver has no capacity for such an unselfish art. Like the George Washington of folklore, he cannot tell a lie. In contrast to Ulysses and the Danaid bride, he cannot tell fables for his group because *his posture is the scientific one deprived of all commitment save to self.* Circumspect and detailed in his accounts of latitude and longitude, flora, fauna, land configurations and everything but human right and wrong, he cannot tell a lie about his bowel movements in Lilliput or the abuse of the Brobdingnagian farmer.[89] He cannot speak untruth about his country when he describes it to the ruler of the Brobdingnagians (he only leaves out the negative details *until questioned*). His final offer, the offer of the truth of gunpowder, encompasses one of the great discoveries of *fruit* as opposed to *light* that Bacon praises, and gunpowder is no lie. At the end of part 4, Gulliver claims under the influence of the Houyhnhnms that he has "chose[n] to relate plain Matter of Fact in the simplest Manner and Style; because my principal Design was to inform, and not to amuse." Having wiped out the noble lie containing a deeper truth of the *mythoi* that construct the human group, he finally can only be the Sinon of the "truth" telling that destroys a culture—can only look at himself in the mirror and hope that solipsistic and prideful pretense at Houyhnhnmdom will get him through the desperation of his self-contempt.[90]

While Gulliver's name suggests his gullible nature and his incapacity to fathom the multitudinous uses of language or of journeying, while his scientific literalism allows him to maintain his fidelity to a narrow *truthfulness*, his solemn witlessness creates satire in Swift's hands that does not detract from the Gulliver/Ulysses contrast. Gulliver's narrative is always literally accurate and crudely self-serving, as if he had visited Pope's Ulyssean lands and seen them only as vehicle and never as tenor for an education about the uses of academies or history or curiosity or pleasure-and-education. For centuries, criticism has divided over whether Gulliver's admiration for a truth telling that human beings lack, especially in the land of the horses, represents a sick misanthropy or a proper admiration. If we regard Gulliver as a Ulysses manqué, then the function of his love of the literalistic and empirical becomes clearer. He dissolves dissimulation into lying and myth into pseudoscience so that the communal functions of literature disappear in dullness and solipsism. As Robert Stock has pointed out to me, Gulliver is metaphorically always the imitator of the gait and whinny of the horses he meets.

Probably by reason of his Puritanical education at Emmanuel College, Gulliver avoids the role of dissimulating mythmaker until he is pressed to tell embarrassing truths about his society. When he is so pressed in Brobdingnagia, he lies, lies until his inconsistencies are exposed, lies to no good or edifying purpose, lies to preserve no crew or family. An Emmanuel College man, he has been trained in literalistic Calvinistic and dissenting habits of reading and in science, and based on his affiliations with Dutch learning, religion, and trading ambitions, he is as nonconforming and as committed to "science" as the Commonwealth Protestants were.[91] He studies surgery with the Dutch, arranges for his final voyage in Leyden, and learns mathematics and navigation in the same city, famous for its Calvinistic theology (and work on the scientific optics that seems to inform parts 1 and 2).[92] He depends on the Dutch for correction, adopts their nationality as his own while generously avoiding the extreme Calvinistic habit of trampling on crucifixes, and further proclaims his Dutch connection when the Dutch authority on the pirate ship he encounters is so enraged at his Christian profession as to persuade a group of heathen pirates to turn him loose on the wide sea with but a canoe.[93] In short, he is the product of that mixture of Calvinism and scientific inquiry—pessimism about human nature and optimism about the conquest of nature—celebrated in Rembrandt, Vermeer, and the Dutch East India Company, a man totally incompetent in Ulysses' lands of wise myth.

◆§Gulliver's Visits to Homeric Places in Part 3

Gulliver's Travels is not, in surface form, a comic epic in prose or a mock epic, as other great works of the period such as the *Dunciad* or Fielding's *Joseph Andrews* are.[94] It is mock-epic commentary. Told by a plain-style scientific literalist, *Gulliver* includes none of the inflated diction and misplaced use of epic stylistic devices the mock-epic genres use.[95] Rather, Gulliver unwittingly offers mock-truthful prose that mirrors the mock-truthful follies and crimes of an anti-epic age whose leadership, unlike Harley and Bolingbroke as Swift saw them, "cannot tell a lie" on behalf of the group. Gulliver visits the eighteenth-century equivalents of Homer's fabulous loci without learning anything. In the landscape of myth, he avoids the constructively mythic to mirror in his truth-telling foolishness the incongruities of modern culture.

Gulliver part 3 is the most obvious example. Though often criticized for its episodic character, it is designedly so after the structure of Ulysses' journey. Created to mock the darting chiliastic/scientific expectations of the Commonwealth dreamers and their successors, it moves from misapplied deductive science (the floating island of the astronomers) to its misapplied inductive counterpart (the Sirens), then to the scientific search for "objective" history (Hades), and finally to the search for physical immortality itself (the Elysian fields).

Homer's floating island, Aeolus' place floating in the sea, the equivalent of Swift's flying island of Laputa, holds the astronomer King Aeolus according to the Pope-Broome commentary, and Gulliver's comparable island floating in the sky holds the Laputian chiliasts and quadrivialists (musicians, mathematicians, astronomers, and astrologers) who lead the Laputians into apocalyptic predictions connected with astral and planetary peculiarities (Atlas, as an astrologer, is compared with Aeolus in the Pope-Broome commentary).[96] Whereas Aeolus' sons and daughters commit incest with one another, the wives and daughters of the astronomers, denied the payment of their sexual debt by the males of the Laputian community, only descend to the Balnibarbian mainland to consort with the Lagandans. The abstracted astronomers meanwhile play along with the music of the spheres, "bearing their part in whatever instrument they most excelled."[97] And they make their own volcano. While the brass appearance of Aeolus' isle in Pope-Broome comes from the volcanic night fire reflecting on its waters, Laputa has within it the artificial volcanic cave a hundred yards beneath the surface of the adamant, in which burn twenty lamps that cast a stupendous reflection and in which sits the lodestone that permits the island to bounce up and down over the lands beneath as if it were a sort of volcanic rock.[98] According to the Pope-Broome commentary, Aeolus' temptation for Ulysses' sailors is an allegorical rendering of avarice and idle curiosity, the former having its counterpart in Laputa's colonialist oppression of the lands (and classes) beneath it and its exaction of tribute from them, and the latter in the "intense Speculations" that make it impossible for Laputans to "speak or attend to the Discourses of others, without being rouzed."[99] Indeed, Laputa's society for knowledge creation, composed of powerful scientific groups who at once rule the underclasses that do not share in their knowledge and waste their resources on speculative projects, is Bacon's House of Solomon without press agentry.[100]

The Grand Academy of Lagado's sirenism of the inductive sciences sings beneath Laputa's music of abused deduction, the academy being Balnibarbi's equivalent both of the empiricist pursuits of the Royal Society and of the Pope-Broome sirens. Whereas the Pope-Broome sirenic academy studies eloquence and the liberal sciences to justify wrong, corrupt manners, and subvert government, thereby wasting the patrimony of the country, the toil at Lagado's academy uses empirical means to create a land filled with "Folly and Beggary."[101] Lagado's academy, resembling the College of Experience in Plattes's *Macaria*, requires that the "Professors contrive new Rules and Methods of Agriculture and Building, and new Instruments and Tools for all Trades and Manufactures, whereby . . . one Man shall do the Work of Ten; a Palace may be built in a Week . . . as to last forever without repairing." Lagado's academicians, like Bacon's guardians, promise a land in which "all the Fruits of the Earth shall come to Maturity at whatever Season [they] think fit to chuse, and increase an Hundred Fold more than they do at present; with innumerable other happy Proposals."[102]

And Lagado is a divided land, like that of the Sirenusae. The Siren country in Pope's translation is a dichotomous landscape, part "beautiful country" and part desert ("In verdant meads they sport, and wide around / Lie human bones, that whiten all the ground; / The ground polluted floats with human gore, / And human carnage taints the dreadful shore.")[103] Similarly, when Gulliver reaches his siren landscape of Lagado, he sees an equally dichotomous landscape: first, a patrician Munodi supervising his traditional estate of verdant meads laid out in georgic order and then the scientists overseeing the ruination of the Grand Academy of Lagado. Where the crops and people of Munodi's farm prosper, the beauty is evident: "We came into a most beautiful Country; Farmer Houses at small distances, neatly built, the Fields enclosed, containing Vineyards, Cornground, and Meadows." Gulliver does not "remember to have seen a more delightful Prospect."[104] But outside Munodi's ancient-seeming estate with its classical architecture and neat farms lies the Grand Academy of Lagado's desert. Not one Lagadan agrarian scientist recognizes the sickness of an agriculture that, ignoring Munodi's classical gardens and house "built according to the best Rules of ancient Architecture," has destroyed the implicit ancient rotational system of vineyards, wheat fields, and meadows.[105] Yet even Gulliver recognizes the injury: "I never knew a Soil so unhappily cultivated, Houses so ill contrived and so ruinous, or a People whose Countenances and Habit expressed so much Misery and Want," and "except in some very Few Places, I could not discover one Ear of Corn, or Blade of Grass."[106] The subversions of the Sirenusae's academy parallel the efforts of the Lagadan academy to undermine and pour contempt on Munodi's regime, and the academic Siren's "abuse of knowledge and . . . coloring of evil" parallels the academy's abuse of animals, plants, the blind and ill, and even human language. Things substitute for words in the academy's effort to create precise discourse after the manner of Bacon, John Wilkins, and a host of seventeenth-century advocates of artificial languages.[107] When Swift equates the Royal Society and the Baconian experimental scientists with the academy of the Sirenusae, he mocks eccentric and unethical scientific experiments.[108] But his main target is the very idea of a "Royal Society" or scientific academy collectively sharing information, creating collaborative normal science, and dissecting or reversing natural processes without consideration for the past, human community, or the environment.[109]

In "Hades" on his subsequent Glubdubdrib trip, Gulliver visits the place of sorcerers and magicians, where historical figures and immortal beings relate intertextually with those in Ulysses' Hades. Ulysses' Hades includes the heroic dead from the Trojan and Theban past, whose appearance *in propria persona* sets aside all questions of historical authenticity and "presence." But whereas Homer's souls from the past appear to suggest that history can be known directly, Swift's Hades totals up the errancy of scientific history, the uncertainty of Richard Bentley's detailed positivistic commentary and history. If Glubdubdrib presents sympathetically and attractively Eustathius and Didymus, those commentators on Homer used by Pope and Broome whom Swift also uses to create the intertextual dimension of *Gulliver's Travels*, it reserves only scorn for the new theoreticians of history and science—for Gassendi and Descartes, who were popular with some Commonwealth theorists, and for modern heroes and great families mounted high by "Perjury, Oppression, Subornation, Fraud, Pandarism," "Sodomy . . . Incest," and the "prostitution of their own Wives and Daughters."[110]

The country of Luggnagg correlates with the "Elysian fields." There live the modern immortals who are the equivalents of Homer's Hercules, the man who husbands Hebe, or Youth, and enjoys "perpetual youth," a "reputation that never grows old." This immortality belongs to people who serve humankind in Broome-Pope.[111] Facing the possibility of seeing in Luggnagg a similar immortality, Gulliver fancies *his* immortal state as one in which he, as a Struldbrugg, and all his fellow Struldbruggs, will grow rich (at least he will); come to full maturity in the arts and sciences and in wisdom; grow learned in astronomy, riparian science, geography, and history; and, conversing around the table of intellect, teach the hopeful young by example and wisdom how to prevent the "continual Degeneracy of human Nature."[112] (Recall that Ulysses rejected immortality with Calypso and accepts the mortality assigned to him by Tiresias in Hades.) But when Gulliver sees Struldbrugg-land's this-worldly immortals, he finds no Elysian fields—only the material immortality produced by the "extension of human empire" to the creation of endless senility, Bacon's deathless world carried to its logical conclusion. Luggnagg tells us the "gifts reserved for Age," as Eliot puts it in *Four Quartets*.[113]

➛ Lands of Pygmies and Giants in Parts 1 and 2

Three other less obvious intertextual patterns make Gulliver invert the Ulysses of the commentaries: the parallelisms between Lilliput and Troy and Gulliver and Polyphemus in part 1, parallels between the Brobdingnagians and other Homeric giants in part 2, and the opposition between Odysseus' return to Ithaca and Gulliver's to England in part 4.

Troy and Phaeacia are backdrops to Lilliputian education. Swift's specific manipulation of size in *Gulliver* parts 1 and 2 depends on the new science of optics and the eighteenth century's interest in near and distant magnification. But the manipulation of size is also a Homeric game; the commented *Odyssey* uses the pygmy metaphor to speak of collectivities and the gargantuan one to speak of the individual. The Lilliputian episodes examine England's collective political enterprises and set forth a Moresque satire of human collectivities, while the Brobdingnagian ones look, through Juvenalian eyes, at heroic individual vanity and heroic efforts to attain beauty in an unheroic age.[114] Beneath this manipulation of the new optics for satiric purposes lies the Odyssean intertext and its manipulation of size. Swift presents the mock heroism of the Lilliputians and the clumsy incivility of the Brobdingnagians as distortions of Phaeacia, Troy, and Cyclopsland.

Both Lilliputian and Brobdingnagian counterparts appear in the *Odyssey*. To the Cyclops, Pope's Ulysses is a "pigmy wretch" and therefore an object of contempt; but to the short Phaeacians, he appears godlike in beauty and size and flatters them by showing how he avenged himself on their Cyclopean enemies.[115] At first Lilliputia appears to be a place where a new Hercules will repeat his bagging of the pygmies, but it soon becomes more—a hybrid of the land of the paradisal Phaeacian garden and the defeated Troy where the palaces burn. Its liberator is a Gulliver who, endeavoring to play Hector, becomes its Polyphemus. In Phaeacia, everything exists in the activities of the common—in storytelling, music, feasting, and gardening. Such a world, according to the Pope-Broome commentary, did suggest to some critics a corrupt Epicureanism, but Pope and Broome assert that in Phaeacia the joy is appropriate and innocent, it being the "most glorious aim of a king to make his subjects happy and diffuse an universal joy thro' his dominions.[116] Phaeacia's untroubled island becomes the more delightful to Ulysses because, having just experienced the sorrows and triumphs of the Trojan War, he can here unwind and tell his "war stories."[117] And Swift develops a subtle, if not insistent, parallelism between Gulliver in Lilliput and Ulysses in Phaeacia in the early sections of part 1 and later between Gulliver and

Ulysses among the Trojans as paradise turns monstrous. As Ulysses encounters the Phaeacians in perpetual feast, the Lilliputians begin by giving him what, in their terms, is a gargantuan feast.[118] As Ulysses appears to the Phaeacians to be a godlike man or a god, Gulliver appears to be a giant to be lodged in a defiled Lilliputian temple. The Phaeacian palace includes an elaborate and verdant garden, and the whole of Lilliputia appears to Gulliver "a continued Garden."[119] As some critics believe "*Nausicaa* had conceiv'd a passion for *Ulysses*," according to the Pope-Broome commentary, so in Lilliput an "excellent Lady" is said to have "taken a violent Affection for [Gulliver]."[120] The Phaeacians are a "simple, . . . credulous" and "lazy people," pleasure loving and effeminate, with a penchant for games according to Pope-Broome.[121] In a similar vein, Gulliver notes the simplemindedness of the Lilliputians in analyzing his person, their diversions in the form of rope dancing (seeking preference in the government and court), stick leaping before the emperor to gain blue, red, and green threads (sycophancy to the monarch and chief minister to obtain the award of knightly order), battle gaming on Gulliver's handkerchief (petty dynastic wars), and purporting to cut an egg correctly (sacramental disputes).

But the difference between the Phaeacians and the Lilliputians, between the epic Mediterranean and Walpole's England, lies in the Lilliputians' innocent-seeming posture, their cuteness cloaking malice. Whereas the Phaeacians stand in awe of the heroic world but do not emulate it, the tinier Lilliputians, fancying themselves a heroic people, resent Gulliver's extinguishing the "Trojan" fire that burns their queen's palace, and they plot to kill him for saving them from a "Trojan" fate. Full of self-inflation, they emulate Ulysses' putting out the eye of the giant, Polyphemus, by planning to put out both of Gulliver's eyes and starving him to death in the meantime (the applications to England's treatment of Harley and Bolingbroke are obvious).

All of this may go to the failure of education. The mock Phaeacia observed by Gulliver, which at first seemed pleasant, cute, harmless, and full of lovely gardens, becomes monsterland because of its neglect of learning for role and for charitable humanity within role responsibility. Lilliputia's education comes out of Plato's *Republic* seasoned with the practices of some of the continental Protestant countries in central Europe where a national system of education had taken root in Swift's time. Lilliputian boys who will rule, like those in Plato's *Republic*, are taken from their parents and placed in "common nurseries," kept busy, taught the cardinal virtues and religion, and prevented from conversing with servants except "in the Presence of a Professor . . . whereby they avoid those early bad Impressions of Folly and Vice to which our Children are subject."[122] Lilliputian girls are placed in nurseries where the nurse is forbidden to tell frightening or foolish stories—Swift's equivalent of Plato's false stories—and where they receive a female education almost equal to the male's. Whereas ruling-class Lilliputian females discontinue their education at twelve, ruling-class males continue to fifteen, "which answers to One and Twenty with us."[123] Schools are devoid of love and natural affection between parent and child or teacher and child, and though much of Lilliputian education may parallel what Swift seriously advocates, it is without generosity. Children of tradesmen receive proportionally less education, and cottagers' and labourers' children receive none. No one in this society is taught kindness or responsibility. Beneath the utopian surface of a benevolent education lies the malevolent depth of a role-structured society lacking all preparation for aristocratic *noblesse oblige* and all lower-order provision of education for role. Charity schools do not even exist; in Lilliput, the poor receive no education. The education in the land constructs the ingratitude and malice of the Lilliputian ruling class and the Leviathan spirit of the masses. To the Lilliputians, Gulliver appears the barbarian that the Pope-Broome commentary says the Cyclops race was, but at this point he is actually governed by a simple kindness that is as close as he ever comes to a heroism. This kindness disappears from his temperament in the later parts of the book.[124]

◦ The Brobdingnagians and Other Commentary Giants

Though to Gulliver the Brobdingnagian giants appear demanding and to the reader they seem inhumane (in their treatment of him as a show animal and circus performer), Brobdingnagian education is actually as humane as Lilliputia's is corrosive. The individuals in Brobdingnagia may be physically and sometimes morally ugly, but their institutions have the innocence and humanity of those of Dacier's Odyssean giants lodged between the second and third stages of Cyclopean reconstruction after the great Atlantan flood (as already noted, this period is also mentioned by Bacon). The Pope-Broome commentary on the Cyclops episode tells us, after Plato's *Laws* (III, 677Aff.), that when the Platonic flood had subsided, three manners of life succeeded among mankind.[125] The first (i.e., the Cyclopean) was rude and savage; men were afraid of a second flood and therefore inhabited the summits of mountains, without any dependence upon one another. Each was absolute in his own family.[126]

Polyphemus seems to be an exaggerated form of such a creature: he even lacks a family (as does Gulliver through most of Swift's work). The second stage became "less brutal; as the fear of the Deluge wore away by degrees" and the Cyclops "descended toward the bottom of mountains" to begin some social interaction. The third stage after the flood "was more polish'd; when a full security from the apprehensions of a flood was establish'd by time." The giants, now to inhabiting the plains, created commerce and "enter'd into the societies, and establish'd laws for the general good of the whole community." The commentary adds that the Cyclopeans "maintain'd the first state of life in the days of *Ulysses*; they had no intercourse with other societies, by reason of their barbarities, and consequently their manners were not at all polish'd by the general laws of humanity."[127]

Of course, in the passage Dacier and Pope-Broome cite from the *Laws*, Plato describes a flood that destroyed all civil society save for the giant families who lived on the mountain tops. They herded goats and cattle and knew none of the arts of war, metal making, or lawyering. As the giants came down from the hills, their families who lived in the foothills gradually diminished in stature, turned to farming, and created property boundaries, erecting stone defense walls around their common farms. Those who came together to form a society were governed by separate laws and experienced difficulty in creating a polity. They therefore chose "certain men common to them who look over the customs of all the clans," men "especially agreeable for the community." These men they "present[ed] . . . for the approval of the leaders and chiefs of the populace" to be "lawgivers" (III, 681–D). Brobdingnagian culture rules through a simple polity like that mentioned by Plato, Dacier, and Pope and Broome. The culture respects farming and simple forms of community; has a king who displays Plato's group's abhorrence of war; and, as Plato's people are great builders in stone, the Brobdingnagians throw up stone temples three thousand feet tall and a hundred feet thick.[128] Further, as Plato's group, recently come to law, has a simplified legal system, so also Gulliver's Brobdingnagians make laws that do not consist of more than twenty-two words, each offered without precedent and understood by everyone.[129]

In Plato, diminishing size represents a movement toward the present. One may regard the Brobdingnagians as representing the civilization of the past and the Lilliputians as coming to be under the aegis of the decay of nature. Temporally the Brobdingnagians seem to reflect the Cyclopean descendants described in Plato's *Laws*. Their size clearly sets them in a former age but not the earliest one, as the "Treatise, which always lay in *Glumdalclitch*'s Bedchamber," demonstrates. The writer of the treatise shows how "diminutive contemptible, and helpless an Animal" the giant Brobdingnagian race is and how inferior to the animals in speed, sight, work habits, and defensive capacity. This section therefore shows how nature has "degenerated in these latter declining Ages of the World, and could now produce only small abortive Births in comparison of those in ancient Times."[130] As a projection out of the past, Brobdingnag practices some few vices of Plato's later corrupt civilization, such as avarice and the desire for victory. The farmer who puts Gulliver on display does so out of sheer greed, but the country generally lacks the other "civilized" amenities produced by the modernist education and research known to our modern Ulysses. It has no mercenary standing army, no taxation system permitting a national debt, and no cynical parliament or bevy of lawyers.[131]

The praise of the modernism implicit in the gun and the gunpowder so loved by Bacon comes to a head when the king pronounces Gulliver to be a member of the "most pernicious race of little odious verman that nature ever suffered to crawl upon the surface of the earth" (Gulliver has just given an account of Europe). To recover the king's respect and to ingratiate himself, our dwarfish voyager offers to show the king how to "make a certain powder" to discharge balls that will destroy "whole ranks of an army," destroy city walls and sink whole ships, "divide hundreds of bodies in the middle, and lay all waste before them." When the king encounters gunpowder, the very pride of Baconian scientific industrialism as it has been eulogized by the mouth of the movement's Moses (see chapter 2), his wonder at how such an "impotent and grovelling . . . insect could entertain such inhuman ideas . . . wholy unmoved at all the scenes of blood and desolation" incites him to forbid Gulliver ever to speak of such matters again.[132] There is some progress that Brobdingnagia will not tolerate.

Simple as the giants are, they stubbornly pursue what is, to Gulliver's way of thinking, a generally defective education but one close to Swift's normative essayistic statements on it: "The Learning of this People is very defective; consisting only in Morality, History, Poetry, and Mathematics; wherein they must be allowed to excel. But, the last of these is wholly applied to what may be useful in Life; to the Improvement of Agriculture and all mechanical Arts; so that among us it would be little esteemed. And as to Ideas, Entities, Abstractions, and Transcendentals, I could never drive the least conception into their heads."[133]

The country's learning is directed to right conduct and understanding the creation without manipulating it or creating theory directed toward its manipulation. The Brobdingnagians study mathematics as Arbuthnot would have it studied—as the basis for work in agriculture and mechanics and as a substitute for the endless unguided and random experimentation of the virtuosi.

Brobdingnagians' moral training appears to include no study of the uses and limits of power, perhaps because Swift believed the strong always incline to some element of tyranny over the weak. In a basically benign culture, the exploitation of Gulliver "laborious enough to kill an animal ten times my strength" goes unpunished. Though Swift respects simplicity and elite leadership in government, he also argues that in any political system, "the Limits of Power deposited with each Party ought to be ascertained."[134] Believing in clear limits to power and clear responsibilities for those holding it, he does not eulogize the enhancements to those limits coming from such scientific inventions as the gun and does not condone grandeur's insensitivity to the consequences of its actions.

➎Ulysses' Return to Ithaca and Gulliver's to England

Ulysses' decision to return to a Penelope protected by Minerva rather than to stay with the Calypsos and Circes of his journey makes him prefer humane wisdom and the care of the family to the pleasures of the journey.[135] Gulliver's contrasting returning choice in part 4 of the "two young Stone Horses" over his wife places bestiality ahead of humanity.[136] Gulliver's journey to educated madness culminates in his visit to a Houyhnhnmland that is the inverted equivalent of Circe's witch haven. He lands on the island of the horses in "desolate Condition," so desperate that he does not recognize to what extent the Yahoos are his own species and so disturbed in his wits that when he sees the talking horses, he thinks, as if he were Ulysses among the pigs in Circeland, that "they must needs be Magicians, who had . . . metamorphosed upon some Design," diverting themselves with a stranger.[137] The Homeric reversed intertext, Circe's island, according to Pope and Broome, makes Mercury or "Reason . . . the God of Science" teach statesmen how to regulate their desire for pleasure by using the moly's "fruits of instruction . . . sweet, agreeable, and nourishing" to empower the statesman-Ulysses to overcome pig-heaven by study.[138] The Swiftian equivalent assumes a modern Circean power making humankind forget itself as a species compact of reason *and* passion, in "doubt to deem himself a God, or Beast; / In doubt his Mind or Body to prefer," and doubtful that he is a "Chaos of Thought and Passion, all confused."[139] For Swift, in my view, as for

Pope, the height of bliss is not rationality but charity, a passionate/rational direction. In the *Dunciad*'s Circe section, an old wizard extends the *"Cup of Self-love"* (p. 393) whose taste makes its drinker forget "former friends, / Sire, Ancestors, Himself" (bk. 4, ll. 518–19) until—possessed with self-love and forgetful of all responsibility, yet retaining a human shape—he pursues only aristocratic recreation, "turn[ing] off to roll with Hogs, / To run with Horses, or to hunt with Dogs" (bk. 4, ll. 525–26). As Pope observes in his note, the wizard's effects are clean contrary to Circe's. Whereas she took the human shape away from the men she converted to pigs and left their human minds, self-love does the opposite, leaving the human shape but taking the mind somewhere else.[140] Self-love, the pride of Lemuel Gulliver that has taken his mind elsewhere, lies at the heart of his mad melancholy.[141]

Self-love makes Gulliver look at himself "often in a glass" to habituate himself to the sight of a human creature. It results in his fancying that he is incapable of lying and without most of the other vices of the Yahoos, and it renders him incapable of detecting the melancholy and anger that separate him from love for his human family and race. He only, Puritan that he is, admires Houyhnhnms who procreate without desire or sense of sexuality and breed by the books.[142] They educate only in their version of the four cardinal virtues, "TEMPERANCE, *Industry, Exercise . . . Cleanliness*," and appear to know nothing of faith, hope or charity.[143] Gulliver is the perfect avatar of the new generation—scientific, calculating, governed by the eighteenth-century international businessman's self-interest (note the echo of Martinus when he fails to turn his discoveries over to the Secretary of State primarily because the potential colonies he discovers would not be easily conquerable or profitable).[144] Gulliver's "Vein of melancholy" leading to "Disgust of his own species" culminates a journey that begins with his leaving his wife five months pregnant to go on his trip. It incubates during his travel with Captain Purefay (Purefaith) from Calvinistic Leyden; strengthens with the growth of the defects that lead to the mutiny of his men and his sharing in the addled regions of Nuyt's (night's) land, 1st St. Peter, Sweers (Swears)

I, and I Madsuyker de Wits (Madseeker of Wits); and culminates in Horseland. That at the end he comes home to Bedlam is fully predicted.

The Houyhnhnms who further Gulliver's mad development are not new to Swift. Talking horses also appear in books 17 and 19 of Homer's *Iliad*, when Achilles' horse Xanthus weeps for Patroclus' death and later predicts Achilles' death (bk. 17, ll. 435 ff; bk. 19, ll. 446–63).[145] When Dacier interprets the former passage, she argues that if fables can make animals speak, Homer could certainly make Achilles' immortal horse speak and weep even as Virgil made Pallas' horse do.[146] The virtues that Gulliver assigns to his Houyhnhnm hosts begin with Homer: Spondanus cites numerous classical authorities on the intelligence and loyalty of horses.[147] The prophecy by Dacier's Xanthus to Achilles concerning the approach of his death, anticipated by the horse's weeping for Patroclus' death in book 17, certifies his conveying divine prophecy and divine intelligence in the manner of Balaam's ass.[148] Pope and Broome repeat the Dacier/Spondanus interpretation.[149] However, though Swift's talking horses may have divine intelligence, they do die—unaccompanied by passion or grief. They are not in "doubt to deem [themselves] a god, or beast; / In doubt [their] minds or bodies to prefer" because they represent a hypnotic model of humankind: the transcendence of the middle state of passion that can become charity and of the familial love that can become nurture.

Gulliver's vision of them is more a product of his own melancholy than of their perfection or his love of divine intelligence. Captive to a Circean vision of a society based in simplicity, truth, order, and the four cardinal horse virtues, endeavoring to exemplify that society to humankind, Gulliver abandons *specifically* human virtues having to do with care for family and kin, the primary virtues belonging to Ulysses *and* to the Portuguese Pedro de Mendez. In the conclusions of the *Odyssey* and *Gulliver*, both Ulysses' and Gulliver's wives think their husbands dead at the time of their return. Both rejoice when they discover the return. But how different the husbands' responses! When Ulysses returns to Penelope,

> Touch'd to the soul the King with rapture hears,
> Hangs round her neck and speak his joy in tears . . .
> The ravish'd Queen with equal rapture glows,
> Clasps her lov'd Lord, and to his bosom grows.
> Nor had they ended till the morning ray:
> But *Pallas'* backward held the rising day. (Bk. 23, ll. 247–60) [150]

When Gulliver's wife and family "receive [him] with great Surprize and Joy" and his wife takes him in her arms and kisses him, he is filled with "Hatred, Disgust, and Contempt . . . by reflecting on the near Alliance I had to them" with a sense of their "Smell . . . intolerable" and disgust at the prospect of copulating with his wife. [151] The return of the hero metamorphoses to the misanthropist's anger at the species rather than Ulysses' handling of his neglect of his own affairs and the great disorders in his realm. Gulliver's neglect, rather, continues with his residence in the stable, his impotent railing against his own civilization, and his beholding of "[his] Figure often in a Glass" while he rails against the pride of his own species. [152]

Gulliver's scientific, "Dutch" detachment in his voyage for the new lands of knowledge and science has become the isolation of Narcissus. In the lands he has visited, a Baconian and Commonwealth style of education, science, and rationalistic government have created malice and madness in the ruling groups, have denied all familial and natural ties, and have posited a power of human action beyond human nature. As we have already suggested, *Gulliver* is not a mock epic or "little epic," as the fictive persona pseudo-Ricardus Aristarchus (Richard Bentley), in his essay "Of the Hero of the Poem," says the *Dunciad* is. It is not an action in imitation of an epic in which the epic's standard stylistic and plot devices clothe outlandishly a hero vain, impudent, and debauched. [153] In *Gulliver*, the reverse happens. The conventions are those of the scientific travel writing beloved of the Royal Society, and the virtuosi are imposed on the grand landscape of epic.

Their "detachment" and "isolation" shrink them and their hero, Gulliver, to complete and self-centered isolation. The ancient in education has become paradigmatic for the modern in the profoundest sense, a sense Bentley, the scientific philologists, and editors never understood.

The *Dunciad* completes this end-of-the-world project by showing the destruction of the culture of the city as a Periclean school, the killing of all holistic learning, and the apotheosizing of heroic Dulness at the end of a few decades of the new order.

CHAPTER FIVE

Adam Smith and Utopia as Process

AdAM SMITH PUBLISHED his *Theory of Moral Sentiments* (1759) sixteen years after Pope completed his last version of the *Dunciad*, and only seventeen years later he issued his *Wealth of Nations*, celebrating the bourgeois enterprise and nonascriptive social world that Pope, Swift, and the other Scriblerans had despised as Dullness. He celebrates this new and coming world in wholly nonreligious terms save for his faith in the invisible hand. The Scriblerans—finding little hope in the Baconian-Comenian millennial thrust toward universal popular knowledge and a research and education seeking the mastery of nature—favored an educative culture and education that would promote responsibility in aristocrats as rulers and in the populace according to role. In contrast, Smith, seeking a mastery of nature comparable to that found in the Commonwealth people, paradoxically founds his educational hope on secular state-sponsored compulsory education for the masses.[1] He does so though in almost every other arena his positions are antistatist ones.

Wealth is a utopian work, not least in its educational proposals, a "real-world" fiction footnoting Bacon and setting the Whig or liberal educational agenda for over a century. (Incidentally, the skeptical reader need not agree that *Wealth* is a utopian work since, whatever its genre, it sets the stage for later utopian educational writing by the Utilitarians.) Writing over a century after Bacon and against the background of a culture in which Latin and Greek learning were much in decline among all elites, Smith abandons the models provided by canonical literature, particularly Homeric and Virgilian. His new persuasive model is plotlessly novelistic rather than epic, and novelistic mimesis in *Wealth* tells us how to conduct a utopian market society, how providence creates it, and how compulsory education assists it. Because by 1776 the idea of the Baconian search for light and fruit through education has triumphed, the question now concerns how light is to become a fruit sufficiently distributed to feed the industrial masses.

THE WEALTH OF NATIONS AS STRAIGHT-FORWARD OR IRONIC UTOPIA

Wealth is not your traditional utopia. There is no island society controlling nature and evil, no paradise satisfying all human wants and creating peace, and no humankind living according to a generally rational and pleasurable balance. Few of utopia's good results are promised without qualification. But *Wealth* does promise that its system will make things as good as they can be, which is all any serious utopia can promise. However, Smith's rhetoric countenances positions arguing that *Wealth* assiduously avoids utopian hopes or claims. For example, in book 4, chapter 2 of *Wealth*, he identifies the constraints that make tariff reduction difficult: for example, securing domestic monopolies, promoting domestic investment, protecting nascent manufacturing industries, sustaining local industry deemed necessary to national defense (even when not), tariff retaliation, and supposed tariff protection of the domestic employment market. At the end of this enumeration of impediments, he concedes that "to expect, indeed, that the freedom of trade should ever be entirely restored in Great Britain is as absurd as to expect that an Oceana or Utopia should ever be established in it."[2] Notice that Smith projects some golden time when trade *was free*; free trade is now to be "restored" to the degree possible as, in Bacon, science is to bring back Eden to the degree possible. But insurmountable public prejudices and private interests now seem to prevent the immediate realization of utopian hope, though the general premise of the book is that they can eventually be surmounted.[3] Smith's persona is always that of the dour Scotsman looking reality in the face to see its full possibilities, however limited.

Several scholars have questioned whether *Wealth* should be treated as a utopian book in the sense that it is unrealistic. For example, Karl Polanyi argues that any work proposing a society organized totally on the basis of an unregulated "free market" is pejoratively utopian, but he also argues that Smith does not fully propose such a society.[4] Richard Teichgraeber III argues that *Wealth* is not free market advocacy but an effort to show that the complete free trade advocated by some prior eighteenth-century thinkers is overly optimistic: Smith therefore is trying to set limits on utopian hope, to show what policy changes England and Europe will have to employ to introduce a feasible free trade in mid- to late eighteenth-century Europe.[5] (The argument is historically irrelevant since Smith's most powerful followers, the Utilitarians, never used his arguments to seek limits on overly optimistic views of what the free market could do and generally argued for a completely uncontrolled market, even in matters of usury. As in Smith, only education was given over to the state in their utopian designs.)

Marxist criticism has also implied that Smith's work is utopian either in the serious or in the mystificatory sense. For Karl Mannheim, liberalism is the second positive wave after Chiliasm. One can extrapolate from this that if liberalism is the second wave in the Western postmedieval tide of utopian hope, then Smith is its prophet, and *Wealth* is the classic piece of liberal utopianism, both legitimizing the movement toward a freer market economy that was beginning to come into existence in the English-speaking world and also enhancing the impulse toward such an economy. In contrast to the implicit in Mannheim, Ernest Bloch regards *Wealth* as purveying a false utopian consciousness:

> Characteristics of false consciousness, which were subjective, came to light in the "selfish system" of Adam Smith, and those characteristics were not wily and filled with discord, as so often found in Calvinism, but subjectively honest and harmonious. They were the characteristics of the conviction, of the good conscience of the respectable merchant and entrepreneur who, in fact, believed in honest gains. First of all, in the interplay of supply and demand, he thought of himself as a kind of benefactor of the consumers. Of

course, he thought mainly of the solvent consumer, those with whom he could make money by selling the products of labor gained from the surplus value pressed from the workers. But the good conscience gained strength by supposedly relating the capitalist interest constantly to that of the consumer, making the customer satisfied. The good conscience of mutual advantage was also eased by *embellishments* since everyone was regarded as a free trader of increasing exchange power whose unmistakable self-interest was compensated by the general commercial interest that was developing everywhere. Throughout all this, the capitalist economy appeared as the only natural economy that one had finally discovered. And it was this economy that Smith praised ceremoniously as utopian. This [commercial] interest itself was influenced in a utopian way, or rather the false consciousness of interest, but it was quite an active one.[6]

Bloch also observes that this utopian sense of the free, nonexploitative play of the market does somewhat describe small business in Smith's Edinburgh but hardly pictures how the East India Company with its repertory of coercive tools worked. Whether Smith creates an honest utopian hope to mobilize society to allow for the play of the market or the falsehood that everyone is served by its play does not matter here. What matters is that *Wealth* and its supporting writings depend on the techniques of fiction for their power. The source fictions are no longer those of the classical epic or Plato's *Republic* but those of the eighteenth-century novel with its verisimilar surface, especially in the treatment of the invisible hand, the division of labor, and the role of education, and it is to these fictions and their live counterparts in the heads of people mobilizing for change or stasis that Smith addresses his construction.

NOVELISTIC TECHNIQUE AND THE INVISIBLE HAND

While Smith's *Wealth* contains almost no data in the ordinary sense accepted by modern social science, it is the textbook basic to many forms of modern social science. Its history of the movement from hunter to pastoralist to agriculturalist to merchant is a fictive, stylized

history, largely unsupported by research.[7] Some of its material about
the legislative, taxing, and commercial practices of European and
some prominent Asian countries is accurate and quite telling, but
much of that information is also questionable.[8] In a few cases, the
work includes information about prices and changes in prices over
time that appears to be accurate.[9] But most of the "empirical force" of
the work resides "ordinary life" presentations, exactly what Henry
Fielding or Tobias Smollett give us. We see commonsense emblematic or exemplary pictures of how a landlord feels when he looks out
at his vast fields, how pins or clocks are manufactured, how people
barter and divide labor, how poor people live and feel, how university
lecturers and students behave, how monopolists conspire, and how
apprentices work. None of these is drawn from ordinary life observation or from serious ethnology. Though ordinary life and common
sense are Smith's supposed data, his scenes are really exemplary, having no local habitation and name but instead possessing a certain
novelistic verisimilitude. What further gives the picture of how whole
economies work a persuasive character is Smith's connection of all of
his material into a systemic analysis, in this case a providential system.
The central teaching of *Wealth* is that providence guides self-interest
so as to make human beings productively and inadvertently serve one
another.

The first version of Smith's paradigmatic fable of providential self-
interest appears in *Theory of Moral Sentiments*, where the notion of
an invisible "divine" hand regulating nonpurposive, unplanned economic competition first appears in *the* "fable" of the unfeeling, egocentric landlord, in which a self, contemplating what it can have,
becomes the emblem of a whole society spontaneously and invis-
ibly organizing itself for material gain according to the dictates of
providence:

> It is to no purpose that the proud and unfeeling landlord views
> his extensive fields and, without a thought for the wants of his
> brethren, in imagination consumes himself the whole harvest that
> grows upon them. The homely and vulgar proverb that the eye is

larger than the belly never was more fully verified than with regard to him. The capacity of his stomach bears no proportion to the immensity of his desires and will receive no more than that of the meanest peasant. The rest he is obliged to distribute among those who prepare, in the nicest manner, that little which he himself makes use of, among those who fit up the palace in which this little is to be consumed, among those who provide and keep in order all the different baubles and trinkets, which are employed in the economy of greatness; all of whom thus derive from his luxury and caprice that share of the necessaries of life which they would in vain have expected from his humanity or his justice. The produce of the soil maintains at all times nearly that number of inhabitants which it is capable of maintaining. The rich only select from the heap what is most precious and agreeable. They consume little more than the poor, and—in spite of their natural selfishness and rapacity, though they mean only their own conveniency, though the sole end which they propose from the labours of all the thousands whom they employ be the gratification of their own vain and insatiable desire— they divide with the poor the produce of all their improvements. They are led by an invisible hand to make nearly the same distribution of the necessaries of life, which would have been made had the earth been divided into equal portions among all its inhabitants and thus, without intending it, without knowing it, advance the interest of the society and afford means to the multiplication of the species. When providence divided the earth among a few lordly masters, it neither forgot nor abandoned those who seem to have been left out in the partition. These last too enjoy their share of all that it produces. In what constitutes the real happiness of human life, they are in no respect inferior to those who would seem so much above them. In ease of body and peace of mind, all the different ranks of life are nearly upon a level, and the beggar who suns himself by the side of the highway possesses that security which kings are fighting for.[10]

For all his realist's persona, Smith never offers evidence from research on the consumption of resources for the truth of his claim. He includes no possibility that both conspicuous consumption and waste might govern the behavior of his prudently grandiose landlord. The scene comes to us as so objective, even negative, in its picture of the greed and indifference of the landlord and the gargantuan appetite that consumes him that we, for the moment, suspend all judgment as to Smith's accuracy in the remainder.[11] We do not ask whether in fact the exemplary unfeeling landlord is likely to consume little more than his servants and peasants or whether his "vain and insatiable desires" end with the consumption of "little more than the poor." We do not speculate as to whether the action of degrading, torturing, and punishing the poor may not in itself be one of the satisfactions of wealth and power. (Remember that the highland clearances take place in Smith's lifetime.)[12]

The landlord mythos consciously or unconsciously counters the biblical parables of the self-satisfied man who, on the eve of the time when God requires his soul, says he will "tear down his barns and build greater barns" because he has a good harvest *to store up* (Luke 12:16–21) or of the self-important Dives who ignores the Lazarus begging by his door (Luke 16:17–31). Indeed, the net effect of Smith's parable is to remove the anti-acquisitive sting from such biblical tales through a counterparable that implicitly makes the barn builder and Dives unwitting servants of universal egalitarian improvement and prosperity. The *Theory* passage contains one of Smith's primary inventions—the idea of a providence ("invisible hand") governing selfishness to create universal benefit. The invention converts to complete seriousness Mandeville's hive fable averring that private vices are public goods; Smith's selfishness drives the landlord to seek to produce more than he can possibly consume, as in the general Christian mythos the divine scheme makes more of the sum of things than any one person's partial evil can destroy.

Wealth, published seventeen years later (1776), generalizes the novelistic fable of the rural landlord to whole industrial societies. Smith uses the "invisible hand" in *Wealth* exactly as he does in *Theory* but relocates the design argument of *Moral Sentiment* from the rural estate to the capitalistic marketplace, positing what F. K. Mann has called "the related concept of the self-regulating market and of nonpurposive social formations."[13] In *Theory* the insatiable landlord is led by an invisible hand to share his massive output with his peasants in order to serve his own greedy interest; in *Wealth*, the individual capitalist grasps the invisible hand of providence as he invests in industries that bring maximum returns. Intending "only his own gain," so Smith's *Wealth* mythos goes, the capitalist also is led "by an invisible hand" to promote the good of society:[14]

> But the annual revenue of every society is always precisely equal to the exchangeable value of the whole annual product of its industry, or rather is precisely the same thing with that exchangeable value. As every individual, therefore, endeavours as much as he can both to employ his capital in the support of domestic industry, and so direct that industry that its produce may be of the greatest value[,] every individual necessarily labours to render the annual revenue of the society as great as he can. He generally, indeed, neither intends to promote the public interest, nor knows how much he is promoting it. By preferring the support of domestic to that of foreign industry, he intends only his own security; and by directing that industry in such a manner as its produce may be of the greatest value, he intends only his own gain, and he is in this, as in many other cases, led by an invisible hand to promote an end which was no part of his intention.[15]

Unlike *Theory*, *Wealth* presents us with a class of central figures through whom the invisible hand works, capitalists looking out over their fields of industry. Smith may have gotten the idea of a providential selfishness producing the same effects as charity not only from Mandeville but from a tradition extending from Chrysostom to Pierre Nicole, though none of these thinkers made organized selfishness the motor of whole or good societies. Smith's conviction that society, governed by a certain invisible hand or providence and liberated from mercantilist bureaucracy, can create massive wealth leads him to subscribe to the ideas that nonpurposive social formations are necessary to human well-being and that collective social planning based on altruistic motives has no purpose since God made "the immense machine of the universe" to create the "greatest possible quantity of happiness" without government meddling.[16]

Though Smith disapproved of David Hume's arguments about divine wisdom and providence in his *Dialogues concerning Natural Religion*, he also virtually eliminates traditional ideas of Wisdom and Providence from his assumptions and postulates no divine force encouraging us to learn that has an echo in the human scientific/cognitive faculty.[17] As Wisdom is no longer the governing force in the natural and educational worlds, so also Christian charity (or self-sacrifice) and the common weal no longer motor the good society. *Theory* valorizes sympathy as the source of moral good between acquaintances, but even sympathy appears in *Wealth* to be unnecessary and potentially hurtful, since though people, in a "flourish[ing] and . . . happy" society may help each other out of "love, . . . gratitude, . . . friendship," at a lower level workable societies may exist "as among different merchants" for utility rather than love.[18] Natural law tells us that organized societies cannot survive when their members seek only to hurt one another, but their members can compete with one another in ways that appear hurtful yet actually help one another. This is true because where intellectual interpretations of human motives and God's purposes come into play, we often "imagine that to be the wisdom of man, which is in reality the wisdom of God."[19] In short, the wisdom of God by implication subsists, if at all, in the competitive market.

One may contrast Smith's landlord scene with that describing another landlord, Fielding's Squire Allworthy, in *Tom Jones*, and his use of his fortune: "I have told my reader . . . that Mr. Allworthy inherited a large fortune; that he had a good heart, and no family. Hence, doubtless, it will be concluded by many that he lived like an honest man, owed no one a shilling, took nothing but what was his own, kept a good house, entertained his neighbours with a hearty welcome at his table, and was charitable to the poor, i.e., to those who had rather beg than work, by giving them the offals from it; that he died immensely rich and built an hospital."[20]

This *noblesse oblige* paragraph prefaces Allworthy's discovery of the foundling Tom and the history of his efforts to educate Tom and protect him from himself and others. Tom, without identifiable parents and caught in the religious opposition between Square and Thwackum, in the lifestyle opposition between libertinism and pious emptiness, has only the generosity of Allworthy as his flawed protecting deity (in imitation of the ancient epics) and the vision of Sophia, his self-consciously named beloved, to guide his journey. The thrust of the novel that follows is that wealth exists in consequence of no appetite for wealth and for the well-being of others. Through the generosity of the master of the house, it functions to construct the happy, well-fed household, though happiness and being well-fed are not the end of existence.

Allworthy's household is not the kind through which Smith's invisible hand or version of providence moves because Fielding's providence belongs to the order of tragic joy and not of material proliferation. Tom's comic suffering—his birth as a bastard, his childish peccadilloes, his rejection on mistaken grounds by Allworthy, his drunken ecstasy at Allworthy's escape from death, his endless separation from his Sophia, his affair with Mrs. Waters, and his duel with Fitzpatrick ending in jail all providentially shape him from an improvident youth to a fit husband for Sophia. His comic suffering and escapades *have made him*—through Jenny Jones's mistaken identification as his mother, through Bridget Allworthy's timely death leaving Jenny to uncover his identity, through Mrs. Waters's real identity with Jenny Jones but not with Tom's mother, through Dowling's revelation to Tom in prison, and through Jenny/Mrs. Waters's more significant revelation that Bridget Allworthy is his mother and he is not guilty of incest. All of his painful separation from parent and protector and would-be spouse change Tom Jones from an irresponsible doubting Thomas at the beginning of the novel to the satisfactory domestic epic hero who can marry the sophic woman at the end.[21]

Smith's novelistic story takes quite a different turn.[22] It has no plot shaping the hero in the heroic wars of experience and no providence guiding the hero through his suffering to a spiritual Penelope. His providence blesses greed, and rather than promising marriage and reconciliation to an exemplary social group after suffering, it promises a better life for everyone so long as they all pursue untrammeled selfishness. Certainly in traditional belief, a providential myth including suffering is closely entwined with the utopian one. Gonzalo announces it a little too readily at the end of the *Tempest* (5.1.205–13).[23] All of the chiliasts argue that, in the midst of the turmoil of the times, divine providence is bringing in their chiliastic kingdoms of God, and even the far more pessimistic Pope and Swift routinely look to a divine providence that controls the course of history.[24] The removal of this kind of providence from the human search for meaning and from human education represents a major new move in the annals of utopian educational literature. For whenever the notion that the inner faculties do not guide one toward learning declines, whenever experience is denigrated as educating one in how to discover meaning in suffering, whenever history becomes entirely a matter of human construction, then the notion that education must be compelled grows. Smith's fiction of a providence that works through landlord and capitalist greed rather than through suffering is a momentous restructuring of the fictions by which human beings have been invited to live. Smith presents more than the Calvinistic Protestant notion of prosperity *as the sign of election.* In him the greed and material success of the landlord do not *confirm* any transcendent endorsement or any moral rectitude. They are themselves the election given by an invisible hand. In conventional religious terms, the landlord is a reprobate, "proud and unfeeling," lusting after his production with "immensity of desire," inattentive to the "wants of his brethren," hardly one who consciously or unconsciously cares for the least that Matthew 25 has as its subject. Yet, he is the hope for the good society.

FICTIONS ABOUT THE WORKFORCE

If the fiction of the invisible hand is Smith's major one, his complementary minor fictions do almost as much work. In looking for utopianism in *Wealth*, we cannot expect a hope-construction process empowered by an integrated fiction—the island, the perfect social order, the wise rulers. Rather we are overwhelmed by a montage of fictions, constructions, historical and semihistorical anecdotes designed to create new social structures. Through these fictions, *Wealth* does purport to describe how the commonwealth can move to an ideal state and how providence can lead it. It offers in them a practical manual that can serve as an appendix to the assumptions in *New Atlantis* about material progress and the perfective role of invention and machinery. Smith never directly describes divinely knowledgeable scientists who can extend human empire to accomplish everything possible, and one critic has argued that Smith was oblivious to the industrial revolution, to the importance of "machine production," and to the whole force of technology, reducing all these changes to the division of labor.[25] The critic is wrong. Smith *does* recognize the importance of new machinery to the world that he visualizes. He admits that machines have "much facilitated and abridged" labor. He concedes that machines transforming the labor process have been invented both by workmen on the job and by "philosophy or speculation," presumably exactly the kinds of philosophy exercised in Bacon's Solomon's House.[26] Smith further asserts that one must expect an investment in machinery to repay one's outlay.[27] Of course, his political processes are different from Bacon's because he writes for a Hanoverian merchants' state rather than a Stuart absolutist one; for a state with no invisible monarch, no invisible college of scientists, no scientists working in secret, no vague Faustian promise of a better life. Smith's utopia contains efficient workers making cheap pins and clocks and hoeing cheap potatoes, but Bacon's notion of a scientific/industrial world vastly more productive, comfortable, and materially satisfactory remains central. Progress is still central.

In *Wealth* the progress seen as a visionary possibility by Bacon seems already here or just around the corner if we can but make a few reforms:

> The real recompence of labour, the real quantity of the necessaries and conveniences of life which it can procure to the labourer, has, during the course of the present century, increased perhaps in a still greater proportion than its money price. Not only grain has be-

come somewhat cheaper, but many other things, from which the industrious poor derive an agreeable and wholesome variety of food, have become a great deal cheaper. Potatoes, for example, do not at present through the greater part of the kingdom, cost half the price which they used to do thirty or forty years ago. The same thing may be said of turnips, carrots, cabbages; things which were formerly never raised by the spade, but which are now commonly raised by the plough. All of the garden stuff too has become cheaper. The greater part of the apples and even of the onions consumed in Great Britain were in the last century imported from Flanders. The great improvements in the coarser manufactures of both linen and woolen cloth furnish the labourers with cheaper and better cloathing; and those in the manufactures of the coarser metals, with cheaper and better instruments of trade, as well as with many agreeable and convenient pieces of household furniture. Soap, salt, candles, leather, and fermented liquors, have, indeed, become a good deal dearer; chiefly from the taxes which have been laid upon them. The quantity of these, however, which the labouring poor are under any necessity of consuming, is so very small, that the increase in their price does not compensate the diminution in that of so many other things. The common complaint that luxury extends itself even to the lowest ranks of the people, and that the labouring poor will not now be contented with the same food, cloathing, and lodging which satisfied them in former times, may convince us that it is not the money price of labour only, but its real recompence, which has augmented.[28]

No data is presented in support of the proposition, no cost of living analyses, no analyses of average consumption levels in 1576, 1676, and 1776, no ethnology of what constitutes poverty in differing economic circumstances, no pictures of comparative access to resources to grow food and make housing in various rural and urban circumstances.

Much of the new "luxury" produced by the nascent market economy about which Smith writes comes about through a definitional move that makes soap, salt, candles, and leather largely unnecessary—even luxuries—for the industrious poor. The new "needful luxuries" possessed by the working poor consist in sufficient grains, vegetables, fruits, cloth, and tools. In the market sector of the British economy, linen manufacture in Scotland and coarse wool manufacture in West Riding are increasing the quantity and quality of good cloth available.[29] And in this increase of luxury for the working poor consists the "flourishing and happy" character of Smith's new society.[30]

Though Smith's fiction promises no Baconian technological fireworks—no control of weather or the forms of animals and plants—it offers its own miracles. For example, Smith observes, a pin could scarcely be made by one workman in one day working by himself. However, that same pin, given the division of labor, can be multiplied 48,000 times by twelve to eighteen men dividing the task into minute parts. Each man, in short, makes about 3,000 pins in a day. A smith by himself can make only a thousand nails in a day, but under a proper division of labor even boys can make 2,300 nails per day each.[31] In this fiction one does not find out what tools have to be made for the boys to make the 2,300 nails, how the workshop has to be constructed, what other resources have to be provided to make the nail factory possible. The narrative is similar to the contemporary one communicated in television advertisements, describing how one American farmer feeds thousands of people worldwide. The message does not examine the labor that goes into plant breeding, farm machinery development and manufacture, fossil fuel by-products used, and food transportation and packaging. Without referring to Bacon, Smith tells us that science has made machinery and people far more productive, that agriculture and manufactures have constantly been improving since ancient times, and that wages have risen in England because "the improvements of agriculture, manufactures, and commerce began much earlier than in Scotland."[32] If there is an economic problem in the transformation of life by the invisible hand and the division of labor, it is that the "wealth and wanton luxury of competitors" may produce a market glut and make commodities available at very low prices.[33]

The fiction of fluid community follows from the fiction of the universal creation of luxury, as if rootedness in village, family, local culture, and love of place had no economic implications. In a country without restrictions on the movement of labor, workers will soon move to those geographic areas and into those trades or professions where they are useful and needed. As apprenticeship restrictions disappear and labor further divides its tasks, having been made mobile by the factory system, clocks, watches, the products of the "trades, the crafts, the mysteries," will all come to market more cheaply and benefit the public with a better life. Everywhere one climbs to greater heights in the world of material comfort, especially if the present constraints on trade and the sale of labor are eliminated, even if one has to curtail the use of "soap, salt, candles, leather, and fermented liquors."

TWO NIGHTMARES ARISING: MALTHUS AND STUPIDITY

Smith's hopeful dreams are complemented by two nightmares that are designed to move us more rapidly in his direction. First, as Robert Heilbroner has observed, the luxury of Smith's utopian prospect is tempered by his assumption that as the demand for labor grows, population will grow and even outgrow the resources available, in a Malthusian-style apocalypse. Second, increasing people's material productivity through the division of labor will make workers useless for virtually all social and intellectual purposes aside from production. As we have already noted, Smith's smooth, self-sustaining upward path in a market economy must somewhere turn into a trajectory that descends to a final stage in which both wages and profits of stock must be very low. Heilbroner gives the reason for this: "In a country fully peopled in proportion to what either its territory could maintain or its stock employ, the competition for employment would necessarily be so great as to reduce the wages of labour to what was barely sufficient to keep up the number of labourers, and, the country being already fully peopled, that number could never be augmented. In a country fully stocked in proportion to all the business it had to transact, as great a quantity of stock would be employed in every branch of trade as the nature and extent of the trade would admit. The competition, therefore, would everywhere be great, and consequently, the ordinary profit as low as possible."[34]

The country that has reached such a dismal no-growth equilibrium will also be a country in which money will bear almost no interest and only the very rich will be investors, creating an economic stasis combined with overpopulation, which Heilbroner calls a situation of "Malthusian precariousness."[35] Heilbroner shows that beneath these "Malthusian" assumptions lie two further quieter Smithian assumptions: first, that population growth, especially among the poor, will be very high in the new economy and will ultimately consume any increase in productivity occasioned by the division of labor; and second, that as productivity increases, many more children of the working classes will survive, making the supply of labor eventually outstrip the demand and depress wages. Thus, if Smith predicts a modest material utopia in the near term, his long-term prediction admits of a possible stasis and decline produced by the very system he proposes. Apparently the near-term benefits are worth the long-term price, for the benefits receive virtually all of the attention.

Smith's Malthusian-style argument comes close to recognizing the pollution and environmental issues raised by scientific/industrial civilization and ignored by Bacon and the Commonwealth utopians, to the consternation of the Scriblerans. At no point does Smith spell out what he means when he speaks of the population that a country's "territory could maintain," but presumably he is speaking of the exhaustion of environmental resources with population growth.[36] Yet he does not explore this theme in depth or propose a cure for the problems, perhaps because touching the theme of the limits to growth set by the exhaustion of environmental resources would destroy much of his utopian fiction, creating conditions under which the mechanisms whereby self-love and greed could not serve social ends. When population limits have been set by the environment, can the self-love and self-protection that encourage the poor to "bear more than twenty children," as Smith puts it, also mysteriously be a force for social good? Can these work toward the good society when individual survival and reproductive interest push against the social need for limiting population because of exhausted resources?

If population growth has no cure in Smith, his second nightmare, the solipsistic stupidity that the market system's division of labor develops in the worker, does have the statist cure of compulsory education. The utopianism of *Wealth*, its development of a theory of non-purposive social formations that will lead to a significantly improved society, differs from other utopian dreams in that instead of proposing a perfected social order as its end, it offers the *perfective means* to such an order and, in addition, *a dream of freedom* where, driven only by greed and ingenuity, we can do what we want to do.

Yet we are allowed to infer that the eighteenth-century equivalents of Robert Bellah's solipsistic *Habits of the Heart* will injure the social fabric. Smith admits that ignorant and stupid workers, in a society without a "common," will destroy the social order. But then he also tells us—if ever so subtly—that the price of freedom is the surrender of our children to the state. The nightmare is put to rest by the violation in education of Smith's laissez-faire views: that is, by the imposition of a mass, state-based compulsory education that defies Smith's earlier vision of liberty or the remainder of his antistatist views.

While Smith is extremely candid in addressing the social costs for the individual worker of the kind of market system and division of labor that he advocates, he proposes universal education as their solution. The stupidity created by the extreme division of labor developed under late forms of mercantile capitalism and early market versions of the same system will be remedied by schools. Though the seeds of a new industrial, acquisitive order had been planted in England's fourteenth-century wool manufacture, competitive market capitalism, as opposed to its mercantile alternative, began to dominate British incentive systems only in the second half of the eighteenth century.[37] The mid-eighteenth-century decline of protectionism was hastened by the destruction of manorial farming and rural "learning-by-doing" education, by the weakening of the peasantry consequent to the eighteenth-century enclosures of the common lands and the virtual disappearance of the open field system, by the removal of peasants and villagers from England's and Scotland's deserted villages to the industrial cities, and by the decline of the guilds. All of these changes meant advancing disarray for the experiential apprenticeships and learning-by-doing systems where rooted education—in situ education attached to place—went ahead. The children of the anomic masses needed to be controlled and prepared for the new kind of workforce. The second half of the eighteenth century saw the growth of wealthy industrial groups, especially in western England, where industrial misery was also on the rise and where industrialists had grown increasingly impatient with government regulation and protection. Few of them saw that the government could serve them by educating children to serve their factories, but Smith saw what they did not—the need for a new education to resocialize youth, especially poor and urban youth, to the assumptions of progress, science, and industry and to deliver them from their systemic stupidity.[38]

Before introducing his proposal for compulsory public education, Smith goes after the old education based on corporatist or mercantilist views, the guild and medieval college. First, he attacks the common form of popular education related to economic development available in his time, the apprenticeship system of the guilds, for its inefficiency and restraint of trade. Second, he makes a parallel attack on standard forms of elite education, the "medieval" university and endowed "public" education, as higher forms of guild education. Smith's attack on the primary available form of popular advanced education, guild education, comes in his first book in *Wealth*. A long account in chapter 10 of the implications of the division of labor focuses on the artificial inequalities created by European labor policy, especially by the apprenticeship system still alive as a vestige of mercantilism.[39] In treating guild apprenticeship education and training, he argues that the English and European guild policy of his time "restrain[s] the competition in some employments to a smaller number than would otherwise be disposed to enter into them" and creates further injustices mandating apprenticeship periods so varied among the various European countries that the periods mandated must be *prima facie* arbitrary, making the young worker give up and turn to idleness.[40] Indeed, in Smith's view, most credential-related education could be eliminated. Though the clock was difficult to invent, once it had been invented, according to Smith's fiction, one could explain to a young person in a few days or weeks how to "apply the instruments" and construct one. Guild education had not prevented "insufficient workmanship" from being "exposed to public sale" since bad workmanship generally resulted from fraud and not incompetence. Furthermore, by creating a labor monopoly and shortages of finished products, such an education advantaged the "finishing" over the "raw" end of work, the town over the country, and heavily over sparsely populated areas.[41] Taking a position that reflects his bias against most forms of social organizational activity of a collaborative sort and anticipating the modern assault on unverified credentialism in the United States after the Griggs versus Duke Power decision, forbidding non-job-related impediments to the securing of a job. Smith argues that even the most casual conversations among people bearing the same credential are likely to become conspiracies against the public interest.[42]

Education of an endowed formal, nonguild type receives a similar treatment much later in *Wealth*, in book 5. There Smith discusses how the minimalist state or sovereign should expend tax revenues or grant monopolies to specially chartered companies to enhance the national wealth in the areas of defense, justice, and public works for developing commerce. Among the disapproved forms of monopoly is the education used to develop the skills of elites, especially endowed or provincially supported education. Whether practiced in the school, college, or university, it receives the same laissez-faire reproach as does the guild apprenticeship system. Supported by monopolistic tolls, such endowed education encourages lazy, incompetent teachers and professors indifferent to students, assembling them in collegiate corporations existing primarily to enable their members to protect one another:[43]

> If the teacher happens to be a man of sense, it must be an unpleasant thing to him to be conscious, while he is lecturing his students,

that he is either speaking or reading nonsense, or what is very little better than nonsense. It must too be unpleasant to him to observe that the greater part of his students desert his lectures; or perhaps attend upon them with plain enough marks of neglect, contempt, and derision. If he is obliged, therefore, to give a certain number of lectures, these motives alone, without any other interest, might dispose him to take some pains to give tolerably good ones. Several different expedients, however may be fallen upon, which will effectually blunt the edge of all those incitements to diligence. The teacher, instead of explaining to his pupils himself the science in which he proposes to instruct them, may read some book upon it; and if this book is written in a foreign and dead language, by interpreting it to them into their own; or, what would give him still less trouble, by making them interpret it to him, and by now and then making an occasional remark upon it, he may flatter himself that he is giving a lecture. The slightest degree of knowledge and application will enable him to do this, without exposing himself to contempt or derision, or saying anything that is really foolish, absurd, or ridiculous. The discipline of the college, at the same time, may enable him to force all his pupils to the most regular attendance upon this sham-lecture, and to maintain the most decent and respectful behaviour during the whole time of the performance.[44]

To break the complacency of the endowed colleges and public schools, students should be allowed to change institutions, teachers, and tutors as their sense of good teaching dictates. Teachers should no longer possess the vested authority created by the combination of the collegiate credential system and required attendance at lectures. School, college, and university teachers supported by endowments will then find themselves in the situation of free enterprise dancing and fencing masters, who have to teach well or get out. Smith does concede that the endowed "public schools"—presumably the Eton and Westminster variety—are less corrupt than the universities in that students going to these schools at least have to learn something, namely Greek and Latin, partly because the schoolmaster has to depend partly or wholly on fees from his students, and the schools have no monopoly on instruction in the areas where they teach. In the universities, in contrast, the "youth neither are taught, nor always can find any proper means of being taught, the sciences, which it is the business of those incorporated bodies to teach."[45]

Vesting scholarships to colleges also constrains competition. Were university teachers freely to market their wares and students to choose their own teachers, many higher education institutions would wane, unprotected by the present monopoly privileges of the professions that depend on their graduate degrees in "art, law, physic and divinity" to "force a certain number of students to such universities independent of . . . merit or reputation." Indeed, the special privileges granted graduates in these professions act as a "sort of statutes of apprenticeship."[46] The education of women escapes Smith's censure—essentially because there is no formal public or endowed system of education for women, and what they are taught informally suits them to the ascriptive role system of society:

> There are no public institutions for the education of women, and there is accordingly nothing useless, absurd, or fantastical in the common course of their education. They are taught what their parents or guardians judge it necessary or useful for them to learn; and they are taught nothing else. Every part of their education tends evidently to some useful purpose; either to improve the natural attraction of their person, or to form their mind to reserve, to modesty, to chastity, and to oeconomy; to render them likely to become the mistresses of a family and to behave properly when they become such.[47]

Women derive universal advantage from education in every part of their lives whereas men seldom derive any good from even the most difficult parts of what they learn.

The form that Smith's "utopian" education takes may surprise one. The combination of his remarks on women's education with his attack on endowed education would seem to suggest that he favors an education directed purely toward the narrowest conceptions of stereotypical vocational and social role. But paradoxically, the king of the free marketeers, the prince of those who would limit state power over the economy, proposes the greatest surrender of power to the state made in the history of modern cultures. The first prominent Britisher after the Commonwealth to make such a proposal, he puts all of his educational faith in the coercive power of the state.[48] Having rejected most of the educational system common in his period, he might be expected to extend the competitive, "survival of the fit" aspects of his theory to call for an educational system that would ask children to struggle and fail or survive in the factory and marketplace without educational assistance.[49] That was, after all, to be increasingly the lot of children in a rapidly industrializing United Kingdom as child laborers filled the factories. Alternatively, he could have argued for the equivalent of educational vouchers to allow for a public tax-supported system of education based on market principles, as has his disciple, Milton Friedman. But, though he warns against a number of violations of what he sees as market principles in both the apprenticeship and university systems, *Smith does not argue that the fundamental system of education for the masses of workers in a state in which the division of labor prevails should be a market system. He rather opts for a state-sponsored compulsory system.* In doing this, he contradicts another distinguished educational thinker having antistatist tendencies, Joseph Priestley, the high priest of the dissenting academies and of scientifically based education. In his *Essay on the First Principles of Government* (2nd edition, 1771), Priestley had argued that the "establishing of [education] by authority would obstruct the great ends of education," cramp and confine it, and produce a conformist model of humanity instead of allowing diversity to flourish as variety of commerce flourishes in an uncontrolled market.[50]

It should be observed that Smith does not insist on compulsory education primarily on the grounds of quality, as some early and mid-nineteenth-century parliamentary investigations of the "dame" schools and conventional private elementary and secondary schools were to do, but on the grounds of the utopian need for an intellectual "common" in an otherwise ideally self-aggrandizing society and also on the grounds of the stupidity created by the division of labor. He poses the essential question as follows: "Ought the public, therefore, to give no attention, it may be asked, to the education of the people? Or if it ought to give any, what are the different parts of education which it ought to attend to in the different orders of the people? And in what manner ought it to attend to them?" Smith's answer turns to education to create the sense of the social unit. Education is the one purposive social formation basic to the utopian hope of *Wealth*. The remainder is nonpurposive stuff—the elimination of social directives from public bodies, faith in the absence of public constraints and in the wisdom of the invisible hand, reliance on the force of pure competition and on the individual desire for "sympathy," respect, and material grandeur.[51] Smith's rationale for universal publicly supported education in a modern commercial/industrial state is simple: "In some cases the state of the society necessarily places the greater part of individuals in such situations as naturally form in them, without any attention of government, almost all the abilities and virtues which that state requires," while "in other cases the state of the society does not place the greater part of individuals in such situations, and some attention of government is necessary in order to prevent the almost entire corruption and degeneracy of the great body of the people."[52] That is, the social need determines whether a society ought to have a publicly supported universal system of education or some other form of formal education or no system at all.

Smith's evolution of socioeconomic orders brings society from hunting to pastoralism to agriculture to the mercantile and then to the market commercial/industrial system.[53] Each of these stages has its own exigencies and greater or lesser need for publicly supported education and training, and the commercial system current in the eighteenth-century United Kingdom has *most* need for a universal system of education because, requiring nothing but repetitive actions, it destroys all informal need for learning as part of social adaptation. The division of labor that exists in industrial, commercial societies has made the self-education commonplace in "barbarous societies" impossible because too little of the total social system can be understood by industrial workers whose "whole life is spent performing a few simple operations."⁵⁴ In barbarian societies every man is a warrior, statesman, husbandman, and shepherd, but in a "*civilized*" one (italics mine), where in consequence of the division of labor most people perform only a few simple operations, almost every man is stupid. The workers' minds perforce becoming "as stupid and ignorant as it is possible for a human creature to become."⁵⁵ The laborer degraded by the division of labor also becomes cowardly and worthless for all private and civic judgment. If stupidity and cowardice are the natural lot of the greater portion of the citizens of "improved and civilized" societies, it might appear that the condition of barbarity would be intellectually preferable, but Smith does not explore this possibility, rather trying to remedy the defects through compulsory education. If general stupidity and cowardice are the lot of "the great body of the people" in "improved and civilized society" when the government does not act to counter this natural outcome of the division of labor, if the equitable regulation of a country's market depends on the vigilance of its citizens, then the common people, and not just the elite classes, must be educated.⁵⁶ The specific answer to the destruction of a common by the division of labor is for the children of all of "the common people" to receive, at public expense, instruction in how "to read, write and account" early in life.⁵⁷ Elsewhere Smith argues that his preferred compulsory education will teach children to write, "to read," to "account," and to learn "elementary geometry and mechanics," the most "sublime" and "the most useful sciences." The state must pay for much of this education because parents among the poor have neither the time nor the money to provide an education for their children and often require all of their income to subsist: "The public can facilitate this acquisition [of knowledge] by establishing in every parish or district a little school." The master must be subsidized by the public; if he were to depend on payments by the children's families, "he would soon learn to neglect his business," because "the children of the poor are to be taught for a reward so moderate that even a common laborer may afford it, the teacher being partly, but not wholly, paid by the public" as in Scotland.⁵⁸ The education of "the common people" requires the primary attention under the commercial system because the elites get all the education that money can buy; if they are poorly educated, it is because they have had poor masters. Further, they have leisure as adults to educate themselves, and their duties being various, they are required to learn as part of adaptation to role.[59]

The activities of a complex society are so varied that presently only the elites can make the connections necessary to understand it. For Smith the possibility of making systemic connections in an arena of experience is crucial to its comprehension.[60] But with the division of labor at an advanced stage, the activities of the laboring class are so simplified and routinized that the laboring group—indeed, most people—have no understanding of the complex workings of their society. Their ignorance and cowardice will jeopardize the whole social fabric. (So far as I can determine, Smith does not argue for education, as Patricia Werhane asserts, on the grounds that without it "the worker . . . slips back into identifying herself with her work," while with it, the progression of the mind will help one to judge one's work rather than becoming identified with it.[61] The function of education in the lives of workers as Smith envisages it is to give them a sense of how the whole social engine works, not only the capacity to judge their work or commodity.)

What Smith proposes to use to educate the whole social body and give it an understanding of itself is pretty thin stuff: writing, "accounting," and reading—reading confined to English, eliminating instruction in Latin, and rooted in practical "instructive" books.[62] It is not clear how this education will counter the soporific and degrading effects of the division of labor and make workers bright, brave, and worthy in their private and civic judgments, but Smith assumes that development. Perhaps he assumes that given literacy, the products of the public press and printing would do the job, the very Grub Street productions hated by Pope and Swift. But civic competence need not be assumed. To make certain that the compulsory effort bears fruit, Smith would have the state (the "public") oblige everyone to undergo an examination in essential knowledge before participating in any corporation or setting up a trade in an incorporated village or town.

Compulsory education will improve "military exercises" and give every citizen the "spirit of a soldier," as the Prussians had long assumed; it will do more by creating a market-oriented society's common and will protect it against "enthusiasm and superstition," vulgarity, and disrespect.[63]

After Smith the Whig or liberal agenda comes increasingly to include a proposal for compulsory education as necessary to the brave new world that industry and science are creating. However, the basic reasons that Smith offers for a public investment in education soon drop out. Between Smith and John Stuart Mill there is little interest, in this wing of British thinking in education, in creating the equivalent of the common or the village market square, where the multiform activities of society can be seen to come together and be comprehended, where workers can be awakened from intellectual torpor. The school itself becomes the agent for the socialization of children to competitive behavior and for the suspension and submersion of critical intellect. And one finds little mention of what is happening to the lilies of the field as the Coketowns and Manchesters and Coventrys of the north and west develop.

Historians of education such as Michael Katz and Raymond Callahan have described the mid-nineteenth- and early twentieth-century alliance between capitalism and the public schools by picturing a late nineteenth-century formation of an implicit alliance between the two, fusing with education the process of mass industrialization and the application of the methods of "scientific management." But the contract between the two forces came at least a century earlier. The movement to fuse capitalistic business enterprise and compulsory schooling was not covert and not the result of a recent application of business practices to schooling but lay at the very foundation of the English and American public schools, created by late eighteenth- and early nineteenth-century members of the Scottish Enlightenment and the English Utilitarian movements who were empiricists in philosophy, admirers of Adam Smith's vision of a material prosperity created by market economics and of Francis Bacon's vision of a new Atlantis. The group included many protégés of Adam Smith: Jeremy Bentham and James Mill, Henry Brougham, William Ellis, and J. A. Roebuck. As these major figures developed their agendas, other figures given to applications such as Joseph Lancaster, the period's monitorial system advocate, and George Combe, the phrenologist, turned their theories into practice.

CHAPTER SIX

Utilitarian Compulsory Utopia

S MITH'S SUCCESSORS in the construction of educational utopias and schools did not retain his sense that state-sponsored compulsory schools should serve the creation of a social and intellectual common. Smith did argue that state-sponsored education had a vocational purpose and concerned reading, writing, and arithmetic as the tools of trade and industry, he asserted that "scarce a common trade" does not apply the principles of geometry and mechanics, and he approved of women's education as entirely related to the "female" occupations.[1] As a man of limited traditional religious commitment, he deemphasized the schools' role in establishing religious hegemony, the basis for the primary compulsory national systems in the rest of Europe (i.e., Prussia, the Netherlands, and Scotland) to the degree that they enforced such compulsory attendance.[2] However, he saw the schools as having an ethical purpose beyond vocationalism in that they were basic to the formation of intelligence and a common social interest.[3] The job of education was to liberate workers from the stupidity that industrial age routines imposed on them, to provide an understanding of the general social and intellectual worlds that the routinized vocations serve, and to help workers understand the whole social fabric so that they might act constructively in relation to it.[4]

In contrast, the next generation of Smithians, the Utilitarians— Jeremy Bentham, James Mill, Henry Brougham, J. A. Roebuck, William Ellis, and their followers—largely removed "the common" from educational ideology (the idea returned in various specious forms in the "melting pot" ideology of the twentieth century) and devised embodiments of an individualistic and competitive education that would power industrial progress and extend human empire everywhere. In doing so, they prepared the way for the compulsory education enacted in the 1870s. Three aspects of Utilitarian invention in the early nineteenth century (primarily prior to the 1830s) are crucial to the formation of utopian visions and actions: Bentham's *Chrestomathia*, the most significant Utilitarian print-based educational utopia (developed from Bentham's Panopticon for prisons); James Mill's Associationist educational psychology, promising a technology for social control that would realize utopia; and Joseph Lancaster's monitorial schools, providing a model for how cheap compulsory education that might feed both Chrestomathic education and capitalist progress might work. The alternatives to these thrusts came from the utopian socialist Robert Owen. While Foucault's beloved Benthamite Panopticon was never really constructed, Bentham-style panoptical schools were—all over Britain and the United States with an application and rigor that makes the Panopticon for prisoners appear insignificant.[5]

UTILITARIANS AND *CHRESTOMATHIA*

The Utilitarian reformers cite many reasons for creating state-based secular, compulsory education and teacher training: for example, the desire to regularize the lives of urbanizing populations and prevent vagrancy, crime, and gangs; the need to regulate education and restrict abuses in private and dame schools; the hope of preventing child labor; and the necessity of developing the young workers' industrial work skills. The system they devised also promised the scientific/technical skills to extend human empire and the competitive skills to make the extension a capitalistic one.

In 1816, Bentham's *Chrestomathia* proposed his Chrestomathic School, an educational utopia as much set off from the muck and mire of daily life as Prospero's magic island. It, in turn, became a prime catalyst for Utilitarian educational and political organization as such prominent Utilitarians as Mill, Ellis, Brougham, David Ricardo, and Francis Place (a member of the British and Foreign School Society pushing for general use of the monitorial system) involved themselves in efforts to bring Bentham's fantasy alive as an institution. Bentham's assistant, John Herbert Koe, did much of the early organizing toward the effort; later, Henry Brougham was brought into the discussions, as were other prominent political figures, from time to time. Since William Ellis — the school reformer of another generation and a leader in the marine indemnity business discussed in the next chapter — was active in the Utilitarian group's 1820s discussions of education, one must assume that he talked with the others about *Chrestomathia.*[6] Though a strict Chrestomathic School was never founded, Bentham later described the Hazelwood School, founded in 1819 at Edgbaston near Birmingham, as confirming his theory, and of course University College, London, was also to some degree parented by *Chrestomathia.* Further, since Bentham put his weight behind the monitorial schools, they were, in their post-1820 form, both a building block and an outgrowth of his utopianism though a few such schools existed prior to *Chrestomathia.* Part of the genius of the Utilitarians in educational reform as in other areas was like that of the Hartlib-Comenius-Durie circle: to form networks of people in the schools, business, politics, and the bureaucracy who could carry an agenda forward and to keep working on the agenda for an extended period.

According to Bentham, *crestomathic* means "conducive to *useful* learning." The day school in *Chrestomathia* is therefore an institution for pursuing strictly useful (utilitarian) learning. Indeed, *Chrestomathia* proposes, on its title page, both a systemic and a class orientation: the systemic factor requires the "extension of the *new system of instruction* to the higher branches of learning" (emphasis mine), essentially to secondary and higher education in the sciences and technology, and the class factor directs that extension. It is "for the *use of the middling and higher ranks in life*" (emphasis mine).[7] By the middling ranks, Bentham means the ranks of the shopkeeper and management classes, who require literacy and scientific knowledge for their work in business and industry in the new order yet do not need the knowledge of classical languages still demanded of lawyers, medical doctors, and theologians.[8] The higher classes would presumably be people of title. Thus, the conquest of nature potentially involves both the Whig and Tory classes, though Bentham must have known that his primary appeal extended to the Whigs and philosophic radicals. He never defines the lower classes; by exclusion, they would have to comprise the unskilled industrial masses, the marginally employed, and the unemployed. From his actions elsewhere in supporting monitorial elementary schools for the lower classes (see later discussion), we can infer that in the radical utopia they were supposed to receive education only at the beginning levels of literacy and numeracy.[9]

Bentham's "new system of instruction" uses the monitorial method in which students teach students in an endless competition. The school room-construction and surveillance methods are to be those proposed for prisons in Bentham's *Panopticon*, making the eye of the schoolteacher, representing the social collective, control students *as the prison warden's eye controls prisoners* in the *Panopticon*. Since the social collective exists in the eye of the single master teacher and not in any discursive identification of the common profit of the group characterizing ancien régime institutions, the school makes no effort to create a common. In drawing the analogy between prison and school, Bentham unabashedly makes clear that invisible control comes first among the school's goals: "By the *Panopticon* principle of construction [of the classroom], security in this respect, is *maximized*, and rendered entire: viz., partly by *minimizing* the distance between the situation of the *remotest Scholar* and that of the *Master's eye*; partly, by giving to the *floor* or *floors* that inclination, which, to a certain degree, prevents remoter objects from being *eclipsed* by nearer ones; partly by enabling the Master *to see without being seen*, whereby, to those who, at the moment, are unseen by him, it cannot be *known* that they are in this case."[10] Though the common disappears in this arrangement since it allows for no negotiation among individuals, so also do privacy and individuality before the all-seeing eye of the master teacher, the Prospero surveillant over his little social world betokening the larger regimentation demanded by society. (Foucault is wrong in imagining educational surveillance as beginning with the Enlightenment efforts to discipline and punish; it is clearly basic to Prospero's order.) Beneath the master teacher, teams of surrogate teachers or "monitors" maintain a strict meritocracy of drill as they herd their little groups of students through the desired performances. Punishment is sure because everything is seen; surveillance prevents all mere *"sport,"* *"wantonness,"* and *"idleness."* Further, the problem of evil is solved through the creation of a permanent register of "bad boys" that precludes serious evil.

For Foucault, the creation of this sort of social discipline along panoptical lines (itself the creation of a nascent group of social sciences) required not only a panoptical use of space so that the potential of surveillance would be ever-present. It also required a constant control of the activity overseen through hierarchy, surveillance, observation, and writing (or record keeping), exercises to ingrain habit, and common tactical drills in which the permitted and the forbidden are distinguished.[11] All of these would create a regimented social solidarity in the panoptical prison and in the military, and all are proposed for the Chrestomathic school and present in the monitorial school on which Bentham bases his proposals (discussed later). At the end of the line comes the examination, the final authoritative grading of the individual's performance and the manifestation of his (*mostly his*) conformity to the norms demanded.[12]

To reinforce his idea of what a monitorial Chrestomathic school for older children (ages seven to fourteen) should be, Bentham places in the appendices to *Chrestomathia* two letters written in 1814 by leaders of the Edinburgh High School describing the use of monitorial practices in the teaching of Latin and Greek to students older than those in the common primary level monitorial school (since Bentham wishes to eliminate Latin, the Edinburgh example cannot be exact). In one of the letters, James Pillans, the rector of the school, tells how his school works as a system. The duty of the monitor is to: "1 . . . take care that each boy shall construe a portion of the new lesson; 2 . . . see that his division understands the syntax and construction of the passage; 3 . . . take care that the right meaning be always given to the passage in all its parts; and, 4 . . . mark on a slip of paper the names of the boys who fail in saying." After the lesson, the various divisions or groups under the various monitors assemble under the tutelage of the headmaster, and the students receive encouragement to appeal any of the translation decisions of their student monitor. If the appeals are justified, the appellant takes the place in the line of merit of the student who has mistranslated, and the monitor loses a place, presumably in the monitors' line of merit: "This system binds both the monitor and pupil to careful preparation at home; the former, from the fear of detection and exposure by a boy far below him in the class; the latter, both by the infallible certainty of his being called on to say, and reported if he fail; and by the honorable desire of rising in the class, and proving that he knew the lesson better than the Monitor." Pillans also emphasizes the centrality of the element of surprise—not knowing when one is to be called on or appealed. In an additional essay, James Gray, a teacher in the school, argues that the system eliminates student restlessness while other students are reciting, the wasting of student time (since everyone is concentrating on everyone else's possible errors), and all corporal punishments. The teacher who was once a "tyrant" and an "enemy," because of corporal punishment, now comes before the students with a "reciprocity of kindness and *docility*" (emphasis mine).[13]

Bentham announces pedagogical principles to undergird the proposed school, reflecting monitorial and panoptical controls on space, time, repetition, and tactics, principles that in fact give the student an epiphenomenal sense of individualism related either to Associationist psychology or market competition. The *contiguous proficiency* principle means that the satisfaction of being a monitor depends on one's being placed over other students and nearer in power to the adult teacher. The *Panopticon* principle means everyone is seen by the adult teacher without being seen. The *place capturing principle* means that students are constantly ranked according to performance on the drills and exercises; the *scholar jury principle* means that students are pitted against one another to judge mistakes; the *comparative proficiency principle* provides for a long-term sum and average of the daily rankings of students. The *delation-exacting principle* means that the public exposure of faults in a published register will be enough to shame students into behaving. The *proficiency principle* demands perfect performance as opposed to promise or skillful analysis of the background of a problem. And the *gradual progression principle* means that exercises proceed from easy to difficult and the school records the scholar's progress in a register to be confirmed by public performances before the adult teacher and various school visitors and sponsors. The learning system, pitiless in its application, relies on externalized behavior, "right" answers, emulative motivation, and social stigma, enforced by the all-seeing eye, all-public records, and external visitations.

All critical education is eliminated from the curriculum. There are *no scientific experiments, only scientific drill*—a Baconian dream proposed without reference to Bacon's call for critical analysis defying the intellectual idols (Bentham refers to Bacon, often to correct him slightly, more than a half a dozen times in the work). In the school's Stage I, the children of the middle and upper classes are to know the disciplines Bacon described as creative of "light" (for example, Mineralogy, Botany, and Zoology), and in its Stage II, they are to move into the applied sciences resulting in the "fruits" of progress such as Hydrology, Galvanism, or Animal Chemistry. In Stages III, IV, and V, they are to work at the vocational application of these sciences to industry in Mining, Surveying, Pathology, Surgery, Technology, and Bookkeeping. Since Bentham assumes Adam Smith's division of labor is a desirable social organization, appendices 6 and 7 of *Chrestomathia* include an elaborate discussion of how the various technological operations used in the crafts and industry are to be taught and offer a taxonomy of such operations.[14] Obviously such an expansion of the curriculum in the sciences does not come without an elimination of those subjects that might lead the student to question the behavioral system of the school, the all-seeing eye, and the human or environmental consequences of an unfettered pursuit of "progress." The subjects to be eliminated are the fine arts and *belles lettres*; the arts of war and navigation (contrary to Smith's view); and finally and most important, the "moral arts and sciences": divinity, ethics, law, politics, and most of all logic—as Bentham puts it, "by some called Metaphysics."[15] The subjects that might call the system into question give way to make space for those that will speed us into the coming brave new world.

Though the proposed education appears to ask only that the student perform well for the cult of progress, Bentham argues that the proposed education will also lead to personal growth in self-respect and to relief from ennui, sensuality, idleness, and mischief. Given his program, this growth must come from the surveillance of the all-seeing eye and not from any conscious teaching of an ethical code, as its *conscious* emphasis goes to developing business-style "useful subjects" supporting entrepreneurial capitalism and creating new business pursuits and employments. These are envisioned as activities that will create mental strength in one's business, eliminate unscientific superstition, and enlarge "each scholar's field of occupation": "The more things [the student] is more or less acquainted with, the more things he is fit for, and the better chance he has acquired of meeting with some *occupation*, (pecuniary-profit-yielding or not,) according to his *condition*, which shall be at once within his *power*, and suited to his *taste*." [16]

To support his interest in industry and technology and the emphasis on the material world, Bentham proposes a taxonomy renaming the sciences and technologies to clarify their relationship to one another, using a Baconian or Bishop John Wilkins–style "real character and philosophic language." The proposed language names the equivalents of Wittgensteinian "simples," all useful languages consisting, in Bentham's view, in predication concerning the names of corporeal things, incorporeal or inferential things, and fictitious entities or qualities. [17] Obviously a "real" character can most easily name the "simples" in things that can be seen. [18] Hence, in the ideal curriculum, the objects presented will be named so that one may ascertain both their nature and how they are connected to every other object, and everything studied will appear rationally and sequentially. Every study will move from the natural to the artificial, the corporeal to the incorporeal, the concrete to the less concrete, and the cause to the effect in a curriculum as structured and putatively cohesive as any 1960s National Science Foundation "Bruneresque spiral," based on Jerome Bruner's *Process of Education*. [19]

Utilitarian Compulsory Utopia

JAMES MILL AND SCHOOL PSYCHOLOGY
AS UTOPIAN TOOL

Bentham's pedagogical principles derive from the school application of an Associationist psychology, reformulated by James Mill and perfectly suited to the construction of a regime of surveillance, temporal control, rote drill, and examination. This psychology empowered the dream that education could reinvent human nature for the machines of industry, science, and competitive work. In the old regime that prevailed prior to the French Revolution and the collateral reforms in England, control issued from religious and political structures, using direct or threatened violence here or in the afterworld, its power rehearsed in catechetical instruction, church courts, public rites of recantation, witch burnings, and the like. Much of the control was vested, as in any conservative community, in cultural habit. After Adam Smith, the new materialists, to create a new set of habits, increasingly call into question the old psychology and control systems.[20] The older faculty psychology really has no place for control even as modern developmental psychology springing from Piaget does not. As represented in Comenius's and Pope's writing, faculty psychology, dividing the mind into the sensorium, memory, imagination, reason, and intellect, moves the mind, as it is educated, upward to more and more universal comprehension, as experience and inner discipline dictate. It employs the sensorium to study the surface appearance of things, the imagination to view their appearances and structures through applied mathematics (and related disciplines), the reason to study pure structures themselves through pure mathematics, and finally the intelligence to synthesize the harmonies and relations among structures into a systemic unity.[21] This psychology— originally formulated for medieval and Renaissance education by Boethius and Aristotle and promoted by all pre-Associationist psychologies—made the maturing child's mind move developmentally through concrete and partial stages to the abstract and complete system.[22] But since the movement of the mind toward learning appeared inwardly impelled, psychology could have little to do with education since it did not explain how the school could control the student's development. Montaigne's schoolroom festooned with whips seemed to offer the only control vehicle available, and plenty of accounts of traditional schools in the late eighteenth and early nineteenth century remind us that Montaigne's child-hells still existed. But Associationist psychology, assuming that rationality was a construct created outside the child (or adult), that the societal control creating classroom "rationality" mitigated the coercive force required to make students fit the emergent society, promised a "kinder" space for schooling.

Of course, everything was coercion, only on a subtler scale than that of the old regime. Associationist theory had always included social control and the construction of rationality as putative productive outputs, at first in adults. In 1650, Thomas Hobbes published *Human Nature and the Elements of Law*, arguing against the old faculty psychology and in favor of a more "scientific" account that would treat all objects as emitting motions, vibrations, or waves moving the organs of sense through the air or ether.[23] Supposedly, ear, eye, skin, tongue, and nose, receiving the "waves," interpret them as sounds, sights, pains, tastes, and smells that then mysteriously become motions in the mind, retained in the memory and the imagination of things. The mental motions then organize themselves inside the head into the sequences that, by an unknown mechanism, allow for prediction, planning, and speech as the record of mental images, often for completely random or irrational sequences: "The cause of the coherence or consequence of one concept into another, is their first coherence, or consequence at that time when they were produced by sense. As for example: from St. Andrew the mind runneth to St. Peter, because their names are read together; from St. Peter to a stone for the same cause; from stone to foundation, because we see them together; and for the same cause, from foundation to church, and from church to people, and from people to tumult. And according to this example, the mind may go from almost any thing to any thing."[24]

Since the associations are wild, the job of monarchic habituation, in Hobbes's view, is to make certain that what is "associated" in the mind actually fits together in the object world and does so in such a way as to sustain the monarchic authority system. Later the Tory Hume's *Treatise on Human Nature* (1739) assimilates Hobbesian Associationism to argue that education, reconceptualized as habituation, could also change people for the better in society; a simple idea, an image, impression, or sensation becomes associated with another because of its resemblance to that other "idea," its contiguity to it in time or space, or its causation by the other.[25] Since habit and repetition fix everything in the mind, the accidental and fortuitous association of ideas constitutes "learning," and traditional learning simply makes vivid those images, ideas, and associations that a priest-ridden society wishes to vivify, all past and future education being fundamentally habituation.[26] The trick for Hume, then, is to change education so as to habituate people to proper, Humean ideas. By the 1740s, the Whig/liberal psychologists who operated at the other end of the political spectrum from Hume and Hobbes saw that Associationism could serve their scientific/industrial school, and David Hartley, in 1749, gives Hobbesian-Humean theory a particularized pseudo-physiological base: supposedly external objects create vibrations that the nerves' medullary substance transmits to the brain. There the sensations-become-vibrations turn into "ideas," and their subsequent association with other sensations or ideas depends on their synchrony or succession, all of this controllable by habituation: "Sensations may be said to be associated together, when their impressions are either made precisely at the same instant of time or in contiguous successive instants."[27] Since the associations have no rational basis, the persons rearing the child must control the synchrony and succession of ideas to which he or she is exposed in order to force rationality through habituation: "all that has been delivered by the ancients and moderns, concerning the power of habit, custom, example, authority, party prejudice, the manner of learning the manual and liberal arts etc., goes upon this doctrine as a foundation."[28] Finally, following Hartley, Priestley in 1778 applied Associationist principles to create a technology for private education in the private dissenting academies.[29]

Utilitarian Compulsory Utopia

The dream of full social control through employing Associationism in publicly supported, compulsory schools appears two years after *Chrestomathia* in James Mill's 1818 entry on psychology for the
Encyclopedia Britannica. Mill proposes Associationist principles of si-
multaneity, succession, and habituation as the basis for a compelled
public education.[30] Education cannot "assume its most perfect form"
until "the science of the human mind has reached its highest point
of improvement"—that is, Associationist psychology.[31] The current
language of educational psychology—presumably that of the faculty
psychology derived from Boethius, Aristotle, and the schoolmen—is
inadequate; the new psychology must depend "upon a knowledge of
the sequences which take place in the human feelings or thoughts."
Upon this new knowledge, "the structure of education must be
raised." According to Mill, psychology's present vague naming of the
Associationist sequences precludes any of the precise labeling of their
concrete appearance in external behavior that would allow education
to shape the individual.[32] Since the business of education is control of
the individual's mental life ("to make certain feelings or thoughts take
place instead of others . . . to work upon the mental successions"), Associationist psychology's purpose, as applied in the schools, will be to
furnish a tool capable both of changing human beings into rational
creatures, as defined socially, and of creating benign social change.
The understanding and manipulation of the "sequences" or "associations" of ideas and the subsequent habituation of people to have correct associations is *the* great scientific study that will give rise to the
new education, which will teach people to be happy by giving them
the power to know and choose the means and the ends that please
them. Absolute habituation will create absolute freedom, absolute
pleasure.

Part of the job of the new education and psychology will be to get
rid of the old order's impediments. After paying tribute to Rousseau
and especially Helvetius for making clear that everything in experience habituates and affects the "train of feeling," Mill launches into
his own analysis of education's physical inhibitors (physical handi-
caps, sickness, disorders of the nerves and brain), its environmental

inhibitors (inadequate food, overwork, work on minutiae required by the division of labor), and its roots in preschool education in the family. All must be changed. Family education, properly directed by the spirit of Plato's censor, should seek to take the element of story-telling (or superstition) and fear out of childhood so that children can see events in the order of the "most invariable and comprehensive sequences and assess the consequences of their actions in pleasure and pain exactly as nature provides consequences." It must get rid of those "terrific trains of ideas . . . passing in [children's] minds, when they go into the dark . . . which have nothing to do with the order of events . . . and often exercise over them an uncontrollable sway during the whole of their lives." If "an order of ideas, corresponding with the order of events, were taught to come up in the minds of children when they go into the dark, they would think of nothing but the real dangers," and "their conduct would be nothing but that which prudence, or a right conception of the events, would prescribe." The same strictures apply to educating children against a servile fear of wealth and power or contempt for the poor or against political, religious, or national prejudice.[33] Knowing that "intelligence is power," previous premarket cultures have resisted teaching workers the truth about cause and effect, about how natural events create human pleasure and pain, or how using scientific insight one may achieve one's individual ends. The leaders of premarket cultures have wanted to keep the world divided into oppressors and oppressed through controlling who is educated.[34] The new education will be drill—directed to the creation of a better society through the development of habits destructive of the old society's deference to the ancien régime's aristocratic or mercantilist assumptions. Education for the new world can have no truck with the muck and mire of the old. For Mill, child labor, with its Dickensian cruel exploitation of children but also with its childhood real-world learning and development, is out. Education for place and community is also out. Mill's rationale is that since the acquisition of the intelligence to manage a rational society requires a full concentration on the "real" sequences of events and the suppression of random associations, it ought not to be interrupted in childhood by the labor of the market, the search for bread, or guild education. It ought, in short, not only to be public and compulsory but separated from traditional community, from objects and situations outside the school, and centered in routines associated with texts and experiments that rehearse the new order. Implicitly it is to be the vanguard of the new order, separating children from quotidian customary work and responsibility and seating them in the schoolroom until they are fifteen or sixteen years of age, following the principles both of Bentham's Chrestomathic utopian plan for future schools and of the extant monitorial schools.[35]

THE LANCASTRIAN SCHOOLS AND THE DESTRUCTION OF THE COMMON

Undergirding the Whig 1820s–40s proposals for a national system that creeps toward compulsory schooling and related teacher training are Mill's approved models, Bentham's never fully implemented Chrestomathic plan, and Joseph Lancaster's and Andrew Bell's monitorial schools. These last include an easy-to-master regimen of surveillance, temporal and behavioral control, repetitive exercise and drill, constant examination, and public manifestation of conformity to norms.[36] The Lancaster-Bell system was the model for that already used in the Edinburgh High School by James Pillans. Lancaster especially furnished the Utilitarians with their pedagogical model in that his system sought to create cheap *secular* schools for working-class children and succeeded through prescribing a student-teacher ratio of 500 to 1 (Lancaster calls for one monitor for every ten pupils and one adult teacher for every fifty to one hundred monitors). To support the 500 : 1 ratio, the schools trained some children as monitor-teachers, who would "teach" the other children for a halfpenny per week.

The system's "education," like the economic system it served and served to create, was fiercely competitive and based on rote. After each monitor was taught a lesson from a printed card, he used the same card method he had just learned to teach his fellow students. He was to encourage the students under him to compete with one another, discern one another's mistakes, and where possible also discover his own mistakes. Unlike the old grammar school master or the master craftsman in the guilds, who was expected to be, above all, literally the master of his material, Lancaster believed that the new style monitor-teacher needed to know nothing. The monitor who is able to read, "can teach, ALTHOUGH HE KNOWS NOTHING ABOUT IT [the subject]."[37] The whole *modus vivendi* of the school is to become competition—the displacement of rivals in mechanical tasks.

School was to become conditioning or the control of associations. As F. W. Garforth has put it, an Associationist psychology that "after a somewhat mechanical model, emphasizes the manipulation of man and the means of manipulating him, lends itself to a mechanical concept of education in which the stress is on teaching rather than experiences to be explained." Thus, it "is not . . . surprising . . . that James Mill and other utilitarians likewise committed to association psychology were so strongly attracted to the monitorial system of teaching introduced by Bell and Lancaster." Its "appeal lay . . . in its cheapness" and its conformity to the Associationists' "conception of education as the presentation of prestructured experience, here in the form of 'programmed' information which once correctly ordered by a skilful teacher according to the laws of association, could be presented by any number of unskilled apprentices."[38] The competitive, society-forming logic of the Lancastrian system not only arranged children from top to bottom according to their skill in handling the drills; it made the meritocratic ranking manifest in constant examination. Numbers indicating the students' places in the hierarchy of merit were hung each day around their necks, and each lesson involved an effort to rise in the scale by beating out the person ahead. Lancaster's principle book on pedagogical method begins with the sentence, "To promote *emulation*, and facilitate learning, the school is arranged into classes" (emphasis mine).[39] According to this treatise, prizes are to be given regularly to the best students, the best groups of students and the best monitors, and monetary prizes are to be used to honor learning. For example, to reward penmanship, a student ranked number one three times is to receive a halfpenny prize. And finally, to reward excellence over the long haul, schools included an "order of merit," an

aristocracy made up of boys who had consistently distinuished themselves by their diligence in "teaching others" or "improving in [their]
own learning." Thus, what was happening to the House of Lords as
the group of industrial magnates grew and came into the peerages
through wealth also happened, in a simulated fashion, in the Lancastrian schools.[40]

The monitorial authority system was not to be challenged any
more than was the all-seeing teacher in the Chrestomathic school.
The monitor in short became the eye of the all-seeing teacher. His
commands were to be terse and instantly obeyed: "Go," "Halt,"
"Sling hats." Lancaster asserts that "the practice of giving short commands aloud, and seeing them instantly obeyed by the whole class,
will effectually train the monitor in the habit of giving them with dig-
nity and propriety."[41] A student violating the system faced punishment that might include having cards hung about his neck indicating
how he had offended. Sometimes four- to six-pound wooden logs or
pillories were tied around the necks of offending boys, and at times
shackles and other exotic devices were used. Occasionally offenders
were put in a sack, or in a basket, and suspended from the roof of the
school in the sight of the other pupils, who, according to Lancaster's
assertion, frequently smile at the "birds in the cage."[42] Sometimes offenders would be yoked together by a piece of wood and required to
parade around the school, walking carefully to avoid hurting one another's necks or falling down. Sometimes "kings" were crowned with
tin or paper fools' crowns and preceded by heralds who called out
their faults; and sometimes boys were confined after school with
shackles. The system hardly required beatings.

Monitorialism found support initially in private pilot form among
a national group of prominent citizens and became the basis of
their arguments for publicly supported compulsory education for the
poor. Monitorialism lay behind Brougham's effort to achieve a leg-
islatively sponsored compulsory education in the 1820s and 1830s and
Roebuck's similar work in the period.[43] The monitorial system came
to be widespread indeed if we are to believe parliamentary testimony.
In 1820, Henry Brougham, speaking in Parliament, estimated that the

privately supported monitorial schools of the time included 200,000 students in 1,520 schools out of a total of around 650,000 in all day schools. If "children of the rich" who were in school (Brougham estimated the rich at half of the total school population) came to 300,000, or about half of the school population, then the remainder of the school population could not have been more than 350,000. Thus, nearly two thirds of the English working-class children who went to school attended monitorial schools.[44] There, if Lancaster is to be believed, they were taught to submit to the contest in the system without questioning its central authority, exactly as, when they became adults without labor protections, they were taught to submit to the dominant economic structures of the early nineteenth century.[45] The school population apparently went up rapidly. In 1835, Brougham estimated that a little over half the population of children, about 1,300,000 children of all classes, were receiving some sort of day school education, an increase of 650,000 over 1820, but he also notes that the preparation of students in endowed schools serving poor people, especially monitorial schools, has fallen off and that more poor parents are paying for their children's education, perhaps because of the growing dissatisfaction with schools made up exclusively of drill.[46] Still, the monitorial method remained long after the reaction against it set in, and it remained both in Britain and he United States until well into the twentieth century. Though David Allsobrook correctly argues that the Utilitarians had little direct influence on middle-class education, that observation skirts the locus of their real effort in the period.[47] The first target of their early work was to demonstrate that private thrusts in the direction of universal education could help the "destitute" or "the working classes."[48] In the 1810s–20s they did not seek much serious general influence on middle-class education, especially at the higher levels, but rather supported a few experimental middle-class schools such as Hazelwood at the secondary levels and reserved their efforts in more advanced education until the 1840s and later (see chapter 7).

Monitorial schools were the beginning of a system for delivering education to the masses, and the first "teacher training" in England was actually the training in Lancastrian schools of child monitors as masters of drill and competition. While educational histories commend Lancaster's innovative methods — teaching children to write by printing in sand, using alphabet and word reading cards, teaching spelling by writing, and drilling in arithmetic tables with slates — these cheap innovations derived importance from their enabling Whig/liberal educators to demonstrate the feasibility of universal compulsory education and its effectiveness in promoting the now dominant economic system. Lancaster's devices and drill in using them were central to formalized adult teacher training when it came: David Stow, the founder of the first British teacher training college in 1827, under the auspices of the Glasgow Educational Society, was powerfully influenced by Lancaster and Bell — as his book, *The Training System*, illustrates — though he softened the system somewhat.[49]

The Chrestomathic plan was never realized in the lower schools, but it did in part form the basis of the organization of University College, London (1828), and through *Chrestomathia*, University College, and schools like Hazelwood, it probably influenced the general choice of subjects in Victorian Britain. Foucault speaks of the discipline mechanism that is a "functional mechanism that must improve the exercise of power by making it lighter, more rapid, more effective, a design of subtle coercion for a society to come," a regimen that sees all, controls time, creates rote exercises and drills, and normative public displays of conformity.[50] All of these parts of the discipline mechanism are evident in the development of Utilitarian-style education, both the fictions and the embodied experiments. What Foucault does not examine is how this mechanism spread. For civilian spaces, its spread, I think, comes largely through the mechanism of the new schools. Foucault also does not examine why the mechanism spread — what the society-to-come is that so draws both school creators and the consumers of schooling. That society-to-come is the Atlantis proposed by Bacon combined with the market economy proposed by Smith, now made seemingly necessary by the enclosures, the appearance of unorganized and anomic, sometimes revolutionary urban masses. The schoolyard is the new sea surrounding the utopian island of the school. Monitorial schooling was not just a technology that made the new order; it had a vision, however perverse.

Though the tradition described eventually triumphed in a modified form in the 1870s, it did not go wholly unchallenged any more than Baconianism went unchallenged in Tory times. The chief socialist educator of the time, Robert Owen, decrying the education sponsored by his capitalistic opponents, envisaged a system that appropriated, for secular purposes, the assumptions of the first of the utopians discussed in this book, Sir Thomas More.[51] As the inventor of the infant school movement and of the cooperative movement that controls large sectors of the economy in Scandinavia, parts of the United Kingdom, and the American Midwest and Great Plains, Owen pioneered the movement that Engels and Marx were both to use and to deride as *utopian* in the pejorative sense.[52] Seeking to create a cooperative, community-based attitude in his schools, Owen not only forbade corporal punishment but also demanded an emphasis on the affective and artistic side of learning, encouraging cooperative planning among the children who were to become part of his villages of unity. In an undated letter contained in the Combe archive, he speaks of how he came to see that his workers at his New Lanark mill had been degraded by their industrial circumstances and could only be redeemed, starting with the children, by a change of their circumstances, so that their society was based on mutual affection.

Owen's disciples formed schools modeled after the New Lanark one all over Britain, including one having six hundred students in Edinburgh (the "capitalistic" alternative infant schools, based on Lancaster's work or Samuel Wilderspan's, were much more widespread). Owen was well aware of the differences among the utopias that he and the Utilitarians sought through education, the one at least superficially communitarian and collectively based, the other superficially individualistic and meritocratic in principle. Indeed, he remarked in one of his essays that though Lancaster and Bell might have found the best manner of teaching, the matter of their education was such that it might render children "irrational for life."[53] For his part, he recommended that children be educated "as though they were literally all of one family," and he argued that their characters should be formed "by excluding all notions of reward, punishment, and imitation."[54] To him, a child who is properly educated learns what he is "in relation to past ages, to the period in which he lives, to the circumstances in which he is placed, to the individuals around him, and to future events"—in short, that he belongs to a corporate society with groups of communities and a history.[55] In Owen's view, the education proposed and supported by his friends and fellow intellectuals Bentham and Mill did not create a common sense of humanity or serve the social order he hoped to create. The battle was joined in the 1840s and 1850s.

One word more: though John Stuart Mill is not properly part of this history since he contributed little to the utopian educational thrust of the Utilitarians, his autobiography (1873) does give one some picture of what Utilitarian education might have been like at the personal level for the classes of people assumed to be capable ruling and therefore of critical reflection. James Mill's encouragement of his son assumed that he would work at reading the Greek philosophers and historians and that he would study logic and Benthamite political economy. His insistence that John Stuart Mill act the role of teacher to his brothers and sisters, perhaps in imitation of the monitors, tells us how deeply the philosophy of Bentham and Lancaster had penetrated even into his household practice. The crucial difference between this education and that proposed in *Chrestomathia* or the monitorial schools is that it is sustained by individual attention from James Mill, his twisted paternal kindness, and his penchant for endless critical debate. At the same time, when ultimately John Stuart Mill suffered a bout of severe depression, it is not to his father's sort of education that he turns, since he sees it as emptying his inner person, denying all capacity for affection, and destroying fellow as well as natural feeling. He turns rather to Wordsworth and Carlyle and the poets. His implicit critique of what his father did to him is, of course, at one with that given Gradgrind by his daughter in Dickens's *Hard Times*.[56]

CHAPTER SEVEN

The Second Generation Utilitarians

THE 1840S–60S REFORMERS AND
UTILITARIAN STRATEGY

T HE INITIAL "practical utopian" work for a universal education that would train people in science, industry, and competition came from the Mill, Bentham, and Lancaster group of the 1810s–20s, but they did not complete the work. They established infant-level monitorial schools for very young children throughout Britain and parts of the United States, but after the 1820s their movement required experimental schools that would move children toward creating "New Atlantis" at the more advanced educational levels.[1] Keeping the vision alive after the negative 1846 parliamentary report on the monitorial schools also required a new praxis since the critics of the monitorial schools argued in the report that these schools taught too narrow a range of subjects, encouraged only rote, and taught badly what they endeavored to teach.[2] The 1830s–60s battle for a long-term institutionalization of utopia required day-to-day work on theoretical positions, "model" schools, and teacher training institutions. It demanded that a coalition of educators, policy makers, and literary leaders (e.g., George Eliot) shape public opinion so as to demand government initiatives toward universal compulsory education. In this second thrust, phrenology plays the role in forming the psychology of the schools that Associationism played in the first, and the direct teaching of laissez-faire theory supplemented some of the endless combat of the monitorial mode. Phrenology provided a solution to problems that Associationism created by emphasizing an almost infinitely malleable mind that could be shaped by education. Anticipating the measurement of intelligence, it reassured the world that where education failed, the fault lay with natural deficiencies in the child and problems with his or her inheritance. It therefore provided the rationale for a compensatory education directed toward those whose phrenological bumps meant that they would not learn certain things or had to learn them in different ways. By making eduation appear to be a science based in physiology, as later forms of Associationism had also done, and a science based in pseudo–physical anthropology, phrenology provided a rationale for racism in education both in England and in the United States. It also enabled the reformers who followed in the steps of Mill and Bentham to assume that they were doing something based in science, something that the children of the workers needed, whether they wanted it or not. Clearly the education that emerged after the 1870 Elementary Education Act was designed *for* the working classes and not *by* them. It was created in the "progressive" Utilitarian circles populated by "forward-looking" businessmen who were dedicated to the ideals of Adam Smith and who thought they knew what workers needed.

The model educational practices developed in the second generation Utilitarian schools served the cause of enacting legislation requiring workers' children to go to school. The schools showed Whig/liberal industrial leaders that education could serve capitalism. They demonstrated to the government that the populace would tolerate a school requirement.

Phrenology was crucial to the new utopian thrusts. It developed in Germany in the late eighteenth century, and many people thought its claim to a comprehensive knowledge of each individual and its compensatory educational strategies entitled it, like Associationism, to the school center. The eleventh edition of the *Encyclopedia Britannica* observes: "The sarcastic suggestion which originated with Christopher North of moulding children's heads so as to suppress the evil and foster the good was actually repeated in good faith by a writer on phrenology, but experience of the effects of malformation leads one to be sceptical as to the feasibility of this mode of producing a social Utopia."[3] By 1911, the *Encyclopedia* could joke since Utopian phrenology had been largely discredited. But in the early and middle nineteenth century, the "science" heralded an education that would be the mold for children's heads and would make a benevolent capitalism outrival utopian socialism's promise for the masses. For the prophets of the new order, progress in this world would replace a dubious afterworld, and model schools led by teachers would become the beachheads in the war on nature and poverty. The history of educational reform in this period both confirms and belies Mannheim's assumptions: liberal capitalistic and socialistic views did vie for the control of the schools, but the battle did not lead from capitalist schools to socialist schools, as Mannheim's Marxist theory of history and the sociology of knowledge suggests. The two forms of schooling dueled until socialist schooling was killed by the sheer political clout of the Whig/liberal establishment.

Political histories of the reform creating universal state-supported education in Britain represent it as occurring in about eight stages:

1. A Utilitarian, Henry Brougham, pushes the 1818 Parliamentary Select Committee report concerning "the education of the lower orders of society" arguing for state involvement in the education of elementary school children and brings forward the 1820 Parish Schools Bill, only to see it fail.[4]

2. J. A. Roebuck (also a Utilitarian) produces the failed 1833 plan for a compulsory education for all children in Great Britain and Ireland from six to twelve years of age, providing for infant, industrial, and normal schools.

3. The 1833 first Reform Parliament allocates £20,000 to be apportioned equally between the National Society, which supported the Church of England–related monitorial schools, and Brougham's British and Foreign School Society promoting Lancastrian-style monitorial schools.

4. The 1833 Factory Act's anti–child labor legislation provides for the education of laboring children for a few hours per day (revisited unsuccessfully in 1843).

5. The Privy Council's Education Committee develops in 1839, under James Kay-Shuttleworth, an administrative agency to dis-

tribute the national elementary school grant (now £30,000) and to provide for the role of school inspector.

6. Parliament in 1858 establishes the Duke of Newcastle's commission to study what the national educational policy should be.[5]

7. The Education Department in 1866 extends schooling opportunities to some additional children and relates elementary school state grants to attendance and test scores.

8. The 1870 Elementary Education Act enables all parishes and boroughs to create school boards and levy a school tax, empowering any school board that wishes to make attendance compulsory for children between the ages of five and thirteen (1876 saw attendance made compulsory in all districts).[6]

So the story goes. But this is only the history of public acts. Behind this legislative and governmental history lie the Utilitarian prophets' visions, a deep historical mobilization of networks of support for utopian schooling ideals and utopian schools, and a Utilitarian exploitation of the fear of socialism and continental revolution.

Many utopianists led in the creation of a new climate of opinion, but the two activists who created the central mobilization binding the new schools to science and industry, George Combe and William Ellis, are the focus of this chapter. Combe was the leading proponent of phrenological theory after the 1832 death of J. C. Spurzheim, one of phrenology's German founders. Ellis was the owner of the Marine Indemnity Company, an 1820s Utilitarian thinker and economic theorist, and a major patron in the 1840s–60s of schools for workers and workers' children. Though the older Utilitarians had fiercely criticized phrenology, Ellis was happy to make Combe, its leading proponent, his ally. Other allies of the movement were American educator Horace Mann, Scottish physician James Simpson, experimental teacher W. M. Williams, school inspector W. B. Hodgson, and, for a time, George Eliot. Several parliamentarians also assisted. The Birkbeck schools that this group created were the heralds of the new post-1870 state-sponsored compulsory schools.

The Second Generation Utilitarians

The effectiveness of the Combe-Ellis group in turning vision into practice and legislation came from three forces. The first of these was their 1820s–40s development of "liberal" theoretical positions and utopian visions that fused Utilitarian and phrenological views and answered the utopian socialists. The second force was their 1840s–50s creation of model schools providing patterns of secular education and "new world" accomplishment in working-class children (one can include the 1830s if one includes Horace Mann's Massachusetts work under Combe's influence). And third, they exerted an influence over the 1850s–60s climate of opinion surrounding the legislative studies required for the development of the national educational policy passed in the 1870s.[7] The central activity took place in the 1840s and early 1850s, but before we look at that activity, it may be useful to look at what prompted it and at what utopian socialism and Chartism were saying to the industrial masses.

A UTOPIAN VISION TO ANSWER SOCIALISM

The revolutionary events on the Continent in 1830 and 1848, the rise of British utopian socialism, and the revolt of the British Chartists made clear that all was not well in the cities of an industrializing Europe.[8] For the capitalist-oriented school reformers, education was to be the palliative limiting worker misery, and the road to a better society.[9] It was the answer to Owenite socialism and the appeal of that movement to collaboration as opposed to competition.[10] And it answered the labor unrest of Chartism and the specter of continental socialism.[11] Education was to right the temporary problems of the industrial revolution while providing the populace with industrial capitalism's rationale.

Utopian socialism, like one version of More's *Utopia*, predicates itself on circumstances creating people. For example, from Owen's utopian socialist perspective, the circumstances of private property without shared ownership and shared community institutions create society's problems. Owenism, therefore, emphasizes an education of children and adults to learn the values and actions necessary to communitarian or cooperative living and enterprise (as other communitarian groups such as the Hutterites or the kibbutzim have done in their educational institutions). By 1813, Owen had published part of his *New View of Society*, and by 1816 he had published it all. Following Helvetius and William Godwin, the radical political thinker, Owen proposed that people do not so much create their environment as their environments ("circumstances") create them. The only possibility for creating a different character in people is to educate them differently from infancy. Like the phrenologists, Owen believed in an evolving world, governed by a power that "so formed man, that he must progressively pass from a state of ignorance to intelligence."[12] The progressive movement of things will come as humankind discovers that "individual happiness" can be increased only as people "increase and extend the happiness of all around."[13] Instead of the Utilitarian and individualistic assertion of the "greatest good for the greatest number," Owen calls for the communal increase of happiness for all. A rationally instructed child will see a destructive child as produced by circumstances and as needing help rather than warranting anger, and the education and training of children properly done will promote every individual's happiness without regard to religion, political party, nation, or "climate" (probably meaning race).[14]

In his New Lanark factory, the base for his first socialist-style experiments, Owen abolished childhood labor (for children under the age of ten) and provided his workers with community housing. In the "New Institution," a kind of school and playground that was the first infant school, he provided the workers' children between the ages of five and ten with school instruction. The New Institution was designed to separate children from previous societies' errors and from the faults of untrained parents. It allowed children to participate in collaborative activities (including play) where they were instructed never "to injure . . . playfellows" and always "to contribute all in [their] power to make them happy." The goal was to create group meaning even in such educational activities as reading.[15]

Owen was aware that his educational proposals lay at the antipodes from those of Lancaster and the Utilitarians with their mandating of incessant competition and drill. Though he commends them for initiating the education of industrial workers' children, he observes that children taught using their schemes may "yet acquire the worst habits, and have their minds rendered irrational for life." Their system trains the child not in thinking but in "retain[ing] incongruities without connection," in endeavoring to become "what is termed the first scholar in the class." Such a system "destroy[s] the mental powers of the children." [16] Even the Malthusian nightmare, foreshadowed by Smith and articulated by Malthus in 1798–1803, makes no sense to Owen because it does not include a calculation as to how much more production might be possible in a rationally educated, socially responsible society providing full employment to its members. [17]

In 1817, for a meeting of the establishment leaders in Britain, Owen wrote a revision of his earlier work, now entitled *New View of Society . . . Report to the Committee for the Relief of the Manufacturing and Labouring Poor*, in which he again proposes a social organization quite like that found in More's *Utopia*. [18] He argues that the poor should be organized into groups of about twelve hundred people, each group settled on a thousand acres of land or more, supervised by skilled craftsmen and teachers, and dedicated to communitarianism in their industrial production, education of children, leisure time activities, meals, and care of their needy. Their work is to be both agricultural and manufacturing, and if a similar group is formed voluntarily by people with means, it is to be self-governing. Owen's 1820 "Report to the County of Lanark" elaborates this principle and specifically takes on the laissez-faire economists' arguments that "individual interest" is the "cornerstone to the social system," treating such positions as the most "anti-social, impolitic, and irrational, that can be devised." [19] In Owen's early work, one sees the roots of three later movements: the cooperative movement that has had such a powerful influence in the Scandinavian countries and in much of rural America, the communitarian movement that issues ultimately in the communes of the 1960s, and the formal socialist movement revised by Marx and Engels.

In the early 1830s, Owen had a peak period of influence with a sector of the labor movement interested in cooperative production. In

1834 the Grand National Consolidated Trades Union espoused his cause. But as the 1840s wore on, his influence waned or was absorbed in broader movements, partly because he himself, like the Utilitarian authors described later in this chapter, remained a patronizing patrician throughout his career, hoping to create utopia from above.[20]

The second revolutionary movement, Chartism, opposed Owenite socialism on the question of the means to ameliorate the conditions of industrial workers. As the main wing of the left/liberal workers' movement, it aimed to alter the lives of industrial workers through the reform of basic political institutions rather than through changing conventional property concepts.[21] As Marx was to observe, the abrupt reforms that Chartism's "People's Charter" proposed—annual parliaments, equal electoral districts, universal male suffrage, the abolition of property requirements, and a secret ballot—became the basis for the entry of a whole new class into the political realm. Opposing Owen's elitism, it turned to popular demonstrations and violence and thus anticipated other, more forceful forms of the labor movement. Though its tools were radical, ultimately Chartism was based on less radical property assumptions than was the Owenite movement. Hence, in its formation of model schools, the capitalism-oriented Combe-Ellis group was able to forge a coalition with moderate Chartists to discredit the violent wing of the movement (see later discussion).

The central educational opponents of the Owenites and Chartists were the heroes of this chapter: Combe and Ellis. A brewer and businessman, and Owen's educational antagonist by dint of personal experience, Combe bitterly opposed labor unions and increasingly advocated market economic views as the socialist alternative gained strength.[22] In 1820 he visited New Lanark and Owen, but he remained an outsider to Owenite ideals. In contrast, his younger brother, Abram, joined up with Owen's cause in the 1820s and set up an Owenite colony at Orbiston near Edinburgh—the first serious Owenite colony, since Owen's own New Lanark was more a manufacturing plant with amenities than a full-blown socialist experiment.[23] Eventually Abram bankrupted himself at Orbiston and died, leaving his children in George's care in 1827, which contributed to the latter's permanent resentment of his brother's movement. At the beginning of the socialist experiment, George, already a persuaded phrenologist, was modestly sympathetic to socialism's utopian aims but not to its means. In writing about his brother's colony in 1827, he argues that it might be a good thing if it had resources, overcame its physical obstacles, and taught the laws of nature (presumably phrenology). He is sympathetic enough to allow that he would be willing to fill his brother's leadership role if he did not have to pursue his professional life.[24] Even in 1827, he writes about Owen to a Mrs. Kemmis to say that Owen's first object ought to be to surround the individuals whom he wishes to improve with external circumstances that call forth their higher sentiments. But to do this properly, he and his followers would have to know what human nature *is* and would need to start with phrenology to know the true sources of happiness (Owen was also an amateur phrenologist). They would have to use more than the single principle Combe attributes to Owen, namely that what is good for the social body is good for the individual. In Combe's view, the indiscriminate application of this principle means that Owen ignores all individual differences.[25]

As Owenite influence waxed with the 1830s and then waned with the development of Owen's eccentricities such as free love and spirit tapping, the Combe of the 1840s came to have a stronger resentment of socialism, exhibited a more feverish support of capitalistic principles, and expressed a greater contempt for worker revolts. For example, in 1848 he writes to William Ellis that all of the *isms* that the revolutions of 1848 have proposed, including socialism and communism, will fail because running an enterprise requires the kind of cultivated intellect *that workers do not have*. Even companies run for the joint benefit of worker and owner can hardly succeed if they become the general rule, for the leaders of such companies, where they are successful—labor and management alike—are exceptional people. The class assumption must be frozen in place. Combe never suggests that working-class children could be educated toward management or cooperation or social sharing. For him, the leaders of labor "constitute the great obstruction to a thorough-going scheme of national secular education."[26]

Having set aside revolt as a solution to the malaise of the working classes, Combe replaces it with education. It is not accidental that in 1848, the year of the industrial class revolution against King Louis Philippe in Paris, he decided to become the principal mover in the establishment of the Edinburgh Secular School (or Mr. Williams' Secular School), one of a string of schools also supported by his compatriot, William Ellis. His purpose from the outset was to develop a working-class school with a curriculum teaching the physical sciences, phrenology, physiology, and Smithian economic theory. By the late 1840s, Combe's commitment to the elimination of cooperativist ideology was complete. In 1850, Ellis writes to Combe, with a full sense of class solidarity, that the working classes are uninformed or misinformed: the result of their "neglected or misdirected education" is "misconduct, communism, destitution, and discontent."[27]

In Combe's perspective, both capitalism and socialism propose to be communitarian routes to a better world, but the difference is that capitalism understands ignorance to be the root of the problem, not selfishness or private property (it would appear that the Church, with its emphasis on pride as the root of evil, should have favored some sort of Owenism, as Christian Socialists were to do later). Capitalism works out its communitarianism through the joint stock company, instead of planned community schemes for holding common property. On May 8, 1850, Combe writes to remonstrate with George Henry Lewes about Lewes's piece in the *Westminster Review*:

> In page 131, column 3d, you advocate Socialism and Communism, and say that Socialism is extending its influence in this country "into different sections of the more educated classes." I wish much that you would define what you mean by socialism and communism? Do you mean community of wives & goods? Or do you mean joint stock companies? I hear people putting these different interpretations on these words. . . . I acknowledge the force of what

you say on page 130, last column, in favour of the people; but I have had some knowledge of them in CIVIL affairs, & my observations lead me to the conclusion that IN CONSEQUENCE OF THEIR IGNORANCE, the men among them who promise most largely too often lead them in their own benefit societies & stores; & lead them to ruin. I saw 300 of them placed under my Brother Abram in Orbiston in Lanarkshire on the principles of communism & socialism; & through ignorance, & also through self-seeking, they consumed £20,000 & produced nothing.[28]

For Combe, ignorance of the "truth" of laissez-faire economic theory and phrenology causes revolutionary activity. On December 30, 1854, he wrote a letter to Lord John Russell, then lord president of the privy council dealing with education and a parliamentary leader in the consideration of educational reform, about the political success of the Swiss/French socialists in the canton of Zurich, which already provided compulsory education (he later published the letter). He argues that the movement to socialism by the canton masses derives from a defect in their curriculum, their being "very little instructed in regard to the natural foundations of morals and social institutions" — that is, in Smith, Malthus, and laissez-faire theory.[29] Their ignorance is fostered by an ignorant left. While in Zurich this left destroys proper compulsory education, the superstitious right does so in Prussia. There, the forces of repression prevent the emergence of a new world through using, for their purposes, the theological interests that control the Prussian schools. Combe's route to a good society through education on the Continent ends with blockades put up by ignorant peasant and urban working classes that do not understand capitalistic theory (and therefore adopt revolutionary utopianism) *and* by conservative churches that sustain conventional despotism. In Combe's view, England can take another road.

Ellis takes similar views. In a letter to Combe concerning the Zurich affair, he argues that the "mischief felt in Zurich" does not originate in the scriptural or unscriptural character of its universal and compulsory education but in the failure of the Zurich schools to "embrace instruction in the elementary principles of Economic science."

(At the same time, he argues against Combe's expressing his position to Lord Russell that England is ruled by the upper and middle classes using the military to keep the people in line.)[30] Ellis had always opposed radical labor, probably because he participated in the 1820s Utilitarian group's discussions of education and undoubtedly knew the older Utilitarians' economic and educational ideas discussed in chapter 6.[31] His 1820s Utilitarian group, according to both Mill's and his own memoirs, engaged the London area Owenites in a series of debates that really began the British dialogue between capitalistic and socialistic assumptions. At about the same time as he debated the Owenites, he began his fulminations against other branches of the labor movement, in 1824 attacking the Luddites in the *Westminster Review* while at the same time ostensibly joining in labor's cause by becoming a member of the London Mechanics Institute and contributing money to the British and Foreign School Society. In the 1820s, he already advocated for free education and a Malthus-derived population control, and in 1829 he published his profoundly Utilitarian and capitalistic *Conversation upon Knowledge, Happiness, Education etc.*, a work that Brougham caused to be read all over the country.[32]

As concerns education, the 1830s were a hiatus for Ellis. From the mid-1820s to the mid-1840s, he reared his family and grew wealthy in London's insurance industry, attempting little practical work outside his Marine Indemnity Company (he told Combe that he felt a certain uneasiness and self-reproach in leaving the school issue alone for so many years).[33]

Ellis's awakening to action as an educational leader came in the mid-1840s. A master of the Lancastrian British and Foreign School Society, at its school in Camberwell, invited him to prepare a course in elementary market economics for older boys. When Ellis had prepared and printed his lessons, the leader of the Borough Road Lancastrian movement, the center of the national movement, ignored them. Ellis was sufficiently vain to feel resentment at the snub, and once he turned to the idea of educational reform as a bulwark against socialism and labor unrest, he was not about to be turned aside. Between 1846 and 1848, he presented his market economics program to about a dozen headmasters with a view to getting them to use it in their schools, and having only marginal success, decided to create his own schools, supporting his first one in February 1848—the very month of the revolution against Louis Philippe and of worker unrest throughout continental Europe. He makes clear that the events of 1848 propelled him into action on a broader stage: "I should mention that shortly after the outbreak at Paris in February 1848, an attempt which I then made to draw the attention of influential public men to the importance of teaching the Elementary principles of Economical science in all primary schools, brought me into communication with the Rt. Hon. W. E. Gladstone through whom I expressed a willingness to give, if invited, a course of lessons in that branch of knowledge to the young masters in the Battersea Training College."[34] Battersea was the normal school created and administered by James Kay-Shuttleworth, later to be regarded as the architect of the national school policy supported by Parliament in 1870.[35] However, the persons at Battersea to whom Gladstone passed Ellis's offer apparently did not subscribe to his ideas at this point either.

Having failed with a complacent establishment, Ellis began a sophisticated movement to coopt the moderate Chartists, arguing for educational reform as opposed to street violence as the route to a better world, proposing to them model schools as the immediate political tools in the battle against radical labor movements. Not accidentally, the first model school that he supported had as its teacher William Lovett, the leader of the moderate Chartists.[36] From 1837 on, William Lovett had worked with the London Working Men's Association on an educational position that identified ignorance (deriving from the unequal distribution of educational opportunities) as the basis of poverty, inequality, and injustice. Under the auspices of the Moral Force Chartists (as opposed to the Fergus O'Connor group, who believed violence to be necessary to reform), the 1840s Lovett occupied himself with the practical aligning of working-class Chartists with such middle-class reformers as Ellis.

Given Lovett's moderate position on violence, it is no surprise that in 1848 he attracted the attention of an Ellis obsessed with revolt in

Europe: "Among the Chartists, there is a section that calls itself the 'Moral Force' Chartists. . . . Wm. Lovett is one of their chiefs & he is a very high-minded, honorable man—not entirely free from the prejudices of his class, but open to conviction and improvement & at last nearly persuaded of the soundness of the conclusions of economical science. . . . At my persuasion and with my assistance they have opened a school there for 'Secular Education.' Many very intelligent people are assisting them—among others Mr. Hickson of the Westminster Review. And I have undertaken to go up by and bye & give the upper Class lessons once a week in the Laws of Social Life."[37]

In fact, Ellis provided the resources so that Lovett could open and head the first precedent for the Birkbeck Schools at the London Mechanics Institute, and Lovett allowed Ellis to make a first foray into the reform of education.[38] In the late 1840s and early 1850s an "enlightened" Ellis became one of Combe's important correspondents, seeking to teach children economics and "the conditions of well-being" so as to avoid the Malthusian curses of overpopulation, filth, and improvidence. Indeed, part of Ellis's objection to the labor organizers of the 1840s was based in the same Malthus-like sentiments that Adam Smith espoused (see chapter 5) and that Dickens's Gradgrind favors. For example, in April of 1848, Ellis wrote to Combe:

> These organizers of Labour seem always to ignore the great law of Population. Let them & their followers persevere in such a course— increase productive power as they may, all that they can do will be to ADD TO THE NUMBERS of the miserable. If on the other hand they will cease to ignore this law, the tendencies of society as regards the direction of its productive powers are sufficiently good to create little or no uneasiness on that score. Why do not the great mass of labourers participate in profit now? Because they have no Capital. Why have they no Capital? Because their parents were improvident, they themselves are improvident—& their children will be so if we do not strive to prevent it.[39]

Lovett's and the moderate Chartist reformers' path to the better society was not always easy. Though Birkbeck schoolchildren may have been relatively easy for Ellis and Combe to set on the Utilitarian/phrenological road to utopia, the adult workers who took night classes at their schools appear to have been less easy to manipulate. For example, W. M. Williams, one of the teachers sponsored by Combe and Ellis, wrote to Combe about adult worker-pupils who made it clear that they would not attend his classes in Social Economy (i.e., classical capitalistic theory) since such theory was "only an invention to justify the repression of the working man." Williams says these the worker-students "are the leading Chartists and socialists and some of the most energetic and influential men among the working classes of Edinburgh, warm friends of the school [i.e., of Combe's Birkbeck-style school], mostly phrenologists." These workers "believe that they have already gone far ahead of the antiquated doctrines of political economy and patronizingly deplore that such a friend of progress as George Combe should be still sticking fast in the middle of them," and they go on to accuse Williams of teaching Smithian doctrines because his patrons and paymasters, Combe and Ellis, require it.[40]

In consequence of this confrontation, Williams turns the class into a debating society, as he describes in the same letter to Combe: "On the first night when I opened the discussion in favour of competition not one could be found to say a word on the same side, the whole of the speakers were against one, and the second night only one spoke on the side of competition." Finally, a strategy of intimidation works: "I did not hesitate to ridicule their ignorance of political economy when I found their great guns obviously blundering, as they did constantly, even in the application of the most frequently used terms such as capital, value, etc." His "principal object at present is to get them into dilemmas and in every way possible demonstrate to them how very ignorant they are of this same Political Economy they denounce so confidently." Even so, one of the fathers of children in the school stops at the teacher's place to say that Political Economy is taught in the school as "a sort of sop to the rich & middle classes to get their interest in favour of the school; and as a set off to its heterodoxy in other respects." He adds that his family lets its children attend the "Social

Economy on account of the other subjects, but they take care to teach them a very different philosophy when they get home."

Contrary to the Chartist/socialist workers, the second generation Utilitarian/phrenologists see themselves (and are sometimes seen) as visionaries moving the world toward the true laissez-faire utopia. For example, William Ellis remarks in 1856 that Lord Ashburton may classify Ellis and Combe, the two leading exponents of a universal education in the sciences and the social sciences, with "Robert Owen & look upon us as visionaries and propagandists, & shrink from associating with us lest he might promote our ulterior views." William Pyper writes, in the *Edinburgh Advertiser*, about "St. Simon Robert Owen, Benbow Carlisle" and other recognizable utopians and then adds phrenologists of Combe's ilk as "another class of theoretical visionaries."[41] Combe seems to think of himself as a utopian when he speaks of his brother's work with an Owenite colony and then remarks that, to realize its goals, it lacks sufficient resources and a proper knowledge of human nature—that is, phrenology. And one of Ellis's last writings, *Thoughts on the Future of the Human Race*, attacks those who regard the prospect of massive improvement in a whole society or people as "Utopian" in the pejorative sense.[42] Utopia as capitalists might dream it was precisely what he and Ellis sought.

In contrast to Chartism or Owenite socialism, the Combe-Ellis version of laissez-faire educational theory assumes that people behave badly under old (i.e., eighteenth- and early nineteenth-century) market capitalism not because of a bad environment or nurture, nor because they do not read or do arithmetic, but because they are born with defective heads and cannot use phrenology to fix them.[43] They do not understand science, technology, or laissez-faire theory. They have not been taught the arts of individual competition and of self-improvement communicated by the study of economics, phrenology, hygiene, proper ventilation, or temperance. They have not been taught to improve. For though the human nature assumed by the second generation Utilitarian phrenologists is not as malleable as Owen's, they do assume that it has improved in the march of the progress of the superior Anglo-Saxon peoples across the centuries, and that it can improve further.[44] In their long-term march toward a "Paradise in erthe here," the central figures in the Combe-Ellis movement, like the Owenites, express little respect for afterlife-oriented revealed Christianity. However, this does not mean they call for an immediate restructuring of the conditions of this life as the Owenites do; they believe that market capitalism is natural and just, and that, as Ellis's economic theory baldly asserts, in the short term we receive everything that is certain in this life and generally get what we deserve. The pre-Darwinian evolutionary assumptions of Ellis and Combe and their followers (Ellis lived to see and admire Darwin's *Descent of Man*) told them that what they could hope for was the gradual conquest of nature through science, a "continued" progress in the improvement of human material conditions, and a long-term moral evolution inspired by education and phrenology.[45] The better future state that humankind can hope for it will slowly make for itself as it struggles to improve all of the mental faculties to their full godlike capacities through phrenology, pre-Darwinian evolution, and the laissez-faire system.

George Combe's *Lectures on Popular Education* (1833), published at the time that the first parliamentary grants for schools were being considered, define the group's phrenological and evolutionary assumptions.[46] Lectures I and II set forth an evolutionary picture of the emergence of the lower and higher orders of creatures, culminating in a humankind differentiated by cranial shape and requiring a phrenologically based education. Whereas nonhuman creatures achieve perfection by nature (bees build perfect hives and so forth), humankind achieves its fully evolved status only through education: "Comparing the civilized Christian inhabitants of modern Europe, with the ignorant, ferocious, filthy, and helpless savages of New South Wales, we perceive a vast advance: but I do not believe that the limits of attainable perfection have yet been reached even by the best of Europe's sons. All, therefore, that I venture to hope for is, that man, by the proper employment of the means presented to him, may arrive at last at a condition of enjoyment of his mortal existence, as great, in relation to his rational nature, as that of the lower animal is in relation to their natures."[47]

Though Combe does not clarify how the Australian aborigines can be both helpless and ferocious (racism is a staple of much phrenological rhetoric), he goes on to describe how we may achieve the perfection awaiting us: we must get rid of Latin and Greek in the elementary schools, add practical studies related to industrial life, adopt universal compulsory public education on the Prussian model, study a wide range of the sciences, relate them to manufacturing, and teach correct animal, moral, and intellectual habits.[48] (Combe and Ellis were later to have second thoughts about Prussia.)[49]

Influenced by his physician brother Andrew and the German phrenologist J. C. Spurzheim, Combe argues in the *Lectures* that the "study of the structure, functions, relations and laws of . . . [the] vital parts" of human beings are the primary future scientific study. As knowing the principles of biology and health prolong life, so knowing the laws governing the faculties of the mind will enable individualistic human beings to construct the best possible world. Psychological study illuminates God's governance of the moral world and the extent and limits of human freedom in utopia construction, and it will ultimately permit individuals to understand their mental organs and maximize happiness:[50]

> The Creator has obviously invited us to study the means by which He executes His secular providence and to accommodate our conduct to its laws. In submitting these means to our cognisance, He presents to us a practical revelation of the course of conduct which He desires us to pursue in order to work out our own enjoyment in this world. Is it not true, therefore, that in the endowment of objects and beings with specific qualities and modes of action, which we cannot alter, God maintains his supremacy; while in enabling us to discover these, and to modify our conduct in relation to them, He bestows on us all the freedom compatible with our subjection to a superior Being?[51]

The Second Generation Utilitarians

In the presence of phrenology, people will recognize their limitations and be "all that they can be"—the beginning of the notion of compensatory education and the initial seed for the notion that education can change people but only within the limits imposed by inherited endowment.[52] While the early Utilitarians assume that utopia construction can be powered by the introduction of the "correct" system of associations to a seemingly infinitely malleable human mind, Combe and his fellow phrenological educators—Hodgson, Williams, Simpson, and Horace Mann—assume inherited characteristics that are moderately malleable and bettered within limits by education, the basic assumption of most education since.

Given this assumption, the construction of the good individual and laissez-faire society requires a different process than the monitorial schools' exclusive attention to rote and emulation (though the monitorial and pupil-teacher systems are still used part of the time). The teacher must shape the whole: the students' intellectual powers, their "organs of veneration" (to respect Combe's version of natural law-and-religion), and their acquisitive organs so that they understand "the modes of producing and attaining riches" prescribed by natural law.[53] The Combe of the *Lectures* recognizes that he is, in some sense, the heir of Francis Bacon, but for his money the post–Bacon Baconians have concentrated too much on observation and too little on the pragmatic consequences of knowledge for ethical decision making.[54] Though Combe includes most of what Bentham argues for in *Chrestomathia*—the basic subjects, reading, writing, arithmetic; and the mathematical and scientific subjects, algebra, geometry, natural history, chemistry, anatomy, physiology, and natural philosophy—he as an ethicist would also give some small role to the subjects that inform decision making: philosophy of mind, literature, poetry, painting, sculpture, and natural religion, the subjects that might lead to a total transformation of human beings and a new social order.[55]

Since Combe's alternative to socialism is secular education, his utopianism during a time of revolution appears in his 1848 pamphlet,

The Second Generation Utilitarians

What Should Secular Education Embrace, pushing for deistic education based in this-worldly research and experience.[56] He does not recognize state control of education as coercion and, unlike most social change advocates from Machiavelli through Marx, invites no violence or military coercion to alter things: a soft-handed educational reform encompassing all children and eventually all adults does the job. The argument assumes that: (1) Reformation Christianity and its education believed in a miraculous divine interference in the world that neither experience nor science supports; (2) in fact, the divine presence and intervention in the world occurs through the operation of natural laws or the "Wisdom of God" as represented, for example, by William Paley; and (3) guided by the likes of Paley, anyone else who wishes can study the Wisdom revealed by astronomy, anatomy, physiology, chemistry, and economics can help produce through education the good society.

The leg of the Combe-Ellis utopian educational theory supplied by Ellis moralizes laissez-faire economic theory to make it a tool in ethical education. Since Ellis lived to a great age, he is both the last of the first generation Utilitarians and the first of the second generation ones, doing his 1820s work as a discussant with the early Utilitarians, then gaining wealth as an insurance executive in the late 1820s–early 1840s, then working thereafter as a practical school reformer who paid for the Birkbeck schools, taught in them, and wrote extensively in behalf of his view of reform. From early in his career, he believed that he could identify the conditions of "well-being," summarizing them in the conclusion to his *Lecture of Education, Government and Competition*:

> My general outline of the conditions of well-being is thus finished. . . . Summed up in a few words, it runs as follows: An abundant supply of the necessaries and comforts of life is requisite for well-being; but can only be obtained by a general prevalence of industry, skill, knowledge, economy, sobriety, honesty, and punctuality. Two large classes of means are available for the cultivation and

diffusion of these qualities: the Governmental means, which secure to every individual the full enjoyment of the fruits of his earning, and the Educational means, which provide adequate instruction and training for every human being. Neither of the classes of means, more particularly the latter, can be hoped for in perfection, except through that quality—that master quality—that keystone of the social arch—Parental forethought.[57]

Governmental intervention to provide for a national educational system and government monitoring of trade to make certain that it is "free" (i.e., untrammeled by monopoly or class restrictions) are the twin cornerstones to building a better world.[58]

For Ellis, the Malthusian impediments to utopia—overpopulation and improvidence—can be overcome through education in the laws of nature covering production and reproduction (though I have not found Ellis anywhere explicitly referring to methods of birth control). In warning of the Malthusian nightmare, Ellis is at one with Combe in offering the Malthusian theory's almost certain inferno as avoidable if we will only reach for Smith's paradisal production increases. As Combe puts it:

I . . . recollect . . . meeting with only two works which approached to the solution of any portion of the enigma which puzzled my understanding. These were "Smith's Wealth of Nations," and "Malthus on Population." The first appeared to me to demonstrate that God actually governs in the relations of commerce; that He has established certain natural laws which regulate the interests of men in the exchange of commodities and labor; and that those laws are in harmony with the dictates of our moral and intellectual faculties, and wisely related to the natural productions of the different soils and climates of the earth. [Combe then discovers that all ruling elites pursued principles directly opposite to Smith's, i.e., regulated trade.] . . . Malthus . . . appeared to me to prove that God reigned, through the medium of fixed natural laws, in another department of human affairs—namely, in that of population. . . . Malthus demonstrated . . . that the Creator has bestowed on mankind a power

of increasing their numbers much beyond the ratio of the diminution that, in favorable circumstances, will be caused by death; and,
consequently, that they must either, by ever-extending cultivation
of the soil, increase their means of subsistence in proportion to
their numbers, or expose themselves to the evil of having these re-
stricted by disease and famine, to the amount which the actual production of food will maintain.[59]

As we will observe in chapter 8, Gradgrind's children in Hard
Times are Combe's favorite reading. The passage comes as close to a
"limits-to-growth" statement as Combe and Ellis ever make, but they
turn their argument in directions opposite to those proposed by recent Club of Rome limits-to-growth theorists by proposing an endless increase in industrial production, combined in Ellis's case with a
vague hope for population control. We will all die of famine if we do
not produce more; education will make us see this, and help us produce more. At the same time as Combe and Ellis seek to demytholo-
gize conventional organized Christianity, they use appeals to natural
religion, awe, and contemplation to cast themselves as the warm-
hearted successors to the theorists of selfishness who comprise the
Mill-Bentham generation of Utilitarians. In 1846, Parliament conducted an analysis of the defects of monitorial education based on
pure emulation, and shortly thereafter, monitors were replaced by
what were called pupil teachers in many schools, to what effect it is
not clear.[60] As part of this process, Lord Ashburton wrote to Combe,
"What I am anxious to establish . . . is, that the same principle, which
dictates free trade, enlightened medical practice, & successful social
legislation should guide us also in education, in all of our acts of cooperation with nature" so that educational inquiry asks the question,
"How does nature work in the case, to produce the result I require"
and "How can I bring about the conditions in which nature will so
work?" The spirit in which this is done must be "far different from the
cold irreverent tone of Bentham." Ashburton's warm spirit is a spirit
of cooperation with the works of God while the debased one is based

on a selfish "desire to extend man's power & the contemplation of its success," but it leads essentially to the same kind of education.[61]

MODELS AND NATIONAL EDUCATIONAL POLICY

Warm-heartedness and cooperation with nature, the tools necessary to the making of utopian places, had to begin in the "model" school, in itself a Renaissance island set aside from the quotidian world of traditional community to create a new person.[62] If, for the leaders of the educational reform movement, the raw capitalism and industrialism of the early nineteenth century provided the base metal of utopian hope, the first steps in its golden transformation had to come from model schools that would illustrate what the new world could be like. As school utopias developed, the evils of the last generation—ignorance, pollution, filth, alcoholism, and noncompetitive, spendthrift behavior—were to be cured. The Ellis-Combe faction's privately funded Birkbeck schools for the industrial working and the shopkeeper classes provided models for what the new government schools would be like under a national, universal education policy—offering evidence that working-class education could serve useful purposes.

Even prior to the 1840s development of the Birkbeck schools, James Simpson, a physician friend of Combe's from Edinburgh and a phrenologist, argued in his 1836 *The Philosophy of Education with its Practical Application to a System and Plan of Popular Education as a National Object*, that five circumstances make the time ripe for a nationally supported education: (1) the advocacy of such schools by a broad section of the press; (2) the sense of national pride that would not allow Prussia, the smaller German states, France, and the United States to outstrip England; (3) the government dialogue about the issue from the time of Lord Brougham's 1818 speech on the matter, the work of the Commons committee of 1818 that followed from his speech, that of the Roebuck committee of 1833, and that of the Lord John Russell's and the Earl of Kerry's committees in 1834 and 1835; (4) the development of societies all over the nation to support new forms of education; and finally and most important (5) the appearance of schools suggesting that improved education along the new lines is possible.[63] Simpson notes:

> In the possession of Infant schools, alone, we have an advantage fully equaling all that is enjoyed by the countries alluded to as before us in other respects, but which have not yet adopted these, the only means of efficient moral training. There are, in England, schools of real knowledge [i.e., scientific knowledge], in which almost every thing is taught recommended in chapter V. of this treatise. There are Dr. Mayo's school at Cheam in Surrey, Messrs Morgan and Emmertons at Hanwell Middlesex, and the establishments of the Messrs Hill at Hazelwood, near Birmingham, and Bruce Castle at Tottenham, near London; and it is well known that these schools serve as models to others, and that this system of imparting real useful knowledge to the young is extending. In Mr. Bruce's Academy, in Newcastle-upon-Tyne, in addition to the useful branches, which need not be enumerated, the following philosophic courses are taught: chemistry, electricity, magnetism, and pneumatics, as connected with physical geography, meteorology, &c.; natural history, with reference especially to the mechanism and physiology of the human frame making Paley's Natural Theology the text book, mental philosophy, the evidence of Christianity,' &c.[64]

Simpson then goes on to list similar schools in Bath, Liverpool, Bristol, Belfast, Edinburgh, and Glasgow and even a couple on the Continent. One cannot read long in the writings of the school leaders cited by Simpson or in the 1840s writings of Combe and Ellis before recognizing that they see their "model" institutions as the forerunners of a new secular national educational system that will supersede the religious domination of education and the piecemeal system being practiced. That the Ellis-supported Birkbeck schools were supposed to be models for what national educational policy and a national future should be is most strongly indicated by the fact that when the national Elementary Education Act passed in 1870 and full compulsory education in 1876, Ellis allowed the schools he had founded to pass away, satisfied that they had had the desired influence on the formation of national educational policy.[65] Obviously many other schools that had existed before the act, such as the Renaissance grammar schools, continued as before. The Birkbeck schools were designed to model what the required tax-supported compulsory schools were to be.

Ellis called his Birkbeck schools model schools, and one cannot accuse him of indifference or tokenism in their creation.[66] Not only did he pay what it took to start them and keep them going; he was, for some years, fully engaged in their development, doing some teaching of workers' children by day and of adults by night. He paid for nineteen Birkbeck schools in whole or in part, and in the case of the Edinburgh equivalent of a Birkbeck school supported by Combe (Mr. Williams's Secular School), Combe makes clear in a letter to Henderson's Trustees appealing for assistance that he was able to plan for and set up the school because Ellis contributed one hundred pounds to it.[67] The seven schools that were in operation in the London area by October 1850 had sizable enrollments of paying and nonpaying scholars, and Ellis supplied most of what their fees did not pay. In 1850, he gave the number of paying students in the major London area Birkbeck schools as follows: the first Birkbeck had 330 boys and 45 girls, the Finsbury school 260 boys, the South Islington school 120 boys, the Paddington one 66 boys, the National Hall School 150 boys and 33 girls, Mr. Bank's school 130 boys, and Mr. Holmes's school 280 boys.[68]

In general design, the Birkbeck schools covered the ages after the infant school—seven through the midteen period, using a modified version of the monitorial system for some teaching and, for the rest, demonstrations and lectures.[69] They taught science and the usual Utilitarian subjects, but most of all they promised full indoctrination in laissez-faire theory. Combe wrote to Ellis of a meeting with parents and interested parties connected to Mr. Williams's school in Edinburgh, during which "Mr. Williams explained the monitorial system, & his method of trying school offenses by juries; & we concluded by distributing small prizes, & we appealed to the boys to name the individuals entitled to the three highest prizes—each a six pence."[70]

The circular for one school indicates that its students will be taught how "the comforts and necessaries of life are produced," how full production requires "industry, skill, economy, and security to property," and what are the "advantages of the division of labour, of the cooperation of labour and capital, and [of] the arrangements which facilitate interchange."[71]

Sustaining the vision of a new world to come and not to be produced by violence required, like Virgil's projected empire in his sixth book, epiphanic manifestations of that world to come, designed to sustain people in the hard work of creating it, to show that the promise was real and to mark development in the direction of the new city. Part of these epiphanic efforts to sell the new schools consisted in "showings forth"—public displays at the model schools of what their students had learned of the matter requisite to the production of a happier world—especially interrogations before parents, educational theorists, and influential business people.[72] One public display went as follows in the Combe-Ellis school in Edinburgh, according to a letter from Combe:

> Mr. Williams then examined the youngest children, of 7 & 8 years on the names & properties of objects, & they defined "transparent," "elastic," "opaque," "porous," "frangible," "tough," "durable," etc. with great readiness and precision with the objects before them.
>
> Mr. Williams then examined the older boys on the mechanical powers, "the lever," "screw," "pulley," "inclined plane," "wheel & pinion," etc. etc. and they showed great intelligence.
>
> He next examined them on the bones, muscles, heart, lungs & blood vessels, the stomach, liver, intestines & other digestive apparatus, the absorbent vessels & the skin, and they showed a most satisfactory knowledge of the local situation, general structure, and functions of all those parts.
>
> I then examined them on the uses of all this knowledge. We placed before them a fetal & an adult skeleton, & I asked them how the one grew to the size of the other. They described the absorption of the waste matter of the body by the absorbent vessels & its dis-

charge by the skin, bowels, lungs, & bladder; then . . . the disposition of new matter, by the blood vessels, bone to bone, muscle to muscle, nerve to nerve etc.; they next described how wholesome food in due quantity was necessary to supply the blood with those elements, & pointed out the consequences to health and growth of too little, too much or ill chosen food.[73]

The students go on to discuss the uses of fresh air, cleanliness, and exercise, and the rules of nature providing that obedience to God-given law with respect to cleanliness, air, exercise, and so forth will bring happiness.[74] The emphasis of these interrogations is always on how individual responsibility in observing the laws of cause and effect will produce a better future for the individual and for society.

The process of giving students exercises in definitions often involves what was called an "object lesson," an exercise using ordinary language to sort things into pseudoscientific categories. John Angell, the Birkbeck teacher at Manchester, speaks of his young students (four to nine years of age) being asked to name things that have properties in common with sugar: "The little children amused the audience very much by the energy and vivacity they displayed but principally by the various substances which they mentioned as possessing individual properties in common with the sugar, one little boy being required to mention other things besides sugar which possessed the property of whiteness, called out in a peculiar manner that made the audience laugh 'a shirt,' another boy thinking he could improve the answer called very eagerly 'a DICKEY,' another little boy called out 'SLAPDASH' which I found upon explanation to mean 'whitewash'."[75]

Though this exercise may ask for something between science and vocabulary drill, much of the training that passes for science is pure indoctrination in market capitalistic theory, presented as if it had some scientific validation—this from thinkers who have no use for religious teaching not validated by empirical evidence. For example, Combe reports to Ellis on an interrogation that took place on August 2, 1851, in which children of various ages from Mr. Williams's school are quizzed on the scientific subjects, demonstrate chemical apparatus, do phrenological analyses, and finally demonstrate the principles of capitalism. After the children have been asked to define wealth, capital, and the principles of the advancement of civilization through capital, their discussion focuses on the so-called laws of nature:

> Here the point was brought out very forcibly that these laws are facts founded in nature, and that man can neither alter them, nor escape from their consequence. If of 1000 persons forming an entire community, 900 consume all they produce, & 100 save, what will be the consequence? Do the 100 by saving & becoming capitalists benefit or injure the 900 labourers who have consumed all? Would the 100 benefit the 900 most by giving them gratuitously all they had saved, or by giving them it only on condition of labouring & producing more? From past experience, what would the 900 be likely to do with the earning of the 100, if given to them gratuitously? What would happen if the 100 gave each of the 900 the exact full value of his labour without stipulating for any profit to themselves?[76]

After dismissing as irrelevant what Marx was later to call "surplus value," the questioning continues with a further interrogation designed to show that the progress of civilization depends on leaving sizable profits to capitalists: no one has a right to be idle, those who do not consume all of their earnings but invest them are the saviors of progress, the "idle rich man" who does not invest is as worthless as the idle poor man, and both laborers and capitalists do good by continuing in their respective places (the prospectus for Combe's school, significantly issued in 1848, calls attention to the revolutions on the continent and the unrest among the lower classes that purportedly better education will remedy).[77]

Sometimes the epiphanic events involved quite large audiences. For example, on May 18, 1850, Combe reports to Ellis on an examination before three hundred persons of young children in the scientific subjects of geography, physiology and physical science and of older ones in arithmetic, algebra, geography, and physiology, the last of these with an eye to social policy: "To give you an idea of how far they were able to go, I told them that Dr. Stark had reported that the mean age of the gentry & professional men in Edinburgh at death was—43 years, of master tradesmen, Clerks etc. 36½. And of Artizans, labourers, porters etc. 27½—and asked them whether God was kinder to one of these classes than to the other two. 'No!' 'How then do you account for the third class dying so young?' 'They are dirty, live in bad houses, drink too much, are ill fed, and have hard work.' Explain how dirt makes them die soon? They applied the physiology of the skin admirably in their answers."[78]

The remainder of the questioning focuses on how through education the working class is to learn to be cleaner and less alcoholic. One student suggests that the filth, alcoholism, and poor ventilation of the people's houses might be improved by the employment of scavengers to handle the problems. Thereupon Combe dismisses the idea by "showing" that such a policy would be too expensive, require too many scavengers, and promote too many fights between the dirty people and the scavengers. If the working classes are to live longer, they will have to take care of themselves.[79] That unjust wages, long hours, filthy factory conditions, unsafe machines, and exploitative management contribute to the community health problems never appears in the discussion.

Finally, some of the epiphanies became printed gospel. Consider, for example, a pamphlet supposedly recording an examination on social economy on May 23, 1850, conducted by George Combe and James Simpson. The children questioned are nine to thirteen years old. Combe begins the celebration by telling the children that the study of social economy looks at those laws of nature explicating how wealth is created and distributed that, upon deeper thought, tell us of the nature of humankind, the construction of the external world, and the relationship between the former and the latter. Under questioning, the children describe how natural laws may be discovered and argue that to compensate for their natural weakness, human beings must know what they can extract from nature and must use their minds, varying in capacity, in differentiated productive activities.

The case of two men was supposed, one with strong intellect and well informed but with a weak body, the other with a weak mind and ignorant but with a strong body, both engaged in the cultivation of the land, and the children were questioned as to their comparative powers of production, their position at the end of ten years, and the manner in which they could best cooperate. Their answers affirmed that at the end of the ten years, the first (the well-informed person of strong intellect) would have saved the most wealth; and that both would gain if the latter were to place himself under the guidance of the former and receive wages for his labour, by which arrangement he could produce more than when left to himself. In this manner, and with the aid of additional examples, the distinction between the capitalist and the laborer was shown to be a result of natural inequalities in the capacities of men for producing and accumulating wealth.[80]

There follows a catechism in which the interrogator, now Dr. James Simpson, leads the children to prove that hiring laborers at low wages leads to more production than hiring them at slightly higher ones and will eventually lead to their betterment.[81] Then comes another in which the law of supply and demand manifests itself in the operation of a fishmongery; and a third involving definitions of value, money, and bills of exchange.[82] Such egregious oral displays of the children's acceptance of the mythology of the patrons as constituting the laws of nature, such a thorough-going rejection by children of the claims of their own group, made patronage an endearing art.

Constructing utopia means creating teachers worthy of utopia or at least of model schools—a major theme since Prospero took up his book. As teacher training of the monitors heralds the monitorial reform, teacher training comes to be systematized in the model Birkbeck-style schools to create teachers who can herald the future. Robert Cunningham, a proponent of teacher education, wrote a very insightful letter to Combe from Philadelphia in January 1839 in which he told of the problems in the early teachers' seminaries, as he labels them. For example, the one at Andover seemed dedicated to teaching teachers only what they needed to know but not the art of communi-

cating that knowledge.[83] In contrast, many teacher education institutions appeared to be connected to no conventional colleges or
advanced faculties and, by implication, lacked strength in subject matter. For Cunningham, questions arising were whether teacher education should be assimilated into the remainder of higher education
and whether public support should extend to candidate teachers
emerging from among the poor. In Britain, the reformers recognized
that the development of teacher training colleges and "enlightened"
consumers of the schools would be necessary to the accomplishment
of a reform agenda. For example, on October 27, 1851, Combe writes
to his brother Edward: "I cannot avoid asking, 'Supposing we had a
Bill [i.e., a national education bill] of our own framing, how would it
work?' Every enlightened educationist answers, 'Very imperfectly, because we want instructed Teachers, & instructed Committees.' PRAC-
TICALLY, therefore we cannot bestow too much attention on in-
structing Lecturers & sending them forth to instruct the people,—
not merely to induce them to VOTE for an EDUCATIONAL BILL, but to
qualify them to manage the schools under that Bill well, after it becomes an act of Parliament."[84]

The idea that model schools could illustrate not only student performance but what teachers could do often occupied the second
generation reformers. For example, in June 1854, some of Combe's
friends took him to see a "ragged school" in Kingston, where he saw
a middle-aged teacher holding a religious primer and trying to teach
some children to read, a nearby helper teaching reading by showing
children doggerel and asking them to repeat each line, and a second
helper reading the miracle of the loaves and fishes and showing a
picture of Raphael's cartoon of it. Combe laments that though the
women had excellently shaped heads and large anterior lobes, they
lacked "all knowledge of things' use to be learnt & how to teach
them," unlike the teachers in the Birkbeck schools.[85] If Utilitarian
teacher training in England began as the training of monitors, its second generation reform, influenced by David Stow and the Glasgow
Normal School, recognized subject matter. To get students to adopt
politically productive attitudes, normal schools had to train teachers

to take those attitudes.[86] The descriptions of conventional teaching that appear in the second generation accounts are as horrific as those in Montaigne—accounts of dame schools, Sunday schools, church-conducted schools, grammar schools, and schools for women. The more detailed and accurate accounts appear in the write-ups of the government visitations to schools done as part of studies of the national educational condition. The reformers—Combe, Ellis, Williams, Hodgson, Simpson, and their allies—are regularly angry about bad teaching. Ellis is particularly vehement, writing in a letter to Combe: "General Routine may have much to answer for as regards the life & sufferings of our Soldier, but he is a model of enlightened proficiency compared with the besotted & learned professor of the same name who, under the pretense of educating the young, excludes from their notice, as far as he can, all modern science & crams them with dead language & obsolete fables & opinions."[87]

When Lords Granville and Russell and the Duke of Argyll proposed a national educational policy in 1855 and Prince Albert supported it, Ellis asked, "Where are the teachers to carry out his [Prince Albert's] instructions?" and lamented the lack of provision for colleges or universities for training teachers to do what Albert proposed.[88]

THE CLIMATE OF OPINION

Much of the battle over nineteenth-century education has been characterized as a battle over whether the church or secular authorities would control the greater share of a public tax-supported school system when it came into existence.[89] But the battle was not only for control of the schools; it was also for the "hearts and minds" of the populace over what life's reward system is. The second generation reformers, knowing the continental higher criticism, especially Strauss's *Leben Jesu*, were skeptical of afterlife heavenly cities and of emphases on their compensations for life's trials. The matter is put precisely by Combe's letter to W. J. Fox in 1853: whereas revealed religion is a kind of opiate of the masses, natural religion is their goad in an industrial system. Revealed religion is false in its emphasis on the standard credal doctrines—the incarnation, salvation by grace, sin, the efficacy of the crucifixion, and the like—and it is particularly so in its emphasis on an afterlife of glories distorting the individual worker's sense that the this-worldly system gives people what they deserve.[90] Combe's long letter to Horace Mann on the subject makes clear that he had lost belief in an afterlife, and Mann replies with arguments in favor of the doctrine but also with a plea that Combe not reveal his skepticism lest he hurt the school project.[91]

Religious controversy and uncertainty as to afterlife "utopias" gave the reformers their power, for in the battle with the Church of England over religious control of the coming national system of schools, they knew that they would win not because they had a popular view of the afterworld but because they had adopted the only position that could unite the British nation. Supremely aware that it would be quite impossible to produce a consensus for schools controlled by the Church of England, they relied on Catholic emancipation, the sizable Jewish population of London and some other urban centers, and the appearance of widespread skepticism as to the truth of Christian doctrine in order to place the formation of the schools in hands like theirs.[92] Combe notes in his journal on April 4, 1853, that in a presentation to the Commons on a national system of education, Lord John Russell went out of his way to note that Combe's proposal for a secular system included the notion that political economy (read "market economics") and natural theology should be taught in the schools—but that most of the people entering into the debate and favoring a secular system wanted no religious or ethical instruction to enter the school. They wished religion to be taught by ministers of religion only. Combe remarks in his journal: "His scheme is to give money for education based on religion to all sects who will take it & teach their own creeds." In Combe's opinion, "He will not succeed in carrying such a measure."[93] While deploring sectarianism, the reformers were careful to speak respectfully of "religion" and of the scientific truths announced by divine Wisdom, but they were not so aware that "natural religion" itself had sectarian implications to those in England who emphasized the absolute character of religious revelation apart from natural confirmations (perhaps the English equivalents of Kierkegaard) and to those who were atheists.[94] In a discussion in 1852, one of Combe's interlocutors, Hewett Watson, argues that the school that Combe had founded in Edinburgh should not be called Mr. Williams's Secular School because it taught a sectarian natural religion. As Watson asserts, "Natural religion is as offensive to the Catholic, Calvinist, & Socialist Atheist, as any of these dogmas can be to him," and Combe has no right to exclude the children of "Catholic, Calvinist, & Socialist Atheist people by teaching only his own religion."[95] However, this level of sophistication with respect to the difficulty and complexity of creating a genuinely pluralistic system of schooling, respectful of all credal formulations and yet attached to none, is not often found in these debates.

The policy debate was carried ahead in the reviews and in novels, especially in the *Westminster Review* and in George Eliot's novels. Her circle and that of the second generation reformers affiliated in the early 1850s when she developed the second phase of her basic intellectual position as the effectual editor of the *Westminster Review*, the first phase having developed in the 1840s out of her friendship with the Brays and the Hennells and having immersed her in the higher criticism of the Bible, Owenite socialism (though she never had much use for Owen), Chartism, Emersonian transcendentalism, and a range of "progressive" positions. At the *Review*, Eliot widened her interest to include reform in general, politics, history, philosophy, science, and education. Combe first met Eliot in 1851 on a visit to Coventry and remarked in his journal on her fine phrenological profile and the great intellectual powers represented in her translation of the many languages used in Strauss's "higher critical" *Leben Jesu*. His conversations with her concerned religion, economics, and politics.[96] When John Chapman took over the *Westminster Review*, Combe supported him for a time, always somewhat skeptical of his business sense. In 1851–52, while editor of the *Review*, Eliot visited Ellis's home several times.[97] The initial links between the Combe-Ellis group and Eliot as the editor of the *Westminster Review* seem to have been based less on a common interest in educational reform and more on the Combe-

Ellis group's patronage of the *Westminster Review* for its religious positions. Both groups had an interest in promoting through the *Review* the higher biblical criticism demythologizing conventional religion. Both groups sought through the *Review* to promote skepticism as to the conventional versions of Christian revelation and the standard versions of Gospel harmonies, and both knew Strauss's demythologizing *Leben Jesu*. Eliot translated and published it in 1844; Combe made a note about it in his diary as he traveled in America in 1853.[98] In a letter on January 27, 1852, Eliot complains to Combe that William Lombe is being obstreperous about getting the return of a hundred pounds that he had contributed for publication of an abridgement of Strauss.[99] An 1853 letter shows that though Combe has little respect for organized religion in any of its forms, Eliot tries to suggest that it may be changing for the better and writes that "even narrow orthodoxy is beginning to shrink from the doctrine of eternal punishments"; she argues against any effort to make the biblical writers all say the same thing or to find the idea of eternal life in the Mosaic books.[100]

But though religion was the original basis of the alliance, through the *Review* Eliot and the second generation Utilitarians were also able to promote the new world beyond special revelation and advance the meliorist potential of science, technology, and scientific/technological education. For example, on November 21, 1851, William Ellis remarks on the possible limited use of journals for disseminating of educational ideas: "I sent, as you requested, a copy of my little book to Miss Evans—a page for the notice is more than the work deserves although the subject & the review might occupy more to advantage. The kind of work going on at Leith under the auspices of . . . Williams is what we must mainly depend upon for the furtherance of what we both have in view."[101]

In the July 1852 number, Eliot as the de facto editor of the *Review* published Combe's essay on "Secular Education," concerned with Ellis's *Education as a Means of Preventing Destitution*, Church's *Rise and Progress of National Education in England*, and the first, second, and third reports of Williams's Secular School (i.e., the Birkbeck School in Edinburgh, in the initiation and management of which Combe and Ellis had had a hand). Eliot's role in the publication of Combe's essay is telling. On January 27, 1852, she writes to Combe asking him to review Ellis's book, a reprint of the reports and speeches of the National Public School Association and their opponents, and a report on the "State of Education in the Sandwich Islands" for the April number of the *Westminster Review*.[102] On February 24, 1852, she has received Combe's article and, while indicating that she has removed a couple of Ellis quotations from the article, expresses her "great interest and admiration," praising it for "serv[ing] the cause it advocates and the reputation of the *Review*."[103] The alliance continues after the article has been received. On April 8, 1852, Eliot writes to Combe to reassure him that the *Review* still supports phrenology and would like an article on it for October.[104] Later she writes to inform him that she has secured Dr. James Coxe for the task.[105] On June 7, she writes to Combe to assure him that she will soon publish an article on the "hereditary transmission of qualities," a phrenological educators' theme.[106] The reformers were aware that journals having a general circulation to the intellectual class could be of some service to their cause. (The literature-school contact went from literary people to the schools also. Eliot's friend from Coventry, Charles Bray, visited one of Ellis's schools in late 1851 to hear the children talk about the benefits of machinery and asked to return again to see more of the school.[107] Even in late 1854, W. M. Williams, the former teacher at Combe and Ellis's Edinburgh school, visited Bray at Coventry and was invited back.)[108]

In the 1852 *Review* article, Combe begins by announcing that his sorts of philanthropists are the prophets of a "distant date which they themselves may never see," people who are "misrepresented, misconstrued, accused of hardness of heart" in the present and thwarted by those whom they would help, presumably the working classes.[109] To show what they are about, Combe says he will treat three points: the necessity of educating the people, the kind of education to be given them, and the means of supplying it.

Under the rubric of necessity, he repeats Smith's argument that without education, stupidity comes to be so rampant as to endanger the whole of society, given the division of labor. He then displays the evils of the industrial system for the working classes—starvation, disease, criminality, irresponsibility toward children, overpopulation— and argues that while the working classes without the vote may be toothless, once they have the vote they will bite their masters unless they are educated, as the case of the United States proves.[110] Well aware of Eliot's antipathy to conventional ecclesiasticism, he lands on the church party for its insistence on ecclesiastical control of education and argues that what schools in a society riven by sectarian division can teach is the manifestation of God in the world: that is, science. He also argues for some kind of universal teaching of "standard English" so that those who speak a regional dialect or Gaelic can understand the oral version of the written script that they are reading, a position that would eliminate regions and regionalisms in language. As the ecclesiastical party does not recognize, in his view the misery of the masses is temporal misery—lack of food, clothing, and shelter (this almost a century after Smith has blessed the luxury visited on the masses by the new order!); the party's members resemble the American slave holders who would banish slave learning but send in missionaries to save slave souls. Teaching theology without teaching "Political Economy" or "physical, physiological, and economical causation," the ecclesiastical party believes that "providence will evolve temporal prosperity out of moral and religious duty duly discharged," whereas in fact gardening, milling, and farming—the production of the necessities of life—all require applied scientific and economic knowledge and not theology.[111]

As to the kind of education to be given the masses, Combe would have the schools teach (1) things that exist (as would Bentham and the first generation Utilitarians); (2) the things' modes of action; (3) human nature; (4) the adaptation of the things of nature to the human creature, a phrenological obsession; and (5) wonder at the laws of nature and nature's God: "Under such a system of instruction and training, the laws of nature, by which health and disease, poverty and riches, honour and disgrace, and every other worldly enjoyment or suffering are produced, would become the fingerposts and trumpet tongues of Providence warning the people that 'in this direction lies happiness—in that misery.'" Science and wonder joined become the true this-worldly religious revelations. Both can be taught in the schools and are the basis for ethical behavior.[112] All of this is larded with implicit attacks on the schools controlled by the clergy, on the universities, the irrelevance of classical education to mass needs, and the confinement of mass education in a scientific age to reading, writing and arithmetic.

Combe then reviews Ellis's book and accomplishments, beginning with his teaching of economics at the Lancastrian Camberwell school in 1848 and afterward his founding and supporting of the (then) eleven Birkbeck or Birkbeck-style schools, arguing that instruction in Nature, natural transformations, and good habits should come neither in Sunday schools nor in clerically controlled schools but from secular schools supported by taxes from the community of every district. Schools cannot survive on the sorts of voluntary subscriptions that shored up the Lancastrian schools. Finally, sectarian education should be given outside the tax-supported schools, and though standard educational work may modify conventional religion, it will strengthen true natural religion. Indeed, the existence of working-class atheism testifies to the absence in the extant conventional schools of scientific education concerning God's creation. It does not derive from the paucity of biblical education.

Combe then approves of Ellis's catalogue of the subjects of education: study of the causes (as opposed to the effects) of things ethically discerned, the study of the consequences of action, the "division of labour, interchange, partnerships, buying and selling, and credit and confidence" as making labor productive, and the study of "honesty, fidelity, punctuality . . . order," and sobriety as leading to the well-being of all. Indeed, education replaces what religion had once claimed: "The task of creating the virtues belongs chiefly to the educators of the people."[113] In this context, Combe praises the London Mechanics Institute Birkbeck lessons on competition, overpopulation, and undereducation, taught by a Mr. Runtz at that institute, a segue that permits him to return to the theme of the need for the teaching of economics in the schools.

In reviewing Richard Church's "Rise and Progress of a National Education" addressed to Cobden, the great parliamentary advocate of reform favorable to the working classes, Combe treats tax-supported universal education as the proper next step in Cobden's program to liberate the masses and adds a coda concerning Mr. Williams's Secular School as already carrying into action the agendas of Ellis's book and his review.[114]

The 1852 review of educational books does not end the intellectual commerce between Eliot and the Combe-Ellis circle. On November 13, 1852, Eliot consults with Combe about an essay to be written for the *Westminster Review* by W. B. Hodgson, Combe's protégé, on the need for a substitution of modern for classical languages in the curriculum, suggesting that Hodgson's proposed essay needs to be broader and that Combe can indicate how to broaden the topic.[115] In the October 1853 issue she publishes Hodgson's completed essay defending the study of the sciences and the modern languages in early schooling, and the April 1854 *Review* includes a version of Combe's phrenological "Criminal Legislation and Prison Discipline" which she had shortened and revised from Combe's submission. But though the prison piece was published in 1854, the Eliot-Combe friendship was essentially over by October of 1853. When Eliot began her sexual relationship with George Henry Lewes, Combe and Ellis cut her off as an immoral woman.[116]

Eliot often appears in the critical literature as a Victorian sage who adumbrates her will for humankind's future and her sense of moral necessity through the elaborate organization of her novels, including her organization of the education of her characters. However, she is no Utopian, for with Comte and the other continental thinkers who emphasized the importance of the community and the communal and the glacial nature of change in human communities, she does not expect rapid change to be productive: "Utopian pictures help the reception of ideas as to constructive results, but hardly so much as a vivid presentation of how results have been actually brought about, especially in religious and social change." [117]

Still, she shows the marks of the Combe-Ellis faction. Though by the time she began to write *Scenes of Clerical Life* in October 1855 she had come under Combe's condemnation for a year, her work continues to evidence the Combe-Ellis educational and phrenological theories, the latter learned not only from Combe but from Bray, from her editing the last two volumes of G. H. Lewes's *Problems of Life and Mind*, and from reading Comte. [118] She includes frequent reference to phrenological configurations in her novels: Lawyer Dempster's bump of benevolence in *Scenes of Clerical Life*, Latimer's defects of organization in "The Lifted Veil" (1859), Felix Holt's large "veneration" in the novel carrying his name, Arthur Donnithorne's "approbation" in *Mill on the Floss*, and so forth. Latimer's "Lifted Veil" account, contrasting the phrenological "scientific" education that emerges from the Combe-Ellis faction with the public-school classical education of the religious right and the English elite, gives a comic rendition of how a phrenological analysis was done and the educational prescriptions to which it led:

My brother was to be his [Latimer's father's] representative and successor; he must go to Eton and Oxford, for the sake of making connections, of course: my father was not a man to underrate the bearing of Latin satirists or Greek dramatists on the attainment of an aristocratic position. But, intrinsically, he had slight esteem for "those dead but sceptred spirits," having qualified himself for forming an independent opinion by reading Potter's "Aeschylus", and dipping into Francis's "Horace". To this negative view he added a positive one, derived from a recent connection with mining speculations; namely, that a scientific education was the really useful training for a younger son. Moreover, it was clear that a shy, sensitive boy like me was not fit to encounter the rough experience of a public school. Mr Letherall had said so very decidedly. Mr Letherall was a large man in spectacles, who one day took my small head between his large hands, and pressed it here and there in an exploratory, suspicious manner—then placed each of his great thumbs on my temples, and pushed me a little way from him, and stared at me with glittering spectacles. The contemplation appeared to displease him, for he frowned sternly, and said to my father, drawing his thumbs across my eyebrows:

"The deficiency is there, sir—there; and here," he added, touching the upper sides of my head, "here is the excess. That must be brought out, sir, and this must be laid to sleep."[119]

Latimer says he hated the phrenologist, and perhaps rightly so, for the system that the narrator describes as emerging from this session is a wholly compensatory one emphasizing systematic zoology, botany, natural history, science, and the modern languages and created to remedy Latimer's supposed problems with "organization." It eliminates his literary and imaginative interests, as Utilitarians prior to John Stuart Mill felt that one must with ordinary or working people, and substitutes scientific/organizational ones: "I [Latimer] was very stupid about machines, so I was to be greatly occupied with them; I had no memory for classification, so it was particularly necessary that I should study systematic zoology and botany; I was hungry for human deeds and human emotions, so I was to be plentifully crammed with the mechanical powers, the elementary bodies, and the phenomena of electricity and magnetism. A better-constituted boy would certainly have profited under my intelligent tutors, with their scientific apparatus; and would, doubtless, have found the phenomena of electricity and magnetism as fascinating as I was, every Thursday, assured they were."[120]

"On the sly" Latimer reads Cervantes and Shakespeare and rejoices in the natural world "glad of the running water," "watch[ing] it and listen[ing] to it gurgling among the pebbles, and bathing the bright green waterplants, by the hour together," confident without analytic evidence "that there were good reasons for what was so very beautiful."[121] "The Lifted Veil" is a melancholy, improbable story of a clairvoyant and vacillating hero, unchanged by the remediation provided to alter his phrenological deficiency of organization.

But Eliot also picked up on Combe and Ellis's broader educational themes in her early fictions, giving them a plausibility and meaning that no essayistic presentation could. Her interest in Utilitarian economic theory, in the Combe-Ellis sense that self-interest should be the motor of society, is complicated by her interest in Comtean sociology. She believed, as they did not, in the community factor in the evolution of individuals and groups, and her faith in sacrifice, benevolence, and sympathy as the motors of the good society remained undiminished long after she had left orthodox belief. Her sense of how the economy ought to be organized seems to have been partly a conventional laissez-faire one, but she developed it in a direction implying that the true service of self-interest also became the service of social interest when accompanied by sympathy and cooperative association. Her Comtean sociology included a heavy dose of interest in a complexly articulated social group having many classes and functional vocational groups.[122] As a novelist experienced in the lives of desperate working-class people, capable of seeing and imagining the forces that shape and educate people outside the school, she writes novels that perpetually remind us, as Combe and Ellis do not, that people cannot be made wholly by schools.

All of this admitted, Eliot sometimes displays a sense of her intellectual roots in the phrenological Utilitarian educators when she describes schools and schooling and is not just referring to phrenology. Her "flesh and blood" critiques of conventional schooling and her positive pictures of what schooling could be embody the usual Utilitarian topics: the frivolousness of conventional women's education, the need for women's education in "men's" subjects, and the irrelevance of the Latin/Greek education offered at public school and university.[123] She describes the limited uses of the dame schools, the incompetence of clerical teachers, the inadequacy of the Sunday schools teaching the Bible and basics to otherwise unschooled children, and the usefulness of the night schools to uneducated adults.[124] Eliot is aware of new developments in education. David Faux in "Brother Jacob" attends the Mechanics Institute and Will Ladislaw goes to a meeting in Middlemarch concerning a similar institute.[125] Recalling the phrenological Utilitarians' critiques of Owen, Dorothea plans to use her money to initiate a village that will be a "school of industry" until Sir James and her uncle persuade her that such a learning community would be too risky, perhaps evoking Orbiston, where Combe's brother had failed in the 1820s, or other 1820s–30s socialist learning communities from the period when Middlemarch is set.[126]

Since Eliot writes about an earlier England to mirror the problems of her own time, she cannot easily represent a school explicitly conducted along narrowly Utilitarian or laissez-faire principles. However, Robertson's remark that Eliot lacks knowledge of the monitorial system developed by Andrew Bell and Joseph Lancaster is surprising, given her connections to Ellis and the second generation Utilitarian schools' continued use of a version of monitorialism, and it is also wrong.[127] A metaphor in the "Amos Barton" part of *Scenes of Clerical Life* speaks of Mr. Cleves as the kind of clergyman who was the "surest helper under a difficulty, as a monitor who is encouraging rather than severe."[128]

Adam Bede shows Bartle Massey fusing day schools for children with night schools for adults, a characteristic of the Birkbeck schools, and *Felix Holt* demonstrates the enthusiasm for fusing the labor movement with the educational movement developed by Lovett and Ellis. Though Bartle's school operates fictively in a much earlier period than did Ellis's schools, within his male preserve Bartle pays tribute to the Birkbeck combination of day classes for children with night ones for adults and educates his adult working-class students with patience and sympathy. With the two teenaged students who come to him for help in calculating "bills of parcels," he employs Birkbeck's object lessons fixing on possible real world situations. If the students wish to learn to do sums for "bills of parcel," they must both do sums in school and make up summing problems for themselves at work. If the student is a shoemaker, he must learn to count stitches by fives, price them, count the number made in an hour and a day, and calculate the wages per day and then the wages at that rate for a year for three or ten workmen, and so forth.[129] Bartle is quite vehement in his teaching, and he may be laying on the passion as a compensation for some phrenological defect that he perceives in his students.[130] At the same time, however, he hates women and his school is the only one in the village, a comment on the deficiency of rural women's education.

Again *Felix Holt, The Radical* (1866) seems to replicate the kind of experience that the William Lovett whom Ellis patronized had had in the 1830s and 1840s. Felix supports the Radical Party, a branch of the Liberals in the 1833 election conducted after the passage of the Reform Bill. Though the novel is not a strict roman à clef, it glancingly recalls the Chartist splits of the 1830s. Harold Transome embodies the elitist top-down tendencies of many of the Liberal and Radical leaders, concerned in the abstract for the "welfare of the working man." Holt represents the Lovett-style forces in labor that in the 1840s advocated educational reform as the path to worker freedom, and finally, Transome's lawyer-supporter and rabble-rouser Matthew Jermyn represents the Fergus O'Connor–style Chartists who sought reform through violence. Though Holt attempts to prevent the riot that occurs among the workers, a disturbance created by the elites that manipulate them, he inadvertently participates in an action that kills a man. Michael Bincey's testimony in his favor argues that he favors "schooling and bringing up the little chaps" and that he tried to set up a school for working-class children. Further, Mr. Lyon testifies that Felix Holt wanted to set up a night school for the working men of the district that would convert "them somewhat to habits of soberness and due care for the instruction of their children." [131] That Felix Holt resembles Lovett in some respects is natural, given the fact that Eliot first knew Ellis in 1852, shortly after he had formed his alliance with Lovett setting up the Birkbeck day and night schools at Lovett's London Mechanics Institute. Of course, by 1866, when the novel was published, Chartism had been replaced by more aggressive forms of the militant wing of the labor movement in Britain, especially those attracted to Marx, and the issue of a compulsory national schooling policy was on the national agenda.

In 1868, Eliot published a sequel to *Felix Holt*, a piece entitled "Address to Working Men," supposedly by Felix Holt and spoken in the wake of the granting of the franchise to male members of the working class. The speech has been called an unradical piece, not even Tory-Democrat, and certainly it argues for a complexly articulated class-based society.[132] However, the more pressing claim of the speech is for class-based solidarity in the common interest. It wants a transformation of the concept of class interest into a concept of class functions, better labor leadership, respect for the world of traditional culture not previously accessible to the classes, adherence in labor communities to the cooperative movement (presumably Owenite structures), and schools for labor's children: "Let us demand that they [union members] send their children to school, so as not to go on recklessly breeding a moral pestilence among us, just as strictly as we demand that they pay their contributions to a common fund, understood to be for a common benefit. . . . To find right remedies and right methods. Here is the great function of knowledge: here the life of one man may make a fresh era straight away, in which a sort of suffering that has existed shall exist no more."[133]

Eliot then cites the French sixteenth-century discovery of how to stop bleeding through tying off arteries as an example. Eliot was as aware of the evils of capitalistic urban industrialism as was Mrs. Gaskell or Zola. Once one sets aside the negative examples of education for an industrial age gone wrong, once one sees where her two positive exemplars, Bartle Massey and Felix Holt, point, it is not difficult to see her common ground with the phrenological Utilitarians who had rejected her. But the grounds for hope in her work are gradualistic and empathic, not Smithian or Utilitarian. They are not Marxist either.

The degree to which electoral reform could save the industrial system was to become even more uncertain two years later after the Franco-Prussian war of 1870–71, the Paris Commune, and the widespread appearance of Marxist and socialist revolts elsewhere. But Eliot had spoken her piece. It is not surprising that her last novels, *Middlemarch* (1871), *Daniel Deronda* (1876), and *Theophrastus Such* (1879) do not mention the issue of compulsory general education as a national policy even by indirection, save to show a variety of people needing sound education.

The Second Generation Utilitarians

Numerous critics have observed that in Eliot, the real always aspires toward a condition of ideality—as if in a Vermeer painting—but the reverse is also true: the movement toward the utopian comes, if at all, in the vestments of ordinary life, and Eliot's real sense of how her characters are educated comes in her picture of their learning from history, from their communities, from developing sympathy, and seeing into each other's situations. Finally, of course, she does present a kind of rough justice as operating in history, giving people eventually what they deserve in this life, and she offers a range of sympathetic characters such as Dorothea Brooke for whom the education of the lower orders represents a great cause. In her concern for the implications of the higher criticism, for phrenology as an explanation of why people are as they are and why they need special kinds of education, for the education of the lower orders, for secular justice apart from afterlife considerations, and for the duty of the affluent to the poor, she is at one with the second generation Utilitarians. The other great novelist of her generation, Dickens, was not.

CHAPTER EIGHT

Dickens's Utilitarian Dystopia and the Death of the Social Commons

B Y THE MIDDLE of the nineteenth century, what Mannheim describes as liberal utopianism had gradually hardened into classical, liberal "ideology" throughout the British Isles and the northeastern United States. Though secular compulsory education was not enacted as a national policy in Britain until the complementary bills of 1870 and 1876, Whig/liberal interests controlled the government for most of the period between 1840 and 1876. The polluted and overcrowded cities of an industrializing England had been described by Blake, Wordsworth, Mrs. Elizabeth Gaskell, and others, but aside from Swift and the Scriblerans, the major figures who wrote about education did not question the environmental efficacy of the vision of scientific/industrial education promoted by the utopias treated in this book. Few questioned whether children were getting a square deal.

Some reaction had begun: the Romantic writers—especially Wordsworth and Blake—had begun indirectly questioning the developing consensus for a compulsory scientific/industrial education by representing crucial education of childhood as occurring neither in schools nor in universities. For them, it came in visionary and panentheistic experiences prompted by the evocative presence of unusual natural landscapes, special kinds of dreams and visions, and childhood books.[1] To such writers, the very institutions society had provided to make children know the material world seemed to prevent their knowing the important transcendent things. In addition, Blake attacked the "dark Satanic mills" of the new industrial order that blighted England's "green and pleasant land" where an innocent

Jerusalem might be built. John Stuart Mill, in his *Autobiography* (1873), demythologized the education his father provided him (Thomas Carlyle called it the "autobiography of a logical Steam-engine"), but that deflation counted for little in national policy discussions.[2] In any case, the education J. S. Mill received was not exactly the education that his father advocated for the children of the working poor. Further, the Romantic and Millian analyses of education ignore the power relationship dictating how capital, government, and education in science and technology unite to determine humankind's interaction with the natural world.

Dickens makes up for these deficiencies in his 1854 *Hard Times*, which was appropriately dedicated to Thomas Carlyle. In *Chartism* (1829) and *Past and Present* (1843), Carlyle created Romantic neomedieval critiques of the Whig/liberal theory and placed the ideal reconstruction of society in the hands of a patriarchal community of heroes. His works, and those of his followers, also prepared the way for certain uniquely British sorts of socialism.[3] *Hard Times*, as Carlyle's offspring, is not a socialist polemic. However, its satire, launched from the vantage point of a demand for empathic, almost religious vision, argues for the social construction of the imagination at the expense of a solipsistic visioning of the meaning of human enterprise.

Though Dickens deals with some form of education in most of his novels, only in *Hard Times* does he consider the second generation Utilitarians.[4] The novel does not attack only Bentham or James Mill, as has been commonly supposed (such attack would have been pointless, since they were no longer around). It excoriates Ellis, Combe, and the schools they created, the schoolmasters and teachers they promoted, and the pedagogical styles they made canonical. It further presents pedagogical styles and power relationships that duplicate those of the Birkbeck schools and their simulacra. There is some evidence in Mrs. Ellis's letter to Combe of January 21, 1853, that Dickens himself or his reporter made a detailed examination of the Birkbeck schools. Mrs. Ellis objected to having a writer from a publication called *The Bouquet* write about the Birkbeck schools and notes in passing what damage the wrong writer can create: "Dickens is about as clever a word-monger as can be wished—& yet see from his ignorance what a sad mess he has made of the Schools—and yet he sent a Shorthand writer to take down the lessons."[5] Since Dickens himself was an accomplished writer of shorthand, he may have been the reporter.

Mrs. Ellis's letter was written over a year before *Hard Times* was serialized in *Household Words*. The remarks are made in response to an account in *Household Words* of the Birkbeck schools at the Mechanics Institution and the National Hall, published on December 25, 1852. On December 28, 1852, Ellis tells Combe of Dickens's story: "I sent you last Friday a copy of the last number of the *Household Words* containing an account of the Schools at the Mechanics Institution & at the National Hall a la Dickens," observing also that the article "is more likely to do us good than otherwise although I would rather see so important a matter as Education treated more seriously."[6]

Since the article sets down the basic polarities in terms of which Dickens treats second generation Utilitarian education in *Hard Times*, it deserves a full accounting. It begins with Dickens (or the "we" of the story) leaving the Chancery Court, where he was presumably gathering information for *Bleak House*.[7] He goes to the nearby Birkbeck School at the London Mechanics Institute, where he hears children singing in a social harmony that outdoes the Chancery's will and property controversies. The school has three hundred and fifty students divided into three classes (under eight years, eight to eleven years, and over eleven), which are subdivided into "the quick and the slow" students; these groups are taught by five teachers and an unspecified number of monitors.[8] The reporter's direct observation of teaching begins with an "Object Lesson" given to the eight- to eleven-year-old children in which the teacher has a penny in his pocket and asks the students to guess what it is on the basis of the cue: "I have something in my pocket which I am always glad to have there."[9] "We were old enough and worldly enough to know what he meant; but boys aspire to fill their pockets with so many things that, according to their minds, the something in the teacher's pocket might be string, apple, knife, brass button, top, hardbake, stick of firewood, crumbs, squirt, gunpowder, marbles, slate, pencil, pea-shooter, brad-awl, or perhaps small cannon."[10] On the basis of the clue that the object could burn a hole in a boy's pocket, the children eventually guess a piece of coal. The teacher then announces that numerous objects of this kind are together building a monument to a great man who made the penny loaf "bigger" through the Corn Laws—that is, Sir Robert Peel of Corn Law fame. After much further cuing, the children guess that the object is a penny. *Hard Times* includes no such guessing game centered on an object at McChoakumchild's school, but the effort to guess what is on the teacher's mind appears in both schools.

The next Mechanics Institute exercise, like the classifying and vocabulary drills in *Hard Times*, requires that the students define the qualities of the penny. Its being hard, brown, heavy, stamped, and copper are easily ascertained. The children also discover that it is, "O-p-a-k-e" (having some trouble with the spelling), since it will not do for a spy glass, and "Malleable," though the word is not exactly understood. A serious discussion then arises as to whether the object is odorous and tenacious until Master Square, who for some time has endeavored to enter the labeling fray, asserts that it is "INORGANIC," which leads to a distinguishing between living and dead—organ-filled and inorganic—matter. This exercise eventually ends in the display of copper ore, pyrites, and so forth.[11] Though the tone of the *Household Words* treatment of the Mechanics Institute school is far more respectful than that given McChoakumchild's in *Hard Times*, one finds in the contrast between the teacher's coin and the fantasy-attached objects that the boys putatively carry in their pockets a parallel to the novel's dichotomizing of the worlds of construction and of utility, of Sleary's circus and Gradgrind's school.

Though the monitorial schools' method of numbering children according to performance appears only in the *Hard Times* account, the schoolchildren in *Hard Times* and *Household Words* compete constantly for the teacher's favor in guessing games that pose as education. The exercise in defining the qualities of the coin parallels Bitzer's magnificently successful and sycophantish *Hard Times* definition of a horse.

In the *Household Words* essay, the succeeding lesson at the Mechanics Institute works with eleven-year-old and older children and concerns capitalistic theory: definitions of wealth, capital, wages, and the division of labor—functions served in *Hard Times* by the pressure in the school of the capitalist Bounderby himself. As the students receive cues, out come what the author calls "stereotyped" answers, which are alike in concept though differing in form of phrase. The lesson then continues with a catechism in the "truths" of laissez-faire capitalism, showing how people justly get higher or lower wages under the capitalist system because they do more or less valuable work. They are more or less trained or skilled, and they act with more or less care or industry in their work. Further, the students learn that workers, if they are to be workers at all, must be clean and sober. They then soberly articulate the role of Malthusian population expansion, Smithian sympathy, and economic cycle wage fluctuation as they look at what they can expect from work in the future. Finally, the reporter concludes this section with a picture of a well-educated child who emerges from the school. In the essay's imagination of him, he becomes a man sitting with "square bold head, . . . beside the neatest of wives," arguing with his son about how to dispose of some of the capital he has acquired with his wages: "It is too much to hope that he will ever be Prime Minister."[12]

The final class described in *Household Words* is an evening class for both boys and girls conducted at the National Hall school by Ellis himself. It is concerned with wages as measured both in monetary units and in the commodities that they might purchase. The lesson demonstrates that "wanting" wages does not give one a right to have them and that wealth is only increased by the increased skill, labor, and industry that lead to increased productivity, allowing more wealth to be divided among the workers. The only reference to the portion of production taken by capital as opposed to labor is Ellis's cuing a student to respond that "the proportion between capital and wages never alters suddenly."[13] No analysis of conspicuous consumption on the part of owners and capitalists appears. In fact, the only issue of conspicuous consumption discussed is that of the drunken laborer who drinks up all of his wages until he runs out of money to drink up. As one youth with half-boots puts it, the product of great progress in educating and "civilising" youth would be that people "would not marry till they knew beforehand how they were to feed and educate their children."[14] Both Malthus and Smith are front and center, and the entire function of the lesson is to argue that poverty and woe in modern life can be alleviated by greater productivity based on more knowledge and prudence, since questions of distribution and resource cannot exist in this discussion. Ideology has swallowed all the commonsense information that the Sissy Jupes of the world have acquired from experience.

The author ends the article with a bittersweet observation that blooms into a full novel in *Hard Times*: "The imaginative faculty in all these children, and also (last but not least) their religious principles, are we assume to be cultivated elsewhere. Such cultivation, we are well convinced, is no less important to their own happiness and that of society than their knowledge of things and reason; and it should be steadily borne in mind that no amount of political economy, and no working of figures, will or can ever do without them. Still, that in its influence upon the well-being of the children and upon the future of the country to which they belong, this is an important and useful labour, we are quite sure we need not insist."[15] By the time *Hard Times* was published, the labor of the Birkbeck School did not appear to be so useful and the death of the imagination and of the religious side of humankind seemed much more threatening.

Between December 1852 and August 1854, when the last installment of *Hard Times* was published, Dickens saw more clearly the connection that had always existed between the Combe-Ellis school and the indoctrination of the children of workers who made up the industrial scene in Britain. The strike at Preston near Manchester in Lancashire began in the fall of 1853 and did not end until April of the following year. Dickens did a reading in December of 1853 in Birmingham at the Mechanics Institute, where W. M. Williams, who had been the lead teacher in Combe's school in Edinburgh, was now the science teacher. In his Birmingham speech, Dickens appealed to all sides in the industrial struggles of the day to perceive their common profit and their common need for a share of the power, and he visited the endless Preston strike in January of 1854.

These events and others like them probably led him to perceive the monstrosity of the claims made in Ellis's lesson and the other lessons on Political Economy that he, or his recorder, heard. On April 21, 1854, he wrote to Mrs. Gaskell that part of the *Hard Times* scheme would be to treat of the "monstrous claims at domination made by a certain class of manufacturers, and the extent to which the way is made easy for working men to slide down into discontent under such hands."[16] In December 1853, he published in *Household Words* James Lowe's account of the misery of the strikers and the mood of the manufacturers leading the lock-out.[17] In February 1854, he published his own account of the Preston situation, in which, in his own voice, he attacks the kind of sentiment that Ellis is earlier described as evoking from his students: "Certainly," said I. "I read, even in liberal pages, the hardest Political Economy—of an extraordinary description too sometimes, and certainly not to be found in the books—as the only touchstone of this strike. I see, this very day, in a tomorrow's liberal paper, some astonishing novelties in the politico-economical way, showing how profits and wages have no connexion whatever; coupled with such references to these hands as might be made by a very irascible General to rebels and brigands in arms."[18]

While Ellis in the lesson described in *Household Words* does not cue his students so as to evoke the notion that wages and profits have absolutely no relation, he does get them to say that the ratio between capital and wages never alters suddenly. In short, massive increases in worker productivity would not alter much what the wage earner would receive. In the Preston article, Dickens goes directly after the kind of Political Economy that Ellis and his teachers are getting students to mouth:

> In any aspect in which it can be viewed, this strike and lock-out is a deplorable calamity. In its waste of time, in its waste of a great people's energy, in its waste of wages, in its waste of wealth that seeks to be employed, in its encroachment on the means of many

thousands who are laboring from day to day, in the gulf of separation it hourly deepens between those whose interests must be understood to be identical or must be destroyed, it is a great national
affliction. But, at this pass, anger is of no use, starving out is of no
use—for what will that do, five years hence, but overshadow all the
mills in England with the growth of a bitter remembrance?—political economy is a mere skeleton unless it has a little human covering and filling out, a little human bloom upon it, and a little human
warmth in it. . . . Gentlemen are found, in great manufacturing
towns, ready enough to extol imbecile mediation with dangerous
madmen abroad; can none of them be brought to think of autho-
rised mediation and explanation at home? I do not suppose that
such a knotted difficulty as this, is to be at all untangled by a morn-
ing-party in the Adelphi; but I would entreat both sides now so
miserably opposed, to consider whether there are no men in England, above suspicion, to whom they might refer the matters in
dispute, with a perfect confidence above all things in the desire of
those men to act justly.[19]

After *Hard Times* had been published, the Ellis-Combe circle had
far more reason to resent Dickens than it did after the *Household
Words* essay. Harriet Martineau, whose *Lessons in Political Economy*
Ellis used in his schools and whose little lessons in laissez-faire economics Dickens mocks in *Hard Times*, attacked Dickens for misrepresenting the incidence of industrial accidents in his journal. She also
attacked him for misrepresenting the industrial life he was writing
about, his representations being no more like the real thing than
"Ogre and Tom Thumb."[20]

Dickens's critics also objected to his *Hard Times* presentation of
Utilitarian education as killing the imagination, a theme already developed in the *Household Words* essay. Jane Sinnett of the *Westminster
Review* attacks Dickens's representation of the Utilitarian suppression
of fantasy:

We suppose it is in *anticipation* of some change of the present educational system for one that shall kill "outright the robber Fancy,"
that Mr. Dickens launches forth his protest. . . . We are not aware

of such a system being in operation anywhere in England. On the contrary, it is the opinion of various continental professors, very competent to form a judgment on this subject, that more play is given to the imagination and will be by the English system of instruction than by any other. If we look to our public schools and universities, we find great part, too great part, we think, of the period of youth and adolescence devoted to the study of the mythology, literature, and history of the most poetic people of all time. . . . If there are Gradgrind schools, they are not sufficiently numerous to be generally known. Now, at the very commencement of "Hard Times," we find ourselves introduced to a set of hard uncouth personages, of whose existence as a class no one is aware, who are engaged in cutting and paring young souls after their own ugly pattern, and refusing them all other nourishment but facts and figures. The unpleasant impression caused by being thus suddenly introduced into this cold and uncongenial atmosphere, is never effaced by the subsequent charm of narrative and well-painted characters of the tale. One can have no more pleasure in being present at this compression and disfigurement than in witnessing the application of the boot. . . .[21]

Yet Dickens was more right than Sinnett allows. From Bentham's elimination of literature to James Mill's picture of the need to suppress erroneous fantasies about the dark to Ellis's and Combe's fear of too much literature and classical writing, one finds a consistent tradition that denigrates the eicastic imagination and privileges statistics and disembodied abstractions, occasionally applied to oversimplified putative real-world situations. The same fear of the religious imagination appears in Dickens's picture of the actual operation of two Birkbeck schools.

Many critics have discussed how Dickens targets Utilitarian education while privileging the fantasies of fairy tales and circuses as an alternative, and many have spoken of the I-it dehumanization implicit in Gradgrind's Utilitarian education. However, they have not demonstrated what Dickens's target is. Bentham and Mill cannot be the target, as I have mentioned, since they are long dead. The Lancastrian schools are in retreat by the 1850s. Sinnett's allegation still seems to stand: "If there are Gradgrind schools, they are not sufficiently numerous to be generally known."[22] Sinnett asks exactly the right question: satire is worthless if it has no real-world correlative at some level of mimesis. But Dickens's dystopian representation of the power relationships mythologized in *Hard Times* could not be *more* accurate. He writes about large capital in the figure of Bounderby, educational reformer and sponsor of schools in the figure of Gradgrind, "experimental" teacher in the figure of McChoakumchild, applied science and technology in the personified elephants and snakes of Coketown and the pits surrounding it, and labor—unorganized and organizing—in Stephen Blackpool and Slackbridge.[23] On the fringes of these central and symbiotic power relationships he places the declining "aristocracy" in the form of Mrs. Sparsit, Bounderby's housekeeper, and Mr. James Harthouse, Tom Gradgrind's friend. One finds the products of the new schools—the fink Bitzer, the cheat Tom Gradgrind, and the hollowed-out woman Louisa Gradgrind. And he locates what is left of allowed vital religious and empathic imagination in Sleary's circus.

In the world *outside* the novel, one finds an equivalent stand-in for large capital in Ellis and a hundred others, for the educational reformer and sponsor of schools in Combe or Simpson and their like, for the experimental teacher in W. M. Williams, for applied science and technology in the elephants and snakes of the reality of Preston and Manchester, and for labor—unorganized and organizing—in the labor union movement centered in the north. Finally, one finds the intellectual sources of the movement in the intellectual equivalents of Gradgrind's two allegorically named children, Adam Smith and Malthus. What is left of what is allowed of the religious and empathic imagination—"Sleary's Circus"—exists for Dickens's England in the romantic novel, the fairy tale, and in Carlylean or Wordsworthian mystical writing.

Hard Times is not only about characters or events. It mythologizes the central power relationships of the new utopian order—and then satirizes them. Bounderby, the capitalist, and Gradgrind, the hardware dealer turned Utilitarian, educational theorist, and reformer, are friends as Ellis and Combe were in real life. The friendship of Bounderby and Gradgrind is affirmed in a series of family and power structure relationships: Gradgrind's worthless son Tom goes to work for Bounderby, and his daughter Louisa marries Bounderby without sexual attraction or affection, but out of some vague desire to serve Tom in an incest of the imagination. When Gradgrind sees his children abandoning the Utilitarian, imageless world to watch Sleary's circus, both Gradgrind and Bounderby go out to impose discipline on the sources of the fun by finding the circus culprits. In chapter 2, Gradgrind, Bounderby's friend, visits McChoakumchild's classroom along with a government inspector of schools who reinforces the rote of the school. This trio tell us that together, the government, the educational reformers and their business allies, and the trained teachers control the model school agenda.[24] Gradgrind later confirms this account when he becomes a parliamentarian allied with the decadent Harthouse, also a parliamentarian. For the "irresponsible" Utilitarian parliamentarians, one could supposedly substitute Brougham, Russell, Ashburton, or a number of other parliamentary figures who were correspondents of Brougham and Ellis and active in the development of the national school policy in the period between the revolts of 1848 and the passage of the Education Act of 1870 (though the fictional equivalence is loose).

The notion of a conspiracy between the government's developing school policy favoring Utilitarian forms of education and the childchokers in the schools is reinforced by Dickens's calling up the Roman government's massacre of Bethlehem's innocents in the title of his second chapter, "Murdering the Innocents." Bethlehem's massacre emblemizes the choking of children in the McChoakumchild school. It foreshadows the ultimate emotional destruction of the only students given full discussion: Louisa, Tom Gradgrind, and in another way, Bitzer. The school's massacre, in its preparation of robotic ideologues and emotional/religious idiots, finds its external outcome in the massacre of the adult innocents, the workers of Coketown, so tellingly described by Stephen Blackpool.[25]

The coalition between capital, business, and school begins to come apart only when Louisa (née Gradgrind) Bounderby flees from her home, after having been spied upon with the decadent Harthouse in what looks like a love scene; the coalition ends when she tells her father that his school—his child-rearing Eden, the "land of milk and honey" that he believed himself to have created for her—was an endless Sinai wilderness. (Like Combe expounding on the limitations of the Golden Rule, he is interrupted in the process of proving that the Good Samaritan was a Bad Economist.) Gradgrind's wilderness exists both within Louisa and in the environmental desert that is Coketown: "How could you give me life, and take from me all the inappreciable things that raise it from the state of conscious death? Where are the graces of my soul? Where are the sentiments of my heart? What have you done, O father, what have you done, with the garden that should have bloomed once, in the great wilderness here?"[26]

Two chapters later, when Bounderby appears and demands that Louisa return to his house as his wife by twelve o'clock the next day, Gradgrind, chastened by this previous recognition scene with Louisa, resists. Part of his resistance turns on his perception that he may not have "been quite right in the manner of her education."[27] Thereupon, Bounderby abandons the Utilitarian myth of Baconian-Smithian competitive education and turns to the brute myth of the self-educated man, risen from being "tumbled out of doors, neck and crop, and put upon the shortest allowance of everything except blows." This brutal education he now deems education fit for a woman like Louisa.[28]

Ultimately, Bounderby's respect for the red-in-tooth-and-claw school of economic/educational thought gives way to a trust in his own red teeth and claws. But by this time, the power structure that has dominated the novel has disintegrated—not only the alliance between Bounderby-as-capitalist and Gradgrind-as-parliamentarian in determining Louisa's fate but also the alliance between Harthouse-as-parliamentarian and Tom Gradgrind that makes Stephen Blackpool the suspect in the robbery from Bounderby's bank. Stephen's plight suggests official complicity in his framing and official protection of elite crime. Bitzer allies himself with young Gradgrind on the basis of the myth that they have a common Smithian self-interest that is as good as compassion.[29] Finally, Thomas Gradgrind Jr. has to flee to Sleary's disreputable circus to escape from Bitzer's world of pure self-interest and from the law that protects only property. He goes to Sleary so that he can find a bit of empathy and can flee "many thousands of miles away."[30] What the collapse of the power structure at the center of the novel suggests is not that the workers will revolt to struggle loose from their chains (though Dickens presents them in a world where they have every reason to do so) but that the denial of nature itself will tear down the whole edifice of business-and-education designed to destroy both the inner heart and the outer green world.

The denial of nature means the denial of what children naturally know by being alive and caught up in the flow of events: the suppression of the basic human growth and development patterns that philosophers and psychologists from Plato to Comenius had recognized; the stunting of the human imagination and human needs for affection and fun; and finally the destruction of the light and air that feed the nonhuman organic world.

THE DENIAL OF WHAT CHILDREN NATURALLY KNOW

The "Murdering the Innocents" scene begins with Mr. Gradgrind asking Sissy Jupe, the daughter of a circus horse rider (in one of the public epiphanies of education so common to the Birkbeck method), what her father does. As part of the word and category mongering that, in real life, passed for education in these public displays, Gradgrind then relabels her father "a veterinary surgeon, a farrier, and a horsebreaker." He further asks a child who has spent her whole life with horses to define what a horse is. The child, in Dickens's phrase, is "thrown into the greatest alarm" by this question and then told: "Girl number twenty unable to define a horse." Though the class comes together in one of those group assemblies where the monitorial groups are dissolved in a general meeting, the monitorial practice of calling students by their numbers persists. Thomas Bitzer, the pet of the classroom, answers when Sissy cannot supply the expected rote definition: "Quadruped. Graminivorous. Forty teeth, namely twenty-four grinders, four eye-teeth, and twelve incisive. Sheds coat in the spring; in marshy countries, sheds hoofs, too. Hoofs hard, but requiring to be shod with iron. Age known by marks in mouth."[31]

The teaching of the kind of category parroting that Bitzer masters was held up to admiration in Birkbeck circles. For example, Mrs. Ellis writes as follows about a lesson given by a Mr. Shields at the Peckham Birkbeck School:

> As far as I can recall to mind, something like the following was the order of the lesson:
> Maize
> Shape Conical
> Colour, yellow—white etc.
> Qualities, vegetable—organic, foreign, opaque, hard, edible, wholesome, nutritious, farinaceous, valuable etc.
> Each quality he had fully explained—the vegetable, because grown in the ground, organic, having organs . . . [32]

Bitzer, who has a name instead of a number and may therefore be a monitor, has no horse sense beyond the memorized words that will please his masters. He no more knows horses than Gradgrind knows education, and all that Bitzer has learned is the kind of educated sycophancy that makes him a willing tool throughout the book; that is, the sycophancy that comes "naturally" in the numbering and sorting classroom, whether the Lancastrian or Birkbeck variety.

Gradgrind's and McChoakumchild's teaching process then continues with a James Mill–style objection to the childhood imaging of things in fictive realms: "Would you paper a room with representations of horses?"[33] Two domains that are crucial to the education process, according to Piagetian and post-Piagetian development psychology, disappear in Gradgrindian education: experience and imagination. All that is left is what poses as science; namely, the exercise of guessing at the authority figure's answers.

The denial of experience continues through the book, especially in the life of Louisa. Endless lectures and work with "cabinet" collections—shells, minerals, and all sorts of specimens given their proper taxonomical names—render the little Gradgrinds incapable of seeing a face in the moon or hearing of the cow that jumped over the moon or entertaining any other fantasy. When Louisa, beginning puberty, gazes into the fire and wonders about her future, combining her experience of the fire with a visionary picture of the future, her mother chastises her for wandering from the straight and narrow laid out for her by lectures and experiments.[34] When, in the scene already cited, she tells her father that he has taken all life out of her, she is speaking not only of the expression of her sexuality and of her forced marriage but also of the denial of all of the holistic experience that must be prior to any mental organizational or categorizing efforts: the denial of the whole world of fairy, fantasy, and romance and of the spiritual conditions that make it possible to find meaning in experience. At the end it is not accidental that Louisa finds her alter ego in a Harthouse, whose cynicism has rendered all experience meaningless.[35]

DENIAL OF BASIC HUMAN DEVELOPMENT PATTERNS

The education that Gradgrind and McChoakumchild offer ignores the development of Louisa's sexuality and affectional needs and, presumably, those of all the other students in the school. In the early part of the novel Louisa is fifteen or sixteen, and she is not much older when her father and brother place her as an offering on the altar of Hard Facts, as a propitiation to the Bounderby she despises.[36] Her father is aware that she is moving from girlhood to womanhood and, in his quest for quantification and commodification, gives no hint that he recognizes her capacity for sexual or affectional choice (the kinds of desires expressed in Louisa's diatribe). But the denial of Louisa's developmental self, or its suppression, is not unique.

On a less developed scale, McChoakumchild's school chokes precisely because it recognizes none of the need for fantasy and fun in the intellectual and affectional development of its children and adolescents. It does to all of its children what Gradgrind does to his daughter. Almost the first words from Gradgrind, the Utilitarian, are: "In this life, we want nothing but Facts, sir; nothing but Facts!"[37] In contrast, Dickens's fiction argues that what we *want*, what we desire, and what we need, as children and adolescents, is almost everything else. It fictionalizes the notions that a child, encountering a world "out there" and learning what needs to be learned, is an organism capable of differing levels of cognition and analysis as he or she develops an ability to go beyond the authoritarian, competitive game of searching for the authority figure's "right answers." This natural developmental pattern is entirely lost on Gradgrind, on McChoakumchild, *and* on Bounderby. For them, children and workers are empty vessels waiting to be filled with correct ideas and correct work behaviors as measured by their masters. Indeed, Dickens's first satiric mention of the metaphor of the vessel and the liquid filling it as standing for the student and the education of that student with "facts" ("the inclined plane of little vessels then and there arranged in order, ready to have imperial gallons of facts poured into them until they were full to the brim") reflects a metaphoric understanding of education as old as Quintilian and as recent as the Utilitarians.[38] But it is a metaphor for an education that altogether ignores the capacity of individuals to learn and develop by themselves or with the assistance of a community of seekers that goes beyond the teacher, government, or business.

As part of its denial of developmental patterns, the Gradgrind school of education, following James Mill's prescriptions against fantasy, does not ask of students that they take responsibility for their lives or undertake responsible work tasks. Predictably, Tom Gradgrind emerges from the school capable only of sycophancy and of guessing at the "right" answers. Equally predictably, Bitzer's trained sycophancy, when out of power, gives way to the gospel of self-interest, as he turns on Tom Gradgrind when the possibility of power appears.[39] The denial of concern for children and their developmental reality appears in Coketown's repetitive severing of parent and child—a severing that occurs from the circus household of the Jupes to the elite households of Gradgrinds and Bounderbys. This denial of familial affection founds the twisted relationship, amounting to a sort of imaginative incest, that Tom and Louisa Gradgrind develop, and it allows for the continuation of these warped patterns into other sectors of Coketown's life: Bounderby's refusal to accept Stephen Blackpool's separation from his drunken wife; Bounderby's refusal to accept his wife's rejection of him and his failure to allow her to return to him except on his terms; Sparsit's pandering to Bounderby's need for an "aristocratic" maid and her concomitant private hatred of him; and the workers' hatred of management and cowering acceptance of their oppression.

The education provided at Gradgrind's establishment and the modes of being in Coketown mirror and are symbiotic with each other. Both deny any natural developmental patterns. There is no green and pleasant land within Coketown's souls or in the landscape. As the managers, made competitive by Bounderby's pressures and his espionage, recreate themselves and their children in a robotic mode, the workers are forcibly rendered mechanical in Coketown. Kept from expressing their common interest effectively, they live almost identical mechanical, routinized lives in look-alike surroundings. Coketown *is* their education, even though many of them cannot read.[40] As Stephen Blackpool says, "Look how we live, an' wheer we live, an' in what numbers, an' by what chances, and wi' what sameness; and look how the mills is alwus a goin', and how they never works us no nigher to onny dis'ant object."[41] Stephen knows what the real education provided by this social system is and that no utopia lies around the corner.

Dickens makes explicit the metaphoric similarity between the competition and standardization forced in the educational establishment and that forced in Coketown:

All the public inscriptions in the town were painted alike, in severe characters of black and white. The jail might have been the infirmary, the infirmary might have been the jail, the town hall might have been either, or both, or anything else, for anything that appeared to the contrary in the graces of their construction. Fact, fact, fact, everywhere in the material aspect of the town; fact, fact, fact, everywhere in the immaterial. The M'Choakumchild school was all fact, and the school of design was all fact, and the relations between master and man were all fact, and everything was fact between the lying-in hospital and the cemetery, and what you couldn't state in figures, or show to be purchaseable in the cheapest market and saleable in the dearest, *was not, and never should be, world without end, Amen* (emphasis mine).[42]

Dickens undoes Coketown's standardized, materialist construction of the material and immaterial with his blasphemous version of the conclusion of the liturgical postcommunion canticle.

THE DENIAL OF THE IMAGINATION'S ROLE IN CREATING THE SOCIAL SENSE

The imagination denied becomes the perverse imagination. The children in the Gradgrind school and household cannot, on "factarian" grounds, construct fictions. On factarian grounds, power dictates that rooms cannot be papered with horses or carpeted with flowers, nursery rhymes and astronomical myths cannot be told, no "idle storybook" can come into the house, and the fairy tale, romance, and world of the circus must be marginalized.[43] All of those who have associated with the circus, including the child Sissy Jupe, are suspect.

But the denial of traditional childhood fantasy and the kinds of stories and poems that Bruno Bettelheim credits with giving us sanity and placement in the human group does not altogether displace fantasy.[44] The allegorized, normative myths and epics that we call fairy tales, the stories about the functioning of the social group and of role that Swift and Pope built into their cauterizing satiric critiques of the social, have disappeared from Coketown's conscious education. However, egocentric and solipsistic fantasy projects its own forbidden fairy-tale world onto the weirdness of Coketown. Bounderby's whole life myth is a perversion of the story of the young man who went into the world to seek his fortune: a man who created himself from the detritus of an abandoning mother, a drunken grandmother, a chandler's shop home, an egg-box room, and a vagabond childhood that became the prodigal's sty: "I hadn't a shoe to my foot. As to a stocking, I didn't know such a thing by name. I passed the day in a ditch and the night in a pigsty. That's the way I spent my tenth birthday. Not that the ditch was new to me, for I was born in a ditch."[45] But, in the "real" world of the fiction, the mother is not the rejecting stepmother of fairy tale so much as the son is the reverse-prodigal who has decided to sequester the parent to protect his public fantasy that he has overcome the prodigal's sty. The liberal legend of the self-made man becomes a reversal of the biblical legend of coming home to regeneration.

The other Coketowners also have their upside-down perverse fairy tales. Louisa lives by the unexpressed—probably sexual—fantasies that she sees in the fire. Stephen Blackpool's fantasy of liberation from his wife is almost equally subjective in the social world in which he lives, as is his sight of Rachel as his star when he lies at the bottom of the mine pit.[46] There is Gradgrind's myth that what he and McChoakumchild are providing to the children at the school is fact, by which he means definitional as opposed to experienced reality. Paired with this fantasy is his and Bounderby's imagining of the world of labor:

> [To these two, the laborers] were a bad lot altogether, gentlemen; that do what you would for them they were never thankful for it, gentlemen; that they were restless, gentlemen; that they never knew what they wanted; that they lived upon the best, and bought fresh butter; and insisted on Mocha coffee, and rejected all but prime parts of meat, and yet were eternally dissatisfied and unmanageable. In short, it was the moral of the old nursery fable:
>
> There was an old woman, and what do you think?
> She lived upon nothing but victuals and drink;
> Victuals and drink were the whole of her diet,
> And yet this old woman would NEVER be quiet.[47]

Ultimately the myth of the worker palaces is also captured in a misapplied nursery rhyme. McChoakumchild cannot run his schoolroom without using the fiction of the schoolroom as a nation and the starvation of twenty-five as a minimization of pain to provide the greatest good for the greatest number.[48]

The little myths that keep childhood going have been exiled—only to return surreptitiously and in twisted forms that dominate adult life. The grand social mythos has failed. Religion has failed in Coketown, as it has disappeared from Ellis's school; it has fled as the denominations fight over the workers and give the laborers nothing but teetotaling, statistics, and the superstructural myths of the establishment.[49] There is no story that can create the sense of decency, justice, and community there any more. Most of all, the utopian myth itself has failed.

THE THWARTING OF THE NONHUMAN NATURAL WORLD

The effort to shape human nature to force it to express only competitive self-interest and a positivistic sense of *what is* ultimately results in a transformation of the natural world. *Hard Times* presents a natural world metamorphosed into an inferno by the forces of Bounderby and Gradgrind. There is, of course, the hideousness of the monotonous mill-town urban environment. There is the irony that the town from which all spontaneity and fun have been driven, every vestige of "savagery" has been exiled, has itself become an image of European fear of the savage:

> [Coketown] was a town of red brick, or of brick that would have been red if the smoke and ashes had allowed it; but as matters stood it was a town of unnatural red and black like the painted face of a savage. It was a town of machinery and tall chimneys, out of which interminable serpents of smoke trailed themselves for ever and ever, and never got uncoiled. It had a black canal in it, and a river that ran purple with ill-smelling dye, and vast piles of buildings full of windows where there was a rattling and a trembling all day long, and where the piston of the steam-engine worked monotonously up and down like the head of an elephant in a state of melancholy madness. It contained several large streets all very like one another, and many small streets still more like one another, inhabited by people equally like one another, who all went in and out at the same hours, with the same sound upon the same pavements, to do the

same work, and to whom every day was the same as yesterday and tomorrow, and every year the counterpart of the last and the next.[50]

Dickens's this-world-created Dis answers, consciously or unconsciously, Smith's fiction of the rich man with the field who imagines he can consume it all but who, in his vanity, produces food for many. In Dickens, the vanities of the rich do indeed create the horrors of the poor; witness the comforts and elegancies of life being made in Coketown for the fine ladies "who could scarcely bear to hear the place mentioned."[51]

Later in the novel, Dickens returns to the zoo images of the serpents and the mad elephants to talk of the insanity of the noise and smoke that is the city, but he also describes the grotesquery of the city as a group of fairy palaces surrounded by the dragons or monstrous serpents of the smoke. He then turns the whole materialistic paradise into an ash heap that would have made F. Scott Fitzgerald proud: "The Smoke-serpents, submissive to the curse of all that tribe, trailed themselves upon the earth. In the waste-yard outside, the steam from the escape pipe, the litter of barrels and old iron, the shining heaps of coals, the ashes everywhere, were shrouded in a veil of mist and rain."[52] The steam-engine smoke covers everything with an uncreating smog that reduces the city to a primordial chaos where light dies: "a dense formless jumble, with sheets of cross light in it, that showed nothing but masses of darkness—."[53] As Bounderby avers that the smoke is "the healthiest thing in the world in all respects, and particularly for the lungs," Dickens lays the responsibility for the creation of hell directly at the door of the mill-owning classes who complain of their own ruin when they are "required" to send the laborers' children to school, when their factories are inspected for safety, when they are asked to reduce smoke pollution, when they see a vision of the golden-spoon-in-mouth laborers, or when they face control by the collective social body: "Whenever [the owner] was not left entirely alone, and it was proposed to hold him accountable for the consequences of any of his acts—he was sure to come out with the awful menace that he would sooner pitch his property into the Atlantic.'"[54] The solipsism and egocentrism of the owner class creates the massive violation of nature that is Gradgrind's school and Bounderby's Coketown, a violation that extends to the countryside, where the mines replace the mills, "mounds where the grass was rank and high, and where brambels, dock-weed, and such-like vegetation, were confusedly heaped together," where Stephen Blackpool falls to his eventual death because the lawmakers, influenced by the owners, do not require that the unused pits be closed and fenced in.[55] The massacre of innocents in the school is mirrored itself in the murder of the green world of innocence inside the children and in the environment of Coketown.

Conclusion

WE HAVE EXAMINED utopias suggesting that education rather than the radical social reorganization of adult life can save us, beginning with Shakespeare's culturally conservative *Tempest,* moving to Bacon's radically different *New Atlantis,* and then going on to a series of derived visions of an ideal that issues in educational institutions rehearsing a supposedly better future. We have ended with the little rooms of the Birkbeck schools that look to a more parsimonious, industrious, and hygienic life for industrial workers but also to an increment in their productivity and willingness to accept routine. We began this examination with two questions: *Whence came my World War II superhero's sense that I could learn to master the material universe and, incurring no negative consequences, defeat suffering and evil? Whence came my first grade teacher's related notion of competitive numbering and ranking as basic to learning in the compulsory school?* These questions would be trivial but for the fact that millions of children have had similar experiences across the last century and a quarter.

SCIENCE, TECHNOLOGY, AND DESIRE

To begin with the first question: I have argued that Western culture's effort to achieve a mastery of the physical universe through research and education begins with Bacon and the Commonwealth Baconians and their Solomon's House–style research centers and schools. This millennial effort begins to have implications for children's sociology of knowledge when Comenius invents a Baconian and Protestant educational theory and writes textbooks. The theory is continued and the textbooks are used by the followers of Comenian pedagogy in the dissenting academies. Comenius and his group in England and on the

Conclusion

Continent showed that most people could be reached by reading, writing, and science if proper pedagogy were employed. Bacon's hoped-for research institution becomes reality with the founding of the Royal Society.

Utopian literature, beyond its satiric work, performs planning functions. It invites copycat societies and knowledge-creating social institutions. The remarks by the creators of the new educational and research institutions attributing those institutions to previous fictions make clear that they owe their designs to previous narrative. Their scientific/educational utopias, extending from Bacon to Combe and Ellis, represent a planning process that manufactures hope—often false hope. (Plato was right in arguing that "poets"—that is, the writers of fictions—are dangerous.) Since the utopian fiction comes out of the lying Homeric epic against which Plato warned us, we should be on guard against such fictions, including his own *Republic*. In journeying from Bacon to Bacon's nineteenth-century students such as Bentham or Combe, we have allowed utopian fictions about what new knowledge and related social organizations for the production of knowledge can do for us to bewilder our capacity to project the costs of our trip. This is what Mannheim says utopian imaginings can do. In the case of our study, literary fictions, visions, and eidola (Bacon's idols) have encouraged us to make radically new social and natural arrangements without a cost analysis. We know from studies of how human imaginings anticipate and plan future actions that how we imagine the world affects what we do as individuals; we recognize this from accounts of copycat crimes based on books, films, or other crimes; from studies of the effects of pornography and of children's play as rehearsal; and from examinations of the psychology of planning.[1] We are also beginning to recognize how fiction anticipates social change from investigations of the functions of "superstructures" in the making of infrastructural arrangements.[2] Utopian fictions, whether "intended" to inspire new societies or not, are among the most powerful incentives to infrastructural change.

As the Baconian tradition develops from Bacon to Comenius and the dissenting academies, then to Bentham, Mill, and Lancaster, then to Combe, Ellis, and Eliot, and finally to Lowe and the government bureaucracy, fictive utopias crystallize out institutions in forms that metamorphose the fictions, sometimes only slightly. Fictions become plans, pilot institutions, legislative proposals, and eventually mandated institutions supported by the power of the state: the Royal Society and some of the Commonwealth research communities precipitate out of the substances of Bacon's *New Atlantis*; Comenius and the Commonwealth educational utopias precipitate the dissenting academies; from Smith, Mill, Bentham, and Lancaster come the first generation monitorial Utilitarian schools and more advanced Utilitarian schools; the largely unpublished visions of Combe, Ellis, Mann, and their associates give rise to the second generation schools. The stages in this succession do not seem to me to depend on each other as Mannheim proposes, as thesis, antithesis, and synthesis, but as a succession of trials, errors, and new trials, partially but never wholly integrated to the dominant economic system, though anticipating it in part. The fictions change as Western culture moves from the classical and Renaissance heroic poem to the Enlightenment novel to the Utilitarian's concrete plans and pilot schools.[3] As the movement to discard limits on natural intervention progresses but fails to deliver the promised land in Coketown, it identifies scapegoats for failure: in the earlier stages, the state does not give enough support, then the psychology and economics appear to be imperfect or the schools are poor and disorganized, and then the teachers are untrained. In the second generation Utilitarian stage, "scientific phrenology" provides the escape: that education is impossible "when the bumps are wrong." This and related forms of analysis based on the notions that educability is almost entirely a inherited property, though slightly modifiable by education, then generate various forms of rationalizing IQ and or other ability tests.[4] Since Combe, English-speaking culture has "measured" human beings "scientifically" on unscientific scales. The measuring, changed to accommodate its critics in each generation and basic to the conception of meritocratic fairness, has few serious questioners in the educational/political establishments that have determined how education is to be funded and that still do so. This remains the case even though contemporary biology, unlike phrenology, appears to tell us that each species is stronger if it contains a multitude of individuals possessing a range of differentiated skills. The defect in the rhetoric of "the failure of education" seldom locates the failure in the Faustian project itself—the march in the wrong direction of the project for the enlarging of human empire itself.

Part of what my fellow students and I rehearsed with our superhero comics was uniquely the product of the climate of opinion that developed in World War II and the faith of the time that whoever mastered the technology needed for a superior war machine would win out as good over evil. Later President Truman told the world that God had given the Allies nuclear weapons. But there was a long history of faith in scientific empowerment leading up to this phase. One explanation of it comes from the Laguna novelist Leslie Silko, who has a Navajo medicine man, Betonie, arguing that Western culture was long ago taken over by a kind of witchcraft, summarized in one fictive witch's chant about white people:

> Then they grow away from the earth
> then they grow away from the sun
> then they grow away from the plants and animals
> They see no life
> When they look
> they see only objects.
> The world is a dead thing for them
> the trees and rivers are not alive
> the mountain and stones are not alive.
> The deer and bear are objects
> they see no life.[5]

The witchly growing-away from the earth culminates in the nuclear destruction and attendant genetic deformations that Silko's hero sees implied by Los Alamos.

Demonizing another religion, Lynn White argues that the Genesis command to be fruitful, multiply, replenish the earth, and subdue it gave Christian or nominally Christian cultures the license to impose a man-made regimen on the natural world without regard to the effects of that regimen, an argument that has become a cliché in the analysis of environmental ideology.[6]

Such explanations as Silko's and White's push the beginnings of the environmental crisis to the prehistorical mists where we have no handle on productive analysis or change. Betonie's witchcraft comes into existence in a never-never time and a fictive place, and the command on which White fixes exists from the time of the composition of Genesis, millennia before the industrial revolution. But cultural assumptions do not exist until they are *expressed* and *acted* upon. They cannot be altered until their expression is challenged and acted against. This is not to say that *New Atlantis* created the movement described here by itself. As we have indicated, Western Europe's importation of gunpowder, of certain mining and water-powered cloth-manufacturing equipment, its bringing in of new food plants from the Western Hemisphere, and its rediscovery of the claims of white magic to alter the world prepared the way for Bacon's catalytic fiction. And that fiction found support in the weariness with seventeenth-century butchering religious wars, fought over propositions beyond verification. A widespread millennialism gave the Baconian vision credibility.

But the vision of a scientific community producing new knowledge and applying it for the purpose of enlarging human empire and satisfying human desire had to be created and take hold before much could happen on the road "to the enlarging of human empire." It took hold in the seventeenth and eighteenth centuries. The founding of Baconian institutions at the schooling and research levels had to happen before my comic books could tell me that I, the superhero, could remake the world to fit my desire. My science classes and *My Weekly Reader* had to support the same basic idea, if in less lavish form. As noted in the introduction, I would not always have had such an education. The one fundamental literary journey that modeled education and enterprise for elites in earlier centuries, the epic, essentially celebrated limits. Tragedy, too, modeled the idea of limits. We cannot have our desire as individuals and can only have it partially as social groups, these genres say. Previous versions of Western culture knew this insight from the letter of the epic and tragic texts and from medieval and Renaissance commentaries on them. The hero in the *Iliad* comes home to the desolation of a world lost to him in his predicted death, lost to his dead friend Patroclus, a world also desolated for his enemies—in the form of the Priam at his knee begging for the body of the lost Hector. The hero in the *Odyssey* explores the limits of a phantasmagorical world to come home to his old wife and the problem of ordering his household. That is why Swift uses the *Odyssey* as his primary intertext when he attacks a mistaken empiricism and a mistaken race to learn everything aside from wisdom and gives us a hero who cannot finally manage his own household. The hero of the *Aeneid* may make a new empire, but that empire is only Troy revisited, and we know that tears are at the center of things. While the allegorical versions of the epics developed in the Middle Ages and the Renaissance present the journey to the new home or the old one as a journey to Wisdom or God, their reaching for an infinite goal suggests no transformation of the finite or temporal. Even *The Tempest* and the Scribleran metaphors for the journey suggest that changes in the environment and in human social arrangements cannot go very far before they become madness. Fielding's epic novelistic quests in *Joseph Andrews* and *Tom Jones* celebrate only the household. In them, what we can do to make a decent life does not involve rearranging the world; rather it is a matter of persuading "our selves to become [the] temperate, just, loving and modest innocent mankind" that Henry More saw as the alternative to Luciferian questing. The ancient epics and More's *Utopia* tell us that we must limit desire and destroy our *amor habendi*, and Shakespeare seems to be saying the same thing for all of Prospero's subjects, though not for Prospero. The only reason that Prospero can possess his desire is that he is the monarchic mask of God, the representative of legitimacy and the source of all social cohesion. Even he cannot alter the natural world permanently.

Though the first proposals for schools wholly or very heavily dedicated to science and technology in their subject matter came from the

Conclusion

English Utilitarians and their allies, the appearance of such schools in Britain as a part of the assumed compulsory system occurred gradually after the passage of the 1870 Education Act. Of course, the emphasis of the new working-class schools on arithmetic from the beginning gave a base for the development of skills in science and technology in factory and workshop. But for formal science and technology to become a *de cursu* part of the schools, Hazelwood, University College in London, and the Birkbeck schools had to prove them to be "practical" work for the children who would be the next generation in the factories. They had to show that working-class children could not only learn to read, write, and cipher but that they could employ scientific technology and do routine industrial tasks. The number of science and technology students was to grow radically in the 1850s and 1860s, the Science and Art Department introduced grants for secondary school science and technology in 1872, and Parliament legislated to encourage school science and technology from 1872 until the beginning of the twentieth century.[7] The serpents of environmental destruction wrapping millions in their coils, the syndromes that Leslie Silko and Lynn White visualize, did not emerge in the hinterlands of time but in an industrializing England and northeastern United States between the beginning of the sixteenth century and the third quarter of the nineteenth. The new schools for the new worlds were made brick by brick, and they taught us how to change the world by applied natural manipulation after manipulation, industry by industry.

The enlargement of human empire accomplished through the marriage of technology-based industry and rote-and-technology schools had an impact related to that of the other kind of empire, colonial empire, in stripping the earth. The former permitted the routinizing of labor in exploiting the natural environment; the latter found new environments to exploit. To create a growth system that envisages few limits, children have to be turned over to the state and taught the routines that serve industry and business, and nature has to be opened to a radical human domination without a serious calculation of the possible long-term costs. I came to imagine myself as Superman reclaiming the world from evil with my technological prowess, not alone because my comic book offered me such imaginings but because my local culture and Euro-American culture at large endorsed those imaginings as central to the scientific/industrial project.

The utopian push toward a radical manipulation of the natural world, beyond that customary with agriculturalists or pastoral-nomadic and hunter-gatherer people in medieval Europe and in most other sections of the world until the triumph of colonialism, was itself powerfully questioned, when questioning could have counted, by the most powerful writers of the times—in the eighteenth century by the Scriblerans and in the nineteenth century by Dickens. Their response to utopianism is direct dystopian critique. The same alteration of the natural world was demythologized by the Romantic poets in England and the New England Romantics in the United States and by late nineteenth- and early twentieth-century persons acquainted with the ways of using the land and resources traditional with non-Western small group societies—individuals such as Black Elk, Chief Seattle, and Smohalla. But these critiques did not give rise to practical proposals as to how human beings were to live without the tools that the Utilitarians were espousing. They were never empowered by the business-based political and monetary power and the lobbying networks that the Utilitarians could command. Indeed, one could argue that such persons as Dickens or the Scriblerans were irresponsible or naive, that they did not effectively assume the burden of their insight, as the Utilitarians did, by making things happen politically in education and research. However, *effective* alternative organizing may be too much to ask of them. The individual or social interests to which the literary dissidents appealed were not mobilized by clear and universal evidences of the worldwide environmental consequences of industrialism and capitalism run amuck. There were some evidences. Increasing levels of pollution and increasingly unhealthy pollution were observed from the Renaissance onward.[8] Many critics, from More on, lamented the enclosures and the creation of rootless vagabond populations and urban "rabble," as Marx later labeled them. The market economists and Utilitarians themselves feared population growth, especially after Malthus. The environmental prices that the new science and technology were exacting were evident from the time of Swift and Pope. The human costs, not so evident as the industrial transformation that Adam Smith saw as leading to working-class luxury, became the hell of the industrial revolution seen by the second generation Utilitarians, who tried to help workers individually through schools, and the novelists from Mrs. Gaskell through Dickens and George Eliot, who began a systemic analyses of sorts, though they launched it from the perspective of the fear of worker revolt.[9] The problems that we see today, however, project the problems of earlier days on a global canvas: ozone depletion, massive species reduction, global warming, the desertification of vast areas of semiarid land, and the killing of important rivers and lakes. Meanwhile, developing countries endeavoring to industrialize, feed their people, and provide for other necessities have many of the same problems with interrogating the capitalistic/industrial dream now, especially in the educational arena, that Europe and the United States had in the seventeenth to nineteenth centuries.

The educational utopianism of the Gradgrinds and Bounderbys was part of what made us deny the human and environmental costs, in Dickens's view, and I argue in this book that he is right. The construction of hope led to hopelessness. For those who had faith in the capitalistic industrial system, such as William Ellis, the answer to every industrial problem was to educate the workers to be less improvident, to improve their hygiene, to teach them to drink less, and to make them understand the virtues of market capitalism. Without agreeing with his analysis, one can appreciate the nobility of Ellis's sentiment and the heroic sacrifice that allowed him to create schools for the workers, at great personal expense and after his health was broken. For the opponents such as Dickens, the answer was to provide some difference that might mean hope. As we saw Stephen Blackpool remark in the preceding chapter, "Look how the mills is alwus a goin', and how they never works us no nigher to onny dis'ant object." And as we also saw, later in *Hard Times* Dickens notes the sameness all over Coketown, the emphasis on "fact, fact, fact," and that whatever "you couldn't state in figures, or show to be purchasable in the cheapest market and saleable in the dearest, was not, and never should be."

No one pursued Dickens's description into effective political organizing. That is not accidental. The "onny dis'ant object," the utopian in Mannheim's term, precludes analyses and does not admit data that contradicts the dream, particularly in the case of the power-and-knowledge groups whom the dream serves. The Utilitarian educational party does not develop an analysis that looks seriously at how what is being done to the environment can be reversed or how education can serve such a reversal. For a "scientific" group, it is remarkably dismissive of any position that contradicts its own or interferes with the institutions it is trying to build. On the other side, the anger of the antagonists turns to satire or escape without much analysis or organizing. The antagonists of Gradgrind's and Bounderby's brave new world tend to turn to such values as sympathy or the preference for wilderness country, presented in panentheistic or idyllic terms, over the town or preference of "fancy" over "cold reason." At no point does their analysis go to what the industrial system must do if it is not to destroy the natural system. Nowhere does it ask what the schooling system must do if students are to appear who have that sense of stewardship for the natural world and the human place in it, who have that interactive as opposed to dominative stance toward one another and toward nature, that might reverse the utopian nightmare. No William Lovetts appear among the dystopians. The very facts of school mean that the child does not learn to watch the time and the place. Beyond the school, there is the pollution and artificial environment of the city and the playground separating the school from the rest of the community; inside the school walls are the teachers, as representative of the message to be learned, and the intensity of the drill process, which precludes attention to anything else. Utopia does here what Mannheim argues that utopianism in general does. It suppresses information. That is how I came to be Superman.

Conclusion

My other question involved the derivation of my first grade teacher's organization of my class into a competitively ranked and numbered group. And my answer here is that the production of a competitive student body—all students measured and ranked on the same tasks— did not come from the progenitors of the first dream, Bacon and Comenius, who generally conceptualized the ideal social group in the terms provided by mercantile capitalism with its guilds and coopera- tive associations, or in the terms provided by the equally cooperative work habits of the open field system. Bacon and Comenius and their Commonwealth associates look to a cooperative Solomon's House that is a sort of guild for the discovery of knowledge. They look to the twelve-grade Pansophic school, which has a similar organization, though Comenius, like the continental Protestants, had begun to cre- ate the breakup of Breughel's marketplace community by visualizing a children's social organization divided by age grading. They look to the extended family. However, so far as I can discern, individualism and competition are not yet a prime factor for Comenius and the Commonwealth educators. The joining of a universal education and transformative science to a transformative economic system, the Smithian market one, that is becoming increasingly individualistic, even solipsistic, does not begin in earnest until *after* Smith, with the Utilitarians. The interesting transitional figure in the breakup of the sense of community and the privileging of the individual is Adam Smith, who proposes a market system for almost everything but uni- versal public schools. As the first influential British proponent of uni- versal compulsory education, he argues for an education partially funded by the public to teach working people the basic skills, *plus how the body politic functions and what it does*. The purpose of Smith's pro- posed school is to counteract the stupidity produced by the division of labor and to produce an intellectual common.

But in the next generation, the first and second generation Utili- tarians who are largely Smith's apostles (i.e., Jeremy Bentham, James

Conclusion

Mill, Lord Brougham, Joseph Lancaster, J. C. Roebuck, William Ellis, and George Combe) drop Smith's holistic social goals for schools in their utopian educational proposals and implementations. For them, the crucial tasks are the basics and science and technology. The whole game of learning is to be an uncritical rote competition to please authority figures, a competition emulating the market system in manufacturing and marketing. The new schooling, though it was to encompass all members of society, was not supposed to have an adaptive function in relating the species to the environment or in creating the bonds of human community because adaptation and community were not deemed necessary. Modeled partly on the Panoptical prison and partly on the Empire's Indian monitorial schools, the British and Foreign School Society schools and the more advanced Hazelwood and Birkbeck schools bear the promise of social transformation toward solipsism and competition and of natural transformation toward the enlarging of human empire. Working in the rote mode of the monitorial schools but also in other modes, the Birkbeck schools taught reading, writing, arithmetic, science, and market economics as working-class tools—putatively to give everyone an equal shake but actually as indoctrination. The monitorial students from this tradition of schooling, with their signs from 1 to 10 about their necks indicating where they rank in the meritocracy of reading, writing, spelling, and numbers, are the predecessors of my reading, arithmetic, and spelling groups and of the capitalistic/industrial meritocracy.

One may question how the system got to me from the London Mechanics Institute or Mr. Williams's school in Edinburgh. The monitorial system had supposedly been replaced by the pupil-teacher system after the parliamentary report of 1846, but there is evidence that it continued long after 1846 both in Britain and the United States. The pupil-teacher and the monitorial systems differed little in pedagogical technique.[10] Indeed, long after the monitorial system was supposedly replaced by the pupil-teacher system, Kay-Shuttleworth writes about it as identical with the pupil-teacher system in pedagogy in 1861, in connection with a discussion opposing payment by results as a mode of salarying teachers: "[Robert Lowe's design can] be briefly described as an attempt to reduce the cost of education of the poor, by conducting it by a machinery—half trained and at less charge;—to entrust it to a lower class of ill-paid teachers, and generally to young monitors as assistants;—to neglect the force of a higher moral and religious agency in the civilisation of the people—and to define natural education as a drill in mechanical skill in reading, writing and arithmetic."[11]

The next step, after the eventual triumph of a national system of schooling had become only a matter of time, was to integrate the whole system as a competitive one, to make the teachers engage in a race as unrelenting as that of the students and monitors. This was done through a payment-by-results system, still being used in changed form in some schools across the world, paying teachers for the outcomes that they wrung from their students in reading, writing, and arithmetic and extending the race to all teachers and schools in the British national system. As early as 1862—after the Newcastle Commission report of 1861 was done, Lowe proposed the Revised Code providing for payment of teachers by results. Though the system predated the Forster Act of 1870 creating a national schooling policy, it continued for almost thirty years after 1870. Robert Lowe, a Utilitarian and correspondent of Combe, cut from the same cloth as Ellis and the first generation Utilitarians, was the head of the national government's Education Department and oversaw the payment-by-results scheme of pupil and teacher testing.[12] Unlike Ellis and Combe, he controlled both the public purse and national policy; the Newcastle Report gave him the power to extend the Utilitarian rote-and-meritocracy scheme to teachers and inspectors of schools. As Brendan A. Rapple has shown, the net effect of payment by results was a narrowing of education to those areas where results counted in the payment of the teacher: (1) the climate of the school; (2) the capacity of the teacher; (3) pupil attendance, calculated without reference to illness or other impediments; and (4) student results in reading, writing, and arithmetic. Results in the last three areas, especially the last, quickly appear to have become the central concern, as teachers sought to secure a decent salary.[13] As the system made the students and monitors into competitive producers of rote answers, it made the teachers themselves into the masters of such production beause their salaries depended on the "results"; the system, as the Duke of Marlborough observed, served to introduce "a mercantile spirit" into the art of classroom teaching.[14] The schools that emerge from the 1870 Forster Act are not precisely the Bentham-Mill-Lancaster or the Combe-Ellis schools. Some of them do make an effort to teach geography, grammar, and history, and few seem to have taught Ellis's favorite, political economy, possibly because the behavior system of the payment-by-results school enacted most of competitive ethos the liberal reformers wanted taught. Still, Ellis was disappointed.[15] But the new schools reflect the ethos of the Utilitarian systems. Since similar systems were installed in the United States at first by Horace Mann and later by other American educators, and (absent the payment-by-results system in most schools) they became part of the standard toolkit for teachers, including the toolkit for northern Wisconsin, we have the answer to our question about the source of my first grade teacher's vision positing competition as the essential form of learning in compulsory schools.

The competitive ethos empowered the payment-by-results notion that education depends on constant expert testing—at first by the phrenologists, then by the inspectors of schools, and then by intelligence, aptitude, achievement, and assessment testers. Such persons and their instruments could referee the competition. With testing also came the phrenologists' supposedly scientific theory of the limited educability of non-European people, reinvented by "scientists" in each generation. Limited educability defined by race or head shape implied the need to give compensatory education to make children over as Eliot's Latimer is supposedly made over. And with the routinizing and compulsion came a denial of intellectual authority to teachers and of the inner will to learn in children.

As the push for the enlargement of human empire evoked dystopian responses, so did the cult of emulation and phrenology in education—in details from George Eliot and massively from Dickens.

Conclusion

When the system was fully installed as a state-compelled system, quite a few of the critics of payment by results on standardized measures called attention to the narrowing of the curriculum that this implied and to the lifelessness of classrooms where everything consisted in drill.[16] They also objected to the removal from the curriculum of religious instruction: that is, not just catechetical instruction, which was given outside the school, but alternative imaginings of the world. The inspectors were given a mechanical inspection protocol as to what and how they were to inspect and over what and in what way they were to examine the pupils in writing, arithmetic, and reading. The inspector's routine could have served equally well for factory or military inspectors, and some of them attacked the new regimen's spiritual emptiness.[17] A religiously unorthodox Matthew Arnold, protesting the system as one of its inspectors, spoke of it as forcing inspectors, in words he quotes from Kay-Shuttleworth, "necessarily [to] withdraw their attention from the religious and general instruction, and from the moral features of the school" so that, in his own words "the whole discipline is out of order, and needs instant reformation." When Arnold wrote this, he undoubtedly meant something other than dogma, something like what Dickens described when he noticed the absence of religious and imaginative instruction in Ellis's Birkbeck schools. For Arnold, the whole "movement is a false one," going in the wrong direction. He argues that when one knows the whole system assumes wrong premises, to ask whether it is *effective* is equivalent to asking whether an army is marching at a good pace when it strides in the wrong direction.[18] *Culture and Anarchy*, Arnold's general attack on the failure of British culture to move like Swift's bee toward "sweetness and light," focuses with special vigor on Robert Lowe and on Roebuck as reform leaders: praising people for their material accomplishments "is just the very style of laudation with which Mr. Roebuck or Mr. Lowe debauch the minds of the middle classes, and make such Philistines of them. It is the same fashion of teaching a man to value himself not on what he *is*, not on his progress in sweetness and light, but on the number of the railroads he has constructed, or the bigness of the tabernacle he has built. Only the middle classes are told they have done it all with their energy, self-reliance, and capital."[19]

John Stuart Mill, Arnold, Dickens, and Kay-Shuttleworth all attack the new order in schooling (and the related order in industry) as lacking in "religious sense" and in empathy. They do not note that, as rural England was uprooted, the new schooling also lacked any analysis of local community problems that was not preprocessed, any assigning of mature responsibility to youth, any critical studies that would expose students to non-Utilitarian philosophy, to nonmarket economics, or to literature, music, and art as critical disciplines. When vernacular literature comes into the curriculum, it too does so to reinforce conventional morality, nationalism, and patriotic lore.[20] (This is not to say that earlier systems of teaching did not reinforce the dominant arrangements. It is to say that the liberal regimen was not so different as we would like to believe it to have been.) The new schooling was essentially indoctrination posing as education. As the protocols taken from Birkbeck and Lancastrian school performances evidence, students were taught to seek some sort of better future but not how to analyze critically the promise of the offered utopia.

The absence of the critical was particularly important in an age that envisaged no limits to progress and industrial growth. Consciously or unconsciously, the banning of the critical from the schools, whether critical/conservative in the Scribleran direction or critical/radical in Owenite or Marxist directions, seems to have left education with an unquestioning and unquestioned myth of infinite progress, kindly Panoptical surveillance, political economy as ethics, and routinized work/competition. Part of the price may have been environmental devastation and the invention of a new human nature, supreme over everything but its own blindness to what it was doing. In enlarging human empire to accomplish everything possible, the worlds of school, office, and factory created a different human being to be the emperor—one who is no longer the human species among other species and is not their steward either; one who no longer has confidence that the god within will prompt the learning of what needs to be learned but who requires the coercive power of the state to force learning and to certify that it has taken place. This coercive power now costs more than the military and has a similar role in producing the social. In enlarging human empire, we have lost the human, the adaptive, the critical, and the religious, not only in the terms that a conservative Swift would recognize but in those that Dickens, Arnold, or Kay-Shuttleworth would know.

To the degree that this book has been a test of Mannheim's thesis, it has shown that the issue of how knowledge is to conquer nature affected the social arrangements made for research in organizations like the Royal Society and those made for elementary and secondary schools. The new school community and the new factory community insulated themselves from large-scale environmental change and from the necessity to adapt within environmental limits, one of the requirements of any society that does not despoil its surroundings.[21] In short, as a new kind of individual isolated from other individuals in work and school routines emerged, a new kind of community isolated from most of the exigencies of the community and the natural world also appeared, the precursor of the solipsistic community that Bellah describes in *Habits of the Heart* and of the environmentally displaced community that Wendell Berry depicts in almost all of his work.[22] The solipsistic community and the environmentally displaced community now exist not only in the Euro-American world where Combe, Ellis, Mann, and their allies originally worked but, with the coming of globalization, wherever traditional communities can be separated from their ties with other human beings or from the landscape in which they have long found a place. They exist, like Dickens's laborers, knowing few of the fruits of industrialization and all of its anomie and pollution.

Despite all of this, the reconstruction of the preindustrial relationship with one another and with the natural world is not possible or entirely desirable. Serious reconstruction would mean going to a world of hunger, disease, extremely hard work, and constant uncertainty as to survival.[23] The cry on the right and the left that compulsory education is Fascism or that a full deschooling of society is required seems to imply discontinuities at least as destructive as those produced by the industrial revolution and its accompanying schooling.[24] We could make a conscious effort to eschew fictions about the future when their truth is uncertain. We could try to create an intellectually and culturally neutral education in the schools that would ask serious questions about how we are to relate to one another as human beings and among other species. We could rely less on "scientific testing" when the tests are clearly not scientific and we have no clear knowledge as to what we need as the range of educated adults, given the demands of the rest of the environment. We could allow for more play and more time away from school (and away from play machines in the form of computer games) since we know that play is rich with unstructured learning and adaptation. We could root education much more in the village and neighborhood and give children and youth real responsibility for the community. We could open up adult work spaces for education and observation and work along the lines proposed for adult workers in *Work in America*.[25]

Finally, we could spend more time in immediate contact with environmental change, in view of the evidence that societies living exposed to the alterations of the natural world also conserve that world more carefully. The walls of the school have walled us into a utopia that rehearses a bright future (at least in the suburbs), but they have also walled us away from a natural world that increasingly resents our effort to construct our utopia on a technological island from which we can dominate it. Some of the changes that must be made are happening in some schools and some intellectual sectors — in moving us away from constant competition; in demythologizing assessment and testing; and in opening up the school to the natural world and to adult community responsibility over the long term and not just on a visitation basis — though much present national policy in Britain and the United States goes in opposite directions. If the schools are not now the emblems of the Ithaca to which the journey traced in this book was supposed to lead us, their falling short is not the fault of America's or Britain's teachers. It is the fault of those of us who make and support the myth that there exists a journey through competitive,

Conclusion

scientific/technological education by itself to some "dis'ant object" that is worth reaching, who fund it, and who create its legitimizing tools, including the utopian prospect itself.

As I write these final lines, white powders linger in our post offices and smoke rises on Manhattan from the appropriation of the Kingdom of Science by people who forbid education to most of their citizens and yet use the products of the educational tradition described to destroy its temples. As I write, the president of Russia and the president of the United States—the latter certainly a product of the educational tradition described and the former a product of a parallel tradition—discuss what to do with these appropriations of the Kingdom of Science by people who are only marginally members of that kingdom and also what to do with the appropriations in the form of nuclear weapons created by the most sophisticated products of this educational tradition. It is as if Gulliver were offering the king of Brobdingnagia guns enough to destroy the race and the creation, and this time the king did not know what to reply.

Notes

INTRODUCTION

1. Jo Ann Hoepper Moran, *The Growth of English Schooling, 1340–1548: Learning, Literacy, and Laicization in Pre-Reformation York Diocese* (Princeton: Princeton University Press, 1985), passim.

2. Paul A. Olson, *The Journey to Wisdom* (Lincoln: University of Nebraska Press, 1995), passim.

3. Cf. George C. Homans, *English Villagers in the 13th Century* (Cambridge: Harvard University Press, 1941) for the rote system of the late medieval village; for the rise of Reformation universal formal schooling, see Gerald Strauss, *Luther's House of Learning* (Baltimore: Johns Hopkins University Press, 1978). For the medieval English system, see Moran, *Growth of English Schooling*, 3–63.

4. Moran, *Growth of English Schooling*, 21–63.

5. Early Lutheran and continental Protestant education is largely concerned with the trivium and not the scientific disciplines (though by the eighteenth century it included some admixture of scientific study). The Protestants justified compulsory education with the notion that all people were priests of the Word of God, the text of the Bible, and therefore needed to learn to read the biblical texts in the original Hebrew and Greek and the Latin of their early translations. Even nationwide compulsory education as it appeared in eighteenth-century Prussia and the Netherlands was largely language-based.

6. Martha C. Nussbaum, *Poetic Justice: The Literary Imagination and Public Life* (Boston: Beacon Press, 1995), 1–52.

7. Karl Mannheim, *Ideology and Utopia: An Introduction to the Sociology of Knowledge*, ed. Louis Wirth and Edward Skils (New York: Harcourt Brace, Jovanich, 1985), 136.

8. Mannheim, *Ideology*, 188. Kerry S. Walters argues Mannheim's "utopian" visions have a "non-deceptive, self-transparent quality" bound to class that makes their proponents realize the limits of their vision and avoid "totalization." However, Mannheim, in the citation given, seems to suggest that the utopian person's immersion in vision becomes unconscious and also covers how all experiences are taken. Cf. Kerry S. Walters, *The Sane Society in Modern Utopianism* (Lewiston/Queenston: Edwin Mellen Press, 1989), 66–71. Cf. Job L. Dittberner, *The End of Ideology and American Social Thought* (Ann Arbor: UMI Research Press, 1979), 19. Mannheim's work on the sociology of knowledge anticipates that by Foucault, Kuhn, Toulmin, Popper, Adorno, and others. I do not subscribe to Mannheim's endorsement of the notion derived from Dilthey that particular ages have styles of thought that govern the thinking of individuals. That we succumb to standard ideas often does not mean that we could not do otherwise. For a discussion sympathetic to Mannheim in this area, see Rodney D. Nelson, "The Sociology of Styles of Thought," *British Journal of Sociology* 43 (1992): 25–54; cf. Joan Hart, "Erwin Panofsky and Karl Mannheim: A Dialogue on Interpretation," *Critical Inquiry* 19 (1993): 554–66. However, I do fully subscribe to Mannheim's insistence on the use of context to assist one in understanding the meaning of a work—its "language-games" in Wittgenstein's phrase—so long as one knows that same rules do not mean same outcomes. See A. P. Simonds, "Mannheim's Sociology of Knowledge: A Hermeneutic Method," *Cultural Hermeneutics* 3 (1975): 81–105, esp. 93–98.

9. Paul Ricoeur, *Lectures on Ideology and Utopia*, ed. George H. Taylor (New York: Columbia University Press: 1986), 272–73.

10. Mannheim, *Ideology*, 180. For Mannheim's view of More, see Henk E. S. Woldring, *Karl Mannheim: The Development of His Thought* (New York: St. Martin's Press, 1987), 193.

11. Mannheim, *Ideology*, 181. For a discussion of the problems implicit in Mannheim's idea of a utopia as both an individual's creation and a picture that guides a social movement, see Willard Mullins, "Truth and Ideology: Reflections on Mannheim's Paradox," *History and Theory* 18 (1979): 146–47. The task of this book is to show how Bacon's vision, appropriated in various directions by contending factions, came to guide a

series of social movements directed toward institutionalizing compulsory scientific/technological education.

12. Mannheim, *Ideology*, 182.

13. Diane Knight, *Barthes and Utopia: Space, Travel, Writing* (Oxford: Clarendon Press, 1997), 12; cf. Ricoeur, *Lectures on Ideology and Utopia*, 273–74.

14. Roland Barthes, *Sade, Fourier, Loyola*, trans. Richard Miller (New York: Hill and Wang, 1976), 115.

15. Cf. Ernest Bloch, *The Principle of Hope* (Oxford: Basil Blackwell, 1986), 3 vols., passim.

16. Knight, *Barthes and Utopia*, 12.

17. The effort to find a unifying definition for the term *utopia* constitutes a species of Wittgenstein's search for a substance for a substantive. There are, as in the case of most common nouns, family resemblances among the entities named by the substantive. Ricoeur remarks this "scattering," though he does note a "recurrence of themes about the family, property, consumption, social and political organization, institutionalized religion, and so on." Knight (*Barthes and Utopia*, 15) writes that "traditional representations of utopian societies invariably pay attention to the social organization of sexual relationships, with new arrangements for reproduction and child-rearing resulting from the rethinking of sexual difference." However, most of the utopian writings examined in this book do not exhibit much serious exploration of the meaning of sexual difference; one suspects that other survival concerns were more immediate and, perhaps, less threatening. Ricoeur (*Lectures on Ideology and Utopia*, 270) omits the rather consistent theme of the kind and structure of education offered.

18. Judith Shklar, *After Utopia* (Princeton: Princeton University Press, 1957), passim. Karl Popper and others have argued the converse—that utopianism leads to totalitarianism. The issue would, of course, depend on what tools the utopian group accepted as legitimate for the formation of a utopian society and how planning and the emergence of new social forms happened.

19. Brian Longhurst, *Karl Mannheim and the Contemporary Sociology of Knowledge* (Basingstoke: Macmillan, 1989), 68–71. Cf. Colin Loader, *The Intellectual Development of Karl Mannheim* (Cambridge: Cambridge Uni-

versity Press, 1985), 101–11. For the notion in Mannheim of mutually antagonistic utopias and the notion that a shift in utopian mentalities requires a "global shift of the system," see Ricoeur, *Lectures on Ideology and
Utopia*, 275. Mannheim's position here seems to me to be overly simple.
For rhetorical purposes in particular, utopian movements may adopt
utopian fictions or stories that come from radically opposite political
camps without noticing the difference. For Ricoeur's lucid characteriza-
tions of Mannheim's utopian modalities—Chiliasm, liberalism, and socialism, see his *Lectures on Utopia and Ideology*, 276–81. Mannheim's notion that utopianism arises primarily in deeply oppressed classes needs to
be qualified since in such cases as the Peasants' Revolt of 1381, revolt did
not occur among the most deeply oppressed groups but among ascending groups that had a sense of opportunity denied. Mannheim seems
sometimes to have argued that perspective creates knowledge even in the
hard sciences. See Fritz Ringer, "The Origin of Mannheim's Sociology
of Knowledge," *The Social Dimensions of Science*, ed. Ernest McMullin
(Notre Dame: University of Notre Dame Press, 1992), 64–66; for
Mannheim's understanding of knowledge, see David Kettler, Volker
Meja, and Nico Stehr, *Karl Mannheim* (New York: Tavistock Publications, 1984), 64.

20. For a thoughtful discussion of this and other aspects of Mannheim's thought, see Ricoeur, *Lectures on Ideology and Utopia*, 269–84.

21. Alan Scott, "Politics and Method in Mannheim's 'Ideology and
Utopia,'" *Sociology* 21, no. 1 (February, 1987): 41–54; Martin Jay, "The
Frankfurt School's Critique of Karl Mannheim and the Sociology of
Knowledge," *Telos* 20 (summer, 1974): 72–89; Ricard Ashcraft, "Politi-
cal Theory and Political Action in Karl Mannheim's Thought: Reflec-
tions upon *Ideology and Utopia* and Its Critics," *Comparative Studies in So-
ciety and History* 23 (January, 1981): 23–50. For another view, see Susan
Hekman, "Antifoundational Thought and the Sociology of Knowledge:
The Case of Karl Mannheim," *Human Studies* 10 (1987): 33–56; Ruth H.
Jacobs, "Karl Mannheim's Search for a Philosophy Consistent with Rel-
ativism," *Studies in Philosophy and Education* 7 (spring, 1972): 190–209;
A. P. Simonds, "Karl Mannheim's Sociology of Knowledge," *Cultural
Hermeneutics* 3 (May, 1975): 160–87. For Mannheim's eventual turn to a
kind of Platonic intellectual elite as possible arbiter between versions of

knowledge, see Karl Mannheim, *Diagnosis of Our Time* (London: Routledge and Kegan Paul, 1943), 119; cf. Volker Meja, "The Sociology of Knowledge and the Critique of Ideology," *Cultural Hermeneutics* 3 (May, 1975): 57–68.

22. For perfectibilism and utopianism, see Barbara Goodwin, *Social Science and Utopia: Nineteenth-Century Models of Social Harmony* (Atlantic Highlands NJ: Humanities Press, 1978), 4–5, but see also Krishan Kumar, *Utopianism* (Minneapolis: University of Minnesota Press, 1991), 29. Goodwin (7–8) assumes the utopianist is not only a perfectibilist but a non-relativistic thinker, an outsider, and a mechanist, assumptions that appear to rule out most post-Renaissance fictions and movements we call utopian.

23. Certain texts bind together much of the conversation with which this book deals. First of all, most utopias are, in epic terms, fabulous loci—like Nausicaa's lovely land or the land of the lotus eaters or Circe's island. But the epic writers were clear, as we need to be, that what is seen as "utopian" depends on the passions and interests of the seeker. The island of the lotus eaters is paradise to those who crave the lotus experience, as Circe is to those who wish to engage and be transformed by her witchcraft, and Nausicaa is to those who crave a protected innocence. However, from the perspective of passions and interests, one person's utopian search becomes another's dystopian nightmare. The character of the place itself is judged by the character of the person who adjudges it ideal and by the tone of the writer or narrator, who becomes another protagonist in the assessing of eidola. The fact that epics had long been the mediators of educational visions meant that the new educational utopias and dystopias played against their fictions and that this play was often part of the process of communicating meaning and of moving the new utopian fiction beyond relativism. Cf. Olson, *Journey to Wisdom*, 85–116.

24. Krishan Kumar, *Utopia and Anti-Utopia in Modern Times* (Oxford: Basil Blackwell, 1987), 43, argues that "Turgot's two discourses on the advancement of the human race and mind, given at the Sorbonne in 1750, constitute by general agreement the first important statement in modern times of the ideology of progress," an idea that assumes successive increments in the enlightenment of the human mind, but he also indicates

that Bacon's name is "frequently and rightly evoked in . . . support" of
this idea.

1. SHAKESPEARE'S *TEMPEST* AND
EDUCATION BY THE BOOK

1. Cf. Olson, *Journey to Wisdom*, 176, 278, n. 13.

2. Olson, *Journey to Wisdom*, 176.

3. For a discussion of George Buck's treatise and the uses of eicastic education, see Dennis Brooks, "'To Show Scorn Her Own Image': The Varieties of Education in *The Taming of the Shrew*," *Rocky Mountain Review of Language and Literature* 48 (1994): 7–32. Cf. George Buck, "The Third Universitie of England," in John Stow, *The Annales of England* (London: G. Bishop, 1615), [950]–88.

4. The idea of education through cultural production is discussed in Paul Olson, *Journey to Wisdom*, passim; Frances A. Yates, *The French Academies of the Sixteenth Century* ([London]: Warburg Institute, University of London, 1947), passim.

5. Shakespeare did not write these scenes, but he almost certainly had to know their general outlines to write the scenes he wrote. For Hand D, see *The Norton Shakespeare*, ed. Stephen Greenblatt et al. (New York: Norton, 1997), 2017–19 and bibliography, p. 2014.

6. John X. Evans, "Utopia on Prospero's Island," *Moreana* 18 (1981) 18: 69, 81–83; cf. Judith E. Boss, "The Golden Age, Cockaigne, and Utopia in *The Faerie Queene* and *The Tempest*," *Georgia Review* 26 (1972): 145–55.

7. Elisabeth Hansot has argued that pride feeding on the misfortunes of others is at the root of the disorganized commonwealth presented in book I of More's work and that this pride "has little to do with original sin" but is "a form of vanity" (Elizabeth Hansot, *Perfection and Progress: Two Modes of Utopian Thought* [Cambridge: MIT Press, 1974], 62–68). Actually, pride is the form of possession of private property, related to the fallen state, of which Thomas Aquinas writes when he mentions those who hold private property in contempt of the needy; further, the Utopians could not overcome vanity in a Christian world without, in some degree, overcoming the effects of original sin or without becoming the "gentiles who knew not the law" who became "a law unto themselves" (Romans 2:14). The Vulgate, emphasizing the natural, reads, "Cum

enim gentes, quae legem non habent, naturaliter ea, quae legis sunt, faciunt, eiusmodi legem non habentes, ipsi sibi sunt lex" (Romans 2:14).

More's emphasis on the education and acculturation of the Utopians toward the common construction of a good society comports with his natural law respect for free choice and his hopeful imagination that, given a decent tradition, people will exercise choice reasonably wisely in most cases. Much of his polemic against Luther centers on Luther's apparent destruction of the freedom of the will in his predestinarian treatises. Cf. Thomas More, *The Workes of Sir Thomas More . . .* (London: Cawod, Waly, and Tottell, 1557), sig. siiii recto. Utopian bondage is also natural law bondage. The natural law notion and Morean view that bondage began as a punishment for crime conflicts with the alternative medieval theory that makes bondage inherited. See R. W. Carlyle and A. J. Carlyle, *A History of Mediaeval Political Theory in the West*, 6 vols. (London: Blackwood, 1928), 2:3–4, 117–23; 5:21–24. Technically, free Utopians still have a trace of the sense of private property or interest; they have contracts and they are encouraged to look after their own *commodum* or remuneration. (See More, *Utopia*, 102–3, 153, 164–65; for gold, 163.) Similarly, in natural law theory, because human beings require some basic sustenance, they need property to sustain themselves in a selfish world. Positive law, as enacted by a monarch and his councils, simply codifies what natural law prescribes as it applies to local conditions and peoples. A tyrant becomes a tyrant by virtue of preferring his private good to the public good and of his failure to protect natural law in his positive enactments. Cf. Paul A. Olson, "Chaucer's *Parlement of Foules* and the Foundations of Human Community," *Studies in the Age of Chaucer* 2 (1981), 53–69.

8. More, *Utopia*, 238–41, 101–7. Throughout, *Utopia* turns on the contrast between the common profit and private profit, which contrast is also crucial in Cicero's *De Re Publica* and in Chaucer's *Parlement*. For this distinction and its consequences, see Olson, "Chaucer's *Parlement*," 53–69, which also contains a summary of natural law theory through Fortescue.

9. R. W. and A. J. Carlyle trace out the relationship between "golden age" common property before the Fall and private property intended for the common good after it. Carlyle and Carlyle, *History of Mediaeval Po-*

litical Theory, 5 : 4–20. Thomas Aquinas argues that common property accords with natural law but that, after the Fall, property may be acquired and distributed but may never be ethically possessed to the disadvantage of others who need the possessed good. Cf. Thomas Aquinas, *Summa Theologica* (New York: Benziger Bros., 1947–48), 2–2, quest. 66, art. 2–7; 1–2, quest. 94, art. 5. William Budé's address to Thomas Lupset prefacing *Utopia* makes clear that the European "law of nations," with its emphasis on giving wealth to the strong to the detriment of the weak, is not derived from natural law as is claimed by contemporary rulers (More, *Utopia*, 9). Colet makes the same point (More, *Utopia*, 272).

10. *Utopia*'s statement to its own time is that England should practice what is preached by the natural law theory on which its jurisprudence rests. Scholars have emphasized *Utopia*'s inspiration by communal monastic ideals, the first "golden age" book of Ovid's *Metamorphoses*, some aspects Plato's *Republic*, and dozens of other ancient and medieval sources. It essentially rests on the bromides of standard conceptions of natural law, thought to be the basis of all enacted law, whether Protestants or Catholics ruled. Calvin was, of course, later to question the view that the natural law placed in humankind might lead to any form of right conduct. For him, it was placed in humankind to eliminate any possible excuse for natural depravity, though without grace, this depravity is inescapable, as he understands it. Thus natural law has no normative function in the construction of the good society. See Jean Calvin, *Institutio Christianae religionis*, ed. Jean-Daniel Benoît (Paris, J. Vrin, 1957–63), lib. 2, sec. 2, 22 ff.; see also lib. 2, sec. 3.

11. Cf. Thomas More, *The Complete Works of St. Thomas More: Utopia*, ed. Edward Surtz and J. H. Hexter (New Haven: Yale University Press, 1965), 162–67, 447–59.

12. More, *Utopia*, 10–13, 28–29, 34–35, 59–109. Busleyden treats Utopia as a means of saving Renaissance hegemonies from the fate of ancient commonwealths that have crumbled (34–35). Cf. Dominic Baker-Smith, "The Escape from the Cave: Thomas More and the Vision of Utopia," *Dutch Quarterly Review of Anglo-American Letters* 15 (1985): 148–61.

13. More, *Utopia*, 49.

14. More, *Utopia*, 158–59.

15. More, *Utopia*, 159.

16. More says that especially talented children are assigned to scholarship but all children are taught reading ("omnes pueri literis imbuuntur"). More, *Utopia*, 158. (I take "pueri" to mean children rather than boys here.)

17. For a good discussion of the role of a pleasure not *voluptas* in More, see Hansot, *Perfection and Progress*, 62–68.

18. More, *Utopia*, 183, cf. 162–65.

19. Thomas More, *Selected Letters*, ed. Elizabeth Frances Rogers (New Haven: Yale University Press, 1964), 99. For the tradition of this and other ladders to the stars, see Paul A. Olson, *Journey to Wisdom* (Lincoln: University of Nebraska Press, 1995), passim.

20. Olson, *Journey to Wisdom*, passim.

21. More, *Utopia*, 102–5, lxxv–lxxvi, and passim. For More on natural law, see *The Yale Edition of the Complete Works of Thomas More* (New Haven: Yale, 1963), 6:139–41. Utopia is not always a "utopian place" since the fulfillment of natural law in it falls short of Christian charity and other infused virtues that More elsewhere commends. The locus exists to shame an increasingly enclosure-filled England. Dominic Baker-Smith has argued in "The Escape from the Cave: Thomas More and the Vision of Utopia," 148–61, that More, like Cicero in his *De Re Publica* or Plato in the *Republic*, juxtaposes his ideal vision with quotidian political reality to make the problem of rhetorical persuasion central. Baker-Smith also demonstrates the closeness of millennialism and utopianism in pre-Enlightenment Europe.

22. For the continuation of Plantagenet ideas about monarchy into the Tudor and Stuart periods and into Shakespeare, see Ernst Kantorowicz, *The King's Two Bodies* (Princeton: Princeton University Press, 1957), 24–41.

23. Michel de Montaigne, "Of Cannibals," *The Essayes of Michael, Lord of Montaigne*, trans. John Florio, 4 vols. (London: Oxford University Press, 1910), 1:245. For colonialist issues, see Deborah Willis, "Shakespeare's *Tempest* and the Discourse of Colonialism," *Studies in English Literature* 29 (1989): 277–89. Caliban represents the colonized subject, but

he does so primarily as a metaphor for the colonized mind in Europe, the person close to power who has to usurp it to gain it—that is, the grotesque commoners and the Neapolitans.

24. James I had moved to a somewhat Calvinistic position by this period. For Calvin's assumptions about nature and natural law, see William Bouwsma, *John Calvin* (Oxford: Oxford University Press, 1988), 73–74 and passim. For Calvin and natural law, see footnote 10.

25. Robert Silhol, "Magie et Utopie Dans La Tempête," *Études Anglaises* 17 (1964): 447–56, quote at 451.

26. Montaigne, "Of the Institution and Education of Children," *Essayes*, 1: 190–91; 1: 167–68. Shakespeare's utopia, unlike More's, is based on direct violence as prevention and art as incentive instead of *Utopia*'s cultural conditioning. Education and coercion combine with Prospero's universal surveillance, an art certainly not just invented with Bentham's Panopticon or Chrestomathia (see chapter 7).

27. H. Davies, *The Early Stuarts: 1603–1660* (Oxford: Clarendon Press, 1937), 32.

28. It is not certain that Prospero abandons all magic. He promises to break his staff and drown his book, but he retains his robe (5, 1, 51–57), and he appears in the epilogue without "charms" because the illusions of drama have been abandoned.

29. Anthony Hecht, "Paradise and Wilderness: The Brave New World of the *Tempest*," *Yale Review* 81 (1993): 88.

30. For a discussion of eicastic education, see Brooks, "'To Show Scorn Her Own Image,'" 7ff. For Prospero as educator, see Maurice Hunt, "Belarius and Prospero: Two Pastoral Schoolmasters," *Lamar Journal of the Humanities* 15 (1989): 29–41.

31. Henry Cornelius Agrippa, *Three Books of Occult Philosophy*, trans. J. F. (London: R. W., 1651), sig B[1]r–[B1v], sig. Aa3–Aa4. Agrippa speaks of the magician's ascent to the "original world it self, the Maker of al things" (sig. B[1]r). The Florentine Platonists speak of the unitive experience.

32. Sibilla is said to speak what Jove has taught and to be inspired by him; *The Works of Thomas Campion*, 261–62. For the magician's frenzy and inspiration, see Agrippa, *Three Books of Occult Philosophy*, sig. Kk2r ff.

33. Barbara A. Mowat, "Prospero, Agrippa, and Hocus Pocus," *English Literary Renaissance* 11 (1981), 284–85.

34. Northrop Frye has argued that *The Tempest* is not an allegory because Prospero's "revels" speech does not say an eternal world will take the place of the present "dream." However, a dream surrounded by a sleep is also surrounded by a waking reality if one completes the metaphor. Cf. William Shakespeare, *The Tempest*, ed. Northrop Frye (New York: Penguin, 1959), 17. Prospero is not an optimistic chiliast announcing *the Kingdom of God on earth*. After he prophesies the eschaton, he continues to act as if evil will be abroad and has Ariel arrest and bring in Caliban, Trinculo, and Stephano. The power he possesses is fictively other-than-human, and in his private self, when he recovers from his sibylline ecstatic seizure, he describes himself as "vex'd," having a "troubled old brain" and requiring retirement to his cell (4.1.158–62). The equivalent of the eschaton in Virgil is the prophecy of the restoration of permanent empire and the recycling of souls between the divine world of the One and the present world. For the meaning of divine frenzy in the culture of magic, see Agrippa, *Three Books of Occult Philosophy*, sig. Kk2r ff. James thought of himself as having prophetic powers; cf. Robert Ashton, *James I by his Contemporaries* (London: Hutchinson, 1969), 160.

35. Hans Baron, *The Crisis of the Early Italian Renaissance: Civic Humanism and Republican Liberty in an Age of Classicism and Tyranny* (Princeton: Princeton University Press, 1966), 106–137, 122–25, 316–31.

36. For James as Solomon in Stuart iconology, see Stephen Orgel, *The Illusion of Power: Political Theater in the English Renaissance* (Berkeley: University of California Press, 1975), 73; cf. William Carroll Tate, *Solomon's Wisdom, Solomon's Folly: A Study in Early Stuart Iconography*, Ph.D. diss., University of North Carolina, 1996, passim.

37. Stephen Jay Gould, "Bacon, Brought Home," *Natural History* 108 (June, 1999): 28–33, 72–77, especially 74. Gould cites Bacon's contrasting analytic view of the natural world.

38. Donna B. Hamilton, *Virgil and "The Tempest": The Politics of Imitation* (Columbus: Ohio State University Press, 1990), passim.

39. Cf. Ann Pasternak Slater, "Variations within a Source: From Isa-

iah XXIX to 'The Tempest,'" *Shakespeare Survey* 25 (1972): 125–35. Isaiah was a prominent text during the Christmas season when *The Tempest* was performed in 1612. Isaianic prophecies from the *Book of Common Prayer* were read—prophecies in essence repeated in the later Isaianic apocalypses of Isaiah 24:1–27:13, where world-judgment, the salvation of Israel, and a resurrection of God's chosen are adumbrated, and in those of Isaiah 28:1–33:24, where the pattern is repeated in an account of the sin of Zion and its overthrow, captivity, and deliverance under a messianic king. The sibylline oracles had also become apocalyptic works in Renaissance readings (it is not for nothing that the sibyls sit with the prophets in the Sistine chapel). The sibyl's revelations to Aeneas in book 6 of the *Aeneid*, complemented by apocalyptic elements in the *Aeneid* as a whole, acquired a spiritual authority parallel to that of the Bible. The fall of Troy, the struggles of Aeneas to keep alive a remnant, the revelation that the translated empire had been selected by the gods for a divine destiny, and the reestablishment of the empire to ensure a thousand years of peace fulfill the pattern.

40. Lancelot Andrewes, *Seventeen Sermons on the Nativity* (London: Griffith, Farran, Okeden and Welsh, [1898]), 251.

41. Andrewes, *Seventeen Sermons*, 250–59. The fourth eclogue was still being referred to Christ. Andrewes's point is that Virgil did not heed his own prophecy but misinterpreted it. Cf. Lodovic Vives on the fourth eclogue in Virgil, *Opera*, ed. Fabricius (Basel, 1586), col. 52.

42. Cf. Domenico Comparetti, *Virgilio nel Medio Evo*, 2 vols. (Florence: Nuova Italia, [1937–41]), 1:125; 2:88.

43. Ariel acts as an airy spirit in name as well as in most of the dramatic action, and Juno is allegorized as the air in common Renaissance commentary. However, *The Tempest* allows Ariel to prepare the new Aeneas, Ferdinand, for his union with Milan and Miranda through changing his form from his usual guise as a creature of air to assume the water nymph's form given to those who serve Juno in the *Aeneid*. Agrippa says water music "softens the soul, raises the thoughts . . . diminishes pain and fatigue," all necessary effects if Ferdinand is to find divine beauty and an elevated love for Miranda. As a water nymph, Ariel calls out to Ferdinand with the dance of the water waves and sands (1.2.376–83.), cries the iconologically correct penitential cry of Chanticleer (1.2.388–89), and

announces the waterchange of death that appears to have come to Ferdinand's father, paradoxically on his way to finding himself and rebirth (1.2.398–405). For standard interpretation of Juno as air and marriage, see Natalis Comes, *Mythologiae*, trans. Jean Baudouin (Paris: Pierre Chevalier, 1627), sig. [Lii verso]–[Mi verso]. Cartari and Giraldi, among the standard continental mythographers, make essentially the same interpretations. For English mythography see Abraham Fraunce, *The Third Part of the Countesse of Pembrokes Yuychurch* (London: Woodcocke, 1592), sig. [D5r]–[D5v]. Ariel's literal tempest does what Juno's does in Virgil, creating the conditions for love—Aeneas for Dido in Virgil, Ferdinand for Miranda in Shakespeare. But again working contrariwise to the *Aeneid*, Shakespeare makes the woman who emerges as the storm's comfort also the dynastic bride, the equivalent of Lavinia.

44. Marsilio Ficino, *Commentaire sur le Banquet de Platon*, ed. Raymond Marcel (Paris: Les Belles Lettres, 1956), 153–55, 245–46. Ficino's various Venuses found their way into mythographic commentary.

45. Geneva says that Ariel signifies the Zion altar for David's city that devoured the sacrifices. *The Geneva Bible: Facsimile of the 1560 Edition* (Madison: University of Wisconsin Press, 1969), sig. Cccii recto. Ariel's role in the play as a devouring fury is obvious. Cf. Agrippa, *Three Books of Occult Philosophy*, sig. [v2v], sig. Ff2r–[Ff2v].

46. Cf. *Geneva Bible*, sig. Cccii r.

47. The *Geneva Bible* says "thundre . . . shaking, a great noyse, a whirlwinde, a tempest, . . . a flame of a devouring fyre." *Geneva Bible*, sig. Cccii r.

48. *Geneva* associates this speaking from the ground with the idea that the humiliated Zion will speak like a charmer, certainly Ariel's function. *Geneva Bible*, sig. Cccii r.

49. The magician's Ariel, too, is the patron of kingship—in Agrippa's book, a familiar spirit or daemon belonging to the sign of Aries in which signs are placed on those who are "acceptable, eloquent, ingenious and honorable," those who govern through righteous wrath—precisely what Prospero does. Agrippa, *Three Books of Occult Philosophy*, sig. [v2v]–[v3v] and passim.

50. *The Tempest* 1.2.424; *Aeneid* 1, 328ff. Like Arcita in Chaucer's "Knight's Tale," Ferdinand believes he can accept the prison (the island)

if he can but "behold this maid" (*Tempest*, 1.2.494; "Knight's Tale," A, 1223–74). The confusion of a woman with a goddess or wonder, reversing Virgil, is found not only in Palamon's confusion in the "Knight's Tale" but in Palamon's similar confusion in *The Two Noble Kinsmen*, where he speaks of her as something to be wondered at and as a goddess worthy of reverence (2.2.131–35). Citation from John Fletcher and William Shakespeare, *The Two Noble Kinsmen*, ed. G. R. Proudfoot (Lincoln: University of Nebraska Press, 1970). Since Ariel is a spirit of air and Juno was allegorized as the same force, it seems likely that Ariel played Juno in the masque. The interpretation of "when I presented Ceres" at 4.1.167 as signifying that the Ariel actor played Ceres seems incorrect. The more likely interpretation is that Ariel/Juno "introduces" Ceres or points to the Ceres figure in the masque as s/he sings her marriage song. This Ariel/Juno could easily do as s/he sings the lines "Earth's increase, foison plenty" at 4.1.110 ff. If the lines attributed to Juno in the folio text are wrongly reassigned to Ceres in modern editions, the bracketed part of the *Enter Ceres [played by Ariel]* direction that appears in modern editions following 4.1.75 is incorrect. For a standard contemporary text see *The Tempest*, ed. Peter Holland (New York: Penguin Putnam, 1999).

51. Ellen R. Belton, "When No Man Was His Own: Magic and Self-Discovery in *The Tempest*," *University of Toronto Quarterly* 55 (1985): 127–40.

52. Ariel's sermon further reminds the spectators of the personalistic character of the universe with which they deal by stressing the analogies between the storm's punishment and the banquet's disappearance, both reprisals for the displacement of Prospero and his daughter.

53. When Ariel sings a song to protect the king (2.1.295–300; cf. 2.1.302–3), Sebastian and Antonio unwittingly cast themselves as the roaring lions and Bashan bulls of Psalm 22, 12–13 (2.1.306–7) that in Renaissance-glossed Bibles represented the forces surrounding Christ to crucify him. The lions and bulls thus make even the culpable Alonso into the "Rex-Christus" of medieval monarchic myth.

54. Kantorowicz, *King's Two Bodies*, 24–41.

55. Hamilton has identified the Harpy of the banquet scene with the Harpy of *Aeneid* 3 and also mentions the scene in Hades where a Fury keeps sinners such as Ixion and Pirithous from a banquet, but she sees

the grotesques in the scenes as being two separate kinds of creatures and sees the scene as a fusion of events in *Aeneid* 3 and 6. Hamilton, *Virgil and "The Tempest,"* 74–78.

56. Furies and harpies are identified in *Aeneid* 3, 252, and 6, 605. For the fusion in Renaissance understandings, see Virgil, *Opera Omnia*, including the commentaries of Donatus, Honoratus, and Fabricius (Basel: Henricpetri, 1547), cols. 1081–82.

57. While some texts of the play gloss "perdition" as the secular consequence "ruin," given the Virgilian analogy, Ariel really threatens an afterworld punishment, for the betrayal of the monarchs, projected on the present world to obtain repentance ("heart's sorrow. / And a clear life ensuing," 3.3.81–82).

58. Before Alonso decides to "stand to, and feed" (3.3.49), Sebastian and Antonio remark that the banquet persuades them of the possibility of unicorns and a phoenix (3.3.2227), two standard images of Christ. They do not seek the equivalent of phoenix and unicorn, only the Harpy's ephemeral food. The only messiah who appears to them is the Fury demanding their repentance.

59. The Geneva Bible makes what appears in the dream as food or nourishing support into the false friends of Zion, who ultimately appear as its real enemies. Shakespeare reverses the roles in that those who dream they are fed are not Ariel's false friends but his obvious enemies. Ariel's denial of food reveals the real opposition between the Neapolitan forces and Ariel. See Virgil, *Opera Omnia*, col. 1081–82.

60. William Shakespeare, *The Tempest*, ed. Frank Kermode (Cambridge: Harvard University Press, 1954), xxxiv–xxxvi, 67; cf. *Aeneid* 3, 568–718.

61. Interpretation based on glosses in *Geneva Bible*, sig. Ccci v, and on Shakespeare's text. The Geneva Bible commentary says the "drunkards of Ephraim" were "dronken with worldly prosperitie," what the grotesques of the play in their inebriation imagine to be just around the corner: *Geneva Bible*, sig. [Ccciv]. The drunkards of the play are thrown down by a tempest that Ferdinand attributes to hell and the devils; the Isaiah passage says that the Isaiah tempest is God's punishment on the wicked, an interpretation Ariel assigns to his tempest (3.3.53–61). The Geneva Bible commentary makes the tempest a metaphor for Is-

rael's enemies, standing for the Assyrians; the enemies conceptualized in the *Tempest* represent a conspiracy of internal and external forces such as the establishment feared both from the Catholic forces and from the extreme Puritan ones. I use the King James version for quotations in this section as it was newly minted in 1612; I also use the Geneva Bible's glosses.

62. Hamilton, *Virgil and "The Tempest,"* 85–92.

63. Virgil, *Opera Omnia* (Basel: Henricpetri, 1586), col. 707bc; cf. col. 1028c.

64. For additional material on the betrothal masque, see Hamilton, *Virgil and "The Tempest,"* 78–85.

65. D. J. Gordon, *"Hymenaei*: Ben Jonson's Masque of Union," *Journal of the Warburg and Courtauld Institute* 8 (1945): 107–45.

66. For Juno, unity, the cosmic chain of love, and marriage symbolism, see Jonson's "Hymenaei" in *Ben Jonson*, ed. C. H. Herford, Percy Simpson, and Evelyn Simpson, 11 vols. (Oxford: Clarendon Press, 1963) 7:203–42, especially Jonson's notes.

2. *NEW ATLANTIS* AND THE CHILIASTIC UTOPIAS

1. Many critics believe that Bacon was a millennialist of some sort.

2. Of course, James, ever vacillating and secretive, also had a mind to create a marriage partnership with Hapsburg Spain, a design not widely understood at the court and one that failed abysmally as Frederick was destroyed in the havoc of the Thirty Years War. Cf. W. B. Patterson, *King James VI and I and the Reunion of Christendom* (Cambridge: Cambridge University Press, 1997), 314–38.

3. For apocalyptic thought in England, see C. A. Patrides and Joseph Wittreich, *The Apocalypse in English Renaissance Thought and Literature* (Manchester: Manchester University Press, 1984), 2–237; for apocalypse and utopia as parallel in early Renaissance mystical literature, see Derk Visser, *Apocalypse as Utopian Expectation* (Brill: New York, 1996), passim.

4. See Francis A. Yates, *The Rosicrucian Enlightenment* (London: Routledge and Kegan Paul, 1972), passim. For the political context, see Patterson, *King James VI and I*, 156ff. Cf. Yates, *The Rosicrucian Enlightenment*, 1ff. For *The Tempest's* relation to Prince Henry's marriage and the politics of his career, see Hamilton, *Virgil and "The Tempest,"*

38–43. Hamilton includes a useful discussion of the reappropriation of the play to the context of the marriage of Elizabeth and Frederick (41–44).

5. M. A. Everett Green, *Elizabeth, Electress Palatine and Queen of Bohemia* (London: Methuen, 1909), 44–47.

6. For a good account of the Elizabeth-Frederick wedding and its apocalyptic intellectual climate, see Yates, *Rosicrucian Enlightenment*, 1–58.

7. Green, *Elizabeth*, 41.

8. Thomas Campion, *A Relation of the Late Royall Entertainment Given by the Right Honorable the Lord of Knowles, at Cawsome (i.e. Caversham)-House neere Redding to Our Most Gracious Queene, Queene Anne, in Her Progresse Toward the Bathe, upon the Seven and Eight and Twentie Dayes of Aprill, 1613* (London: Printed for John Bulge, 1613), sig. C2r; see *The Works of Thomas Campion*, ed. Walter R. Davis (Garden City NY: Doubleday, 1967), 249–62, 232–34.

9. Josephine Ross, *The Winter Queen* (London: Weidenfeld and Nicolson, 1979), 45. See George Chapman, *The Memorable Maske of Two Honorable Houses* (London: G. Eld, 1613).

10. The Protestant union of Frederick and Elizabeth that both *The Tempest* and *The Marriage of the Thames and Rhine* celebrated did little to strengthen royal power in England or on the Continent. Frederick, crowned the king of Bohemia by the Bohemian Protestants soon after his marriage to Elizabeth, suffered defeat in the preliminary stages of the Thirty Years War at the Battle of the White Hill (1620). After the defeat, he and his spouse fled to Holland, and Maximilian of Bavaria dismembered the Palatinate kingdom. When James tried to create a continental alliance to rescue his son-in-law's Protestant cause, he was successful only in getting Denmark to enter the field. He was himself unwilling to commit England to the fight and angled for a marriage alliance with Catholic Spain at the same time. His Protestant alliance having failed miserably, he continued to try to buttress his authority at home by court ceremony and drama and masque in the mode of *The Tempest*, but here too his reputation declined. The Protestant left grew, and in its camp on the Continent, millennialist and chiliastic hopes for a new world created through education and research also continued to grow.

11. Gould, "Bacon, Brought Home," 28–33, 72–77, includes a nice contrasting of Baconian and Neoplatonic assumptions about nature.

12. "Sir Francis Bacon, at that time one of James' chief officials, was the chief contriver," though Francis Beaumont wrote the words of the piece. John Nichols, *The Progresses, Processions, and Magnificent Festivities of King James the First*, 4 vols. (London: Nichols, 1828), 2:589. The dedication of the play directs the work "TO THE WORTHIE SIR FRANCIS BACON, HIS MAJESTIES SOLLICITOR GENERALL" and says Bacon spared neither time nor travail in the "setting forth, ordering and furnishing of this Masque," a phrase that suggests Bacon controlled the content of the work. Cf. Francis Beaumont, *The Dramatic Works in the Beaumont and Fletcher Canon*, ed. Fredson Bowers, 9 vols. (Cambridge: Cambridge University Press, 1966), 1:126.

13. Beaumont, *Dramatic Works*, 1:124–25.

14. Nichols, *Progresses*, 2:590.

15. Beaumont, *Dramatic Works*, 1:127.

16. Beaumont, *Dramatic Works*, 1:129.

17. The main masque that leads to this conclusion shows fifteen Olympic knights beside two main pavilions of gold cloth with other lesser pavilions behind them. Nearby, the gods (presumably gods) appear veiled and mitered, and above them stands an altar with three candles and four statues symbolizing the marriage. Jove's priests preside at the altar. When the knights are unveiled, they are clad in carnation satin, roses, and wild olive in tribute to the national colors of the two realms and their ruling houses. The masquer knights dance an Apollonian dance to the music of Apollo, not of Pan, dancing as if in prayer and singing as if in sacrifice. And the masquer ladies are to join in the measure, assured that the sins of their dance will be absolved. Then comes the call to the Olympic games and the knightly prayer-song that the new pair will stop Time (or Saturn) in his course by cutting his wings, taking his scythe, and breaking his hourglass. The power of the marriage and of Vulcan's technology will stop Time in its tracks. This passage is followed by the priestly prayer-song for peace and joy to befall the marriage. Finally, the marriage dance puts the marriage in harmony with the *mundana musica* that blesses chaste marriage, in tune with the prayer and sacrifice that leads to absolution. Nichols, *Progresses*, 2:591–600.

18. *Francis Bacon*, ed. Brian Vickers (Oxford: Oxford University Press, 1996), 785. For discussions of *New Atlantis* and Utopianism, see also Robert Adams, "The Social Responsibilities of Science in *Utopia, New Atlantis,* and After," 374–98; cf. Laurence Berns, "Francis Bacon and the Conquest of Nature," *Interpretation* 7 (1978): 1–26; Jerry Weinberger, *Science, Faith and Politics: Francis Bacon and the Utopian Roots of the Modern Age* (Ithaca: Cornell University Press, 1985), passim, esp. 27–28, 32–39, 75–76, 131–39, 153–242. For accounts of Catholic-Protestant religious issues joined in *New Atlantis,* see David Renaker, "A Miracle of Engineering: Francis Bacon's *New Atlantis,*" *Studies in Philology* 87 (1990): 181–94; Robert K. Faulkner, *Francis Bacon and the Project of Progress* (Lanham MD: Rowman and Littlefield, 1993), 233–36. Most citations and quotations from Bacon's works are from *The Works of Francis Bacon,* collected and edited by James Spedding, Robert Leslie Ellis, and Douglas Denon Heath (New York: Hurd and Houghton, 1869–72), 15 vol., hereafter cited as Spedding, with volume and page number.

19. *Francis Bacon,* ed. Vickers, 785.

20. See Robert Faulkner, *Francis Bacon and the Project of Progress,* passim, for an excellent discussion of "Bacon's project of a new science . . . to institute 'the power of man over the universe'" (4); see especially chaps. 4, 5, 6, and 12; cf. Timothy H. Paterson, "Bacon's Myth of Orpheus: Power as a Goal of Science in *Of the Wisdom of the Ancients,*" *Interpretation* 16 (1989): 427–43, esp. 441.

21. For previous analyses of Bacon and Mannheim's analysis of utopianism, see Kerry S. Walters, *The 'Sane Society' of Bacon and Nineteenth Century Utopias,* Ph.D. diss., University of Cincinnati, 1985, passim, and Kathryn M. Olesko, review of *Solomon's House Revisited, Science* 252 (1991): 976; for the *New Atlantis* and More's *Utopia,* see Denise Albanese, "The *New Atlantis* and the Uses of Utopia," *English Literary History* 57 (1990): 503–28. Though Albanese sees the work as essentially an imperialistic work, she argues that it may pay some tribute to the effect of the New World on the Old in that its fiction enacts the possibility of a significant flow of influence and innovation from the new world to the old, an innovation that was already well under way in the use of Native American foods and medicines in Europe in the 1500s and 1600s.

22. Abraham Cowley's ode *To the Royal Society,* in *The Poems of Abra-*

ham Cowley, ed. A. R. Waller (London: Cambridge University Press, 1905), 448–53, says "Bacon, like Moses, led us forth at last" (450) and from the "Mountains Top" saw the promised land of scientific investigation; Joseph Glanvill calls Salomon's House in *New Atlantis* a "Royal Society" created for "Enquiries into the Works of God." For a full assessment of the significance of these and other quotations attributing the Royal Society to Bacon's influence, see Nell Eurich, *Science in Utopia* (Cambridge: Harvard University Press, 1967), 155–65.

23. For New World concerns, see Albanese, "The *New Atlantis* and the Uses of Utopia," 503–28. For the food sources that come from the New World, see Michael A. Weiner, *Earth Medicine—Earth Food: Plant Remedies, Drugs, and Natural Foods of the North American Indians* (New York: Macmillan, 1980), passim; see also Radcliffe N. Salaman, *The History and Social Influence of the Potato* (London: Cambridge University Press, 1970), 101–3 for mention of protein shortages in seventeenth-century Europe. Cf. *Francis Bacon*, ed. Vickers, 788–89; R. F. Jones, *Ancients and Moderns: A Study of the Rise of the Scientific Movement in Seventeenth-Century England* (St. Louis: Washington University Press, 1961), passim. Bacon may have conceived of Solomon's house as a kind of systematic, institutionalized extension of the Renaissance aristocrat's common patronage of persons like Tycho of Brahe or Kepler or scientists known to James and Bacon, such as Cornelius Drebbel and Salomon de Caus, combined with his common collection of a menagerie or cabinets of curiosi. See Rosalie L. Colie, "Cornelius Drebbel and Salomon de Caus: Two Jacobean Models for Salomon's House," *Huntington Library Quarterly* 18 (1954): 245–64.

24. See William H. McNeill, "American Food Crops in the Old World," in *Seeds of Change: A Quincentennial Commemoration*, ed. Herman J. Viola and Carolyn Margolis (Washington: Smithsonian Institution Press, 1991), 43–59.

25. For a plausible account of American Indian and non-Western tribal science, see Claude Lévi-Strauss, *La pensée sauvage* (Paris: Plon, 1962), passim. He argues that the purpose of "wild science" is not the transformation of nature. For the masque for Grey's Inn, see *Francis Bacon*, ed. Vickers, 54–55.

26. See Laurens Berns, "Francis Bacon and the Conquest of Nature," *Interpretation* 7 (1978): 2.

27. Sharon Achinstein notes that Bacon's search for knowledge was "authoritarian" with "mental activity to be 'guided at every step.'" However, Bacon does not address the manifest impossibility of such a project over the long haul, given the fact that any regime can support research and that the data is democratically available, so to speak. Cf. Sharon Achinstein, "How to Be a Progressive without Looking Like One: History and Knowledge in Bacon's *New Atlantis*," *Clio* 17 (1988): 250; cf. J. C. David, *Utopia and the Ideal Society* (New York: Cambridge University Press, 1981), 135–36.

28. Spedding, 6:121–24.

29. See Julius R. Weinberg, *Abstraction, Relation, and Induction: Three Essays in the History of Thought* (Madison: University of Wisconsin Press, 1965), for a discussion of Bacon's inductive reasoning; see also William Whewell, *History of the Inductive Sciences: From the Earliest to the Present Time* (London: Parker, 1847), vol. 4.

30. For Bacon on alchemists and magicians as imposters and imaginers, see Spedding, 6:127–28, 229–30. For more technical articles on the nature of the scientific methodology proposed by Bacon, see Julian Martin, *Francis Bacon, The State, and the Reform of Natural Philosophy* (Cambridge: Cambridge University Press, 1992), 144, 151–52, passim; Jeffrey Barnouw, "Active Experience vs. Wish Fulfillment in Francis Bacon's Philosophy of Science," *Philosophical Forum* 9 (1977): 78–79; Brian Vickers, "Francis Bacon and the Progress of Knowledge," *Journal of the History of Ideas* 53 (1992): 495–518; William A. Sessions, "Recent Studies in Francis Bacon," *English Literary Renaissance* 17 (3): 356–59.

31. Spedding, 5:398.

32. Spedding, 5:398–408.

33. Spedding, 5:411–12. Practical knowledge like the mastery of gunpowder does not mean professional knowledge. Bacon accuses the ordinary universities of Europe of his day of being wholly dedicated to the professions and caring not for the arts and sciences or the pure pursuit of knowledge (Spedding, 8:126–27). He also urges systems that presage the scholarly journal for the exchange of knowledge among people and

countries and scorns the theater's contempt for the pedagogue, arguing that the choice of teachers is as important as the choice of laws.

34. Spedding, 8:241.

35. On fruit, see Spedding, 8:100–2, 135–53. For Bacon's notion that his enterprise might lead to a recovery from the Fall, see Martin, *Francis Bacon*, 144 ff. On Gulliver's offer, see Albanese, "*New Atlantis* and the Uses of Utopia," 505–9, 520–21; Harvey Wheeler, "Francis Bacon's *New Atlantis*: The 'Mould' of a Lawfinding Commonwealth," *Philosophical Forum* 9 (1977): 293–95, 298–99; Michel Foucault, *The Order of Things* (New York: Pantheon, 1970), 51–52; Barnouw, "Active Experience vs. Wish Fulfillment in Francis Bacon's Philosophy of Science," *Philosophical Forum* 9 (1977): 82–86.

36. "We have consultations, which of the inventions and experiences which we have discovered shall be published, and which not: and take all an oath of secrecy, for the concealing of those which we think fit to keep secret; though some of those we do reveal sometimes to the state, and some not." Spedding, 5:411–12.

37. For Bacon's personal religion, see Perez Zagorin, *Francis Bacon* (Princeton: Princeton University Press, 1993), 50–51.

38. St. Bartholomew is brought in through what one critic has called an engineered miracle. Bensalem's Christianization came through the appearance of a pillar of fire surmounted by a cross, the Old and New Laws symbolically (Spedding, 5:371), and through the related coming of St. Bartholomew's ark containing the Old and New Testaments and certain patristic books "not at that time written," these last perhaps an indication of Bacon's willingness to defer to Lancelot Andrewes's patristic interests. After the miracle of St. Bartholomew's ark and the appearance of the Bible, the members of Salomon's house who approach it identify the appearance of the ark as "[God's] finger and a true Miracle," unusual since the "laws of nature" are God's "own laws," which He "exceedeth . . . not but upon great cause" (Spedding, 5:371–72). Almost nothing is known about St. Bartholomew, save that according to Chrysostom and Eusebius, he went east rather than west with his missionary efforts; possibly this is why he puts Bensalem's Christianizing message on the waters. The miracle of St. Bartholomew's ark is the one miracle in Ben-

salem's world, and it leads to instant conversion, after which comes the cessation of miracles. Hence the study of the light of the Six Days' Work is in fact the study of natural light, and its analogies, rather than the Logos light of John 1. Kumar's observation, following R. W. Chambers, that More's Utopia is "a pagan state founded on Reason and Philosophy" while Bacon's is "latterly Christianized" (Kumar, *Utopianism*, 36), seems to me to mistake rhetoric for reality. Both states are founded on the study of natural law, though Bacon's reveals a far different conception of natural law from that found in More and in traditional Western thought. The Christianity of Bacon's Atlantis exists primarily as legitimization for the House of Solomon's projects.

39. Human beings can, thus, know Christ through nature as well as through grace and revelation.

40. For Solomon and Origen, see Olson, *Journey to Wisdom*, 34–35.

41. For the *De Sapientia Veterum* as an original piece of mythmaking and not a derivative mythological handbook based on someone like Natale Conti, see Timothy H. Paterson, "Bacon's Myth of Orpheus: Power as a Goal of Science in *Of the Wisdom of the Ancients*," *Interpretation* 16 (1989): 427–43; cf. Lisa Jardine, *Francis Bacon: Discovery and the Art of Discourse* (Cambridge: Cambridge University Press, 1974), 173–92; cf. Ronald Levao, "Francis Bacon and the Mobility of Science," *Representations* 40 (1992): 7–9.

42. Spedding, 5:382.

43. I Kings 4:33 says only that Solomon spoke of trees, birds, beasts, and fishes. It does not attribute research or writing about natural history to him. Virgil Whitaker, *Francis Bacon's Intellectual Milieu* (Los Angeles: UCLA Press, 1962), 3–8.

44. Spedding, 6:93.

45. E. A. Burtt, *The Metaphysical Foundations of Modern Physical Science: A Historical and Critical Essay* (London: Routledge and Kegan Paul, 1967), 52–56.

46. Burtt, *Metaphysical Foundations*, 64–65.

47. Burtt, *Metaphysical Foundations*, 82–83.

48. For Bacon's lack of knowledge of contemporary continental science, see Zagorin, *Francis Bacon*, 91.

49. Spedding, 5:398–413.

50. For Bacon's method of manipulating variables, see Zagorin, *Francis Bacon*, 98–99.

51. Spedding, 8:166, 136. Bacon's attack on Wisdom theory may be an attack on the speculations of the theorists of magic, who rely on ideas about Wisdom for their central metaphysical statements.

52. Spedding, 8:168.

53. Spedding, 10:346–53, 387–88.

54. Spedding, 8:167. Cf. B. H. G. Wormald, *Francis Bacon: History, Politics and Science, 1561–1626* (New York: Cambridge University Press, 1993), 284–312.

55. Kate Aughterson argues that Bacon simultaneously fixes "references and yet open[s] meaning and science to the future" through his metaphoric strategy of using seemingly transparent and literalistic prose but prose structurally and metaphorically related to other works, in my view principally the *Timaeus* and Bible. Kate Aughterson, "The Waking Vision: Reference in *New Atlantis*," *Renaissance Quarterly* 45 (1992): 119. Cf. Ronald Levao on Bacon's rhetorical tactic of keeping the reader's mind in motion by suggesting that successive approximations to truth and provisional certainty are possible. Ronald Levao, "Francis Bacon and the Mobility of Science," *Representations* 40 (1992): 1–32.

56. Spedding, 8:72, 70, 93–97; M. M. Slaughter, *Universal Languages and Scientific Taxonomy in the Seventeenth Century* (New York: Cambridge University Press, 1982), 93–95.

57. Spedding, 5:372–73, 407, 409; 6:283.

58. Spedding, 3:727 ff.

59. L. Jonathan Cohen, "Some Historical Remarks on the Baconian Conception of Probability," *Journal of the History of Ideas* 41 (1980): 219–47.

60. Zagorin, *Francis Bacon*, 81 ff, argues that Bacon has a place for theory in his picture of science, and he is correct; what he lacks is a place for systemic analysis.

61. Spedding, 13:124–25.

62. For the conventional mythographic tradition in the Renaissance, see Jean Seznec, *The Survival of the Pagan Gods*, trans. Barbara F. Sessions (New York: Pantheon Books, 1953), passim. See also Paterson, "Bacon's

Myth of Orpheus," 427–43; Jardine, *Francis Bacon*, 173–92; and Levao, "Francis Bacon and the Mobility of Science," 7–9.

63. For Bacon's Democritan materialism, see Zagorin, *Francis Bacon*, 34–36, 79–81, 109–15.

64. For Bacon's use of ambiguous myth to suggest a quest for successive approximations to scientific accuracy, see Ronald Levao, "Francis Bacon and the Mobility of Science," 1–32. Bacon's utopia has to use a somewhat open parable since it suggested a future without much precedent to be realized.

65. Spedding, 6:132–33, 224.

66. Spedding, 5:409.

67. J. A. Stewart, *The Myths of Plato* (London: Macmillan, 1905), 457–64.

68. Spedding, 5:377.

69. Spedding, 5:377–78.

70. Spedding, 5:377–80.

71. See chapter 4 for an examination of how *Gulliver's Travels* parodies this playing with the Platonic account of the evolution of civilization.

72. Spedding, 3:166.

73. More conceptualizes something like medieval political theory's *lex naturae*, a natural law promoting a stable-state society based on understanding humankind's species characteristics. He understands civilization's basis in nature in a manner different from Plato, who thinks that understanding the mathematical forms underlying the seen world is basic to the guardian's task in the formation of civilization.

74. Spedding, 4:339.

75. Spedding, 5:362.

76. Spedding, 5:395–97.

77. Spedding, 5:398–411.

78. Paolo Rossi, *Francesco Bacone: dalla magia alla scienza* (Turin: Einaudi, 1974), passim.

79. J. C. Davis, *Utopia and the Ideal Society* (Cambridge: Cambridge University Press, 1981), 117–18.

80. See John C. Briggs, *Francis Bacon and the Rhetoric of Nature* (Cambridge: Harvard University Press, 1989), 170; Albanese, "The *New Atlantis* and the Uses of Utopia," 515 ff.

81. Vickers, "Francis Bacon and the Progress of Knowledge," 786.

82. Elisabeth Hansot's argument that the separation of the House of Solomon from ordinary civic life is designed "to reassure [Bacon's] reader that the effects of scientific knowledge will not change the nature of a godly society" (Hansot, *Perfection and Progress*, 102) may be correct for those readers in Bacon's time who gave the book only a superficial examination. However, that careful readers would have assumed that the House could exercise such massive control of the natural world and produce experiments that bore "fruit" in practical applications without affecting the structure of civil society seems to me unlikely. Bacon may have left the picture of the government and civic life vague precisely because he wished readers to imagine their own versions of the civic life that would emerge from the new *theoria*.

83. For Bacon's likely homosexuality, see Zagorin, *Francis Bacon*, 12–14.

84. Spedding, 5:398.

85. Spedding, 3:48–51; 4:114–26; 6:457–59; *Letters and Life*, 7:175, 496; 6:64, 60, 205–6.

86. Cf. H. B. White, "Bacon's Imperialism," *American Political Science Review* 52 (1958): 470–89. For a defense of Bacon against environmentalist critics, see Zagorin, *Francis Bacon*, 121–23.

3. BACON'S COMMONWEALTH OFFSPRING

1. James Harrington, *The Common-Wealth of Oceana* (London: J. Streater, for Livewell Chapman, 1656), passim. For a general survey of the utopias of this period and their impact on institution formation, see Amy Boesky, *Founding Fictions: Utopias in Early Modern England* (Athens: University of Georgia Press, 1996), passim.

2. Gerrard Winstanley, *The Works of Gerrard Winstanley, with an Appendix of Documents Relating to the Digger Movement*, ed. George H. Sabine (New York: Russell and Russell, 1965).

3. Gerrard Winstanley, *The Law of Freedom, and Other Writings*, ed. Christopher Hill (Cambridge: Cambridge University Press, 1983).

4. The English Civil War also shaped Comenius; cf. Jan Kumpera, "Vztah Jana Amose Komenského K Anglické Revoluci 17. Století," *Československý Časopis Historický* 22 (1974): 200–28.

5. For the development of Bacon and Comenius as millennialists, see Charles Webster, *The Great Instauration: Medicine, and Reform: 1626–1660* (London: Duckworth, 1975), 21–27. I am deeply indebted to Webster throughout this chapter, though I agree with critics who argue that the movement he describes is more broadly Protestant than Puritan.

6. Webster, *Great Instauration*, 19–21.

7. Durie's education was to include such practical classical writers as the agriculturalist Columella, but his emphasis was on such practical subjects as optics, natural philosophy, medicine, pharmacy, and chemistry and not on the classical authors as sources.

8. For the division of labor among these three men, see Samuel Hartlib, Charles Webster, and John Durie, *Samuel Hartlib and the Advancement of Learning*, ed. Charles Webster (London, Cambridge University Press, 1970), 8–9.

9. Though Charles II's consensus-seeking monarchy found it prudent to found its elite intellectual enterprises on a consensus figure like Bacon, ultimately the "Baconian" method could not be communicated to the classes alone; the accessibility of inductive data meant that its implications could not be confined only to traditional elites such as those in Solomon's House or in the Royal Society. The undermining of the paradigms for research and education supposedly derived from the ancients and communicated through England's most prestigious institutions of research and education was continued from Bacon by George Hakewill in his *An Apologie or Declaration of the Power and Providence of God* (Oxford: Turner, 1630), published in 1627, 1630, and 1635, and by the Polish John Jonston in his *A History of the Constancy of Nature* in Latin in 1632 (Amsterdam, 1632) and in English in 1657 (London: Streater, 1657). Cf. Webster, *Great Instauration*, 19 ff.; cf. Steven Shapin, "The House of Experiment in Seventeenth-Century England," *Isis* 79 (1988): 373–404.

10. Irene Parker, *Dissenting Academies in England* (New York: Octagon Books, 1969), 134; J. W. Ashley Smith, *The Birth of Modern Education: The Contribution of the Dissenting Academies, 1660–1800* (London: Independent Press, 1954), passim.

11. One of the best evidences for the influence of *New Atlantis* on the founding of the Royal Society is the latter's choosing of the House of Solomon's motto as its own; cf. A. R. Hall, *The Scientific Revolution:*

1500–1800 (London: Longmans, 1962), 191. For the consensus-building position of the Royal Society based on the guaranteeing of certain rights or freedoms, see J. R. Jacob, "Restoration, Reformation and the Origins of the Royal Society," *History of Science* 13 (1975): 155–76.

12. Howard Hotson, "Philosophical Pedagogy in Reformed Central Europe between Ramus and Comenius: A Survey of the Continental Background of the 'Three Foreigners,'" in *Samuel Hartlib and Universal Reformation*, ed. Mark Greengrass, Michael Leslie, and Timothy Raylor (Cambridge: Cambridge University Press, 1994), 29–50. Cf. Josef Polisensky, "Komensky, Hartlib a Anglicka Revoluce 17. Století," *Ceskoslovenský Casopis Historický* 26 (1978): 228–48.

13. See Greengrass, Leslie, and Raylor (eds.), *Samuel Hartlib and Universal Reformation*, passim; cf. Webster, *Great Instauration*, passim. For the notion that Webster in *The Great Instauration* describes as Puritan patterns of thought that are generally Protestant in character, see Lotte Mulligan, "Puritans and English Science: A critique of Webster," *Isis* 71 (1980), 456–69. Mulligan may be correct in saying that the patterns of thought that this group developed belonged to Protestantism as a whole in some measure, but the relating of intense Chiliasm and educational reform as a means to the realization of the kingdom of God on earth would not have been so intensely attacked in some Protestant circles as it was had the pattern been universally present in all forms of Protestantism. See later remarks on Broniewski and other critics. In the 1650s Hartlib tempered his millennialism considerably: see Malcolm Oster, "Millenarianism and the New Science: The Case of Robert Boyle," in *Samuel Hartlib and Universal Reformation*, ed. Mark Greengrass, Michael Leslie, and Timothy Raylor (Cambridge: Cambridge University Press, 1994), 145–46.

14. Winstanley, *Works*, 409. The fourth reformer discussed in this chapter, Gabriel Plattes, does not come from Protestant Eastern Europe, but his proposals are sufficiently attractive to Hartlib that the latter disseminates them, fusing them with Comenius's ideas; for a biography of Plattes, see Webster, *Great Instauration*, 47–48.

15. Webster (ed.), *Samuel Hartlib and the Advancement of Learning*, 172–74. However, Comenian thought distinguished itself from Restora-

tion Baconianism that putatively set aside questions of ethics and preference in social formations in that Comenianism endeavored to ask moral
questions concerning scientific findings. Cf. Klaus Schaller, "Die Panso-
phie des Comenius under der Baconismus der Royal Society," *Berichte
zur Wissenschaftsgeschichte* 14 (1991): 161–67. The humanists also asked
similar questions: cf. B. C. Southgate, "'No Other Wisdom'? Humanist
Reactions to Science and Scientism in the Seventeenth Century," *Seventeenth Century* 5 (1991): 71–92.

16. Francis Bacon, *Novum Organum*, book II, aphorism 52 (Spedding
8:347–50).

17. Webster, *Great Instauration*, 506. Hartlib was more heavily influenced by Calvin than were his colleagues; cf. M. Greengrass, "Samuel
Hartlib and International Calvinism," *Proceedings of the Huguenot Society
of Great Britain and Ireland* 25 (1993): 464–75.

18. Webster observes that "the call for universal education begun in
the writings of Comenius was quickly taken up by the puritan social reformers and it was incorporated as an axiom into the reform literature of
the Puritan Revolution." Webster, *Great Instauration*, 114.

19. For a sample, see Webster, *Great Instauration*, index, under Hartlib, associates and correspondents of (596–97). For Boyle's relation to
Hartlib, see Charles Webster, "Benjamin Worlsey: Engineering for Universal Reform," in *Samuel Hartlib and Universal Reformation*, ed. Mark
Greengrass, Michael Leslie, and Timothy Raylor (Cambridge: Cambridge University Press, 1994), 221.

20. Johann Amos Comenius, *Conatuum Comenianorum Praeludia*
(Oxford: G. Turner, 1637), passim.

21. Johann Amos Comenius, *Pansophiae Prodromus* (London: Flesher,
1639), passim. For the circumstance of the publication of the 1630s Pansophic works, see Webster (ed.), *Samuel Hartlib and the Advancement of
Learning*, 110.

22. Johann Amos Comenius, *A Reformation of the Schooles* (London,
Michael Sparke, 1642), passim; cf. Webster, *Great Instauration*, 28 ff.

23. Johann Amos Comenius, *Naturall Philosophy Reformed by Divine
Light* (London: Leybourn, 1651); Johann Amos Comenius, *A Patterne of
Universall Knowledge*, trans. Jeremy Collier (London: Collins, 1651).

24. Johann Amos Comenius, *The Labyrinth of the World and the Paradise of the Heart*, translated by Matthew Spinka (Ann Arbor: University of Michigan, 1972), passim.

25. Johann Amos Comenius, *A Generall Table of Europe* (London: Billingsley, 1670), passim. This is an English translation/summary of *Lux in Tenebris* (Amsterdam, 1670). The original work was published in several editions between 1657 and 1665, among them *Lux ex Tenebris* (Amsterdam, 1665). For additional material on Comenius's millennialism, see Webster, *Great Instauration*, 21, 25–27, 86, 114, 517. Webster establishes that Comenius's millennial hopes and his educational plans were of a piece.

26. Webster, *Great Instauration*, 26.

27. The biblical Sophia is both a revealer of knowledge about the universe and an apocalyptic figure. Cf. Olson, *Journey to Wisdom*, 1–41, 172–99.

28. Johann Amos Comenius, *Physicae* (Amsterdam: Jansson, 1645), sig. 9, 4v.

29. For Bacon's definition of Wisdom as the matter and motion of the atoms, see chapter 2. Comenius appears to retain a much more traditional understanding of Wisdom as the repository of the ideas in the mind of God and their transmitter to matter. For Comenius's atomism, see Ján Mikles, "'Loci Paralleli' Medzi Janom Amosom Komenským A Isákon Cabanom V Atomistickej Filozofii," *Studia Comeniana et Historica* 23 (1993): 12–25.

30. For the development of a greater willingness among seventeenth-century scientists to share findings publicly, see Steven Shapin, "The House of Experiment in Seventeenth-Century England," *Isis* 79 (1988): 373–404.

31. Comenius, *Reformation of the Schooles*, sigs. A2r–B (2–7); [C1]r–C2r (15–18); D2r–[D3]v (26–27); [F2]r (42). Cf. Comenius, *Naturall Philosophie Reformed by Divine Light*, sig. A2r.

32. Comenius, *Reformation of the Schooles*, sig. L2r–[L3]r (82–84).

33. See Olson, *Journey to Wisdom*, 156, passim; Jean Piaget, *John Amos Comenius: 1592–1670* (Lausanne: UNESCO, 1957), passim.

34. Comenius, *Reformation of the Schooles*, sigs. [B4] (13); C[1]r–[E4]r (16–38); [C3]r–[C4]r (20–22); L2r–[L3]r (82–84).

35. Comenius, *Reformation of the Schooles*, sig. [M3]r–[[M4]r (92–94).

36. So far as I can determine, Comenius's *Magna Didactica* was not published in England in Latin; the first publication of an English *Great Didactic* comes in 1896 (London: Black). Some of Comenius's Commonwealth friends did see the work in manuscript.

37. Comenius, *Orbis Pictus*, 24–31, 119–20, 132–35, 194. Cf. *The Orbis Pictus of John Amos Comenius* (Syracuse: C. W. Bardeen, 1887), passim. Cf. Johann Amos Comenius, *Janua Linguarum Reserata: The Gate of Language Unlocked* (London: Young, 1643), passim, organized on the basis of the same assumptions as the *Orbis Pictus* but more advanced and without pictures. The preface to *Orbis Pictus* includes Comenius's theory of pedagogy moving from the sensory to the intellectual; emphasizes the development of wisdom through the initial presentation of the sensory image; describes the visible as a token of the invisible; describes God as Power, Goodness, Wisdom, and a light; includes a good deal of seventeenth-century scientific lore; and presents the industrial crafts and vocations in a quite full review for beginning elementary students. Any teacher using the book would have had a basic grasp of Comenius's pedagogical assumptions.

38. For Hartlib's millennialist appeal to Comenius, see Webster, *Great Instauration*, 33, 77 ff. For Durie, see Webster, *The Great Instauration*, 21, 29, 32–34. Hartlib and Durie mention Pansophia but generally when they are appealing to Comenius.

39. For Hartlib's efforts in behalf of Protestant millennial ideas, see Webster, *Great Instauration*, 40–44; for Durie and millennialism, see Webster, *Great Instauration*, 21–34.

40. Webster (ed.), *Samuel Hartlib and the Advancement of Learning*, 150–51.

41. Webster, *Great Instauration*, 69, 71, 216. Webster (ed.), *Samuel Hartlib and the Advancement of Learning*, 151.

42. Max Weber, *The Protestant Ethic and the Spirit of Capitalism* (New York: Scribner, 1956), passim; R. H. Tawney, *Religion and the Rise of Capitalism* (New York: New American Library, 1954), passim.

43. Webster (ed.), *Samuel Hartlib and the Advancement of Learning*, 145–65 (extended quote from 152).

44. It is difficult to know to what extent Hartlib had a role in the cre-

ation of Plattes's utopia. As Kevin Dunn observes, "the books of this group of men [were] very often communally written" and "were even more often presented to the public in a way seemingly designed to baffle modern scholars"—that is, anonymously or printed as Hartlib's, whoever the author was. Cf. Kevin Dunn, "Milton among the Monopolists," in *Samuel Hartlib and Universal Reformation*, ed. Mark Greengrass, Michael Leslie, and Timothy Raylor (Cambridge: Cambridge University Press, 1994), 182–83.

45. Webster (ed.), *Samuel Hartlib and the Advancement of Learning*, 80.

46. Webster (ed.), *Samuel Hartlib and the Advancement of Learning*, 86.

47. Webster (ed.), *Samuel Hartlib and the Advancement of Learning*, 81–83, quote on 82.

48. Webster (ed.), *Samuel Hartlib and the Advancement of Learning*, 83–84. Walter Charleton, in the period, saw the College of Physicians as a Solomon's House; Webster, *Great Instauration*, 315.

49. For the development of conceptions of rights during the Commonwealth, see A. S. P. Woodhouse, *Puritanism and Liberty* (London: Dent, 1938), passim.

50. B. M. Add. Ms. Ex. Leg. J. Ward, 6271. For Antilia, see Webster, *Great Instauration*, 46–47, 86–87. Webster observes that "despite the utopian guise of *Macaria*, its reform proposals were obviously directed at the English situation" (*Great Instauration*, 359).

51. George Henry Turnbull, *Hartlib, Durie and Comenius: Gleanings from Hartlib's Papers* (Liverpool: University Press of Liverpool, 1947), 69–76.

52. Webster (ed.), *Samuel Hartlib and the Advancement of Learning*, 63. Cf *The Diary and Correspondence of Dr. John Worthington*, ed. James Crossley, 3 vols. (Manchester: Chetham Society, 1847–86), in *Remains, Historical and Literary, Connected with the Palatinate Counties of Lancaster and Chester*, 13:342 (diary completed in vols. 36 and 114).

53. George Henry Turnbull, "Samuel Hartlib's Influence on the Early History of the Royal Society," *Notes and Records of the Royal Society of London* 10 (1953): 128. When Sir John Sadler parodied Hartlib in his *Olbia*

(Hartlib said Sadler made him look like a "fanatick" and Quaker), he ended it with a hymn to a materialized Sophia: "Divine Sophia though I sprawl in clay; / Yet thou art ne'er ally'd." Cf. Henry Dircks, *A Biographical Memoir of Samuel Hartlib* (London: John Russell, [1865]), 24.

54. Webster (ed.), *Samuel Hartlib and the Advancement of Learning*, 48.

55. Webster (ed.), *Samuel Hartlib and the Advancement of Learning*, 132.

56. Nell Eurich observes that both Bacon and Comenius looked for "state support to make possible the new revelations in knowledge, which were to be derived from observation of natural phenomena," and that though Comenius "was less entranced with the scientific laboratory and projected his pansophic theories more into the educational process than Bacon," in effort they are "brothers": "Comenius, as an impressive foreigner in London, played no little part in creating the Baconian legend." *Science in Utopia: A Mighty Design* (Cambridge: Harvard University Press, 1967), 149–50. Eurich's book also contains a useful account of the Hartlib circle.

57. Bacon several times refers approvingly to Jesuit education as the model for primary and secondary education, by which he means the *ratio studiorum*; cf. Spedding 3:277, 416–17; 4:494–95. Based on Sturm's Protestant reforms at Strasbourg, the *ratio* was formally adopted by the Jesuits only in 1599 after some years of discussion. According to the *ratio*, scholars were not to be turned away because they were poor—only for failure to learn. The structure was to be three years of the ABC school; five years of grammar school, including humanities and rhetoric; three years in philosophy, including logic, physics, metaphysics, ethics, and mathematics (primarily the old quadrivium); and then theology for the very good students and the priesthood and teaching for the poorer ones. Teachers could separate students into tracks and give prizes, but students were graded to a standard and not competitively. Teachers were to praise all students. Students lived in college, like the residents of Solomon's House. Cf. *Ratio atque Institutio Studiorum Societatis Jesu* (Rome: Society of Jesus, 1606), passim.

58. Cf. Spedding 1:709–11; 3:277; 4:494–96. Cf. David Cressy, "Francis Bacon and the Advancement of Schooling," *History of European Ideas* 2 (1981): 65–74, esp. 71.

59. Webster (ed.), *Samuel Hartlib and the Advancement of Learning*, 182. A version of this proposal is contained in the Hartlib manuscripts in the Sheffield University Library, box 47, 2, 1r–12v.

60. Webster (ed.), *Samuel Hartlib and the Advancement of Learning*, 182–85. As early as 1653, an educational agenda was put before the British Parliament and nation; it was not passed until the 1870s.

61. Webster (ed.), *Samuel Hartlib and the Advancement of Learning*, 178–85.

62. Hartlib MSS in the Sheffield University Library, box 7, 36, 6; cf., e.g., Hartlib MS 7, 36, 7–8.

63. Hartlib MS 7, 92. "However yf Comenius should fayle of hys personall endeavor to perfect soe vast & admirable a work, whereto no one man's life or ability may easiyly be thought sufficient; yet this prayse & honor he shall not fayle to reap from all lovers of learning, that hee hath kindled a clearer light, then hitherto hath beene used, wherby those may with more speed & fruit order theyre studys, who shall hereafter intend the search & discovery of Truth." Hartlib MS 7, 36, 8.

64. Hartlib MS 7, 51r and 123, 1–2; MS 53, 36, 1rff.; MS 47, 10, 2r–54v. The author of this treatise, probably William Petty (initals W. P.), had already presented to Parliament a "Discourse of the Accomplishment of Englands Reformation." See Hartlib MS 47, 10, 19r.

65. Hartlib MS 47, 10, passim, especially 47, 10, 13r–13v.

66. Hartlib MS 47, 10, 21r, 31r, 32rff. Cf. Hartlib MS 47, 10, 50r–54v.

67. Hartlib MS 47, 10, 38r and 43r–45r; MS 47, 3, 1r–4v.

68. Webster (ed.), *Samuel Hartlib and the Advancement of Learning*, 57–58 7. Turnbull, *Hartlib, Durie and Comenius*, 45.

69. Part of the dialogue concerned the creation of a "real character," a language in which it would be impossible to misrepresent reality without detection because each word would represent a thing and the structure of the language would represent the relationship among the things under consideration. Bacon, of course, had prepared the way for such a concern by speaking of idols or eidola that intervene between cognition and reality, including misleading or imprecise language, a concern shared by Comenius, Cave Beck, John Wilkins, and others. Cf. M. M. Slaughter, *Universal Languages and Scientific Taxonomy in the Seventeenth Century* (New York: Cambridge University Press, 1982), 97–104 and pas-

sim; Gerhard F. Strasser, "Closed and Open Languages: Samuel Hartlib's Involvement with Cryptology and Universal Languages," in *Samuel Hartlib and Universal Reformation*, ed. Mark Greengrass, Michael Leslie, and Timothy Raylor (Cambridge: Cambridge University Press, 1994), 151–61. The artificial language portions of this book were supported by a Fulbright stipend.

70. For Broniewski, see Greengrass, Leslie, and Raylor (eds.), *Samuel Hartlib and Universal Reformation*, 86.

71. Turnbull, *Hartlib, Durie and Comenius*, 452–57.

72. Anonymous, "In Pansophiae Librum Annotationes," Hartlib MS box 18, 22, fols. 1–6. For an analysis of the text see Dagmar Capková, "The Reception Given to the *Prodromus Pansophiae* and the Methodology of Comenius," *Acta Comeniana* 7 (1987): 37–59.

73. Two Lutheran theologians, J. Botsak and A. Calovius, raised the Lutheran objections. Hartlib MS box 7, fol. 96. Dagmar Capková, "Comenius and His Ideals: Escape from the Labyrinth," in Greengrass, Leslie, and Raylor (eds.), *Samuel Hartlib and Universal Reformation*, 86.

74. Paul Wijdeveld tells the story of Adolph Loos's proposing the notion that through "the artist . . . Providence—the 'Holy Ghost'—realized civilization as a cultural flowering in man." Paul Wijdeveld, *Ludwig Wittgenstein, Architect* (Cambridge: MIT Press, 1994) 35. Wittgenstein called the remark "virulent bogus intellectualism." If one were to substitute the word *educator* for *artist* in Loos's statement, one would have a proper characterization of Comenius's hope, and it is not surprising that thinkers who took the old religious categories seriously were bothered by him. Cf. Marjorie Perloff, *Wittgenstein's Ladder: Poetic Language and the Strangeness of the Ordinary* (Chicago: University of Chicago Press, 1996), 224.

75. Bucer, who was in England, during the 1541–42 period, had called for universal education in Strasbourg and shaped much of Sturm's thinking, but he seems not to have pushed for such reforms in England. Cf. Mark E. Vander Schaff, "Archbishop Parker's Efforts toward a Bucerian Discipline in the Church of England," *Sixteenth Century Journal* 8 (1977): 85–103; Webster (ed.), *Samuel Hartlib and the Advancement of Learning*, 207. For the grand scope of the Protestant plans, see Webster (ed.), *Samuel Hartlib and the Advancement of Learning*, 50, 101.

76. Robert F. Young, *Comenius in England* (New York, Arno Press, 1971), 7–9, passim; G. H. Turnbull, "Samuel Hartlib's Influence on the Early History of the Royal Society," *Notes and Records of Royal Society* 10 (1953): 101–30.

77. Webster (ed.), *Samuel Hartlib and the Advancement of Learning*, 69, 494–97; Webster, *Great Instauration*, 96–99, shows that the Baconian agenda of the Royal Society came largely from Hartlib's group and not from the "invisible college."

78. "Later writers have followed Sprat in admitting that a surprisingly large proportion of the leading restoration scientists had been initiated into science during the Puritan Revolution. This applies to almost all of the 'active nucleus' of the Royal Society, and to the vast majority of the 'active members.'" Webster, *Great Instauration*, 492, 502–5.

79. Webster, *Great Instauration*, 492–520.

80. Boyle was interested in Comenian/Hartlibian methods of education during the Commonwealth period, but it is difficult to know to what extent he pursued the agenda after the Restoration. Cf. Young, *Comenius in England*, 92–95. Boyle's membership in the Hartlib group must be separated from his "Invisible College" work; cf. Charles Webster, "New Light on the Invisible College: The Social Relations of English Science in the Mid-Seventeenth Century," *Royal Historical Society Transactions* 24 (1974): 19–42.

81. For more on the dissenting academies, see chapter 4.

82. Parker, *Dissenting Academies*, 135. For additional useful materials on the dissenting academies, see J. W. Ashley Smith, *The Birth of Modern Education: The Contribution of the Dissenting Academies: 1660–1800* (London: Independent, 1954); Herbert McLachlan, *English Education under the Test Acts: Being the History of the Nonconformist Academies* (Manchester: Manchester University Press, 1954); David L. Ferch, "'Good Books are a very great mercy to the world': Persecution, Private Libraries and the Printed Word in the Early Development of the Dissenting Academies, 1663–1730," *Journal of Library History* 21 (1986), 350–61; Diana Harding, "Mathematics and Science Education in Eighteenth-Century Northamptonshire," *History of Education* 1 (1972), 139–59.

83. Ferch, "Good Books," 352.

84. Condorcet, "Fragment sur L'Atlantide," *Tableau Historique des Progrès de l'Esprit Humain* (Paris: Steinheil, 1900), 416–72

85. Letter from Henry More to Hartlib concerning William Petty's Baconian proposals for scientific advancement, republished in Charles Webster, "Henry More and Descartes: Some New Sources," *British Journal for the History of Science* 4 (1969): 371.

4. SCRIBLERAN REVOLT AGAINST EDUCATION
TO EXTEND HUMAN EMPIRE

1. Alexander Pope, *The Dunciad*, ed. James Sutherland (London: Methuen, 1943), vol. 5, p. 381. All references to Pope's poetry and his glosses on it refer to the 15-volume Twickenham edition (London: Methuen 1939–67). *Dunciad* cites often include number and page, even where poetic lines are given in text, to permit consultation with the *Dunciad* glosses; citation of Pope's translations of the *Iliad* and *Odyssey* follow the same pattern.

2. Pope, *Dunciad*, 5:381.

3. For a discussion of Restoration fears of the new mechanists and corpuscular thinkers deriving from Hobbes, see Michael Hunter, *Science and Society in Renaissance England* (Cambridge: Cambridge University Press, 1981), 169–83.

4. Pope, *Dunciad*, 5:385.

5. Pope, *Dunciad*, 5:387–88. Pope makes Hobbes the primary representative of the Baconians in this section. While others move from "plain experience" to "Nature" to "Nature's Cause," the new scientific philosophers, whether Baconians or Cartesian rationalists ("Hobbs, Spinoza, Des Cartes, and some better reasoners"), begin with a priori assumptions, "reason downward," and ultimately, like the Baconians, Cartesians, or Scriblerans, "thrust some Mechanic Cause" into God's place; and conceptualize "a God without a Thought," plainly because they have adopted a definition of natural law that makes the hand of Wisdom irrelevant. In contrast to Newton, who studies whole systems, the *Dunciad* scientists study flies and hummingbirds and seek "to fly to the moon." "Mother of Arrogance, and Source of Pride," Nature has nothing to say to them because they think they know nature's cause from

close-up experiments—no step-by-step movement through the whole system to its cause for them. As ancient ethics was derived from the natural study of physics, mathematics, and metaphysics, the new Baconian or Hobbesian "makes(s) God Man's Image" and finds the source of moral authority to be neither revelation nor Wisdom (natural philosophy) but the self.

6. Pope, *Dunciad*, 5:391–92.

7. Book 1 mocks anti-Sapiential artistic patronage; book 2 pictures popular print culture; book 3 extends book 2 to a history of the progress of "decivilization," and book 4, in the 1743 version, concludes with the apotheosis of "Dulness": the destruction of education and learning seeking Wisdom throughout the realm.

8. Olson, *Journey to Wisdom*, 98.

9. Pope, *Dunciad*, 5:408–9.

10. I disagree with G. S. Rousseau ("Pope and the Tradition in Modern Humanistic Education," in *The Enduring Legacy: Alexander Pope Tercentenary Essays* [Cambridge: Cambridge University Press, 1988], 237) that Pope does not privilege day over night and the other benign sides of his opposites but privileges both contrary states. See William E. Rivers, *Backgrounds of Pope's Satire of Education*, Ph.D. diss., University of North Carolina, Chapel Hill, 1976, and, by the same author, "Pope, Pedagogues and Politicians," *University of Dayton Review* 15 (1981): 113–23. Rivers does not show how reason, light, anamnesis (memory), and logical discipline prevailed in the schools or how this order yielded to educational chaos. What the schools have in Pope's satire is never Apollo's (or Minerva's) armies of Reason. Contrary to Rousseau, the classical Minerva is not emotionally sterile. Indeed, she brings Ulysses home to his love; that is her sole function. The triumph of light and biblical Wisdom does not, in any Popean context, mean that human rationality destroys charity, decency, and kindness or that it relies primarily on violence to order its world. Dissimulation is often for both Pope and Swift an alternative to violence, as are the arts of the epic and mock epic. The understanding of the relationships among instruction, reason and passion, and educational struggle in the Pope/Broome account of the Circe episode makes clear that the function of instruction is not to get rid of passion

but to shape it to constructive, humane goals having to do with the enhancement of human community.

11. For the medieval and Renaissance history of this tradition, see Olson, *Journey to Wisdom*, passim.

12. Cf. Aubrey Williams, *Pope's "Dunciad": A Study of its Meaning* (Hamden CT: Archon, 1968), 143, 131–58 passim. See C. R. Kropf, "Education and the Neoplatonic Idea of Wisdom in Pope's *Dunciad*," *Texas Studies in Language and Literature* 14 (1973): 593–604.

13. Cf. Olson, *Journey to Wisdom*, passim.

14. Pope, *Dunciad*, 5:409.

15. Alexander Pope, *Minor Poems*, ed. Norman Ault and John Butt (London: Methuen, 1964), 6:73.

16. "Eternal Reason" was commonly defined as wisdom in the Boethian commentaries; that is, the wisdom of Proverbs 8:22ff. and of the Apocryphal wisdom books. As the power of natural law that "informs great nature and directs the whole," Wisdom is the force through which kings reign and from whom princes derive their nobility (Proverbs 8:14–16; Wisdom of Solomon 6:1ff.). She is herself a biblical poet and, with her seven pillars, sometimes signified the culmination of the liberal arts (Proverbs 9:1ff). Cf. Olson, *Journey to Wisdom*, passim. These ideas continue in the eighteenth century through biblical commentary and sermons such as William Reeves's *Sermon Concerning the Wisdom of God in the Works of Nature*. In short, in Wisdom's culture, the arts and sciences and natural law order the realm through learning. In Pope's *Essay on Man*, Wisdom structures things as they rise in ordered hierarchies from nothing to God (epistle 1, ll. 43–50). Cf. Alexander Pope, *An Essay on Man*, ed. Maynard Mack (London: Methuen, 1950), vol. 3, pt. 1, pp. 18–19 and notes. In function identical with the Logos of John 1:1–8, she makes the laws that Pope saw Newton unfolding (epistle 2, ll. 29–34). Cf. Pope, *Essay on Man*, 3:59–60.

17. Pope, *Dunciad*, 5:270.

18. Pope, *Dunciad*, 5:336.

19. Pope, *Dunciad*, 5:339–48.

20. For the character of the Royal Society's sense of group, see Hunter, *Science and Society*, 59–86.

21. Michael Hunter, *Establishing the New Science* (Woodbridge: Boydell, 1989), 9–10 and passim.

22. For the Anglican Latitudinarian orientation of Newtonianism, see James R. and Margaret C. Jacob, "The Anglican Origins of Modern Science: The Metaphysical Foundations of the Whig Constitution," *Isis* 71 (1980): 251–67. Cf. Margaret C. Jacob, *The Newtonians and the English Revolution: 1689–1750* (Ithaca: Cornell University Press, 1976), passim.

23. For Hartlib and the Royal Society, see Webster, *Great Instauration*, 98–99, 502, and passim.

24. For the character of mechanism and of Enlightenment experimentalism, see Thomas L. Hawkins, *Science and the Enlightenment* (Cambridge: Cambridge University Press, 1985), 1–157; Margaret Osler, *Divine Will and the Mechanical Philosophy* (Cambridge: Cambridge University Press), passim. The effect of mechanism was to desacralize to natural world preparatory to manipulation.

25. For the foundations of market capitalism before Adam Smith, see Bruce G. Carruthers, *City of Capital: Politics and Markets in the English Financial Revolution* (Princeton: Princeton University Press, 1996), passim.

26. For the influence of Comenius in the dissenting academies, see Parker, *Dissenting Academies*, 134.

27. Great differences separate More's and Shakepeare's modes of thinking about cultural organization; More emphasizes the communal and Shakespeare the monarchic. However, neither defends the permanent alteration of the natural system, and both use cultural artifacts as educative devices. When the Restoration came, Commonwealth proposals for compulsory education in England were shelved. Charity schools substituted for universal compulsory education. Swift thought that they should provide education for the servant classes, who did not have resources to go to other schools in Ireland; cf. Jonathan Swift, "Causes of the Wretched Condition of Ireland," in *The Prose Works of Jonathan Swift*, ed. Herbert Davis, 14 vols. (Oxford: Basil Blackwell, 1939–68), 9:204. Oxford and Cambridge were generally in decline in the period, and Charles II's court frowned on new institutions being founded at either the grammar school or college level. A royalist Hobbes argued that ancient history and classical studies centering in grammar school and uni-

versity dangerously advanced republicanism; cf. David Ogg, *England in the Reign of Charles II*, 2 vols. (Oxford: Clarendon Press, 1956), 1:692–93. Aubrey without effect opposed the tutorials and military academies favored by the rich and proposed the substitution of English and mathematics for Latin studies, all to be done by Swiss or Scottish teachers—that is, teachers from regions where general education flourished (cf. Bodley Aubrey MS A10). And when Locke's *Some Thoughts Concerning Education* promoted many of the attitudes toward instruction earlier encouraged by Hartlib's circle as basic to mass education, it did so *to improve elite tutorial education rather than any universal or compulsory system*.

28. Jonathan Swift, *Irish Tracts 1720–1723 and Sermons*, ed. Louis Landa, vol. 9 in *The Prose Works of Jonathan Swift*, ed. Davis, 14 vols. (Oxford: Basil Blackwell, 1948), 9:264, appendix A.

29. *The Prose Works of Jonathan Swift*, ed. Davis, 12:46–53. Restoration leaders had been suspicious of education and had made few educational proposals. Ogg, *England in the Reign of Charles II*, 1:692–93.

30. *Prose Works of Jonathan Swift*, 12:48–49; 2:52–53, 59; 9:154–55; 12:160–61. Addison and Steele argued that education ought to avoid harshness and all sorts of corporal punishment. Cf. *The Spectator*, ed. Donald F. Bond, 5 vols. (Oxford: Clarendon Press, 1965), 2:114–17, 160–64; 3:105–9; Richard Steele et al., *The Tatler* (Philadelphia: De Silver, Thomas, 1837), 307–8, 338–39.

31. *Prose Works of Jonathan Swift*, 9:204–5. Swift's remark that "it would well become the Wisdom of the Nation to make some Provision in so important an Affair" in the context of the need for all poor children to be trained in charity school in religion, cleanliness, honest industry, and thrift, and then given an apprenticeship, seems to suggest that all poor children should be given an education in charity schools. "Causes of the Wretched Condition of Ireland," in *Prose Works of Jonathan Swift*, 9:204.

32. *Prose Works of Jonathan Swift*, 12:307–8.

33. John Gay, *Poetical, Dramatical and Miscellaneous Works* (New York: AMS Press, 1970), 1:213–19.

34. John Gay, *Fables* (London: Tonson, 1727), sig. B2r.

35. For an account of contemporary educational thought, especially in the later Scribleran period when the last versions of the *Dunciad* were

written, see Rousseau, "Pope and the Tradition," 208–39. Rousseau's brilliant essay, with which I have a number of differences, does not deal with educational thought within the Scribleran group though Scriblerus remains a major fictive commentator on the *Dunciad*.

36. For Pope's early education, see James King, "'I Never Learned Anything at the Little Schools': Pope's Roman Catholic Education," *Education in the 18th Century*, ed. J. D. Browning (London: Garland, 1979), 98–122.

37. For the evolution of Pope's "Epistle on Education," see Miriam Leranbaum, *Alexander Pope's 'Opus Magnum'* (Oxford: Clarendon Press, 1977), 29–31, 131–37, 152–54, 174–75.

38. Leranbaum, *Alexander Pope's 'Opus Magnum*,' 133.

39. Leranbaum, *Alexander Pope's 'Opus Magnum*,' 131.

40. The most helpful material on the possible content of Pope's essay is to be found in Leranbaum, *Alexander Pope's 'Opus Magnum*,' passim; Rivers, *Backgrounds to Pope's Satire of Education*, passim; Vincent Carretta, *The Snarling Muse: Verbal and Visual Poetical Satire from Pope to Churchill* (Philadelphia: University of Pennsylvania Press, 1983), 140–73. Locke's influence on Pope has been debated and possibly overrated, especially in view of the knowledge of Comenius-like educational principles the Scribleran group shows in the Martinus works. However, for a defense of Locke's influence, see J. P. Vander Motten, "Pope, Locke, and *The New Dunciad*," in *Centennial Hauntings: Pope, Byron and Eliot in the Year 88*, ed. C. C. Barfoot and Theo D'Haen (Rodopi: Amsterdam, 1990), 87–96.

41. Pope repeatedly canonizes Newton directly or implicitly; his general appraisal of Newton is sermonized in the epitaph: "God said, Let Newton be and all was Light." *The Essay on Man* begins its crucial set of propositions with a description of "Wisdom infinite" forming the "scale" of "reasoning life." The rest of the poem then presents Wisdom's ladder from God to chaos, constructed according to divine, musical proportions. The entire first half of the work culminates in an ironic echo of Job 40:1–2 and in general biblical Wisdom notions: "Go, teach Eternal Wisdom how to rule / Then drop into thyself, and be a fool!" (epistle 2, ll. 29–30). In the equally ironic context of this passage, Pope demonstrates by indirection how submission to Wisdom accompanies the dis-

covery, rather than the manipulation of its numerical system—its ordered time and regular Sun. The scientist, in discovering, merely submits to what is out there while the pseudoscientist attributes discovery to human powers. Swift, angry at Newton's endorsement of debased coinage in Ireland, generally expresses satiric contempt for him (*Prose Works of Jonathan Swift*, 4 : 231, 122–23), but that contempt must be based on their division over British colonial policy and not primarily on issues of how science ought to be done. See Richard S. Westfall, *Never at Rest: A Biography of Isaac Newton* (Cambridge: Cambridge University Press, 1980), 758.

42. John Arbuthnot, *An Essay on the Usefulness of Mathematical Learning* (Oxford: Anthony Peisley, 1701). Arbuthnot writes of "*Arithmetic, Musick. Geometry and Astronomy,*" 2. Cf. George A. Aitken, *The Life and Works of John Arbuthnot* (Oxford: Clarendon Press, 1892), 66.

43. Arbuthnot, *Mathematical Learning*, 13.

44. Aitken, *Life and Works of John Arbuthnot*, 413.

45. Aitken, *Life and Works of John Arbuthnot*, 416.

46. Aitken, *Life and Works of John Arbuthnot*, 433–35.

47. Pope, *Essay on Man*, epistle 4, ll. 281–82; cf. notes in the Mack edition, vol. 3, pt. 1, pp. 154–55.

48. *L'Odyssée d'Homere, traduite en François avec des remarques*, trans. Anne Dacier (Paris: Rigaud, 1716), 3 vols. In general, both the Pope and Dacier commentaries give interpretations similar to those in the Spondanus commentary, and both cite the same classical authorities; cf. *Homeri Quae Extant Omnia: Opera*, trans. with commentary by Johannes Spondanus, 2 vols. in 1 (Basel, 1583). Spondanus was in Swift's library; see William LeFance, *A Catalog of Books Belonging to Dr. Jonathan Swift* (Cambridge: Cambridge Bibliographical Society, 1988), 21.

49. Cf., e.g., the Geneva 1636 edition of the Virgil's works and the Amsterdam 1746 one.

50. Cf. Donald Foerster, *Homer in English Criticism: The Historical Approach in the Eighteenth Century* (New Haven: Yale University Press, 1947), passim; Thomas M. Woodman, *Thomas Parnell* (Boston: Twayne, 1985), 90–93.

51. For Swift's knowledge of Pope's Homer, see *Correspondence of Jonathan Swift*, ed. Harold Williams, 5 vols. (Oxford: Clarendon Press, 1963–

65), 2:176–77, 381, 444, 446, 458; 3:39, 41, 79, 103. The last passage shows Swift at work on *Gulliver's Travels* as he awaits getting his hands on Pope's *Odyssey*. Pope writes to Parnell about how, after he lost the latter's help, he had to wrestle by himself with Eustathius, Spondanus, Dacier, and a number of other Homeric commentators. See *The Correspondence of Alexander Pope*, ed. George Sherburn, 5 vols. (Oxford: Clarendon Press, 1956), 1:226–27.

52. Alexander Pope, *The Odyssey of Homer*, ed. Maynard Mack (London: Methuen, 1967), Twickenham edition 9:27.

53. Pope, *Odyssey of Homer*, 9:27.

54. Pope, *Odyssey of Homer*, 9:65.

55. Pope, *Odyssey of Homer*, 9:309.

56. Pope, *Odyssey of Homer*, 9:337–42.

57. Pope, *Odyssey of Homer*, 9:353, 361, 363.

58. Pope, *Odyssey of Homer*, 9:431, 442.

59. Pope, *Odyssey of Homer*, 9:395.

60. Pope, *Odyssey of Homer*, 9:221, 257, 406–7.

61. The Broome-Pope commentary consistently distinguishes between Phaeacia's pursuit of relatively harmless pleasure and Circean engagement with its destructive counterpart, between the contrasting extremes of the violence and gigantism of Polyphemus and the effeminacy, luxury, and dwarfish laziness of the Phaeacians. Pope, *Odyssey of Homer*, 9:241.

62. Pope, *Odyssey of Homer*, 9:10.

63. Pope, *Odyssey of Homer*, 10:153, 178, 194, 298.

64. See Parnell's "Essay on the Life, Writings, and Learning of Homer," prefacing Pope's translation of the *Iliad* in *The Iliad of Homer*, ed. Maynard Mack (London: Methuen, 1967), Twickenham edition 7:29–80.

65. See *Prose Works of Jonathan Swift*, 1:69. The notion of the epic writer as a person of encyclopedic knowledge was commonplace. For a more nuanced version that probably comes closer to the Scribleran view of Homer as "a Father of Learning," see Parnell's "Essay on the Life, Writings, and Learning of Homer," in Pope's *Iliad of Homer*, 7:29–80. The defense of ancient poetry as useful because of being allegorical has a long lineage but, in the context of the ancient-modern controversy, ap-

pears prominently in the work of Alexander Ross, who both defended ancient learning and wrote a work of allegorized myth, the *Mystagogus Poeticus*.

66. *Prose Works of Jonathan Swift*, 1 : 80.

67. John Gay, *Dramatic Works*, ed. John Fuller, 2 vols. (Oxford: Clarendon Press, 1983), 2 : 221–75.

68. Cf. *The Letters of John Gay*, ed. C. F. Burgess (Oxford: Clarendon Press, 1966), 7.

69. *The Poetical Works of John Gay*, ed. G. C. Faber (New York: Russell and Russell, 1969), 135.

70. For *The Messiah*, see Pope, *Pastoral Poetry and An Essay on Criticism*, ed. E. Audra and Aubrey Williams (London: Methuen, 1969), Twickenham edition 1 : 111 ff.; Clifford R. Ames, "False Advertising: The Influence of Virgil and Isaiah on Pope's *Messiah*," *Studies in English Literature* 28 (1988): 401–26; cf. Howard D. Weinbrot, "The *Dunciad*, Nursing Mothers and Isaiah," *Philological Quarterly* 71 (1992): 494.

71. *Prose Works of Jonathan Swift*, 1 : 149–57.

72. If the educational books in Harley's library are any indication, his educational ideas would have been as old-fashioned as those of the other members of the Scribleran group. Among its educational volumes the library contains nothing by Bacon and nothing from the Hartlib-Comenius-Durie circle. It does contain Fénelon, Locke, and the advocates of Renaissance English verbal education: Ascham's *School-master*, Mulcaster's *English Grammar*, Wilson's *Arte of Rhetoricke*, Blundevile's *Art of Logicke*, Peacham's *Compleat Gentleman*, Brinsley's *Ludus Literarius*, Coote's *The English School-Master*, plus grammars in a variety of languages. Cf. *Catalogus Bibliothecae Harleianae* (Osborne: London, 1744), a4 : 552–53. Whether Harley and Bolingbroke shared educational ideals is not clear; for Bolingbroke's educational ideas and Pope, see Rivers, "Pope, Pedagogues, and Politicians," 119–20.

73. "The Life of Zoilus and his remarks on Homer's Battle of the Frogs and Mice," *The Poetical Works of Thomas Parnell*, ed. John Mitford (London: Bell, 1894), 129–85.

74. The second Martinus-related work to appear in print was Swift's *Gulliver's Travels* (1726), in which the hero's four voyages flesh out the journeys the Scriblerans apparently had planned as Martinus's culminat-

ing experience over a decade earlier. The next few works concentrate on criticism of the quality of British intellectual life, first in the arts and then in the sciences. Pope's *Peri Bathous; or, Martinus Scriblerus: His Treatise of the Art of Sinking in Poetry* (1728) reverses Longinus's *Peri Utous* or *On the Sublime* and presents a Martinus for whom ancient poetry exists apart from the ancient meaning that Pope's *Odyssesy* encodes as our hero acts as the critical theorist of the bathetic modernists—for example Blackmore, Philips, and Theobald. See Alexander Pope et al., *The Memoirs of Martinus Scriblerus*, ed. Charles Kerby-Miller (New York: Russell and Russell, 1966), 118; Alexander Pope, *The Art of Sinking in Poetry: Martinus Scriblerus' Peri Bathous*, ed. Edna Leake Steeves (New York: Russell and Russell, 1968), liii–lxix. Next come the literary-critical prefatory material and notes attributed to Martinus in Pope's *Dunciad Variorum* of 1729, also included in later editions of the *Dunciad*, altered and developed by Pope up through 1743. Finally, Martinus "creates" Arbuthnot's *Virgilius Restauratus*, which mocks Bentley's practices in textual emendation in the same volume as the 1729 *Dunciad*. Martin the Scribbler's taste for modern poetry and meaningless pseudo-ancient stuff also appears in the *Dunciad*, in both its 1727 and 1742 versions, both of which Martinus prefaces with "Grub Street" tributes and with his own critical essay praising the *Dunciad* as an imitation of Homer's lost poem inflating Margartes, the dunce. In a turn to the sciences, or quadrivium, from Scriblerus's conventional concern with the abuse of rhetoric in abusive politics, Arbuthnot publishes his *Essay of the Learned Martinus Scriblerus concerning the Origin of the Sciences* in 1732, a work in which Martinus exposes the folly of the scholarly genetic fallacy by proving beyond all contention that sciences come from certain monkey-like creatures who taught the ancient peoples of India and Ethiopia. Aitken, *Life and Works of John Arbuthnot*, 360–68.

75. Joseph Spence, *Observations, Anecdotes, and Characters, of Books and Men* (Oxford: Clarendon Press, 1966), 1:560.

76. Pope, *Memoirs of Martinus Scriblerus*, 22.

77. Pope, *Memoirs of Martinus Scriblerus*, 91.

78. Henry Fielding, *Joseph Andrews*, ed. Martin C. Battestin (Oxford: Clarendon Press, 1967), xxxvi–xxxvii.

79. Pope, *Memoirs of Martinus Scriblerus*, 212.

80. Pope, *Memoirs of Martinus Scriblerus*, 98–99.

81. Pansophic theory was essentially designed to make everybody know everything.

82. Pope, *Memoirs of Martinus Scriblerus*, 110.

83. Montaigne had been republished three times since the Restoration (1685–86, 1693, 1700), beginning with his 1685–86 edition. He had been retranslated into an accessible neoclassical translation by Charles Cotton, and Hartlib, in his publication of his *Ready Way to Learn the Latin Tongue* (1654), had included Montaigne's essay on education together with other modernist materials. Comenius's *Orbis Pictus* had been republished six times in England between 1659 and 1713–14 and his *Janua Linguarum* twelve times. I use the entries for these books in Wing's *Short Title Catalogue*.

84. Pope, *Memoirs of Martinus Scriblerus*, 120.

85. Pope, *Memoirs of Martinus Scriblerus*, 123–24. Cf. W. T. Costello, *The Scholastic Curriculum at Early Seventeenth Century Cambridge* (Cambridge: Harvard University Press 1958), passim, which gives one some flavor of earlier scholasticism; cf. Richard Davies, *The General State of Education in the Universities* (Bath: Cooper, 1759), passim.

86. Pope, *Memoirs of Martinus Scriblerus*, 164–65. Harold Williams argues that this structure for four voyages was added by Pope after 1726 and perhaps not long before the *Memoirs* were published in 1741 but that the Laputian and Lilliputian journeys were included in the original Scribleran plans of 1713–14. Jonathan Swift, *Gulliver's Travels: 1726*, ed. Herbert Davis (Oxford: Blackwell, 1941), xiii–xiv. It seems likely that all four voyages were at least vaguely discussed by the Scriblerans, since Pope was working on his Homer in the 1710–20 period and since Swift depends so heavily on Pope's translation in his *Gulliver*.

87. Pope, *Memoirs of Martinus Scriblerus*, 169.

88. The correspondence between the men mentions Pope's translation. Swift, like Pope, may also have used Dacier, and Gulliver mentions Homer's commentators Didymus and Eustathius with modest respect in his visit to Glubdubdrib, though he notes that they "want a Genius to enter into the Spirit of a Poet." Gulliver's pride appears to allow him to claim to know how to recognize such genius. Swift, *Gulliver's Travels*, 181.

89. For travel as employing a scientific episteme and Swift's use of this potential in Gulliver, see Douglas Lane Patey, "Swift's Satire on 'Science' and the Structure of *Gulliver's Travels*," *English Literary History* 58 (1991): 823–27. Patey argues that Swift's critique of science is directed against scientific dogmatism in his age, the imprudence of much of the scientific project, and the physico-theologians who created an easy theology based in analyses of the physical world.

90. Swift, *Gulliver's Travels*, 275–80.

91. For the connections between Emmanuel College, Cambridge, Commonwealth religion, and the reform of education and science, see Webster, *Great Instauration*, 35–37, 435–36. Emmanuel College's commitments in this area continued after the Restoration and into the eighteenth century.

92. Swift, *Gulliver's Travels*, 3.

93. Swift, *Gulliver's Travels*, 138–39, 199, 200–1.

94. For the function of Fielding's use of epic devices, see Homer Goldberg, *The Art of "Joseph Andrews"* (Chicago: University of Chicago Press, 1969), 6–9, 143–45, 229–34, 246–48, 266–68.

95. For alternative perspectives on the genre of *Gulliver's Travels*, see Frederik N. Smith (ed.), *The Genres of Gulliver's Travels* (Newark: University of Delaware Press, 1990), passim.

96. Swift, *Gulliver's Travels*, 148. Cf. Alexander Pope, *Poems of Alexander Pope: The Odyssey of Homer* (London: Methuen, 1967), 9:337–39 (notes). That Swift, as part of a group that had considerable respect for mathematically based science such as Newton practiced, should include the quadrivium arts in his critique should not surprise us. Because of the Irish question, Swift had less respect for Newton than did the other Scriblerans. Moreover, he satirizes obvious abuses in the use of mathematics. The dividing lines between empirical and rationalistic science represented in Lagado and Laputa, commonly seen as originating with Descartes, are not neat. For an account of this complexity, see David Fate Norton, "The Myth of 'British Empiricism,'" *History of European Ideas* 4 (1981): 331–44. In general, the Scriblerans interest themselves in whether scientists analyze whole systems ("Wisdom") or isolate and manipulate a part, as Gassendi and Bacon advocate. For the scientific and topical backgrounds of Laputa, see M. H. Nicolson and N. M. Mohler, "Swift's

'Flying Island' in the *Voyage to Laputa*," *Annals of Science* 2 (1937): 405; Chris Worth, "Swift's 'Flying Island': Buttons and Bomb Vessels," *Review of English Studies*, n.s. 42 (1991): 343–60. Worth (350–51) argues that at least part of *Gulliver* book 3 had its origin in 1713–14.

97. Swift, *Gulliver's Travels*, 146–47.

98. Swift, *Gulliver's Travels*, 151; cf. Pope, *Odyssey of Homer*, 9:338.

99. Swift, *Gulliver's Travels*, 142.

100. Swift's quarrel with the empiricists, Bacon and Hobbes, presented them as freethinkers (*Prose Works of Jonathan Swift*, 2:72; 4:46–47). Swift had little respect for Descartes either (*Prose Works of Jonathan Swift* (1:105, 107; 11:197).

101. Pope, *Odyssey of Homer*, 9:431; Swift, *Gulliver's Travels*, 159.

102. Swift, *Gulliver's Travels*, 161. For Swift's response to Bacon, see Ricardo Quintana, "Two Paragraphs in a Tale of a Tub: Section IX," *Modern Philology* 73 (1975): 15–32.

103. Pope, *Odyssey of Homer*, 9: 432.

104. Swift, *Gulliver's Travels*, 159–60.

105. Swift, *Gulliver's Travels*, 160.

106. Swift, *Gulliver's Travels*, 159. Swift is a bit unfair here. For the effect of research on eighteenth-century English agriculture, see Joan Thirsk, *Chapters from the Agrarian History of England and Wales*, 5 vols. (Cambridge: Cambridge University Press, 1990), vol. 5, passim. Actually, "scientific" agriculture began to have an extreme effect in the improvement of agriculture only in the later eighteenth century; cf. David Ormrod, *English Grain Exports and the Structure of Agrarian Capitalism: 1700–1760* (Hull: Hull University, 1985), 45–60.

107. Pope, *Odyssey of Homer*, 9:169–70. Cf. M. M. Slaughter, *Universal Languages and Scientific Taxonomy in the Seventeenth Century* (Cambridge: Cambridge University Press, 1982), passim.

108. For the Academy's relation to Bacon and to real experiments, see Marjorie Nicolson and Nora M. Mohler, "The Scientific Background of Swift's Voyage to Laputa," *Annals of Science* 2 (1937): 299–334. Jenny Mezciems remarks that *New Atlantis* might have seemed to Swift a type of the modern romantic utopia, an anti-model to set against those of Plato and More; see "Utopia and 'the Thing Which Is Not': More, Swift and Other Lying Idealists," *University of Toronto Quarterly* 52 (1982): 45.

See also Jenny Mezciems, "The Unity of Swift's *Voyage to Laputa*: Structure as Meaning in Utopian Fiction," *Modern Language Review* 72 (1977): 1–21.

109. Hunter, *Science and Society*, 59–86.

110. Swift, *Gulliver's Travels*, 184. Webster, *Great Instauration*, 134–35, 148–49 for Descartes; for Gassendi, see the same source, 116, 134, 176–77, 230, 279, 513.

111. Pope, *Odyssey of Homer*, 9:423.

112. Swift, *Gulliver's Travels*, 194

113. Swift, *Gulliver's Travels*, 194.

114. Cf. Patey, "Swift's Satire," 827–34.

115. Pope, *Odyssey of Homer*, 9:331, 203–259, 315–333. Cf. Dacier, *L'Odyssée d'Homere*, 2:139–40; Spondanus, *Homeri Quae Extant Omnia*, 120–21.

116. Spondanus, *Homeri Quae Extant Omnia*, 66.

117. Dacier, *L'Odyssée d'Homere*, 2:128; cf. Spondanus, *Homeri Quae Extant Omnia*, 107.

118. Pope, *Odyssey of Homer*, 9:260–97; Swift, *Gulliver's Travels*, 7–9.

119. Swift, *Gulliver's Travels*, 13.

120. Pope, *Odyssey of Homer*, 9:228; Swift, *Gulliver's Travels*, 49.

121. Pope, *Odyssey of Homer*, 9:204.

122. Swift, *Gulliver's Travels*, 45.

123. Swift, *Gulliver's Travels*, 46.

124. Swift, *Gulliver's Travels*, 51–64.

125. *The Laws of Plato*, trans. Thomas L. Pangle (New York: Basic, 1979). All quotations and citations are from this translation.

126. Pope, *Odyssey of Homer*, 9:310.

127. Pope, *Odyssey of Homer*, 9:310.

128. Swift, *Gulliver's Travels*, 98.

129. Swift, *Gulliver's Travels*, 120.

130. Swift, *Gulliver's Travels*, 121.

131. Swift, *Gulliver's Travels*, 109–22.

132. Swift, *Gulliver's Travels*, 109–22.

133. Swift, *Gulliver's Travels*, 120.

134. Cf. *Prose Works of Jonathan Swift*, 1:200. For discussions on the limitation of civil power, see *Prose Works of Jonathan Swift*, 2:75–77; cf.

Glen R. Morrow, *Plato's Cretan City* (Princeton: Princeton University Press, 1993), passim.

135. Pope, *Odyssey of Homer*, 9:179–81; Spondanus, *Homeri Quae Extant Omnia*, 71, 238; Dacier, *L'Odyssée d'Homere*, 2: 457; 3: 197.

136. Swift, *Gulliver's Travels*, 274.

137. Swift, *Gulliver's Travels*, 207. The horses, as perceived by Gulliver, combine the roles of Circe as magician with those of her metamorphosed animals. In his view they are human beings metamorphosed into animals, like Circe's pigs, but he believes that as conjurers, they have accomplished the metamorphosis themselves "upon some Design." See Swift, *Gulliver's Travels*, 210.

138. Pope, *Odyssey of Homer*, 9:361; Dacier, *L'Odyssée d'Homere*, 2:361ff, 235–36; Spondanus, *Homeri Quae Extant Omnia*, 137–43.

139. Pope, *Essay on Man*, 55 (epistle 2, ll. 8–13).

140. Pope, *Dunciad*, 393–94.

141. Samuel Monk, "The Pride of Lemuel Gulliver," *Sewanee Review* 43 (1955): 48–71.

142. Swift, *Gulliver's Travels*, 252–53.

143. Swift, *Gulliver's Travels*, 253.

144. Swift, *Gulliver's Travels*, 277–79.

145. See Pope, *Iliad of Homer*, 8:306–8, 390–91. For some of the critical issues that Pope faced with Parnell and Broome in constructing a critical stance toward and commentary on the *Iliad*, see Joseph M. Levine, *The Battle of the Books* (Ithaca: Cornell University Press, 1991), 181–217.

146. Dacier, *L'Iliade d'Homere, traduite en françois, avec des remarques par Madame Dacier*, 3 vols. (Paris, 1711), 3:449; cf. Spondanus, *Homeri Qua Extant Omnia*, 324.

147. Spondanus, *Homeri Quae Extant Omnia*, 321.

148. Dacier, *L'Iliad*, 3:505; cf. Spondanus, *Homeri Quae Extant Omnia*, 356.

149. Pope, *Iliad of Homer*, 8:306–8, 390–91. A parodic Bentleyesque essay, once assigned to Arbuthnot, tells us of all the great horses elevated above human beings by a florid rhetoric, a Caligulan madness, or a mythology in which a horse is something other than a horse. The essay thereby parodies both Bentley's criticism and Gulliver's failure to understand the

relationship between horse and rider; cf. *The Miscellaneous Works of the Late Dr. Arbuthnot* (Glasgow, 1751), 1 : 115 – 41.

150. Pope, *Odyssey of Homer*, 10 : 335.

151. Swift, *Gulliver's Travels*, 273.

152. Swift, *Gulliver's Travels*, 279. For the manner in which the immoderate tone of Gulliver's conclusion invites us to separate ourselves from his position, see Mezciems, "Lying Idealists," 58. The reference scenes in the *Odyssey* invite us to identify with Odysseus' joy.

153. Pope, *Dunciad*, 254 – 65.

5. ADAM SMITH AND UTOPIA AS PROCESS

1. Cf. William Lloyd Bevan, "Sir William Petty: A Study of English Economic Literature," *Publications of the American Economic Association* 9 (1894): 370 – 472.

2. Adam Smith, *The Wealth of Nations*, ed. Edwin Cannan (New York: Random House, 1937), 437.

3. Smith also speaks of utopian hope negatively when he characterizes the prospect of extending the United Kingdom's domestic tax system to the colonies and Ireland as "a new Utopia, less amusing certainly, but not more useless and chimerical than the old one." Smith, *Wealth*, 887.

4. Karl Polanyi, *Primitive, Archaic, and Modern Economies*, ed. George Dalton (Garden City NY: Anchor, 1968), 3–9, 26ff. For Polanyi on the curiousness of the development of what is seen as a self-regulating free market as subordinating the whole substance of society to the laws of the market, see Karl Polanyi, *The Great Transformation* (Boston: Beacon Press, 1944), 68–76.

5. Richard F. Teichgraeber III, *"Free Trade" and Moral Philosophy: Rethinking the Sources of Adam Smith's "Wealth of Nations"* (Durham NC: Duke University Press, 1987), passim.

6. Ernest Bloch, *The Utopian Function of Art and Literature*, trans. Jack Zipes and Frank Mecklenburg (Cambridge: MIT Press, 1988), 112.

7. For critiques of Smith's characterization of earlier societies, see Polanyi, *Primitive, Archaic, and Modern Economies*, 3–26, and Robert L. Heilbroner, "The Paradox of Progress: Declines and Decay in *The Wealth of Nations*," *Journal of the History of Ideas* 34 (1973): 255; for a gen-

eral critique of the common distinctions between hunter-gatherer and pastoral-nomadic cultures, see Paul A. Olson, *The Struggle for the Land* (Lincoln: University of Nebraska Press, 1990), 9, 58–59, and passim.

8. Fernand Braudel, *Afterthoughts on Material Civilization and Capitalism*, trans. Patricia M. Ranum (London: Johns Hopkins University Press, 1977), 101–15.

9. Kozo Yamamura, "Bridled Capitalism and the Economic Development of Japan," in *The Wealth of Nations in the Twentieth Century*, ed. Ramon H. Myers (Stanford: Hoover Institute Press, 1996), 54–79.

10. Adam Smith, *The Theory of Moral Sentiments*, ed. E. G. West (New Rochelle: Arlington, 1969), 264–65.

11. In the literature on Smith that I have studied, I find no analyses of this scene's fictive representation of the poor as richer than the rich.

12. For a critique of Smith's understanding of poverty, see Jacob Ossar, "Adam Smith and Social Justice: The Ethical Basis of the *Wealth of Nations*," *Auslegung* 17 (1991): 128–35.

13. F. K. Mann, "Adam Smith: The Heir and the Ancestor." *Adam Smith: Critical Assessments*, 4 vols. (London: Croom Helm, 1983–84), 1:576.

14. For an elaboration and background, see Jacob Viner, "Adam Smith and Laissez-Faire." *Adam Smith, 1776–1926*, ed. J. M. Clark (Chicago: University of Chicago Press, 1928), 120–27.

15. Mann, *Adam Smith*, 1:576–78. What will make a better world are providence, self-interest, and education. Smith's arguments that self-love and reason are ultimately the same, as Pope puts it (*Essay on Man*, epistle 2, 62–66 and 53–294 passim)—or that private vices such as vanity and greed are public virtues, as Mandeville puts it, are not entirely new. In *The Grumbling Hive*, Jove intervenes to make vanity and self-love, private vices, become virtues and the wheels of commerce. Smith took exception to this work only in the sense that he regarded Mandeville's presentation of private self-interest—vanity and greed, to give these motives their Mandevillian names—as misrepresenting the noble achievements of self-interest.

16. Smith, *Theory of Moral Sentiments*, 347, 235.

17. The reduction of the idea of providence to the development of productive greed may relate to the critique of providentialist notions de-

veloped by Smith's friend David Hume. Hume asked Smith to see into print his *Dialogues concerning Natural Religion*, the framing fiction of which centers in the education of the young, a request that Smith refused because he saw its argument as too sweeping, perhaps because of its assault on the idea of providence. Though *Dialogues* (1779) was published three years after *Wealth* (1776), Smith was probably cautious about Hume's inquiries concerning the ideas of design and providence by 1776. Hume's *Dialogues* effectually weakened the design argument basic to Wisdom theology and educational theory running from the fathers to Pope by answering those who purported to read the designs of Wisdom in nature, including Galileo, Copernicus, and Newton. See Robert H. Hurlbutt III, *Hume, Newton, and the Design Argument* (Lincoln: University of Nebraska Press, 1965). Hume's attack on design became more popular after *The Origin of Species* undermined design arguments from Steno, Hutton, and Lyell that created an evolutionary design case for the existence of God. For the center of Hume's argument see David Hume, *The Natural History of Religion and the Dialogues concerning Natural Religion*, ed. John V. Price (Oxford: Clarendon Press, 1976), 211, 232, 261, 264–65.

18. Smith, *Theory of Moral Sentiments*, 124–25. On laissez-faire economics and Darwinism, see S. S. Schweber, "The Origin of the *Origin* Revisited," *Journal of the History of Biology* 10 (1977): 229–316. For a full exposition of Smith on sympathy and his indebtedness to Aristotle on this topic, see Laurence Berns, "Aristotle and Adam Smith on Justice: Cooperation between Ancients and Moderns?" *Review of Metaphysics* 28 (1994): 71–90.

19. Smith, *Theory of Moral Sentiments*, 127.

20. Henry Fielding, *Tom Jones* (New York: Random House, 1964), 5.

21. For useful hints, see John Unsworth, "Tom Jones: The Comedy of Knowledge," *Modern Language Quarterly* 48 (1987): 242–53.

22. The novelistic-verisimilar as opposed to the researched may be found in almost every chapter in *Wealth*; for instance in the first two chapters, see Smith, *Wealth*, 4, 7, 9, 14.

23. Boethius and Job and the great tragic dramatists such as Shakespeare had proposed, at least in the voices of some of their characters, that the providence of God is most evident in a bad fortune or pain that

either punishes the individual attached to material fortune or tests and refines the person capable of detachment ("we defy auguries; there is a providence in the fall of a sparrow"; *Hamlet* 5.2.155–56).

24. This idea was certainly alive in some quarters in the eighteenth century. Alexander Pope translated Boethius in part and almost certainly used him as he set forth his understanding of the operations of Providence in his *Essay on Man*. See Pope, *Essay On Man*, vol. 3, pt. 1, pp. 50, 73–74, and notes. Boethian ideas receive a hearty endorsement as a mode of construing suffering from the Reverend Abraham Adams in Fielding's *Joseph Andrews* (264–67), roughly contemporaneous with the last version of the *Dunciad*. For a more extended discussion, see Martin C. Battestin, *The Moral Basis of Fielding's Art: A Study of Joseph Andrews* (Middletown CT: Wesleyan University Press, 1959), passim.

25. Thomas K. McCraw, "The Trouble with Adam Smith," *American Scholar* 61 (1992): 366–68.

26. Smith, *Wealth*, 9–10.

27. Smith, *Wealth*, 101.

28. Smith, *Wealth*, 78.

29. Smith, *Wealth*, 84.

30. Smith, *Wealth*, 79.

31. Smith, *Wealth*, 4–5, 8.

32. Smith, *Wealth*, 9–10, 20–21, quote at 76.

33. Smith, *Wealth*, 56.

34. Robert L. Heilbroner, "The Paradox of Progress: Decline and Decay in *The Wealth of Nations*," *Journal of the History of Ideas* 34 (1973): 249.

35. Heilbroner, "Paradox," 249.

36. Heilbroner, "Paradox," 249.

37. Though there emerged in the late fourteenth and early fifteenth centuries a monetarized economic system, supported by banking and lending institutions that could circumvent medieval usury laws, the structure of market—as opposed to mercantilist—capitalism was built slowly. New merchants' groups that were not under the control of any larger society grew up in England, the Low Countries, and the commercial Italian cities; the water-powered West Country weaving industry was located outside the guild-controlled towns to benefit the individual entrepreneur and to provide cheap labor. From time to time the mo-

nopolies of the city guilds were challenged or broken by such figures as the London mayor, John of Northampton. But economic change did not easily progress from a guild- and state-protected base to a market one because large numbers of people had to be persuaded to change directions, political forces strong enough to do in central economic institutions had to be created, and institutionalized systems of motivation had to be altered in both school and factory.

38. Charles Wilson, *England's Apprenticeship: 1603–1763* (London: Longman, 1984), 269–73, 250–51.

39. Smith, *Wealth*, 99–144. Patricia H. Werhane summarizes Smith's objections to the contemporary apprenticeship system as follows: "The most repressive practice was that of apprenticeships. Apprenticeships in Smith's time were encouraged as a means to develop skills. But apprenticeships were generally of long duration with little or no pay. The apprentice was bound to his master and supported by his family. These programs, then, discriminated against those whose families could not afford to support them, they extended the time of apprenticeship far longer than necessary to learn a skill, and they unduly exploited the apprentice. Moreover, apprenticeships did not extend to agricultural labor, which Smith thought required more skill than many other trades. Apprenticeships violated 'the property which every man has in his own labour,' according to Smith, because the apprentice was neither free to control his choice of work nor was he paid for it." Patricia H. Werhane, "Freedom, Commodification, and the Alienation of Labor in Adam Smith's *The Wealth of Nations*," *Philosophical Forum* 22 (1991): 394.

40. Smith, *Wealth*, 118, 122.

41. Smith, *Wealth*, 122–28.

42. Smith, *Wealth*, 128. For a discussion of Smith's failure to address how the social cooperation necessary to the effective division of labor is to be created in a world where "the only effective voluntary associations" are those "of merchants and manufacturers to exploit the consumer and of masters to exploit the worker," see McCraw, "The Trouble with Adam Smith," 367–71.

43. Smith, *Wealth*, 716–18

44. Smith, *Wealth*, 720.

45. Smith, *Wealth*, 721.

46. Smith, *Wealth*, 719.

47. Smith, *Wealth*, 734.

48. I regard the Cromwellian advocate of compulsory education, Comenius, as essentially a continental reformer and his English associates, Durie, Hartlib, and the like, as marginal figures in English intellectual life, though they undoubtedly would have become something else had the Commonwealth survived.

49. C. Daniel Batson, "Do Prosocial Motives Have Any Business in Research?" *Social Justice Research* 9 (1996): 7–25.

50. *Priestley's Writings on Philosophy, Science, and Politics*, ed. John A. Passmore (New York: Collier, 1965), 305–13.

51. For a fuller discussion of these matters, see Jacob Ossar, "Adam Smith and Social Justice: The Ethical Basis of the *Wealth of Nations*," *Auslegung* 17 (1991): 125–36.

52. Smith, *Wealth*, 734.

53. This scheme is implicit throughout *Wealth*, but see especially 653–57.

54. Smith, *Wealth*, 734.

55. Smith, *Wealth*, 734.

56. Smith, *Wealth*, 734–35.

57. During the eighteenth century, poor people were educated, as Frank Smith argues, by a variety of means: by the home and the occupation, especially in rural agricultural areas; in private dame schools; in private day schools; in charity schools supervised by the Society for Promoting Christian Knowledge and first established in 1698; in the school of industry which taught child laborers to read; and, at least from 1780 on, in Sunday schools that taught reading, the Catechism, and the liturgy, the latter institution being much supported by business. See Frank Smith, *A History of English Elementary Education: 1760–1902* (London: University of London Press, 1931), 36–67. For additional material on schooling in the eighteenth century, see Victor E. Neuburg, *Popular Education in Eighteenth Century England* (London: Woburn Press, 1971), passim. It seems likely that many children received no education. In 1820 after a period of growing agitation for increased access to education for the poor, Lord Brougham reported to Parliament that one child in sixteen in England received some schooling. See Hansard, *Parliamentary*

Debates, second series, II, vols. 48–49 (London: R. Bagshaw et al., 1804, 1908), 115–16, 166, 173–75, 180–84, 208, 232–34, 258–59, 268, 281–83, 291, 303–7, 317, 332, 341, 357.

58. Smith, *Wealth*, 737.

59. Smith, *Wealth*, 736.

60. Smith's interest in "connectedness" and the theory of systems probably derives from Condillac. For a discussion of this aspect of Smith's work, see A. D. Megill, "Theory and Experience in Adam Smith," *Journal of the History of Ideas* 36 (1975): 79–94.

61. Werhane, "Freedom, Commodification," 391.

62. Smith, *Wealth*, 737.

63. Smith, *Wealth*, 738, 740. See also R. D. Freeman, "Adam Smith, Education, and Laissez-Faire," *History of Political Economy* 1, no. 1 (1969): 173–86. For an argument analogous to mine concerning the revolutionary character of Smith's proposals about greed and the division of labor, see Albert O. Hirschman, *The Passions and the Interests* (Princeton: Princeton University Press, 1977).

6. UTILITARIAN COMPULSORY UTOPIA

1. Smith, *Wealth*, 736.

2. Karl A. Schleunes, *Schooling and Society: The Politics of Education in Prussia and Bavaria, 1750–1900* (Oxford University Press: London, 1989), passim; Victor Cousin, *On the State of Education in Holland, as Regards School for the Working Classes and for the Poor*, trans. Leonard Horner (London, J. Murray, 1838), passim; John Kerr, *Scottish Education, School and University, from Early Times to 1908* (Cambridge: Cambridge University Press 1913), 161–201.

3. In England and the United States (save in a few northern states), compulsory education did not exist until after the middle of the nineteenth century, and teacher education came with compulsory education.

4. Smith, *Wealth*, 735–40.

5. For Foucault on Bentham's Panopticon as the model for the use of social science–based technologies to control and standardize populations deemed proper subjects of such actions in the new liberal thought, see Michel Foucault, *Discipline and Punish: The Birth of the Prison*, trans. Alan Sheridan (New York: Vintage–Random House, 1979), 205–305.

For some preliminary discussion of Foucault's analysis and general schemes for educating poor children, see Stanley William Rothstein, *Schooling the Poor: A Social Inquiry into the American Educational Experience* (London: Bergin and Garvey, 1994), 4 and passim.

6. Jeremy Bentham, *Chrestomathia* (Oxford: Clarendon Press, 1983), passim. For the Hazelwood School, see Arthur Hill, *Public Education: Plans for the Government and Liberal Instruction of Boys, in Large Numbers, as Practised at Hazelwood School* (London: C. Knight, 1825). See also Hugh Hale Bellot, *University College, London, 1826–1926* (London: University of London Press, 1929), passim. For some useful general background to this chapter, especially in regard to James and John Stuart Mill and systemic education, see Elie Halevy, *The Growth of Philosophic Radicalism*, trans. Mary Morris (London: Faber and Gwyer, 1928), 282–93 and passim.

7. Bentham, *Chrestomathia*, 1.

8. Bentham, *Chrestomathia*, 38–47. The Utilitarians were unusual in wanting at least some education for the lowest classes. Andrew Bell, one of their opponents, says that he does not propose that the "children of the poor be educated in an expensive manner, *or even taught to write and cypher*," and describes leveling educational schemes as confusing the distinction of ranks within both the lower and the higher orders of society. Quoted in Joseph Fox, *A Comparative View of the Plans of Education* (London: Lancaster, 1811), 34. Lancaster tends to be much more concerned than Bell that the working classes be given some sort of education, however limited that education may appear from a distance. See Joseph Lancaster, *Improvements in Education as it Respects the Industrious Classes of the Community* (London: Darton and Harvey, 1803), iii–50.

9. Bentham, *Chrestomathia*, 49; for the implied instruction of the lowest classes in the Bell-Lancaster monitorial schools, see 63.

10. Bentham, *Chrestomathia*, 106. For a discussion of the largest class size practical in a monitorial school, see 124.

11. Foucault, *Discipline and Punish*, 198.

12. Foucault, *Discipline and Punish*, 177–83, 184–94.

13. Bentham, *Chrestomathia*, 130–39. Bentham received a query from one W. Thompson asking a number of questions about the monitorial method and the Chrestomathic scheme including the articulation of the

school and the possibility that, in a school organized by drill, the pupils, as in "the old schools" will "not understand." Letter from W. Thompson of Cork in the Bentham MSS, University College, London, box 18, 176–77.

14. Bentham, *Chrestomathia*, 196.

15. Bentham, *Chrestomathia*, Chrestomathic Instruction Table 1, col. 5.

16. Bentham, *Chrestomathia*, 25–36.

17. Bentham, *Chrestomathia*, 197, 323–30, 407.

18. The concept of material simple entities to be named by definitive names that permit no ambiguity — that is, by a "real character" — is not in itself a concept without difficulties; cf. Ludwig Wittgenstein, *Philosophical Investigations* (Oxford: Basil Blackwell, 1953), pp. 22e–23e. Though Bentham explicitly denies aiming to substitute an entire real character (i.e., a language naming "simples") for all ordinary language, he does want such a language to clarify science and technology and make them more easily learnable. This revives a Baconian and Royal Society interest. Cf. Bentham, *Chrestomathia*, 197.

19. Bentham, *Chrestomathia*, 26, 57–63, and passim. For Bruner, see Jerome Bruner, *The Process of Education* (Cambridge: Harvard University Press, 1960).

20. By fixing the responsibility for educational growth on the individual will and inner development challenged by the beauty of Wisdom, pre-Associationist education centered the creation of the teacher in the discipline and offered no theory of education as habituation (also the case with modern Piagetian theory). Pre-enlightenment cultures both in school and out of school often used the inflicting of torture as an incentive to "correct" behavior, as the case of Prospero makes clear. Cf.Olson, *Journey to Wisdom*, passim.

21. Boethius, *The Theological Tractates*, ed. and trans. H. F. Stewart and E. K. Rand (London: William Heineman, 1918), 382–90 (lib. 5, pr. 4). Cf. Olson, *Journey to Wisdom*, passim, for the medieval/Renaissance tradition.

22. This view was often violated in the actual drill and disciplinary practice of the medieval and Renaissance school and university.

23. Thomas Hobbes, *Humane Nature, or the Fundamental Elements of Policy* (London: Newcomb, 1650), passim.

24. Thomas Hobbes, *The Elements of Law: Natural and Politic*, ed. Ferdinand Tonnies (London: Frank Cass, 1969), 13.

25. David Hume, *A Treatise of Human Nature*, ed. L. A. Selby-Bigge (Oxford: Clarendon Press, 1967), 10–13, 69–78.

26. Oliver Brunet, *Philosophie et esthétique chez David Hume* (Paris: Nizet, 1965), 325, 347–48, 370.

27. David Hartley, *Observations on Man, His Frame, His Duty and His Expectations* (London: n.p., 1749), 65.

28. Hartley, *Observations*, 65.

29. Joseph Priestley, *The Theological and Miscellaneous Works*, ed. John Towill Rutt, 25 vols. in 26 (New York: Krause Reprint, 1972), 22:40–54; 25:5–20.

30. James Mill, *Analysis of the Phenomena of the Human Mind*, 2 vols. (London: Longmans, Green, Reader, and Dyer, 1869), 1:70–126.

31. James Mill, *On Education*, ed. W. H. Burston (London: Cambridge University Press, 1969), 45. This is a republication of Mill's essay as it appeared in a supplement to the fifth edition of the *Encyclopedia Britannica* published in 1824. For the contrasting theory of education of John Stuart Mill, see F. W. Garforth, *John Stuart Mill's Theory of Education* (New York: Barnes and Noble, 1979). I do not believe that the younger Mill's theory of education was widely influential in the period covered by this and the next chapter.

32. Mill, *On Education*, 50.

33. Mill, *On Education*, 95–96.

34. Mill, *On Education*, 105.

35. Mill, *On Education*, 108; for Mill's assertions in favor of secular education for all, see 120–93.

36. Bentham must have known how authoritarian the monitorial schools were, as the Bentham MSS at University College, London (box 165, folder 7, 176) include a copy of Lancaster's list of rules.

37. Joseph Lancaster and Andrew Bell, *The Practical Parts of Lancaster's "Improvements" and Bell's "Experiment,"* ed. David Salmon (Cambridge: Cambridge University Press, 1932), 33. For a life of Joseph Lancaster, see William Corston, *The Life of Joseph Lancaster* (London: Harvey, Darton and Company, 1840), passim. For a sample of the kind of polemic that surrounded Lancaster and Bell, see [Pythias], *Vindication of Mr. Lan-*

caster's System of Education from the Aspersion of Professor Marsh, the Quarterly, British, and Anti-Jacobin Reviews (London: n.p., 1812), 31–61. Coleridge lent his name to an attack on Lancaster. Cf. Joseph Lancaster, *Oppression and Persecution* (Bristol: Evans, 1816), 10. For a sympathetic account of Lancaster's work by someone other than Lancaster, see anon., *An Account of the Progress of Joseph Lancaster's Plan for the Education of Poor Children* (London: n.p., 1808), passim. This treatise claims that one master can teach one thousand children, that arithmetic has been revolutionized by the method, that the method teaches religion without engaging in religious controversy, and that twenty-seven separate towns and cities have such schools already in 1808. Lancaster also had the notion that his methods could be used to enhance industrial production in the workhouses for the poor. See his *Outlines of a Plan for Educating Ten Thousand Poor Children . . . and for Uniting the Works of Industry with Useful Knowledge* (London: n.p., 1806), passim.

38. Garforth, *John Stuart Mill's Theory of Education*, 101.

39. Lancaster and Bell, *Practical Parts*, 1.

40. Lancaster and Bell, *Practical Parts*, 1–55.

41. Lancaster and Bell, *Practical Parts*, 49–50.

42. Lancaster and Bell, *Practical Parts*, 46.

43. Bentham's and Mill's principles and the practice of Lancastrian schools actually became part of the basis of Henry Brougham's 1820 proposals for "Schools for All in Britain," of J. A. Roebuck's 1833 proposal for universal and national education in England, and of a host of later Whig/Liberal Party efforts to achieve compulsory education. These efforts partially failed, but they created a national dialogue about what the national interest in a national system of education might be; what kinds of schools would serve the various possible kinds of social order; what specific sort of social order the United Kingdom ought to envisage for itself; and the respective claims of the individual/contestive and the cooperative in the education of the individual. The second generation of reformers—Combe, Ellis, Hodgson, and their allies (see chapter 7)—completed the project that the first generation Utilitarians had left incomplete. For the evolution of the dialogue about compulsory schools and national educational policy in relation to religious and other questions, see James Murphy, *Church, State and School in Britain: 1800–1970*

(London: Routledge and Kegan Paul, 1971), 1–64. Cf. H. C. Barnard, *A History of English Education from 1760* (London: University of London Press, 1961), 63–70.

44. "The Speech of Henry Brougham, Esq., on the Education of the Poor, Spoken in the House of Commons," *Pamphleteer* 16 (1820): 238–44.

45. For some analysis of the relationship between market economics and Lancaster's system, see David Hogan, "The Market Revolution and Disciplinary Power: Joseph Lancaster and the Psychology of the Early Classroom System," *History of Education Quarterly* 29 (1989): 381–417. For a critique of the notion that the rise of the schooled society merely served the powers that be, see David Wardle, *The Rise of the Schooled Society* (London: Routledge and Kegan Paul, 1974), 148–171. Wardle appears to me to confuse the utopian functions of new forms of schooling with the notion that the bureaucracies controlling the schooling process have allowed the schools to be neutral and serious critics of the basic premises of emerging forms of social organization.

46. Henry Brougham, *Speeches of Henry, Lord Brougham*, 4 vols. (Edinburgh: Adam and Charles Black, 1838), 3:226.

47. David Allsobrook, *Schools for the Shires* (Manchester: Manchester University Press, 1986), 154–75.

48. William Ellis, *Education as a Means of Preventing Destitution* (London: Smith, Elder, 1851), 58–59, 93ff. Eventually the monitorial method was widely used in combination with other methods, both in the United States and in Britain. For an examination of the practice in one U.S. city, see John Franklin Reigart, *The Lancastrian System of Instruction in the Schools of New York City* (New York: Teachers College, Columbia, 1916), passim. For the transmission of the monitorial system to Europe, see Hugh M. Pollard, *Pioneers of Popular Education* (Cambridge: Harvard University Press, 1957), 100–10. For Canada, see George W. Sprague, *Monitorial Schools in the Canadas: 1810–1845*, Doctor of Pedagogy thesis, University of Toronto, 1935, passim.

49. David Stow, *The Training System Adopted in the Model Schools* (Glasgow: W. R. McPhun, 1836), 2–3, 53–66, 96–97, 144–5, 174. Monitorial "teacher training" also influenced George Combe, the Scottish phrenologist discussed in the next chapter, the phrenological guru who

influenced Horace Mann and who in 1838 proposed that America develop training colleges—one year before his friend Mann began to do so. George Combe, *Education: Its Principles and Practices*, ed. William Jolly (London: Macmillan, 1879), 322, lxiii. Combe was also influenced directly by laissez-faire economic theory and Associationist psychology through the late Utilitarian student of James Mill, William Ellis, also discussed in the next chapter. So was Samuel Wilderspan, the pedagogue who founded one version of the infant schools and affected both Stow and Combe. Samuel Wilderspan, *On the Importance of Educating the Infant Poor* (London: Simpkin and Marshall, 1824), 38 ff.

50. Foucault, *Discipline and Punish*, 208.

51. Owen's life (1771–1858) is well known: his success in inventing and managing machinery in New Lanark; his effort to convert it to a cooperative utopia because his workmen were given to drink, dishonesty, and pauperism; his circulation of his early socialist pamphlet *A New View of Society*; his setting up of an infant school there influenced by Bell and Lancaster and the monitorial schools; his friendship with the major Utilitarians; his effort to organize major manufacturers to follow his lead toward social ownership of manufacturing enterprises: his advocacy of villages of unity and cooperation in the late teens; his failed utopia at New Harmony; and finally his advocacy of spirit tapping and free love in his later years. Cf. Margaret Cole, *Robert Owen of New Lanark* (New York, Oxford University Press, 1953), passim.

52. For Frederick Engels's view of Owen, see *Socialism, Utopian and Scientific*, trans. by Edward Aveling (New York, International publishers, 1935), 40–44. For Marx's view of Owen, see Karl Marx and Frederick Engels, *Selected Works* (New York: International Publishers, 1968), 60–61, 193. The Marx-Engels critique of Owen's utopianism as patronizing and unscientifically based on absolutes rather than the historical process appears rather anachronistic in view of later inventions such as the vanguard party and the return to favor of the earlier, more "humanistic" Marx.

53. Robert Owen, *On Education*, ed. Harold Silver (Cambridge: Cambridge University Press, 1969), 134; see also 135–36 for more background on Owen's assertion.

54. Owen, *On Education*, 184, 182. The model school, the teacher train-

ing institution, and the new university, allied to the applied scientific subjects and economics (or political economy), were the tools for creating the new utopias and the vanguard for their creation. Both educational modes had flourished, to some extent, in eighteenth-century Prussia as part of that country's program for the formation of youth, but Prussia in that period was largely a preindustrial country using education to further its pietistic and militaristic goals. While Scotland supposedly had a compulsory system from the sixteenth century on, both school attendance and the enforcement of it in the eighteenth century were poor, and the church controlled its schooling. Many parishes had no education at all.

55. Owen, *On Education*, 185–86.

56. John Stuart Mill, *Autobiography*, ed. Jack Stillinger (Boston: Houghton Mifflin, 1969).

7. SECOND GENERATION UTILITARIANS

1. For capitalism, liberalism, and U.S. schooling, see Michael B. Katz, *Improving Poor People: The Welfare State, the "Underclass" and Urban Schools as History* (Princeton: Princeton University Press, 1995), passim, and Michael B. Katz, *Class, Bureaucracy, and Schools: The Illusion of Educational Change in America* (New York: Praeger, 1971), passim.

2. Sir Llewellyn Woodward, *Age of Reform: 1815–1870* (Oxford: Clarendon Press, 1962), 474–80.

3. "Phrenology," *Encyclopedia Britannica*, 11th ed., 32 vols (London: Cambridge University Press, 1911), 21:540.

4. The bill made the industrial establishment responsible for the provision of the school buildings needed for the education that the Select Committee proposed, while providing that the schools be controlled by the established church and that their costs would be paid by a complex local-national formula.

5. In 1859 Ellis sent a letter to the Education Commission considering a national education policy, urging the teaching of his form of social science; he also urged his views on its chair, the Duke of Newcastle. Ellis to Brougham, Sept. 10, 1859, MS 36, 677, Brougham MSS, University College, London.

6. Combe occasionally backed away from the principle of compul-

sion in education, especially in a letter to Lord Ashburton, on March 11, 1856: "Our government cannot wield despotic power." MS Clark 55, Combe Collection, Scottish National Library (hereafter cited as Combe Collection).

7. The United States was part of the dialogue among the Whig/liberal reformers through Horace Mann, who regarded Combe as his closest friend and named his son after Combe. Though New England and a few other states had a compulsory education policy and so offered a laboratory for Britain, the country as a whole was behind the United Kingdom in its consideration of educational policy since the South did not have universal education until late in the nineteenth century, and Mississippi, as I learned while a consultant for the United States Office of Education in that state, did not enforce its compulsory education laws in regard to African-Americans until the 1960s. Ellis sometimes felt that Massachusetts had more to learn from the Combe-Ellis experiments than they from Massachusetts. Ellis to Combe, Feb. 25, 1853, MS 7333b, Combe Collection.

8. The 1848 and 1870 revolutions on the Continent and mass uprisings of the Chartists, some Owenites, and the continental socialists supply the immediate cause propelling Great Britain toward universal education. The standard reformers' argument is that if the ruling classes fail to provide education, they will face the revolutionary music. In March of 1848, Samuel Lucas, educational leader in Manchester, writes to Combe that the city riots in London, Glasgow, and Edinburgh suggest that society's foundations are tottering; that the French 1848 revolt has had its consequences in Britain. The principle of cooperation may even replace that of competition as the motor of society, a delusion that the *People's Journal* has fostered. If such a principle triumphs, "democratic" roads to wealth will be the new delusions replacing the old truths that wealth is created by "morality, intelligence, thrift . . . forethought." Lucas to Combe, March 8, 1848, MS 7294A, Combe Collection.

9. Combe buys the argument that revolutionary activity may be forestalled by education. In a letter written to Horace Mann on October 24, 1849, after the 1848 rebellions, Combe remarks that the mechanical and useful arts have made so little progress because the world's labor has been done by ignorant men and that both sides in the revolt are at fault—the

old monarchies because they have not given the masses freedom and the uneducated masses because they believe they can run things without having been practically or theoretically prepared for freedom (Oct. 24, Mann 49, Combe Collection).

10. The advocates of capitalistic indoctrination do not appear to have to defend their position often against the criticism that it violates principles of Christian charity. John Smart writes a letter to Combe in which he asks about underpricing "to destroy a weaker": "Where is the so much boasted Christian feeling where it can without compunction ruin a Christian brother?" Smart to Combe, Jan. 18, 1852, MS 7320A, Combe Collection.

11. In a letter to Sir James Clark (April 11, 1848), Combe writes: "This very hour I have received a letter from an intelligent and influential friend in Glasgow . . . in which he says that if the Government do not move speedily in social reform, particularly IN EDUCATION FOR THE MASSES, they will hear from the Chartists in a strain which they little expect! Our people do not want socialism, or communism, but they desire . . . a law for a thorough education of the masses." Combe to Sir James Clark, April 11, 1848, MS 7391, Combe Collection.

12. *Robert Owen on Education*, ed. Harold Silver (Cambridge: Cambridge University Press, 1969), 73.

13. *Robert Owen on Education*, 73.

14. *Robert Owen on Education*, 76.

15. *Robert Owen on Education*, 102–3.

16. *Robert Owen on Education*, 134–37. For Robert Owen's account to Lord Brougham of his founding of the first infant schools, see Owen to Brougham, Brougham MSS, University College, London, Aug. 14, 1846, MS 10,093.

17. *Robert Owen on Education*, 145.

18. Robert Owen, *A New View of Society: Mr. Owen's Report to the Committee . . . for the Relief of the Manufacturing and Labouring Poor* (London: R. Watts, 1817). I find no evidence that Owen read Sir Thomas More.

19. *Robert Owen on Education*, 173.

20. *Robert Owen on Education*, 5; cf. John Saville, "J. E. Smith and the Owenite Movement," in *Robert Owen: Prophet of the Poor*, ed. Sidney Pollard and John Salt (London: Macmillan, 1971), 115–44.

21. For the moderate Chartist leader William Lovett's account of himself with an astute introduction by R. H. Tawney, see William Lovett, *Life and Struggles of William Lovett*, preface by R. H. Tawney (London: MacGibbon and Kee, 1967), passim.

22. To give him his due, Combe was also strongly opposed to British colonialism in India on the basis of the lack of sense of community between the British and Indians, British cruelty and atrocities in India, British greed and lust for domination, and the contempt British rule expressed toward the pride of the Indians. George Combe to Miss Johnston, Oct. 14, 1857, unnumbered letter, Combe Collection.

23. David de Giustino, *Conquest of Mind: Phrenology and Victorian Social Thought* (London: Croom Helm, 1975), 142–44. For Abram Combe's Orbiston colony, see Alexander Cullen, *Adventures in Socialism: New Lanark Establishment and Orbiston Community* (Glasgow: J. Smith and Son, 1910), passim; cf. Ian Donnachie, "Orbiston: A Scottish Owenite Colony," in *Robert Owen: Prince of Cotton Spinners*, ed. John Butt (Newton Abbott: David and Charles, 1971), 135–68. Combe's colony accomplished much before it ran out of money, failing principally because Abram Combe exercised no selectivity in admitting colony members and gave them no education for the cooperative life.

24. Combe to Mrs. Kemmis, May 10, 1827, MS 7383, Combe Collection.

25. Even the socialist principle that the good of the individual is constituted by the good of the whole social body seems questionable to Combe. The Golden Rule should have taught it to Christians long ago, were it a solid principle. Combe to Mrs. Kemmis, May 10, 1827, MS 7383, Combe Collection.

26. Combe to Ellis, April 10, 1848, MS 7391, Combe Collection.

27. Ellis to Combe, April 14, 1850, MS 7307, Combe Collection.

28. Combe to George Henry Lewes, May 8, 1850, MS 7392, Combe Collection.

29. George Combe, *Discussions on Education* (New York: Cassell, 1893), 133. Ellis to Combe, Nov. 30, 1856, MS 7341, Combe Collection.

30. Ellis on September 15, 1856, also urged Combe to communicate his findings on Zurich and the "insufficiency of such [conventional religious] teaching to defend those taught against the advocates of commu-

nism & the instigators of strikes & bread riots" to Lord John Russell, who at that time was the leading politician concerned with educational reform. Ellis to Combe, unnumbered MS, Combe Collection.

31. At twenty-five, Ellis became the chief underwriter for the Marine Indemnity Company and, in that capacity, came to know the older Utilitarians James Mill, David Ricardo, Jeremy Bentham, Henry Brougham, and J. A. Roebuck—the latter two, as we have mentioned, the 1820s–30s leaders in the parliamentary movement toward a general education policy. By the mid-1820s, Ellis had become part of a weekly Utilitarian discussion group made up of James and John Stuart Mill, Thomas Tooke, George Graham, and J. A. Roebuck (Bentham was quite aged by this time). Together they read James Mill's *Elements of Political Economy*, Ricardo's economic writings, and material from logic and analytical psychology. See Ethel E. Ellis, *Memoir of William Ellis* (London: Longmans Green, 1888), 11–16. Ellis writes to Combe of this relationship about thirty years later in the 1850s:

> Among other advantages for which I have reason to be thankful was that of the intimacy of my family with Mr. Tooke, the author of the "History of High & Low Prices," & of other works on Commercial and Economical subjects. In the year 1823 (I was then in my 24th year) he was busy preparing the first of his works for the press. I volunteered to assist him in the capacity of amanuensis. Fortunately for me he accepted my proffered service. The interest which I took in the work as it proceeded induced him to indulge me frequently with expositions & explanations in answer to difficulties that originated in my ignorance & inexperience, & thus began my career as a student of Economical science. Through the same kind medium I was soon afterwards introduced into the circle of the late Mr. James Mill, the well known Historian of British India, & of his distinguished son, John Stuart Mill, at that time combining the . . . enthusiastic energy of youth with the scientific & literary attainments of maturity. Under their influence & aided by their friendly instruction, Economical Science grew within me & at the same time subordinated itself as a branch of the Social sciences in

general; & I pursued its study in common & in harmony with the other branches. (Ellis to Combe, Nov. 3, 1851, MS 7315B, Combe Collection)

For another letter by Ellis reflecting on his relationship to the Mills, see Ellis's letter to George Combe of October 29, 1848, MS 7293B, Combe Collection.

32. Ethel E. Ellis, *Memoir of William Ellis and an account of his Conduct Teaching* (London: Longmans, 1888), 16–20 and passim.

33. Ellis to Combe, Nov. 3, 1851, MS 7315B, Combe Collection.

34. Ellis to Combe, Nov. 3, 1851, MS 7315B, Combe Collection.

35. Combe records in his journal a conversation with James Kay-Shuttleworth in which the latter argues that the Church is the main opponent of the introduction of science in the schools. Journal entry for July 4, 1853, MS 7459, Combe Collection. For Ellis's uneasy relationship with Kay-Shuttleworth, see Ethel Ellis, *Memoir of William Ellis*, 148–49.

36. In 1836, Lovett helped draft the Benefit Societies Act and formed the London Working Men's Association so that he could begin agitating for the reforms that became basic to the "People's Charter" and to the Chartist movement. In 1838, he was the primary author of "The People's Charter." For his pains he was forced to serve a year in prison in 1839–40 for the sedition of cooperating in the authorship and publication of "Chartism: A New Organization of the People." Cf. William Lovett, *Chartism: A New Organization of the People Embracing a Plan for the Education and Improvement of the People, Politically and Socially: Addressed to the Workingclasses of the United Kingdom and More Especially to the Advocates of the Rights and Liberties of the Whole People as Set Forth in the "People's Charter"* (London: J. Watson, H. Hetherington, W. Lovett, 1841). This is the second edition.

37. Ellis to Combe, April 17, 1848, MS 7293, Combe Collection.

38. Edmund Kelly Blyth, *Life of William Ellis* (London: Kegan, Paul Trench and Copany, 1889), 80 ff.

39. Ellis to Combe, April 20, 1848, MS 7293, Combe Collection.

40. W. M. Williams to Combe, July 13, 1850, MS 7336, Combe Collection. Williams's letters to Combe about the process of working out how

to teach new subjects in working-class districts in Edinburgh and Leith and the pedagogy of such teaching are extraordinarily brilliant.

41. Combe to William Pyper, undated but responding to a letter of January 2, 1833, MS 7373 (25087c), Combe Collection.

42. William Ellis, *Thoughts on the Future of the Human Race* (London: Smith, Elder, and Company, 1866), 250–58.

43. Phrenology was supposed to supply limits to expectation and compensatory strategies at the very highest social levels. On July 12, 1858, Combe writes to Sir James Clark about a reading he has done of the head of the Prince of Wales; he finds the Prince's brain to have grown in better directions so that it is much improved from his 1853 reading of it. Combe to Sir James Clark, July 12, 1858, MS 7370, Combe Collection. For an illustration of a phrenological compensatory strategy, see the discussion of George Eliot's Latimer below.

44. De Giustino, *Conquest of Mind*, 64–71.

45. Blyth, *Life of William Ellis*, 284. For Darwin's emphasis on the individual in natural selection as deriving from Adam Smith, see Silvan S. Schweber, "The Origin of the *Origin* Revisited," *Journal of the History of Biology* 10 (1977): 274–83.

46. George Combe, *Lectures on Popular Education* (Boston: Marsh, Capen, and Lyon, 1834), passim.

47. Combe, *Lectures on Popular Education*, 10.

48. For an amusing exploration of the extensions of Combe's position into the debate on classical languages in the United States, see the letter by C. H. Caldwell to Combe, Sept. 9, 1834, MS 232 (25,087), Combe Collection.

49. Ellis writes to Combe in 1856: "The late Educational debate in the House of Commons shows that the public mind is not yet ripe to deal satisfactorily with the question [of compulsory education]. Till opinion ripens into something better, may bigotry succeed in staving off compulsory education and condemnation to a Prussian or Swiss model of perfection." Ellis to Combe, March 13, 1856, MS 7353, Combe Collection.

50. Though Combe argues for a study of secular providence as a key to ethics that does not conflict with the Bible and that will eliminate sectarian controversies in the schools, he has little confidence in the ethical

authority of organized Christianity: He writes to Horace Mann in 1849: "What is the practical conclusion from these facts? That the SUPERNAT-URAL religion is no longer capable of directing social interests. Science has presented an all pervading system of natural causation, moral as well as physical, which has superseded it. Nevertheless the believers in the supernatural control all our schools & most of our public teachings & they shift secular instruction into that form which will render it least hostile to their own principles. The result is, that the people are left without any real religion which is practical & any science of social life based on nature; and in their social, moral, & political conduct, therefore, they are left wholly to the guidance of common sense." Combe to Horace Mann, Oct. 24, 1849, MS 1848, Combe Collection. See Combe to W. D. Hodgson, Nov. 9, 1850, MS Hodgson 50, Combe Collection.

51. George Combe, *What Should Secular Education Embrace*, 3rd ed. (Edinburgh: Maclachlan, Stewart, and Company, 1848), 24–25.

52. Combe's *Lectures on Popular Education* include a veiled reference to sex education in the form of an observation that young women should be given explanations of "all the LEADING organs and their USES." This led to Combe's being accused of offenses against "delicacy," to which he responds with accounts of the amours and sexuality enshrined in classical literature. Combe to William Pyper, a teacher of Latin in Edinburgh, not dated but written in response to a letter from Pyper dated Jan. 2, 1833, MS 7370 (25087c), Combe Collection.

53. Combe, *What Should Secular Education Embrace*, 28–29.

54. Combe, *What Should Secular Education Embrace*, 30.

55. W. B. Hodgson, a phrenologist protégé of Combe's, sets his goals for education in his *Lecture on Education* presented to the Edinburgh Association of the Working Classes on Monday, October 16, 1837: "Education ought to aim at promoting the end of our being,—the great end for which we were created. Allow me to assume that that end is happiness—the greatest good, that is, happiness of the greatest number. It would be easy to show that not merely the Utilitarian system of Bentham, but every moral and religious system, begins and ends at this point, and that every man is in his heart a Utilitarian; . . . I trust I may be permitted to assume, 1st, That education ought to aim at attaining the objects of existence; 2ndly, That the objects of existence are the enjoyment and diffu-

sion of happiness." W. B. Hodgson, *Lecture on Education: Delivered in the Freemasons' Hall at the Opening of the Second Session of the Edinburgh Association of the Working Classes for their Social, Intellectual and Moral Improvement* (Edinburgh: Adam and Charles Black, 1837), 6. For a powerful critique of Utilitarian efforts to aggregate happiness-quotients, see Nussbaum, *Poetic Justice,* 21–27. De Giustino calls attention to the role that phrenology played in the development of attention to individual differences and the development of compensatory education (De Giustino, *Conquest of Mind,* 167). It was also a source of the concept of mensuration that leads into the pseudoscience of intelligence testing, and its assumptions were deeply racist.

56. At least in his later life, Combe had questions about the doctrine of immortality. The Combe Collection includes an eloquent letter from Horace Mann arguing in favor of the doctrine but also asking Combe not to disclose his unorthodox opinions on the doctrine lest the cause of phrenology be injured. Horace Mann to George Combe, June 9, 1855, MS Mann 1, Combe Collection.

57. William Ellis, *Lecture on Education, Government and Competition* (publication data not given), 55.

58. Though nominally advocating free trade in all matters, the reformers placed limits on the parameters of discussion. For example, while they sought to create schools that would legitimize capitalistic enterprise and free trade, they regarded the notion of "free trade" in education, perhaps something like the voucher system, with contempt. The path to a good world required coercion in the realm of education and "freedom" everywhere else. Samuel Lucas, a member of the powerful Manchester group of educational reformers who tended to follow Ellis and Combe, writes to Combe concerning a critic named Baines (Samuel Lucas to Combe, Jan. 2, 1848, MS 7294, Combe Collection):

> Baines' letter is full of fallacies. . . . He talks about free trade in Education—he should rather say in ignorance. Why, according to his principle, every voluntary effort to educate the people is as much a violation of free trade as our Plan is. Free trade in Education would leave the supply of schools to be regulated by the demand for them by the ignorant people; and not to the appreciation of the value

of education by those who are educated and wealthy. Free trade would make education a mere commercial speculation and not a matter for religious sects to interfere in. . . . But as you clearly show there are other parties to the bargain than those who give education and those who receive it; those who provide the article and those who pay for it; there is society who has a right to protect itself from the injuries arising from the ignorance of a portion of the people.

59. Combe, *What Should Secular Education Embrace*, 8–10.

60. Woodward, *The Age of Reform*, 479–80.

61. Lord Ashburton to Combe, March 6, 1855 (summarizing his indebtedness to George and Andrew Combe and announcing the spirit in which he hopes to carry ahead his work on education), MS 7347, Combe Collection.

62. Combe writes to R. W. Smiles that the model schools should probably have been classed as illustrative in that they were designed, along with speeches and other political activity, to show that it "was IMPOSSIBLE to cover the land with SUCH schools on the voluntary principle, & that the working classes should not rest satisfied with any inferior schools." Combe to R. Smiles, Oct. 26, 1850, MS Mann 50, Combe Collection.

63. James Simpson, *The Philosophy of Education with its Practical Application to a System and Plan of Popular Education as a National Object* (Edinburgh: Adam and Charles Black, 1836), 198–205.

64. Simpson, *Philosophy of Education*, 205–7.

65. Blyth, *Life of William Ellis*, 98–119 and passim. For a similar view, see De Giustino, *Conquest of Mind*, 227–29.

66. Blyth, *Life of William Ellis*, passim.

67. Dr. George Birkbeck had nothing to do with the founding of the Birkbeck schools created by Ellis. Birkbeck founded the Glasgow Mechanics Institute in 1823 and the London Mechanics Institute in the next year. For Ellis's financial contribution, see Combe to James Amy, Aug. 2, 1848, MS 7391, Combe Collection.

68. Ellis to Combe, Oct. 16, 1850, MS 7307A, Combe Collection. For statistics on the increase in numbers in the London schools by 1851, see Ellis to Combe, Nov. 3, 1851, MS 7315b, Combe Collection. On Septem-

ber 13, 1859, Ellis invited Lord Brougham to the Birkbeck School in Peckham (MS 30,225, Brougham MSS, University College, London), with the promise that the school would prompt from Brougham Simeon's expression at the Messiah's coming, "Lord, now lettest thou . . ." These were Messianic schools.

69. Letter from George Combe to William Ellis, April 5, 1849, MS 1848, Combe Collection.

70. Ethel Ellis, *Memoir of William Ellis*, 67–68.

71. That the examinations were seen as persuasive devices to educate the public about the new form of education is apparent in a letter from John Angell of the Odd-Fellows Birkbeck School in Manchester. Angell says that his purpose in conducting the public examination is to demonstrate the "desireability, practicability, and advantage to the working classes of makeing SCIENCE the basis of the instruction given in such schools" (i.e., the secular education schools). Angell to Combe, March 2, 1852, MS 7381, Combe Collection. This letter also contains an acerbic critique of employer class assumptions about the understanding and attitudes of working-class people.

72. Combe to William Ellis, April 5, 1849, MS 1848, Combe Collection.

73. Combe to Ellis, April 5, 1849, MS 1848, Combe Collection.

74. Combe to Ellis, April 5, 1849, MS 1848, Combe Collection.

75. John Angell to Combe, May 8, 1852, MS 7322, Combe Collection.

76. Combe to Ellis, Aug. 2, 1851, MS Ellis 51, Combe Collection. Ellis, at least, feared rote learning and in his lessons in social science "avoid[ed] giving the answers to the questions for fear they should give rise to mere teaching by rote." However, it is clear from Ellis's stance that "the answer" is provided by utopian ideology. Ellis to Combe, April 15, 1849, MS 7300, Combe Collection. For a critique of Ellis's manner of teaching the boys using abstract expressions to which they may bring a variety of constructions, see Hewett Watson to Combe, Jan. 14., 1849, MS 7304, Combe Collection.

77. "Prospectus of a School for the Education of the Children of the Working Classes," apparently MS 7368, Combe Collection.

78. Combe to Ellis, May 18, 1850, MS 7392, Combe Collection.

79. Although the reformers sought to alleviate what they saw as appalling conditions in the urban ghettoes, they did not respect the work-

ers. Combe writes a typical opinion on July 28, 1855, when, addressing John Clark, he says that in his experience the education of working men has been "defective" and that this reveals itself in their character: "selfish, opinionative, dictatorial where [they have] power, subservient where [they are] ruled and capricious in [their] likings & resentments." MS Clarke 55, Combe Collection.

80. *Second Annual Report of the Williams Secular School* (Edinburgh: Maclachlan and Stewart, 1851), 27–33.

81. *Second Annual Report of the Williams Secular School*, 27–33. For a phonics-style examination in reading conducted by Simpson on June 17, 1851, see Simpson to Combe, MS 7303, Combe Collection.

82. *Second Annual Report of the Williams Secular School*, 27–33.

83. Robert Cunningham to Combe, Jan. 31, 1839, MS 7350, Combe Collection.

84. Combe to Edward Combe, Oct. 27, 1851, MS Edwcom 51, Combe Collection.

85. Combe journal for June 12, 1854, MS 7429, Combe Collection.

86. Rev. Hugh G. Robinson, principal of the York Training College, argues in his statement to the commissioners studying the state of education in England and Europe in 1861 that teacher training began with Francké's Orphan House at Halle; spread to Magdeburg, Pomerania, and throughout Germany in the eighteenth century; began in France in 1648 and spread slowly there; and began in England only in 1808 with Lancaster's founding of the Borough Road School and his training of monitors. Robinson argues that this step was followed by work in the National Society's school at Westminster, Stow's foundation of the Glasgow Normal Seminary in 1826, and Kay-Shuttleworth's opening of the Battersea Training College in 1846 and says that the character of training college students has become much more professional in the period 1808–60. Cf. *Reports from Commissioners, Session 5 February–6 August 1861: Study of Popular Education in Europe*, 7, 4, 21, part 4, 391–95.

87. Ellis to Combe, Oct. 6, 1855, MS 7347a, Combe Collection.

88. Ellis to Combe, Nov. 25, 1855, MS 7347a, Combe Collection.

89. The conventional histories of education argue that the delaying of the requirement of compulsory education from the 1820s–30s to the 1870s occurred because of the secularist–Church of England contro-

versy, but the fact that writers as diverse and unorthodox as Dickens, Matthew Arnold, and George Eliot in some moods criticized the dismissal of the spiritual, religious, and imaginative from these schools suggests that the issues were not matters of pure dogma. For a version of the conventional secularist critique of the religious position, see Combe's essay for George Eliot and the *Westminster Review*, discussed later in chapter 7.

90. In a letter to W. J. Fox, Combe writes that religious schools will teach the fall of man and the corruption of human nature, the necessity of Christ's atonement, the transformative influence of the Holy Spirit in forming good character, and the necessity of religious education to the proper discharge of religious and social duties in contrast to secular education's emphasis on the unchangeable character of human nature, the necessity that human improvement be based on the development of humankind's natural capacities, the rooting of evil in ignorance, and the necessity of social science education to the proper discharge of social duty. Letter from George Combe to W. J. Fox, April 9, 1853, MS NPSA52, Combe Collection.

91. Letter from George Combe to Horace Mann, June 8, 1855, MS 7347, Combe Collection. Combe describes the yearning for immortality as possibly a projection of human egotism and indicates that for him immortality is the "contemplation of this bright futurity to man" in which "myriads . . . [will] be partakers of a terrestrial existence, immeasurably superior to ours." In general, seventeenth- to nineteenth-century educational utopianism depends on projecting the equivalent of "heaven" on a terrestrial future.

92. During the early 1850s Samuel Lucas was a conduit to parliamentary people for ideas developed by Combe and his allies and chaired an informal committee to develop a plan that would be the basis for a parliamentary national plan for education avoiding sectarian teaching; cf. Lucas to Combe, Jan 1, 1850; Jan 1, 1851; Jan. 8, 1851; Feb. 13, 1851; March 2, 1851 and so forth, MS 7317, Combe Collection. Cf. Lucas letters in MS 7317A.

93. Combe journal entry for April 4, 1853, MS 7428, Combe Collection.

94. In regard to strategy concerning religion, see Samuel Lucas to Combe, Feb. 13, 1851, MS 7317, Combe Collection.

95. Combe journal for September 13, 1852, MS 7428, Combe Collection; cf. journal for June 8, MS 7428. Combe argues that his educational system is not secular but based on "natural religion" and will seem to conservatives a novel religion. Cf. Hewett Watson to Combe, Jan. 28, 1848, MS 7297, Combe Collection.

96. *The George Eliot Letters*, ed. Gordon S. Haight, 9 vols. (New Haven: Yale University Press, 1978), 8:27–28.

97. Gordon Haight, *George Eliot: A Biography* (New York: Oxford University Press, 1968), 102.

98. Combe journal, May 6, 1853, MS 7459a, Combe Collection. Combe also mentions the *Leben Jesu* as he travels in Germany in 1841. Combe Journal, MS 7421.

99. Marian Evans to Combe, Jan. 27, 1852, MS 7325d, Combe Collection.

100. Marian Evans (George Eliot) to Combe, Jan. 22, 1853, MS 7333D, Combe Collection. George Eliot was interested in Combe's ideas on natural religion; she writes on Feb. 18, 1853, that "you promised that I should be one of the few who are to see [the treatise on natural religion] before its ultimate publication—a proof of regard which was very pleasant to me." Marian Evans to Combe, Feb. 18, 1853, MS 7333D, Combe Collection. Cf. Marian Evans to Combe, April 16, 1853, MS 7333E; Oct. 21, 1853, MS 7333E.

101. Ellis to Combe, Nov. 21, 1852, unnumbered MS, Combe Collection.

102. *George Eliot Letters*, 8:33–35.

103. *George Eliot Letters*, 8:35–36.

104. *George Eliot Letters*, 8:40–41.

105. *George Eliot Letters*, 8:43–44.

106. *George Eliot Letters*, 8:46–47.

107. Ellis to Combe, Oct. 3, 1851, MS 7315A, Combe Collection. Though not a very literary couple, the Ellises read Mrs. Gaskell's *Mary Barton* with pleasure and commended it to the Combes with the remark that it contains "no attempt & no pretense to explain the causes of the agonizing misery with which it is chequered." Ellis to Combe, Jan. 28, 1849, MS 7300, Combe Collection.

108. W. M. Williams to Combe, Dec. 24, 1854, unnumbered MS, Combe Collection.

109. George Combe, "Secular Education," *Westminster Review*, n.s. 2, no. 1 (1852): 1–2

110. Combe, "Secular Education," 3–5.

111. Combe, "Secular Education," 10–12.

112. Combe, "Secular Education," 14.

113. Combe, "Secular Education," 25–27.

114. Combe, "Secular Education," 27–32. During this same period, Eliot published an article by Sam Brown, Combe's friend, on "Physical Puritanism" in the April 1852 number of the *Westminster Review*. She also had Andrew Combe's phrenological book on health and education reviewed in the same issue.

115. Marian Evans to Combe, Nov. 13, 1852, MS 7385, Combe Collection.

116. After Eliot took up with Lewes, Combe considered her insane and in violation of the Utilitarian principle of the greatest good for the greatest number, so degrading her own sex that Bray should not admit her into his "female domestic circle." *George Eliot Letters*, 8:129–30.

117. *Essays of George Eliot*, edited by Thomas Pinney (London: Routledge and Kegan Paul, 1963), 447.

118. T. R. Wright, "From Bumps to Morals: The Phrenological Background to George Eliot's Moral Framework," *Review of English Studies* 33 (1982): 35–46.

119. George Eliot, *The Lifted Veil: Brother Jacob*, ed. Helen Small (Oxford: Oxford University Press, 1999), 5–6.

120. Eliot, *Lifted Veil*, 6.

121. Eliot, *Lifted Veil*, 7.

122. Suzanne Graver, *George Eliot and Community: A Study of Social Theory and Fictional Form* (London: University of California Press, 1984), 150–88. Cf. *Essays of George Eliot*, 415–30.

123. Linda K. Robertson, *The Power of Knowledge: George Eliot and Education* (New York: Peter Lang, 1997), 101–24, 145–56; on public schools, see 37–40, 49–59, 41–43, 67–69.

124. On dame schools, see George Eliot, *Silas Marner* (Boston: Houghton Mifflin, 1908), 211; George Eliot, *Felix Holt: The Radical*, ed.

Fred C. Thomson (Oxford: Clarendon Press, 1980), 114. On clerical teachers, see Robertson, *Power of Knowledge*, 40–42. Eliot notes that "the children in the Paddiford Sunday-school had their memories crammed with phrases about the blood of cleansing, imputed righteousness, and justification by faith alone"; George Eliot, *Scenes of Clerical Life*, ed. Thomas A. Noble (Oxford: Clarendon Press, 1985), 155. On night schools, see George Eliot, *Adam Bede*, vols. 3–4 in *The Writings of George Eliot*, 22 vols. (New York: Houghton Mifflin, 1907), 1:231–49, 299–356; Eliot, *Felix Holt*, 218–27, 366–77.

125. Eliot, *Lifted Veil*, 50; George Eliot *Middlemarch*, ed. David Carroll (Oxford: Clarendon Press, 1986), 578.

126. Eliot, *Middlemarch*, 754.

127. Robertson, *Power of Knowledge*, 22.

128. Eliot, *Scenes from Clerical Life*, 53.

129. George Eliot, *Adam Bede* (New York: Harcourt Brace, 1962), 226.

130. Eliot, *Adam Bede*, 220–34.

131. Eliot, *Felix Holt*, 366–77.

132. *Essays of George Eliot*, 415.

133. *Essays of George Eliot*, 428.

8. DICKENS'S UTILITARIAN DYSTOPIA

1. The differences between Romantic and Utilitarian views of education parallel the differences in their views of the uses of poetry; cf. M. H. Abrams, *The Mirror and the Lamp* (New York: Oxford, 1953), 326–35.

2. Fred Kaplan, *Thomas Carlyle* (Ithaca: Cornell University Press, 1983), 534.

3. David Brooks Cofer, *Saint-Simonism in the Radicalism of Thomas Carlyle* (Austin TX: Von Boeckmann–Jones Company, 1931). Cf. Harry Laidler, *History of Socialism* (New York: Crowell, 1968), 99, 319; cf. Norman and Jeanne MacKenzie, *The Fabians* (New York: Simon and Schuster, 1977), 110, 189.

4. Dickens apparently supported some of the efforts of the Utilitarian educators. W. M. Williams writes to Combe from Birmingham that "the general Department of the Institute [the Birmingham and Midland Institute, which Williams headed after he taught for Combe] is at present

but in . . . [an] embryo condition from want of a building. £10,000 must be raised before the land can be given by the Town Council. The subscriptions at present raised amount to about £8,000. Mr. Macready gave a reading from some of the Poets for the benefit of the Building Fund. It was very largely attended & £133 cleared. Above £300 were cleared by Charles Dickens's reading of his Christmas carol etc." This reading took place in December, 1853, when Dickens visited Birmingham and the Preston strike. Williams became the "master of the science classes" at the institute in 1853 after leaving Combe's school in Edinburgh. It seems possible that Dickens's experience with Williams in Birmingham was a disillusioning one, given Williams's skill in pushing the workers toward his position (see chapter 7), a tactic that must have appeared harsh, especially given the context of the Preston strike nearby, labor's general oppression, and the unrest over harsh conditions. Letter from W. M. Williams to Combe, Jan. 15, 1854, MS 7351, Combe Collection.

5. Letter from Mrs. Ellis to George Combe, Jan. 21, 1853, MS 7333, Combe Collection.

6. Letter from William Ellis to George Combe, Dec. 28, 1852 with addendum on Jan. 2, 1853, MS 7385D, Combe Collection.

7. The *Household Words* story may have been written by Dickens on the basis of visiting the school with his stenographer, it may have been composed from the stenographer's notes, or it may have been put together by another author and approved for *Household Words* by Dickens in his editorial capacity. The Ellises clearly think that Dickens is the author. Anne Lohrli attributes the article to Henry Morley and W. H. Wills.

8. Charles Dickens (?), "Rational Schools," *Household Words* 6, no. 144 (Dec. 25, 1852): 337.

9. Dickens, "Rational Schools," 337.

10. Dickens, "Rational Schools," 337.

11. Dickens, "Rational Schools," 337–38 (pages numbered erratically throughout the *Household Words* article).

12. Dickens, "Rational Schools," 340. The next lesson described in the *Household Words* essay offers an object problem in "real-world" arithmetic, like that which Bartle Massey asks that his students offer themselves. It invites the children to conclude how many appetites they have

in a day (the answer is four: breakfast, dinner, tea, and supper) and then, as in Eliot's school, to multiply or add large figures, in this case 365 times 4. Later, the students are asked, as an early lesson in Political Economy, to compare their result with the *one* harvest that comes in a year and to calculate how it can go around. In the case of both of these lessons, the explicit authorial voice is one of respect, though the praise seems so lavish as to border on irony, especially in its treatment of a heavily cued combination of rote learning and guessing.

13. Dickens, "Rational Schools," 340.

14. Dickens, "Rational Schools," 343.

15. Dickens, "Rational Schools." Dickens was later to assert that a utilitarian time needed romance and fairies because they are basic to its greatness. Charles Dickens, "Frauds on the Fairies," *Household Words* 8, no. 184 (Oct. 1, 1853): 97–100.

16. *The Letters of Charles Dickens*, ed. Graham Storey, Kathleen Tillotson, and Angus Easson, 10 vols. (Oxford: Clarendon Press, 1996), 7:320.

17. James Lowe, "Locked Out," *Household Words* 8, no. 194 (Dec. 10, 1853): 345–48.

18. Charles Dickens, "On Strike," *Household Words* 8, no. 203 (Feb. 11, 1854), 553–59.

19. Dickens, "On Strike," 553–59.

20. Harriet Martineau, *The Factory Controversy: A Warning against Meddling Legislation* (Manchester: National Association of Factory Occupiers, 1855), quoted in Charles Dickens, *Hard Times*, ed. George Ford and Sylvère Monod (Norton: New York, 1990), 299–302. All citations and quotations from *Hard Times* are from this edition.

21. [Jane Sinnett], "Belles Lettres" (review of *Hard Times*), *Westminster Review* 62 (Oct. 1854): 604–8; entire review 602–22.

22. [Sinnett], "Belles Lettres," 605.

23. Dickens, *Hard Times*, 21.

24. John Manning, *Dickens on Education* (Toronto: University of Toronto Press, 1959), 141.

25. Dickens, *Hard Times*, 113, 200.

26. Dickens, *Hard Times*, 161.

27. Dickens, *Hard Times*, 178.

28. Dickens, *Hard Times*, 178–81.

29. Dickens, *Hard Times*, 212.

30. Dickens, *Hard Times*, 218.

31. Dickens, *Hard Times*, 9.

32. Letter from Mrs. William Ellis to Combe, Feb. 9, 1853, MS 7333A, Combe Collection.

33. The question that leads to a Gradgrindian excursus of the dangers of fancy and the necessity to stick to facts recalls James Mill's tirade against associations that produce fears of the dark and that cause the mind to relate inwardly things not in actuality related (treated in chapter 4).

34. Dickens, *Hard Times*, 75.

35. Dickens, *Hard Times*, 125–26.

36. Dickens, *Hard Times*, 15, 75–80.

37. Dickens, *Hard Times*, 7. George Combe queries Sam Brown, a lecturer on education who spoke in Edinburgh, about his saying that in nature there "are no laws, only facts, facts, facts." Combe to Samuel Brown, March 23, 1852, MS 1889, Combe Collection.

38. Dickens, *Hard Times*, 7.

39. Dickens, *Hard Times*, 210–12.

40. Dickens, *Hard Times*, 182.

41. Dickens, *Hard Times*, 113.

42. Dickens, *Hard Times*, 22–23.

43. Dickens, *Hard Times*, 8–25, 205–9, and passim.

44. Bruno Bettelheim, *The Uses of Enchantment: The Meaning and Importance of Fairy Tales* (New York: Vintage Books, 1977), passim.

45. Dickens, *Hard Times*, 17.

46. Dickens, *Hard Times*, 200–1.

47. Dickens, *Hard Times*, 23–24.

48. Dickens, *Hard Times*, 47–48.

49. Dickens, *Hard Times*, 22–23, 42.

50. Dickens, *Hard Times*, 22.

51. Dickens, *Hard Times*, 22.

52. Dickens, *Hard Times*, 64, 85–86.

53. Dickens, *Hard Times*, 85.

54. Dickens, *Hard Times*, 85, 96.

55. Dickens, *Hard Times*, 195–200.

CONCLUSION

1. Cf. Dolf Zillman, "Effects of Prolonged Consumption of Pornography," *Pornography: Research Advances and Policy Considerations* (Hillside NJ: Lawrence Erlbaum, 1989), 153–55; Jerome L. Singer, "Imaginative Play in Childhood: Precursor of Subjective Thought, Daydreaming, and Adult Pretending Games," in *The Future of Play Theory*, ed. Anthony Pellegrini (Albany: SUNY Press, 1995), 187–219; Brian Sutton-Smith, *The Ambiguity of Play* (Cambridge: Harvard University Press, 1997), 35–51, 74–90; Alan Garnhom and Jane Oakhill, *Thinking and Reasoning* (Oxford: Blackwell, 1994), 31–39, 313–14, 206–18; Robin Hogarth, *Judgement and Choice* (New York: John Wiley, 1980), 110–29.

2. Richard Harland, *Superstructuralism* (New York: Methuen, 1987), passim.

3. However accurate Mannheim's picture of how "utopia" operates in the sociology of knowledge, his picture of its phases, of a "dialectic" in its phases, is faulty or overly simple, based largely on its Marxist roots and its assumption that whole cultural systems work in an integrated fashion, when the fact is that any culture will include radically discordant elements. Our utopia begins with a Stuart absolutism that may have millennialist overtones. It then proceeds to Commonwealth Chiliasm and the Chiliasm that sometimes found a place in the dissenting academies. The successor Whiggery and liberalism coexisted with a Chiliasm that exists into our time, but it was not in some grand dialogue with Commonwealth religious thought. While Commonwealth thinkers thought they were creating a heaven on earth in anticipation of the millennial one, Whig/liberal thinkers increasingly came to visualize eternity as appearing only as an invisible hand and promising a vague afterlife. While Mannheim's "socialist phase" appeared briefly in Owen's work and recurred in efforts like the kibbutz schools, these phases affected only a small portion of world society, and Soviet education has almost nothing to do with Mannheim's socialist phase. Education and socialization toward a sense of the common have not preoccupied Anglophone societies

as they have some small group societies; cf. Olson, *Struggle for the Land*, passim; Bonnie McCay and James M. Acheson (eds.), *The Question of the Commons* (Tucson: University of Arizona Press, 1987), passim.

4. Cf. Stephen J. Gould, *The Mismeasure of Man* (New York: Norton, 1981), 256–57 and passim; Russell Marks, *The Idea of IQ* (Washington DC: University Press of America, 1981); William H. Tucker, *The Science and Politics of Racial Research* (Urbana: University of Illinois Press, 1994), passim; Graham Richards, *Putting Psychology in Its Place* (New York: Routledge, 1996), 29.

5. Leslie Silko, *Ceremony* (New York: Penguin, 1977), 135.

6. For a summary of White's arguments and those in the White tradition, see Olson, *Journey to Wisdom*, 16–17. However, other critics have shown not only that White misreads the Genesis passage but that centuries of exegesis of the passage do not interpret "subdue" as implying environmental as opposed to human self-conquest. See Olson, *Journey to Wisdom*, 222, n. 2.

7. S. J. Curtis, *History of Education in Great Britain* (Westport CT: Greenwood Press, 1971), 478–96.

8. For the long prospect that includes a damning account of post-Renaissance events, see Committee on Geological Sciences, National Research Council, *The Earth and Human Affairs* (San Francisco: Canfield, 1972), 49–100. For the growth of air pollution in the seventeenth and eighteenth centuries in Britain, see Peter Brimblecombe, *The Big Smoke: A History of Air Pollution in London since Medieval Times* (New York: Methuen, 1987), 63–106; Carlos Flick, "The Movement for Smoke Abatement in 19th-Century Britain," *Technology and Culture* 21 (1980): 29–50.

9. For some useful insights, see Robert Werlin, *The English Novel and the Industrial Revolution* (New York: Garland, 1990), passim.

10. The pupil teacher system, devised by Kay-Shuttleworth in 1846 and based on the monitorial system, involved taking students at thirteen and having them teach all day; having them study with a headteacher to improve their own knowledge of subjects and pedagogy outside of regular school hours; and paying them a small amount to study in grant-aided schools. At eighteen, excellent school teachers might be selected to go to a training college, where they would receive state financial aid to

undergo sufficient training to become a certified headteacher. See Keith Evans, *The Development and Structure of the English School System* (London: Hodder and Stoughton, 1985) 168–71. For the continuation of the monitorial system, including evidences of continuation into the twentieth century both in Britain and in the United States, see notes to chapter 7 of the present volume.

11. James Kay-Shuttleworth, "Letter to Lord Granville," in *Copies of All Memorials and Letters Which Have Been Addressed to the Lord President of the Council . . . on the Subject of the Revised Code, by the Authorities of Any Educational Society, Board, or Committee, or Any Training School*, in British Sessional Papers (London: Her Majesty's Stationary Office, 1862), 429

12. For Lowe as a Utilitarian, see Edwin G. West, "The Benthamites as Educational Engineers: The Reputation and the Record," *History of Political Economy* 24 (1992): 609–19.

13. Brendan A. Rapple, "Payment by Results: An Example of Assessment in Elementary Education from Nineteenth Century Britain," *Education Policy Analysis Archives* 2 (1994): 3–19 (web article at http://olam.ed.asu.edu/epaa/v2n1.html).

14. *Hansard's Parliamentary Debates* (London: T. C. Hansard, 1862, third series): clxv, cols. 1869–70.

15. See chapter 7.

16. Rapple, "Payment by Results," 11.

17. Rapple, "Payment by Results," 4–6.

18. Matthew Arnold, "The Twice Revised Code," *The Complete Prose Works*, ed. R. H. Super, 5 vols. (Ann Arbor: University of Michigan Press, 1962), 2:235.

19. Matthew Arnold, "Sweetness and Light," in *Culture and Anarchy*, ed. Ian Gregor (Indianapolis: Bobbs-Merrill, 1971), 52.

20. Cf. Terry Eagleton, "The Rise of English," in *English Literature in Schools*, ed. Victor J. Lees (Philadelphia: Open University Press, 1986), 62–74; Franklin Court, *Institutionalizing English Literature* (Stanford: Stanford University Press, 1992), passim; for American literature, see David R. Shamway, *Creating American Civilization* (Minneapolis: University of Minnesota Press, 1994), 61–95, 192–94. For a similar use of school history, see Jessie Y. Y. Wong, "Rhetoric and Educational Policies

on the Use of History for Citizenship Education in England from 1880–1990," *Educational Policy Analysis Archives* 5 (1997): 1–14 (web journal at http://olam.ed.asu.edu/epaa/v5n14.html).

21. See Olson, *Struggle for the Land*, 26.

22. See Robert N. Bellah et al., *Habits of the Heart* (Berkeley: University of California Press, 1985); Wendell Berry, *The Unsettling of America* (San Francisco: Sierra Club Books, 1977); and many other works by Berry.

23. In Third World development circles, the requirement of universal primary education appears to many to be the only tool for "breaking the cycle of poverty." Cf. the Oxfam analysis at *http://www.caa.org.au/oxfam/advocacy/education*. This analysis does not examine what alternative forms of education might do or whether the industrial economies building up in "successful" Third World countries are sustainable.

24. For a thoughtful account of the influence of monopoly in the history of education—which does not, however, take account of environmental issues or issues of economic systems and school modes—see Andrew Coulson, "Markets Versus Monopolies in Education: The Historical Evidence," *Education Policy Analysis Archives* 4 (1996): 1–24 (web journal at *http://olam.ed.asu.edu/epaa/v4n9.html*). The present book does not deal with the issue of parent choice and the development of school compulsion.

25. *Work in America: Report of the Special Task Force to the Secretary of Health, Education, and Welfare* (Cambridge: MIT Press [1973]), passim.

Index

Index

Augustine, Saint, 3, 25, 85
Autobiography (Mill), 180, 228
Avianus, Flavius, 4

Bacon, Francis, 41–66; belief of, in progress, 48–49, 51, 273 n.24; Chiliasm of, 41–42, 65–66, 253, 284 n.1, 295 n.5; Christian imagery of, 51–52, 290 n.38, 291 n.39; compared with Shakespeare, 6–7, 28, 29, 31, 33, 40, 43–46, 279 n.37; ideas of, on education, 41, 46–48, 81, 289 n.33, 301 n.57; ideas of, on scientific language, 56–57, 76, 120, 168, 292 n.55, 302 n.69, 328 n.18; impact of, on Adam Smith, 133–34, 144–46, 148; impact of, on Comenius, 259, 296 n.15, 298 n.29, 301 n.56; impact of, on Commonwealth educators, 7, 47, 67, 70–76, 78–84, 86, 300 n.48; importance of, on utopian tradition, 1, 5, 7–8, 13–14, 18, 21, 65–66, 249–51, 270 n.11; as myth-maker, 52, 58–66, 291 n.41, 293 n.64; Royal Society and, 47, 65, 71, 250, 251, 287 n.22, 295 n.9 n.11, 304 n.77; scientific method of, 48–49, 51–59, 289 n.30 n.33, 291 n.48, 292 n.60, 294 n.64; scientific oligarchy of, 46–51, 62–65, 287 n.20, 289 n.27, 294 n.82; Scribleran objections to, 102, 116, 119, 120, 121, 127, 313 n.72, 316 n.96, 317 n.100 n.108; Utilitarian references to, 158, 167, 178, 199
—Works: *The Marriage of the Thames and Rhine*, 41–45, 285 n.10, 286 n.12 n.17; *Novum Organum*, 73; *On the Wisdom of the Ancients*, 58, 291 n.41. See also *The Advancement of Learning*; *New Atlantis*
Baker-Smith, Dominic, 276 n.12, 277 n.21
Bakunin, Mikhail, 11
Barnouw, Jeffrey, 289 n.30
Barthes, Roland, 9

Battersea Training College, 193
Battestin, Martin C., 323 n.24
Battle of the Books (Swift), 96, 108
Beaumont, Francis, 286 n.12
Beck, Cave, 302 n.69
Bell, Andrew: George Eliot's knowledge of, 223; influence of, on Robert Owen, 179, 332 n.51; influence of, on teacher training, 178; monitorial system of, 174, 175, 329 n.37; on working class education, 327 n.8
Bellah, Robert: *Habits of the Heart*, 149, 265
Belton, Ellen R., 34
Benefit Societies Act (1836), 338 n.36
Bentham, Jeremy: attack on, in *Hard Times*, 228, 235; influence of, on Utilitarian movement, 202, 337 n.31, 340 n.55; Panoptical prison of, 162, 260, 278 n.26, 326 n.5; pedagogical principles of, 162–68, 169, 217, 329 n.36; significance of, in educational reform, 7–8, 158–59, 161, 181, 182, 250–51, 259–60, 262, 330 n.43. See also *Chrestomathia*
Bentley, Richard: parodic essay on, 319 n.149; satire on, in *Dunciad*, 93, 131; satire on, in *Gulliver's Travels*, 120, 132; satire on, in Scriblerus papers, 108, 113; satire on, in *Virgilius Restauratus*, 314 n.74
Berry, Wendell, 265
Bettelheim, Bruno, 244
Bible: Geneva, 33, 36, 281 n.45 n.47 n.48, 283 n.59 n.61; higher criticism of, 212, 214–15, 226
—Books: *Canticle of Canticles*, 52; *Ecclesiastes*, 52, 53–54, 55; *Ecclesiasticus*, 53, 93; *Ezekiel*, 76; *Isaiah*, 30–40, 108, 279 n.39, 281 n.45 n.47 n.48, 283 n.61; *Job*, 4, 310 n.41, 322 n.23; *Kings*, 53, 291 n.43; *Logos of John*, 54, 58, 92, 291 n.38, 307 n.16; *Luke*, 139; *Proverbs*, 52, 53, 75, 92, 93, 307 n.16; *Psalms*, 282 n.53; *Romans*,

Index

Index

Index

Jonson, Ben: "Hymenaei," 39, 284 n.66
Jonston, John, 70–71, 295 n.9
Joseph Andrews (Fielding), 117, 254, 323 n.24
Journey to Wisdom (Olson), 273 n.23, 274 n.4, 277 n.19, 298 n.27, 307 n.16, 328 n.20, 353 n.6

Kantorowicz, Ernst, 277 n.22
Katz, Michael, 158
Kay-Shuttleworth, James: involvement of, in educational reform, 183, 193, 263, 264, 265, 338 n.35; involvement of, in teacher education, 344 n.86; pupil-teacher system of, 260–61, 353 n.10
Keckermann, Bartholomaeus, 72
Kepler, Johannes, 25, 54, 57, 101, 288 n.23
Kerby-Miller, Charles, 111
Kerry, Earl of, 203
Kettler, David, 272 n.19
Knight, Diane, 9, 10, 271 n.17
"Knight's Tale" (Chaucer), 281 n.50
Koe, John Herbert, 163
Kumar, Krishan, 273 n.24, 291 n.38

Labyrinth of the World and Paradise of the Heart (Comenius), 74
Lancaster, Joseph: Baconian vision |of, 7, 250–51; James Mill's approval of, 175, 180; significance of, in educational reform, 158–59, 162, 181, 259–60, 327 n.8. *See also* Lancastrian schools
Lancastrian schools: capitalist instruction in, 14–15, 177, 331 n.45; George Eliot's knowledge of, 223; influence of, on adult teacher training, 177–78, 344 n.86; legislative support for, 183, 330 n.43; limitations of, 264; monitorial system of, 174–80, 329 n.36 n.37, 331 n.48; Robert Owen's interest in, 179–80, 186–87,

332 n.51; William Ellis's involvement with, 192, 218
Landino, Francesco, 108
Laud, William, 68
Law of Freedom (Winstanley), 69
Laws (Plato), 61, 125–26
Leben Jesu (Strauss), 212, 214, 215, 346 n.98
Lecture of Education, Government and Competition (Ellis), 200–201
Lecture on Education (Hodgson), 340 n.55
Lectures on Popular Education (Combe), 197–99, 340 n.52
LeFance, William, 311 n.48
Le Guin, Ursula: *The Dispossessed*, 9
Lessing, Gotthold Ephraim, 11
Lessons in Political Economy (Martineau), 234
Levao, Ronald, 292 n.55, 293 n.64
Levine, Joseph M., 319 n.145
Lévi-Strauss, Claude, 288 n.25
Lewes, George Henry, 190, 219, 347 n.116; *Problems of Life and Mind*, 220
Life of Zoilus and His Remains (Parnell), 109
"The Lifted Veil" (Eliot), 220–21, 262, 339 n.43
Locke, John, 110, 313 n.72; influence of, on Pope, 101, 310 n.40; *Some Thoughts Concerning Education*, 87, 309 n.27
Lohrli, Anne, 349 n.7
Lombe, William, 215
London Mechanics Institute, 192, 194, 224, 229, 260, 342 n.67
London Working Men's Association, 193
Longinus: *Peri Utous*, 314 n.74
Loos, Adolph, 303 n.74
Louis Philippe, king of France, 190, 193
Lovett, William, 193–94, 223, 224, 258, 338 n.36

Index

Index

Index

Index

White, Lynn, 252–53, 255, 353 n.6
White Hill, Battle of the, 46, 67, 285 n.10
Wijdeveld, Paul, 303 n.74
Wilderspan, Samuel, 179, 332 n.49
Wilkins, Bishop John, 89–90, 95, 120, 168, 302 n.69
Williams, Harold, 315 n.86
Williams, W. M.: Dickens's knowledge of, 232, 236, 348 n.4; involvement of, in educational reform, 212, 214, 338 n.40; involvement of, with Combe and Ellis, 184, 190, 199, 205, 215–16, 219; teaching methods of, 195–96, 206–8
Willis, Deborah, 277 n.23
Wills, W. H., 349 n.7
Winstanley, Gerrard, 72; *Law of Freedom*, 69; *New Law of Righteousness*, 69
Wisdom tradition: Bacon's attack on, 46, 48–49, 51–66, 292 n.51; Comenian reinterpretation of, 70, 74–77, 81, 84–86, 296 n.15, 298 n.27 n.29, 299 n.37 n.38; as ladder to stars, 25, 78, 91, 100, 277 n.19; Pope's adherence to, 89–94, 100–101, 104, 107, 305 n.5, 306 n.7 n.10, 307 n.16, 310 n.41; in pre-Associationist education, 328 n.20; Pros-

pero and, 31; Scribleran reassertion of, 97, 254, 316 n.96; Smith's attenuation of, 141, 321 n.17; Utilitarian attenuation of, 200, 213
Wittgenstein, Ludwig, 56, 270 n.8, 271 n.17, 303 n.74; *Philosophical Investigations*, 168, 328 n.18
Wordsworth, William, 180, 227, 236
working-class education: Adam Smith on, 149–51, 154–58, 259; Bell-Lancaster system of, 174–80, 327 n.8, 330 n.37; Bentham on, 164, 326 n.5; in Birkbeck model schools, 15, 203–12, 342 n.62, 343 n.71; Combe-Ellis system of, 189–96, 216–19, 343 n.79; curricular limits of, in Utilitarian thought, 259–61; eighteenth-century provision for, 325 n.57; George Eliot on, 222–26; legislative reform of, 181–85, 254–55; Swift on, 99, 308 n.27
Worth, Chris, 317 n.96

Yates, Frances A., 274 n.4, 285 n.6
Young, Robert Fitzgibbon, 86, 304 n.80

Zagorin, Perez, 291 n.48, 292 n.60
Zola, Emile, 225

375